Developing Learning Skills through Children's Literature

An Idea Book for K-5 Classrooms and Libraries

Volume 2

by Letty S. Watt and Terri Parker Street

Oryx Press
1994

The rare Arabian Oryx is believed to have inspired the myth of the unicorn. This desert antelope became virtually extinct in the early 1960s. At that time several groups of international conservationists arranged to have 9 animals sent to the Phoenix Zoo to be the nucleus of a captive breeding herd. Today the Oryx population is nearly 800, and over 400 have been returned to reserves in the Middle East.

Copyright © 1994 by The Oryx Press
4041 North Central at Indian School Road
Phoenix, Arizona 85012-3397

Published simultaneously in Canada

Printed and Bound in the United States of America

∞ The paper used in this publication meets the minimum requirements of American National Standard for Information Science—Permanence of Paper for Printed Library Materials, ANSI Z39.48, 1984.

Library of Congress Cataloging-in-Publication Data
(Revised for vol. 2)

Laughlin, Mildred.
  Developing learning skills through children's literature.

  Vol. 2 by Letty Stapp Watt and Terri Parker Street.
  Includes bibliographies and indexes.
  ISBN 0–89774–258–3 (pbk.: alk. paper)
  ISBN 0–89774–746–1 (v. 2)
  1. Children—Books and reading. 2. Children's literature—Study and teaching. 3. Elementary school libraries—Activity programs. 4. Libraries, Children's—Activity programs. 5. Libraries and education. 6. Children's literature—Bibliography.
  I. Watt, Letty S., 1947–. II. Street, Terri Parker. III. Title
    Z1037.A1L315 1986   011'.6250544   86-2554
                                                 CIP

*For Mildred, our mentor and
more importantly, our friend.*

Contents

Foreword

Twenty-five years ago Dr. Mildred Knight Laughlin pioneered Norman, Oklahoma's first elementary library. She believed the library ought to be the hub of the school with all learning activities radiating from the library media center like the spokes on a wheel. Her library was student centered and the library programs established under her tutelage reflect her philosophy of resource-based learning.

Dr. Laughlin's career in education began in 1939 when she taught the first through eighth grades in a one-room schoolhouse. She received her B.A. from Ft. Hays State, Hays, Kansas, in 1946 and her M.S. in education from the University of Oklahoma in 1950. In 1970 she completed her M.S. in library science and in 1973 she received her Ph.D. in education from the University of Oklahoma. She taught in the Library Science Department of the University of Southern Mississippi in 1972–73. From 1973–79, she taught at the University of Iowa School of Library Science where she continued and expanded their festival of authors. She came to the University of Oklahoma School of Library Science in 1979 where she taught until her retirement in 1991 when she was awarded Professor Emeritus status.

At the University of Oklahoma, Dr. Laughlin established the first Fall Festival of Books in 1980. This festival has become a premiere event featuring noted Newbery and Caldecott award winners and other outstanding authors and illustrators in the field of children's literature. A scholarship established in her honor at the University of Oklahoma is awarded each year at the Fall Festival of Books. She has been an active member of the American Library Association, serving on the Encyclopedia Britannica Award Committee. Her involvement in the Oklahoma Library Association and Oklahoma Association of School Library Media Specialists has paved the way for a strong library media program in Oklahoma. OLA has awarded Dr. Laughlin both the Distinguished Service Award and the Special Merit Award for her involvement in promoting school libraries and reading.

As a professor at the University of Oklahoma School of Library and Information Studies her first goal was to establish the idea of "service." She emphasized that the library media specialist is there to serve students, teachers, administrators, and parents. Dr. Laughlin continually stressed the need for cooperative planning between teachers and media specialists in order to meet the needs of every child in the school and to complement the curriculum. Her tremendous love and enthusiasm for literature has influenced individuals in the field and in school districts where her vision of librarianship has been established. Her creativity in the classroom sparked her students to pursue storytelling, puppetry, creative dramatics, reader's theater, and other art forms that involve children in the learning process. In all areas of professional librarianship, she models effective teaching strategies and demands the best from her students. Because of her high standards of excellence, her students at all levels are eager to achieve the best. A former student said, "She knows how good you can be and so you rise to her standards of excellence."

Dr. Laughlin believes that elementary school media specialists, who are also certified teachers in most states, should play a vital role in curriculum planning, and in cooperative teaching of critical thinking, listening, communicating, and research skills. She also believes that the student must be an active participant in the reading process. From 1970 to 1984, she was invited to lecture to teachers and librarians and to evaluate library programs in schools in Kansas, Oklahoma, Mississippi, Iowa, and Indiana. During these trips she observed that school librarians had a narrow view of their role and that teachers did not expect librarians to participate in cooperative planning and teaching. Therefore, Dr. Laughlin coauthored, with a media specialist and former student, Letty Watt, a book designed to assist teachers and media specialists in using children's literature to augment the reading and language arts curricula. The result was *Developing Learning Skills through Children's Literature* (Oryx, 1986).

The warm reception given this book encouraged her to plan with Arthur Stickney of Oryx Press the publication of a series of similar works applying the same concept and methods to selected specific subject areas of the curriculum. Again, former students of Dr. Laughlin and teachers in the subject areas addressed were coauthors.

Dr. Mildred Knight Laughlin has always been a visionary. Her vision of school libraries and librarianship has inspired and motivated countless educators over the years. Throughout her life, as an educator, wife, and mother, her sense of humor has been life sustaining for all who have been fortuante enough to have been touched by her.

A bibliography of Dr. Laughlin's books:

Laughlin, Mildred Knight, ed. *Reading for Young People: The Great Plains.* American Library Association, 1979.

Laughlin, Mildred Knight, ed. *Reading for Young People: The Rocky Mountains.* American Library Association, 1980.

Laughlin, Mildred Knight and Watt, Letty S. *Developing Learning Skills through Children's Literature: An Idea Book for K-5 Classroom and Libraries.* Oryx Press, 1986.

Latrobe, Kathy Howard and Laughlin, Mildred Knight. *Reader's Theater for Young Adults: Scripts and Script Development.* Libraries Unlimited, 1989.

Laughlin, Mildred Knight and Latrobe, Kathy Howard. *Reader's Theater for Children: Scripts and Script Development.* Libraries Unlimited, 1990.

Laughlin, Mildred Knight and Latrobe, Kathy Howard. *Public Relations for School Library Media Centers.* Libraries Unlimited, 1990.

Laughlin, Mildred Knight and Swisher, Claudia Lisman. *Literature-Based Reading: Children's Books and Activities to Enrich the K-5 Curriculum.* Oryx Press, 1990.

Laughlin, Mildred Knight, Black, Peggy Tubbs, and Lobert, Magery Kirby. *Social Studies Reader's Theater for Children: Scripts and Script Development.* Libraries Unlimited, 1991.

Laughlin, Mildred Knight and Kardaleff, Patricia Payne. *Literature-Based Social Studies: Children's Books and Activities to Enrich the K-5 Curriculum.* Oryx Press, 1991.

Latrobe, Kathy Howard and Laughlin, Mildred Knight. *Multi-Cultural Aspects of Library Media Programs.* Libraries Unlimited, 1992.

Laughlin, Mildred Knight and Street, Terri Parker. *Literature-Based Art and Music: Children's Books and Activities to Enrich the K-5 Curriculum.* Oryx Press, 1992.

Introduction: The Need for a Literature Program

Children's Literature and Its Role in Child Development

A child's need is to be a child. Sharing literature featuring fantasies, mysteries, humorous stories, and real-life experiences helps children formulate meaningful relationships with the world around them. Rebecca Lukens says, "Literature shows human motives for what they are, inviting the reader to identify with or to react to a fictional character."[1] It is through this involvement with the character and action in the story that children come to value themselves. Children can find their own solutions to problems through stories, such as Emma did in David McPhail's *Fix-It* (E.P. Dutton, 1984). After discovering the television broken, Emma entertained herself by reading to her favorite doll. This identity with character and action forms a basis for many of the units incorporated in this work.

Charlotte Huck cites many personal values gained from experiencing fine literature. She says that literature "provides enjoyment . . . reinforces narrative as a way of thinking . . . develops the imagination . . . offers vicarious experiences . . . develops insights into human behavior . . . and presents the universality of experience."[2]

Reading may inspire a child's natural curiosity, creativity, and imaginative behavior. This active imagination can suspend a child's belief in time and allow everyday events and objects to transform into imaginative worlds. In his 1969 Newbery Award acceptance speech Lloyd Alexander said, "Imaginary kingdoms, however, thrive best in fertile soil."[3] Young minds are fertile and deserve only the best literature.

The conflicts faced in real life are found in books as well. When children are faced with a problem in school, reading *Arthur's Thanksgiving* by Marc Brown (Little, Brown, 1983) will help them know how others have dealt with a similar conflict. This same universality applies to conflict with another person, within oneself, or with nature. Marion Dane Bauer says, "Stories help us make sense of our world. They teach us what is possible. They let us know that others before us have struggled as we do."[4]

In recent years the emphasis on whole language has made children's literature an integral part of the curriculum. Reading to children every day is a must. When children are immersed in an environment of reading, writing, and listening activities, language skills develop more naturally. In her Caldecott Medal acceptance speech Gail E. Haley said, "Children who are not told stories and who are not read to will have few reasons for wanting to learn to read."[5]

In a whole language environment children experience authentic language learning. The literature that is read aloud by the teacher, the library media specialist, and the children provides a forum for integrating the children's real life experiences and personal points of view. "Readers who see books as an important part of their lives do more than read words and 'extract meaning'; they create their own worlds as they read."[6]

Literature crosses the curriculum and allows the integration of language arts and reading with science, math, social studies, music, and art. According to Charlotte Huck,

> The content of literature educates while it entertains. Fiction includes a great deal of information about the real world, present and past. . . . All areas of the curriculum may be enriched through literature. Children may start with a story and research the facts; or they may start with the facts and find the true meanings in the stories surrounding those facts. Literature has the power to educate both the heart and the mind.[7]

The underlying goals of the units in this book are to meet the needs of children's imaginative yearnings, use play as a basis for learning, and explore the lives and writings of well-known authors and illustrators.

How the Book Addresses Learning Modalities

Literature provides an easy way to accommodate learning styles. Current educational research demonstrates that children take in information through their primary sensory modes—visual, auditory, and kinesthetic. "While most children use all three of these modalities to some extent, individual children usually acquire skills and concepts better through one channel than the others. Balancing the learning environment, by diversifying materials and techniques to include all three channels, is essential to reach all the students in a class."[8] The units that follow are designed to meet the needs of these learners through activities such as creating bulletin boards, murals, charts, and graphs to stimulate the visual learner; exploring singing, rhythms, sound devices of poetry, storytelling, and readers' theater to stimulate the auditory learner; and using movement, role playing, sculpting, and building to stimulate the kinesthetic learner. Cooking and tasting, too, have a role in reading and acting upon a book.

Dr. Howard Gardner has said in his book *Frames of Mind: The Theory of Multiple Intelligences* (Basic Books, 1985) that "there is a need for a better classification of human intellectual competencies. It seems within our grasp to come up with a list of intellectual strengths which will prove useful for a wide range of researchers and practitioners and will enable them (and us) to communicate more effectively" (p. 60). Gardner has identified seven intelligences—seven distinct ways that we learn and know about reality—each of which can be recognized in the classroom setting: verbal/linguistic, logical/mathematical, visual/spatial, body/kinesthetic, musical/rhythmic, interpersonal, and intrapersonal. Here again acting upon quality literature and the variety of activities found in this book a teacher can touch the needs of each of these intelligences.

How the Book Is Organized

When children have opportunities to respond meaningfully to literature then learning will occur. Units offer students the opportunity to demonstrate and develop decision-making skills, creative responses, and original thinking. Terms such as *classify, infer, select, predict, create, compose, compare,* and *defend* reflect Bloom's taxonomy. Along with Bloom's cognitive approach, careful consideration has been given to the five levels of affective skills defined by Krathwohl: receiving, responding, valuing, organizing, and characterization. These skills in combination are necessary for integrative learning to take place and translate into participatory and enjoyable literature sharing.[9]

Each individual unit identifies objectives to be accomplished by utilizing the ideas presented in the activities. Based on Bloom's taxonomy, knowledge and comprehension are basic to the objectives of each unit. The higher levels of application—analysis, synthesis, and evaluation—become more evident as progress through the grades is made. Each unit lists special objectives and includes an annotated bibliography of seven to twelve appropriate books. Biographical information is given on author/illustrator units. The introductory activity is geared for use by the library media specialist and/or classroom teacher. The emphasis in the units is on collaboration among the teacher, library media specialist, music and physical education instructors, and other special teachers.

Not all books by a particular author/illustrator have been included. Library media specialists may examine their collections for additional titles that could be used. At kindergarten and first grade the material is to be shared aloud with teacher-directed activities. In second grade some activities can be carried out by small groups and individuals. Units for grades three through five offer group activities and a variety of individual activities to be selected by students so they may develop responsibility and build independence in learning.

The variety of objectives at any one grade level will accommodate individual learning needs. Correlation exists at each grade level between literature, library usage, research skills, and classroom learning. Specific objectives are matched to each book at the beginning of the unit so the teacher can easily see what the students will be able to do upon completion of the unit. Each unit ends with a closure activity that brings a meaningful conclusion to the books read and acted upon.

Judgments on the difficulty of a unit must be made by the teacher and library media specialist based on the background and reading ability of the class. For instance, if the "Adventures in Science with Joanna Cole" unit at second grade is too difficult perhaps "Presenting Information with Gail Gibbons," a first-grade unit, is more appropriate. By the same token, in fifth grade one group of readers could read the books of Phyllis Reynolds Naylor while another group reads those of Eth Clifford from the third-grade units.

How the Book Is to Be Used

As in Volume I of *Developing Learning Skills through Children's Literature,* the units are based on children becoming active participants in the learning process. Integration of the curriculum is inherent to all units. Library skills are developed in meaningful situations rather than as isolated concepts.

All of the books have been well reviewed in at least one selected source. Thus, the bibliographies may be used as buying guides. The production dates were provided for audio-visual materials whenever they were available. The choice of authors and themes to be included was based on the availability of in-print materials, the range of writing, and curriculum applications.

A variety of activities is suggested to meet the needs of individual students. Those interested in writing will profit from extensive examination of the works of one author. For instance, in studying the books of Joanne Ryder the children will become acquainted with second-person point of view. Using the style and pattern Ryder developed in her "Just for a Day" series children can apply the stages of the writing process and compose a second-person narration. Through the author/illustrator studies children come to know that person as a friend. Their own writing takes on meaning when children realize that they, too, are authors. In the activities for individual students in Chapters 4, 5, and 6 directions are given directly to the student. The teacher may find it helpful to photocopy these activities and place them on individual index cards. These could be placed in a learning center where children may select and complete the activities of their choice.

Authors from Gail Gibbons to Avi agree that for children to be writers they must be readers. Gibbons says that as a child she was an avid reader. Based on a visit to a friend's farm she says, "I found myself writing and drawing pictures of what I loved and where I wanted to be. The writing became a form of expressing myself."[10] For each of the author/illustrator units it is important that the library media specialist and/or teacher read a biographical account (if available) in preparation for the group introduction. Through the words and experiences of an author's early life children can relate to a real person.

Biographical sources are listed in units about the authors, with complete bibliographic information in Appendix I. In addition publishers, upon request, will often send brochures and pamphlets about an author or illustrator. The Children's Book Council, *School Library Journal, The Horn Book, School Library Media Activities Monthly, Booklinks*, and *Instructor* will often carry biographical information on authors.

Activities such as literature logs, developing criteria for evaluation, use of matrix, picture mapping, story mapping, writing journals, literary notebooks, story quilts, illustrating, and creating dioramas are appropriate for many units. The library media center at all grades provides many opportunities for reading, listening, viewing, and for creative endeavors in art, drama, music, dance, puppetry, cooking, sewing, and storytelling. The arts play a vital role in learning. Regie Routman says, "It is important to allow time for artistic interpretation as another way to respond to text."[11]

References

1. Rebecca J. Lukens, *A Critical Handbook of Children's Literature*, 4th ed. (New York: HarperCollins, 1990), p. 5.

2. Charlotte Huck, Susan Hepler, and Janet Hickman, *Children's Literature in the Elementary School*, 5th ed. (New York: Harcourt Brace Jovanovich, 1993), pp. 8–12.

3. *Newbery and Caldecott Medal Books, 1966–1975.* (Horn Book, 1975), p. 51.

4. Marion Dane Bauer, *What's Your Story?* (New York: Houghton Mifflin, 1992), p. ix.

5. *Newberry and Caldecott Medal Books, 1966–1975*, p. 225.

6. Trevor H. Cairney. "Developing Literature-based Programmes: Getting Kids 'Inside' Books" from *The Whole Language Catalog* by Kenneth S. Goodman, Louis Bridges Bird, and Yetta M. Goodman. (Santa Rosa, CA: American School Publishers, 1991), p. 201.

7. Huck, Hepler, and Hickman, *Children's Literature in the Elementary School*, p. 20.

8. Anthony Coletta, *What's Best for Kids.* (Rosemont, NJ: Modern Learning Press, 1991), pp. 147–148.

9. Beverly N. Parke. *Gifted Students in Regular Classrooms.* (Boston: Allyn and Bacon, 1989), p. 157.

10. *Something about the Author Autobiography Series,* Vol. 12, (Detroit: Gale Research, Inc.), p. 72.

11. Regie Routman, *Invitations* (Portsmouth, NH: Heinemann, 1991), p. 111.

Chapter 1
Kindergarten/First Grade

Everyday Places and Events with Anne Rockwell

Objectives:

1. Realize the library media center is a source for information and activities.
2. Select words that describe a scene.
3. Create a graph.
4. Role play a variety of situations.
5. Create a scene using a specified art medium.
6. Recognize that printed words or pictures represent spoken language.
7. Identify and name warm colors.
8. Identify activities that are appropriate for a designated time and place.

Recommended Readings:

Rockwell, Anne. *Apples and Pumpkins*. Illustrated by Lizzy Rockwell. Macmillan, 1989.
    The fall season offers a family the opportunity to visit a farm to pick apples and pumpkins. (Objectives 5 and 7)

———. *Bikes*. Dutton, 1987.
    This simple transportation book explores bikes of every variety. (Objectives 2 and 6)

———. *Fire Engines*. E.P. Dutton, 1986.
    Parts of a fire engine and the job of a fire fighter are described from a young child's viewpoint. (Objective 5)

———. *First Comes Spring*. HarperCollins, 1985.
    A little bear goes through an entire year changing his clothing and activities to match the seasons. (Objectives 6 and 8)

————. *Hugo at the Window*. Macmillan, 1988.
A visual hide-and-seek is created by the illustrations in this tale of a dog who waits patiently for his master to return. (Objectives 4 and 6)

————. *I Like the Library*. E.P. Dutton, 1977.
Through the eyes of a young child readers share in the excitement of visiting a library. (Objective 1)

————. *In Our House*. HarperCollins, 1985.
Special activities occur in each room of an active, caring family's home. (Objectives 4 and 8)

————. *Our Yard Is Full of Birds*. Illustrated by Lizzy Rockwell. Macmillan, 1992.
From a little boy's point of view readers observe common backyard birds from season to season. (Objective 3)

————. *Root-a-Toot-Toot*. Macmillan, 1991.
Watercolor and pen-and-ink illustrations extend the cumulative tale of a little boy and his toy flute. (Objectives 4 and 6)

Rockwell, Anne, and Rockwell, Harlow. *The Emergency Room*. Macmillan, 1985.
Readers are given a nonthreatening introduction to a hospital emergency room through graphic illustrations and brief text. (Objectives 3, 4, and 6)

————. *The Toolbox*. Macmillan, 1971.
Large, clear illustrations and simple text present common tools. (Objective 4)

Biographical Sources:

For more information on Anne Rockwell see *Something about the Author,* vol. 33, pages 170–74; and *Fifth Book of Junior Authors & Illustrators*, pages 264–66.

Group Introductory Activity:

Anne Rockwell reflects on happy memories of library visits with her children in her book *I Like the Library*. Share some Rockwell family trivia with the children. The article on Anne Rockwell in *Something about the Author* points out that Anne Rockwell's husband, Harlow, who died in 1988, collaborated with her on several books. In recent years their daughter Lizzy has also become an illustrator of children's books, carrying on the family tradition by collaborating with her mother to illustrate *Apples and Pumpkins*. Read aloud *I Like the Library*. Have the children compare the activities and materials available in their library media center with those in the book. Urge the children to discuss the different opportunities offered. If possible, ask a public librarian to visit the classroom to tell about special programs the local library offers.

If the school does not have a library media center, set up a classroom library equipped with some of the media mentioned in Rockwell's book.

Follow-Up Activities for Teacher and Students to Share:

1. After reading aloud *Apples and Pumpkins* by Anne Rockwell, develop a fall bulletin board with the help of the children. Have the children apply watercolors in autumn tones to duplicated leaf shapes to make fall leaves. Explain that red, orange, and yellow are called warm colors. Let the children speculate about why these autumn tones have earned that name. After the paint dries, have the students cut out the leaves and use them as a border. Apples and pumpkins may be cut from construction paper and the children can twist lightweight paper into vines. Arrange these items on the bulletin board to create a fall scene.

2. Read aloud Anne Rockwell's *Bikes* to the class. As a follow-up let the children draw a picture of a bike they would each like to own or use old catalogs to cut out pictures of the bicycle of their choice. Students may dictate captions beginning with "_____ would like a . . ." that briefly describe their "dream bikes." Compile the completed drawings into a class book, *A Bike of My Very Own*, which begins with the words, "Every child would like a special bike of his or her very own."

3. After sharing Anne Rockwell's *Fire Engines* with the class, ask the children to speculate about why the author-illustrator used dalmatians as the characters. As a follow-up, let children create a fire scene by tearing flames from red, orange, and yellow tissue paper. If the children have shared the activity with Rockwell's *Apples and Pumpkins,* ask if these are warm or cool colors. These flame shapes may be arranged and overlapped to create interesting color effects. As a further extension, arrange a class field trip to the local fire station.

4. Read *First Comes Spring* by Anne Rockwell to the class. After the reading give the children time to discuss the changes that take place during the seasons. Rockwell uses the same pattern to describe each of the seasons, that is, descriptions of the yard; the seasonal clothing; repetitive sentences beginning with: "For _(season)_ has come to town. Everyone is busy. What are they doing?" followed by specific seasonal activities. Follow up by creating a simple language experience story loop beginning with "It is Spring. . . ." Have the children dictate the text to describe the season, clothes they wear, and activities in which they engage. Follow the same pattern for each succeeding season. Tape the top and bottom of the paper together to create the story loop. The loop illustrates the cyclical nature of the seasons. Anne Rockwell's *Bear Child's Book of Hours* (HarperCollins, 1987) is another cyclical book that may be used as a further extension.

5. Before reading Anne Rockwell's *Hugo at the Window*, tell the children to study the illustrations of Hugo when he appears. As the book is read, ask them to pretend they are Hugo and use their faces to show how he feels. While sharing the book, give the children time to locate Hugo's friend in each town scene. After reading, tell the students there are many other stories in the pictures of this book. Select one area of the town scenes and show the illustrations again, asking children to tell the stories that are happening in that portion of the pictures.

6. After hearing Anne Rockwell's *In Our House* read aloud, the children may list and describe the activities that take place in various rooms in their own homes. Extend the story into a role-play situation with children pretending to do the many jobs adults do in the home. This activity could be used to reinforce manners and a cooperative environment. For further enrichment read Anne Rockwell's *Come to Town* (HarperCollins, 1987) to the class.

7. Anne Rockwell's *Our Yard Is Full of Birds* is a vehicle to introduce listening for a purpose. Ask the children to listen as the story is read for which birds the father and mother like best and, if desired, the activities the little boy describes himself doing. After reading the story, allow the children to share their answers. Follow with a discussion of the children's favorite birds.

    As a further extension the class may feed the birds by smearing pine cones with peanut butter and then rolling them in birdseed. Loop yarn around the top of the pine cone and hang the feeder from trees or outside a window.

8. After sharing Anne Rockwell's *Root-a-Toot-Toot* with the children, assign character roles and let the children dramatize the story as it is read again. Have the students without roles participate by "reading" the rebus pictures in chorus as they occur in the story. Switch roles and repeat the activity so that all children may take part as both a character and a chorus member.

9. Before reading *The Emergency Room* by Anne and Harlow Rockwell, contact a local hospital or minor emergency clinic to obtain photographs to be used in a learning center. During a discussion of the emergency room, ask the children to think of a word or phrase to describe the photographs. Label these photographs appropriately and place them in the learning center. Read the book aloud. Encourage the children to tell about their experiences with doctors or hospitals. Graph the number of children who have visited the emergency room for stitches, broken bones, surgery, or other reasons. Set up a hospital learning center where students may role play. Encourage individual learners to design a hospital using blocks or other materials.

10. After sharing Anne and Harlow Rockwell's *The Toolbox*, invite a parent or local carpenter to visit the classroom and demonstrate the use of selected carpentry tools. As a follow-up place a toy toolbox, sawdust, wood shavings, sand paper, and small pieces of soft wood in a center for the children to explore.

Closure:

Point out to the class that Anne Rockwell has written many books about everyday places and things to do. At this point she has not written a book about a school. Team with the library media specialist to help the children write a book about their school. Work with the students to decide what experiences and events at school are most important to write about and illustrate. Help put the ideas in order, then have the students dictate the story. Once the class story is complete, have the students illustrate selected scenes. When the book is complete, present it to the library.

Exploring Concepts with Bruce McMillan

Objectives:

1. Understand how real-life experiences are used in writing stories.
2. Listen and look for words that rhyme with each other.
3. Demonstrate the concept of opposites.
4. Accurately and objectively observe and measure living things as they grow and develop.
5. Make and use dial clocks as instruments to measure time.
6. Place numerals in sequential order.
7. Use the body to illustrate descriptive and comparative words.
8. Identify geometric shapes in the environment.
9. Explore simple mathematical concepts.

Recommended Readings:

McMillan, Bruce. *Becca Backward, Becca Frontward: A Book of Concept Pairs*. Lothrop, Lee & Shepard, 1986.
Color photographs of a young girl and her world clearly illustrate the concept of opposites. (Objective 3)

————. *Counting Wildflowers*. Lothrop, Lee & Shepard, 1986.
The numbers one through twenty are illustrated through color photographs of wildflowers, each of which is identified. (Objectives 6 and 9)

————. *Dry or Wet*. Lothrop, Lee & Shepard, 1988.
The concepts of wet and dry are illustrated through a series of paired color photographs. (Objective 3)

————. *Eating Fractions*. Scholastic, 1991.
Colored photographs of food detail the concepts of whole, halves, thirds, and fourths. (Objective 9)

————. *Fire Engine Shapes*. Lothrop, Lee & Shepard, 1988.
Geometric shapes can be found in the bold color photographs of a fire engine. (Objective 8)

————. *Here a Chick, There a Chick*. Lothrop, Lee & Shepard, 1983.
Newly hatched baby chicks were photographed against a bright green lawn to illustrate paired concepts. (Objective 4)

————. *One Sun: A Book of Terse Verse*. Holiday House, 1990.
Monosyllabic rhyming pairs are illustrated by color photographs of a day at the seashore. (Objective 2)

————. *One, Two, One Pair!* Scholastic, 1991.
The mathematical concept of pairs is illustrated in a visual story about getting ready to go ice skating. (Objective 9)

————. *The Remarkable Riderless Runaway Tricycle*. Apple Island Books, rev. ed., 1985.
A runaway tricycle creates its own adventures. (Objective 1)

————. *Super Super Superwords*. Lothrop, Lee & Shepard, 1989.
Positive, comparative, and superlative degree adjectives are illustrated with bright photographs of a kindergartener's day. (Objective 7)

————. *Time to . . . .* Lothrop, Lee & Shepard, 1989.
Both a digital clock in the text and a dial clock in the color photographs mark the hourly passage of time during a young boy's busy day. (Objectives 5 and 6)

Biographical Sources:

For more information on Bruce McMillan see *Something about the Author,* vol. 70, pages 156–60 or *Sixth Book of Junior Authors & Illustrators,* pages 194–96.

Group Introductory Activity:

Before reading *The Remarkable Riderless Runaway Tricycle* by Bruce McMillan, tell the children that the author actually rescued a tricycle from the dump in Kennebunkport, Maine, where he grew up. He says he always brings along his alter ego, that tricycle, when he speaks to groups of adults or children. "I identify with my tricycle that perseveres, no matter what, to get where it's going. . . . You might even call that book my autobiography" (*Something about the Author*, vol. 22, p. 184).

Read the book aloud to the group. Follow up by letting the children discuss the problems the tricycle caused. When necessary, review the illustrations to encourage all students to participate in the discussion. Ask the children how the story might have changed if Jason had been riding his favorite tricycle during its adventure.

Follow-Up Activities for Teacher and Students to Share:

1. Share with the students Bruce McMillan's *Becca Backward, Becca Frontward: A Book of Concept Pairs.* Select pairs of children to work together to demonstrate one concept from the book. As a tasty follow-up drink milk and eat berries or crackers like the photographs show.

2. After reading Bruce McMillan's *Counting Wildflowers* to the class, take the children on a nature hike through the school grounds. Have the students watch for flowers or other designated objects and count them as they are found. If the school setting is inappropriate for an outdoor hike, turn the classroom or hallway into a nature trail. Let the children draw wildflowers, plants, and other natural objects to decorate the area. The objects may be classified by color or size and then counted.

3. Prior to sharing Bruce McMillan's *Dry or Wet* with the class, collect several pictures from old magazines that show wet or dry. Prepare a learning center with two containers, one labeled with a sun, the other with raindrops. Read the book to the children. As a follow-up let the children categorize pictures in the learning center, placing each in the proper container according to the concept each illustrates. Ask the students to discuss how the wet objects could become dry and vice versa. Be sure to extend the book by using the author's suggestion on page 29 of *Dry or Wet* to increase a child's ability to use words effectively.

4. Before sharing *Eating Fractions* by Bruce McMillan, demonstrate the concepts of whole and halves with fruit, corn on the cob, or slices of bread. Have the children compare their portions of food. Now read the book aloud, giving the children the opportunity to question and respond to the picture concepts. As an extension of the book the library media specialist or a parent volunteer could work with the children to make and eat one of the recipes that McMillan offers in the book.

5. Develop a chart showing the shapes Bruce McMillan includes in his book *Fire Engine Shapes.* Include the names of the shapes and place the chart on the wall for the children to refer to later. As the story is read aloud, allow

children to point out and name the shapes they see on each page. Follow up by having the children work in pairs or teams to identify the defined shapes either in the classroom or the library media center.

6. Before reading Bruce McMillan's *Here a Chick, There a Chick* to the class, contact a local farmer, feed store, or county extension service to borrow an incubator and obtain fertile eggs. Share the book with the children. Follow up by incubating eggs in the classroom. Keep a daily chart of children's observations to determine the incubation length, the number of eggs that hatch successfully, and the chick survival rate.

7. Instruct the children to listen for rhyming words in Bruce McMillan's *One Sun: A Book of Terse Verse*. After completing the book, discuss the rhymes children found and give the students the opportunity to develop terse verse of their own based on colors. Let children select and use the correct color crayons or markers to draw an original illustration of a color terse verse of their choice, such as "red bed," "blue shoe," and "black sack." Place the illustrations on a bulletin board or compile them into a class book.

8. Prior to sharing *One, Two, One Pair!* by Bruce McMillan, encourage the children to think about things they know that come in pairs. Tell them to watch the photographs carefully as McMillan's book is read aloud and try to predict what each new pair may be before the page is turned. After completing the book, give the children time to discuss the pairs they saw. Let the children share their reactions when they discover the twins. As a follow up urge the students to find other things that come in pairs and bring one such pair to class to share in a "One, Two, One Pair!" display. If items such as sunglasses or trousers are brought, allow the class to discuss why each is called a pair even though it is only one object.

9. Before sharing Bruce McMillan's *Super Super Superwords* with the students, explain that the photographs and words in the book are about describing and comparing things. As the text and illustrations are shared, encourage the children to discuss the items that are being described and compared in each set. As a follow-up take children to the playground and let them act out some of the comparisons from the book, such as "high, higher, highest" and "loud, louder, loudest." Conclude the activity by trying some comparisons McMillan did not use, asking children to think of ways to illustrate them. End the lesson by having children run to show "fast, faster, fastest" and lining up to depict "straight, straighter, straightest."

10. Share Bruce McMillan's *Time to. . . .* with the children. Draw the children's attention to the clock on the wall behind Bruce McMillan on the back flap of the book jacket. Ask children what is unusual about the clock. When children notice that the numerals are all jumbled at the bottom tell them they will have a chance to "fix the broken clock." Prepare a learning station with a paper plate, the numerals one through twelve on small squares of paper, clock hands, and a brad for each student. Let each child arrange the

numerals around a plate to make a clock dial and glue them in place. The students may affix the hands to the center of the dial by inserting a brad through pre-punched holes. These clock faces may be used as manipulatives to introduce measurement of time by the hour.

Closure:

Culminate this unit with a game called "Kung Thumb," a nearly terse verse title from Bob Gregson's *Incredible Indoor Games Book* (Pitman Learning, Inc., 1982). Assign each student a partner and have them stand facing each other. Using their right hands, the children will simulate shaking hands. Each partner will curl his or her fingers in, locking the finger tips with the thumb on top. The object is for one partner to put the other's thumb down. Grunts and shouts are allowable as if this were martial arts. When the activity is complete, ask the children to recall the books they have heard by Bruce McMillan and the activities they did. Encourage them to discuss their favorite book and activity and tell why they liked it best.

The Joy of Nature with Nancy Tafuri

Objectives:

1. Define the role of an author and an illustrator.
2. Recognize the connection between the season and the calendar months.
3. Communicate feelings and thoughts through oral and written expression.
4. Empathize with a storybook character.
5. Express reading comprehension through art.
6. Identify the theme in a story.
7. Retell a story.

Recommended Readings:

Ginsburg, Mirra. *Four Brave Sailors*. Illustrated by Nancy Tafuri. William Morrow, 1987.
In this lyrical story, four brave mice experience the adventures of the open sea. (Objectives 1 and 5)

Pomerantz, Charlotte. *Flap Your Wings and Try*. Illustrated by Nancy Tafuri. Greenwillow, 1989.

A young bird's wish to fly is fulfilled when he flaps his wings and tries. (Objectives 1, 4, and 6)

Shannon, George. *The Piney Woods Peddler.* Illustrated by Nancy Tafuri. William Morrow, 1981.
A peddler travels the piney woods to swap objects for a shiny new dollar to give to his daughter. (Objectives 1, 5, and 7)

Tafuri, Nancy. *All Year Long.* Greenwillow, 1983.
Seasonal activities depict a calendar year showing days and months of the year. (Objectives 1 and 2)

————. *Early Morning in the Barn.* Greenwillow, 1983.
The barnyard becomes a symphony of sounds as the animals awaken. (Objective 3)

————. *Have You Seen My Duckling?* Greenwillow, 1984.
When a young duckling follows a butterfly, he leads his mother on a chase. (Objectives 4 and 7)

————. *Junglewalk.* Greenwillow, 1988.
A young boy's dream changes his cat into a tiger and his world into the jungles he reads about in his bedtime book. (Objective 5)

————. *Rabbit's Morning.* Greenwillow, 1985.
On his way home one morning a little rabbit encounters many animals and their babies. (Objective 4)

————. *Who's Counting?* Greenwillow, 1986.
A curious puppy counts the numbers one through ten when he finds various animals in the country. (Objective 7)

Zolotow, Charlotte. *The Song.* Illustrated by Nancy Tafuri. Greenwillow, 1982.
Susan hears a little bird singing about the beauty of each season as it arrives. (Objective 3)

Biographical Sources:

For more information on Nancy Tafuri see *Something about the Author*, vol. 39, pages 209–10 and *Sixth Book of Junior Authors & Illustrators*, pages 292–93.

Group Introductory Activity:

Introduce Nancy Tafuri by telling the class that she is both an author and an illustrator. Allow the children to discuss the terms and their meanings. If no one correctly defines the words, explain that an author writes the words in a book or story and the illustrator creates the pictures for the book or story. Point out to the children that in all of her books, whether as an author, illustrator, or both, Tafuri explores the joys of nature and simple activities. Before reading *All Year Long* to the group, ask the children to notice the boy's pet dog, who appears in many of the illustrations. Share the book with the class. Have the children discuss elements common to each season. As an extension of the book, prepare a perpetual calendar using the figures on the final page of Tafuri's book as tags for individual dates. Make a stencil in each shape to simplify the cutting process or substitute dies in similar shapes that may be used on a die-cut machine. Display the calendar on a bulletin board labeled "All Year Long." Change the tags and labels each month.

Follow-Up Activities for Teacher and Students to Share:

1. Before reading Mirra Ginsburg's *Four Brave Sailors,* explain that Nancy Tafuri is the illustrator of this book but not the author. Give the children a chance to explain what part of the book Tafuri created. If no one recalls the proper definitions, review the terms and their meanings with the class. Share Ginsburg's book with the group. Extend the reading by letting the children make folded-paper boats from newspaper by following the directions on pages 17–18 of *Curious George Rides a Bike* (Houghton Mifflin, 1952). If there is sufficient classroom space, construct a sailboat out of large boxes for the children to sit in while pretending to be sailors.

2. Show the children the cover of *Flap Your Wings and Try* by Charlotte Pomerantz. Tell them that Nancy Tafuri is either the author or the illustrator of the book but not both. Ask the group to look and listen carefully to find clues that might help them guess which role Tafuri played. Read the book aloud. After sharing the book, see if anyone recognizes the style of illustrations as being typical of Nancy Tafuri. If not, show the covers of other books she illustrated and point out the similarity. As a follow up have the children describe the body structure of a bird and how it is different from that of other animals. Play Carmen Ravosa's "What Makes a Bird a Bird" (*Records That Teach,* Silver Burdett, P715190, 12 in. LP, n.d.) for the children or sing the song from *Music, Early Childhood* (Silver Burdett, 1981, p. 140). Enlist the help of the music teacher or media specialist to teach the song to the children. As a further extension, share Watty Piper's *The Little Engine that Could* (Platt & Munk, 1961) with the class. Let the children compare the two books to discover the common theme. Ask children to identify how each of the main characters felt when the goal was accomplished.

3. Tell the class that George Shannon wrote the words for *The Piney Woods Peddler* and Nancy Tafuri painted the pictures. After reading George Shannon's story to the children, give the children the opportunity to recall the name of the author and the illustrator. Have the children retell the main parts of the story in sequential order. Let them use a stencil or a rubber

stamp to trace or stamp a pine-tree border around a sheet of paper. Have the children do a pencil or crayon rubbing of a silver dollar in the center of the page. Either a real coin or a plastic replica from a math manipulative set may be used for the rubbing. The finished drawing should reflect a scene from the story.

4. Before sharing *Early Morning in the Barn* by Nancy Tafuri, explain to the children that they will be asked to imitate the sounds of the animals Tafuri wrote about and illustrated. Demonstrate the specific hand motion that will be used to conduct or cue the sounds. As each page is turned, have the children tell about the characters and actions they see. Then signal them to appropriately imitate the sounds of the hungry animals. After reading ask the group to think about the differences in an animal's sound when it is hungry, frightened, or sleepy. Have the children imitate the three different sounds an animal might make in those circumstances. Review the illustrations in *Early Morning in the Barn* as the class sings "Old MacDonald Had a Farm," using animals and sounds from Tafuri's book.

5. A double story occurs in Nancy Tafuri's *Have You Seen My Duckling?* as the wayward duckling chases a butterfly while the mother searches for him. Challenge the children to listen and study the illustrations to discover the two stories in one. After reading the story or sharing the filmstrip (Random House/Miller Brody, 1985), ask the children to retell the wayward duckling's story. Give the children an opportunity to talk about a time when a member of their family may have wandered away and become lost. Let the students discuss the feelings different family members experienced or expressed at that time. Explain that sometimes people lose things as well. Ask the group to think about how they feel when they cannot find a favorite toy. As a follow-up to the book, play a hide-and-seek game. While the "seeker" hides his or her eyes, hide a selected item in the classroom. Let the class give the seeker clues, for example, "hot" if the seeker is near the object and "cold" if he or she is not.

6. Discuss animals and their habitats with the children (e.g., which ones live in the jungle, which are pets, which are farm animals). Share Nancy Tafuri's *Junglewalk* with the students. Then create a junglewalk by hanging paper leaves and vines in the room or a hallway. The children can make and color large drawings of various jungle animals on butcher paper. These may be cut out and placed in the jungle habitat.

7. Share *Rabbit's Morning* by Nancy Tafuri, asking the children to pay special attention to what the little rabbit observed. After reading, have them recall the animals he saw. Explain that the little rabbit was lucky that he didn't get in trouble, but there was another little rabbit who was not so fortunate. Read aloud *The Tale of Peter Rabbit* by Beatrix Potter (Frederick Warne, 1902). Have children compare the two stories to discover similarities and differences. Ask the children to imagine how the two rabbits felt about their adventures.

If the children have already experienced *Have You Seen My Duckling?*, remind them how Mother Duck searched for her baby. Ask them to speculate about what Mother Rabbit may have been doing during little rabbit's morning.

8. Preface the reading of Nancy Tafuri's *Who's Counting?* with a question to the children as the book is displayed: "Who might be counting in this story?" Ask them to look at the illustrations closely as the book is read. The children will enjoy searching for the puppy as he counts. Be sure to have the students identify the curious puppy eating when the story ends. After sharing the book, extend the story by having the children name and associate a number with other animals or natural life in the country. Use the "What if . . ." questioning technique to create a variant of the story. Ask the children to imagine, "What if the puppy lived in an apartment in the city?" Have the children retell the story, one through ten, using that setting.

9. Share Charlotte Zolotow's *The Song* with the class. Let the children discuss ideas about what the bird would sing if he were outside their classroom window. Organize the suggestions in seasonal sequence. Write a class poem about the current season. Use a format similar to Charlotte Zolotow's text about winter. Begin with the color, associate it with the season, and follow with a variety of sensory experiences. Conclude the poem with the sentence, "It is _____ (season)." Read the poem together while playing a bird song recording such as those on *Bird Sounds* (Madacy, SE-2-5501).

Closure:

As a closure activity review the books illustrated by Nancy Tafuri and create a wall mural of nature scenes. Ask the children to select their favorite scene to draw on the mural. This can be done on rolled paper with two or three students working at a time or on individual sheets that can be taped together. Make the mural come to life by allowing the children to add sound effects as each scene is pointed out.

The Graphic Art of Ann Jonas and Donald Crews

Objectives:

1. Recognize that an author's family experiences may be reflected in his or her work.

2. Express changes in tempo or musical rhythms through movement.
3. Role play a variety of situations.
4. Identify various means of transportation.
5. Understand the significance of the dedication page of a book.
6. Develop visual discrimination through identification of hidden objects in a picture.
7. Verbalize a story based on the illustrations.
8. Realize how primary colors combine to form secondary colors.

Recommended Readings:

Crews, Donald. *Bigmama's*. Greenwillow, 1991.
The author recalls his summer visits to Bigmama's, his grandma's farm in Cottondale, Florida. (Objective 1)

———. *Carousel*. Greenwillow, 1982.
Colorful graphics gradually blur, blend, and return to clarity as the carousel begins to move, gains speed, slows, and stops. (Objectives 2 and 3)

———. *Freight Train*. Greenwillow, 1978.
A colorful train takes the reader on a ride through tunnels, past cities, over trestles, and through night and day. (Objectives 3 and 4)

———. *Harbor*. Greenwillow, 1982.
Simple graphics and text explore the variety of boats and ships that may be found in a harbor. (Objectives 1, 5, and 7)

———. *Truck*. Greenwillow, 1980.
Readers of this almost wordless book follow the journey of a truckload of tricycles from pickup to delivery. (Objectives 4 and 7)

Jonas, Ann. *Color Dance*. Greenwillow, 1989.
Young dancers blend the colors of the rainbow in a feathery scarf dance. (Objectives 2 and 8)

———. *Now We Can Go*. Greenwillow, 1986.
Before she can go a young child empties her toy box into her bag to take with her. (Objective 3)

———. *The Quilt*. Greenwillow, 1984.
A new patchwork quilt evokes pleasant memories and dreams in a young girl. (Objectives 1 and 6)

———. *Round Trip*. Greenwillow, 1983.
Stark black-and-white illustrations extend both the simple tale of an all-day trip to the city and, when the book is inverted, the night journey home. (Objective 6)

———. *The Trek*. Greenwillow, 1985.
A menagerie of imaginary animals is hidden in the everyday shapes a young girl sees around her. (Objectives 1 and 6)

Biographical Sources:

For more information on Ann Jonas see *Something about the Author*, vol. 50, pages 106–109. For more information on Donald Crews see *Something about the Author*, vol. 32, pages 58–60 and *Fifth Book of Junior Authors & Illustrators*, pages 88–90.

Group Introductory Activity:

Introduce author-illustrator Ann Jonas and husband Donald Crews by telling the children that many of the Crews family experiences are reflected in their books. Show children the cover of *The Quilt* by Ann Jonas. Explain that the book was written for her older daughter, Nina, who is the girl on the cover. Tell the children that as a child Ann Jonas loved the pictures in children's magazines that contained hidden animals (*Something about the Author*, vol. 50, pp. 108–9). She expressed this love in *The Quilt* by using patterns in the quilt blocks to inspire the events in the child's dream. As the book is read, encourage the children to watch the illustrations carefully to see how the quilt patterns change into dream objects and characters. After completing the book, allow the children to discuss the changes they noticed. If students did not notice them, the teacher may want to point out the balloons, seals, and clowns in the quilt that become part of the circus scenes and the pink cliffs that are really Nina's bed ruffle. If some child notices that Sally was at the foot of the cliffs, ask children to speculate about why Nina woke up on the floor instead of in her bed.

As a follow-up ask the children to bring some pieces of material or a piece of outgrown clothing to show the class. Have the students tell about what they did when they wore the article of clothing or how the cloth was special to them. If desired, a quilt top may be made from these pieces. Ask the media specialist if it would be possible to arrange for a quilt display in the library media center.

Follow-Up Activities for Teacher and Students to Share:

1. Read aloud *Bigmama's* by Donald Crews. The children will discover that the author used his own memories and experiences to tell the story. Follow the reading by having the children discuss their own family traditions and experiences. Have the students bring a photograph from home that portrays a special event from the family's past. Use the photos in a show-and-tell session. Place the photographs on a bulletin board celebrating families. If available, let the children view *Trumpet Video Visits: Donald Crews* (Trumpet Club, 1992, 19 min.) in which the author/illustrator discusses *Bigmama's* and the experiences it reflects.

2. After reading Donald Crews's *Carousel* aloud, have the children pretend to be carousel animals moving up and down as they travel around a circle at a gradually increasing pace. It may be desirable to accompany the movement activity with music that increases in tempo, such as "In the Hall of the Mountain King" from Edvard Grieg's *Peer Gynt Suite* ("Grieg's Greatest Hits," Columbia, PMT-39435).

3. Share *Freight Train* by Donald Crews with the class. Let the children pretend to be a freight train moving across masking tape "railroad tracks" that guide them through the room. Let children identify other means of transportation and discuss when or where each type is most used. As a further follow-up the teacher may wish to create a transportation center, placing the Donald Crews books *Freight Train*, *Harbor*, and *Truck* in the area with toy vehicles for the children to manipulate. Stock the center with old magazines and allow the children to cut out pictures of vehicles and glue them to a "How We Go" mural sheet on the wall.

4. After reading *Harbor* by Donald Crews, have the children listen to the names of the boats in the book as they are read again and try to find a way in which most of the names are alike. Some child will probably notice that most of the boats have women's names. Read the dedication Donald Crews wrote for the book and ask the students if they can guess where the author got most of the names for the ships. If no one guesses that the ships are named after women Donald Crews knows, suggest that idea to them. Remind the group that Big Mama (the container ship) was Donald Crews's name for his grandmother. Nina and Amy are his daughters, and Ann (Jonas) is his wife. Susan H. could be Susan Hirschman, his editor at Greenwillow books. As a further activity have the children examine the illustrations again, telling the story they see in each scene.

5. Before sharing *Truck* by Donald Crews, explain to the children that there is no text in the book. The pictures tell the story. Have the children verbalize the story as they follow the sequence of events in the illustrations. After the group has experienced the book, add a toy truck and blocks to the transportation center developed during the *Freight Train* study. Let the children construct a roadway from the blocks that will carry the truck from a pickup point to a delivery station.

6. Read *Color Dance* by Ann Jonas to the class. Then celebrate the diversity and beauty of color by having a special "Color Day." Ask the children to dress in colors of the rainbow. Play Hap Palmer's "Colors" from *Learning Basic Skills through Music, vol. I* (Educational Activities, OEA 514), having children follow the directions heard in the music. Enlist the aid of the library media specialist or music teacher to help in directing activities. The music teacher may want to sing the song, changing the instructions given to create an original color dance. Have the group listen for tempo changes as the song is sung and show the variation through the speed of their movements.

As a further activity place small pieces of primary colored transparency sheets and an overhead projector in a center and allow the children to experiment with color combinations. The media specialist may wish to share color poetry or stories about color, such as *Mouse Paint* by Ellen Stoll Walsh (Harcourt Brace Jovanovich, 1989) while using colored transparencies to flood the room with the appropriate colors.

7. Read Ann Jonas's *Now We Can Go* to the group. As a follow-up place a dozen of the children's favorite toys in a box along with the matching words in an envelope glued to the outside of the box. This activity center will also need a shopping bag, small suitcase, or other bag. Have each child pretend to be going on a trip and pack the toys he or she would want to take, naming each one. Within the week have the children match the printed word with each toy so that as the child packs his or her bag he or she also identifies the printed word and sets it on a chart. As a further extension have the students select a special trip (e.g., to grandma's, an amusement park, or camping) and tell what they would pack.

8. Before reading *Round Trip* by Ann Jonas, explain to the children that this book takes the reader in a circle, starting and ending at the same place. Read the story, stopping on the last page with the words, "Time to turn around." Remind the group that they were told the story begins and ends at the same place. Ask the students to suggest what the reader must do in order to end at the beginning. If no one guesses that the book must be turned over and read back to front, draw the children's attention to the inverted words at the top of the page and reread the sentence, "Time to turn around." Turn the book over and ask children to notice how the illustrations look different when seen from the new angle. Complete the book. As a follow-up let the children use black finger paint to create a scene or design on white paper.

9. Prior to sharing Ann Jonas's *The Trek* with the children, remind them that Ann Jonas has said she was fascinated as a child by children's magazine drawings that contained hidden animals. Explain that she has used the idea of animals hidden in everyday shapes and objects in her book *The Trek*. The animals that the young girl imagines make her journey from home to school a dangerous trek in her mind. Ask the children to look for the hidden animals as the book is shared and to be prepared to identify them as the book is reread. Follow up by having the children locate and cut out pictures of the animals found in the book. Place these pictures on a poster and attach the printed name of the animal so that the children will begin to recognize the printed name with the animal.

Closure:

Many of the books written by Ann Jonas and Donald Crews are about journeys and transportation. Remind the children that many of the stories are based on personal experiences. Give students time to tell about a personal experience such as taking a walk, a ride, or a trip. Ask an upper grade class to team with the students for a writing project. Have the younger students dictate their personal experience stories. The older students will write them down and read the story back. Together they can make needed corrections. The finished stories can then be illustrated by one or both team members. The final book will then be a blended effort of both students.

Learning Facts with Aliki

Objectives:

1. Respond to literature through discussions, recreation, music, and the arts.
2. Recognize and explain differences and similarities in various forms.
3. Predict action in a story.
4. Identify and express feelings.
5. List and match the five senses to daily activities.
6. Discuss problem-solving techniques.
7. Identify with a book character.
8. Observe changes in people and the environment.

Recommended Readings:

Aliki. *Communication*. Greenwillow, 1993.
    Forms of communication from speaking and writing to the use of Braille are explored. (Objectives 1 and 4)

————. *Digging Up Dinosaurs*, rev. ed. HarperCollins, 1988.
    The role of a paleontologist is explored through text, illustrations, and humorous captions. (Objective 1)

————. *Dinosaurs Are Different*. Thomas Y. Crowell, 1985.
    The differences and similarities of dinosaurs are explained through skeletal forms. (Objectives 1 and 2)

————. *Feelings*. Greenwillow, 1984.
    Children's feelings are depicted through different formats: pictures, poems, dialogue, stories, and demonstrations. (Objective 4)

————. *Jack and Jake*. Greenwillow, 1986.
    The twins, Jack and Jake, keep everyone confused except their sister. (Objectives 1, 2, 6, and 7)

———. *Keep Your Mouth Closed, Dear.* Dial, 1966.
Charles's large mouth causes the family problems as he swallows object after object. (Objectives 1, 2, 3, and 6)

———. *My Five Senses.* Thomas Y. Crowell, 1962.
A young boy demonstrates his awareness of the five senses. (Objectives 1 and 5)

———. *The Two of Them.* Greenwillow, 1979.
The love between a little girl and her grandfather is portrayed through the sensitive text and illustrations. (Objectives 4 and 7)

———. *Use Your Head, Dear.* Greenwillow, 1983.
An absent-minded young alligator gets things mixed up, often causing problems. (Objectives 1, 6, and 7)

Biographical Sources:

For biographical information on Aliki see *Something about the Author*, vol. 35, pages 49–55 and *Third Book of Junior Authors*, pages 8–9.

Group Introductory Activity:

Before introducing the unit on Aliki Brandenberg, arrange for the school counselor to discuss emotions with the class. Make a personal weather wheel for each child in the classroom. Design the wheel so that happy feelings are represented by a bright sun, "in-between" feelings by a sun partially hidden behind clouds, sad feelings by rain and clouds, and angry or upset feelings by storm clouds with lightning. Attach an arrow to the center of the wheel with a brad and write each child's name on the wheel.

Distribute the personal weather wheels to the children and explain that these wheels can be used to show how people feel. Ask the children to decide which picture on the wheel could represent happy, sad, and angry feelings. Give the students time to respond and discuss their ideas for each emotion. Remind the children that sometimes people are not really happy, sad, or upset. Point out that the remaining picture, the sun peeking out from behind the clouds, can stand for those "in-between" feelings.

Introduce Aliki by explaining that this author/illustrator has always found it easy to express herself through art. She says, "I have always felt close to children and to books, and feel fortunate that I can direct what creativity I have to both" (*Third Book of Junior Authors*, p. 8). Tell the children that Aliki has used her writing and artistic talents to create a book about feelings. Read one or two episodes from *Feelings* by Aliki. Ask the children to think about the emotions Aliki discussed and then move the arrow on their weather wheels to describe those feelings. Discuss with the children why it is natural to have and express a variety of feelings.

Post the personal weather wheels in an emotions center. As a follow-up begin each day by recognizing the children's emotions, giving each child the opportunity to move the arrow to describe his or her feelings on that morning. If children's feelings change during the day, they may move the pointer appropriately. Continue to share a few passages from Aliki's *Feelings* each day until the book is completed.

Follow-Up Activities for Teacher and Students to Share:

1. Read aloud Aliki's *Communication* a section at a time. Allow the children to respond to the suggestions, emotions, and ideas expressed in each section. After sharing "There Are Other Ways" have children use body language to communicate a feeling, for example, anger, fear, sorrow, or surprise, or an action, for example, shivering, laughing, or hurting from an accident. Other sections may inspire role-play situations (e.g., "Some Things Are Hard to Say" and "Feed Back").

2. Aliki has written and illustrated many information books for young readers. She says, "Nonfiction needs fascination with a subject, an over-abundance of research, and time to assimilate. The pleasure of these books is writing complicated facts as clearly and simply as possible. . . . I find humor indispensable for making information palatable and fresh" (*Something about the Author*, vol. 35, p. 53). Read *Digging Up Dinosaurs* to the class. As a follow-up bury some well-cleaned bones in a sand tray in the classroom or a sand pit on the playground. Pretend to be paleontologists digging for dinosaur bones. Let children use paintbrushes to carefully brush the sand away from the "fragile fossils." As a further extension let children view the *Reading Rainbow* episode featuring "Digging Up Dinosaurs" (GPN, 1986).

3. After reading *Dinosaurs Are Different* by Aliki, provide for the kinesthetic learner by allowing the children to act out the dialogue and action on page 13 of the text. Let the children bring their prior knowledge of dinosaurs into the activity to extend it by adding more actions.

4. After sharing Aliki's *Jack and Jake,* discuss with the children the problems the twins faced. Have the group brainstorm possible solutions to those problems. Within the story the sister describes different characteristics of Jake and Jack. Ask the students to recall these characteristics and list the differences between the two or simply explain how to tell Jack and Jake apart.

5. *Keep Your Mouth Closed, Dear* by Aliki is an open-ended story. After reading the story to the children, have the students recall and list all of the objects Charles swallowed. Have the children identify the problems that developed because of Charles's actions. Let the children discuss how the

story ended. Because the reader does not know for sure whether Charles learns to keep his mouth closed, have the children predict what might happen next. Ask the students to speculate about how the story might have been changed if Charles had known how to recognize a problem and find a solution using the steps think, predict, and choose. If the classroom or media center has a puppet center, work with the media specialist to allow the children to use a moveable mouth puppet to act out their interpretation of the story.

6. After reading *My Five Senses* to the students, turn back to the pages where multiple things using each sense are listed (page 10). On a chart name the sense, for example, seeing, and have the children list at least five things they see. Follow with each of the other senses. Review and add to the chart throughout the week. On the final day refer to page 21 of Aliki's book and involve the children in learning how to play the game described. Some sample situations in which the children can identify the five senses include: "What if you ran after the ice cream truck and bought a strawberry popsicle?" "What if you stubbed your toe while running?" "What if you climbed the monkey bars?"

7. Read aloud *The Two of Them* by Aliki. Ask the children to sit quietly and think about the story while soft music is played. Tell the children that Aliki says that her stories are based on, "a lifetime of experiences, often my children's. Writing the words . . . is like having to express one's ideas out loud. . . . Such a book can also develop as a need to express a personal experience, as in *The Two of Them*" (*Something about the Author*, vol. 35, p. 53). As the music continues to play, ask the children about their feelings for the event in the story. Allow the discussion to flow into real-life situations the children have experienced. Use the personal weather wheels to identify feelings if desired. Urge the children to compare their feelings to those expressed in the story.

8. Read Aliki's *Use Your Head, Dear* to the class. The children will enjoy meeting Charles again. Remind the students that they first met Charles in *Keep Your Mouth Closed, Dear*. Ask the children to recall the problem the young alligator had in that story. Ask the children if they believe he has learned to solve that problem in this book. Have the group identify the new problem in this story. Follow the discussion by letting children pretend to be Charles after he learned to use his head. Paint with paints, sculpt with clay, and build with blocks.

Closure:

Plan a listening walk for the class. Prior to the walk ask the children to name different sounds they expect to hear. Write these predictions on the board. During the walk note the noises heard. Upon returning to the classroom ask children to recall and list the sounds they recognized. Compare the two lists. Let the children discuss any unexpected or unidentifiable noises they heard. Have the group discuss how they used their other senses during the walk. Urge the children to speculate on how the walk would have been different if they had lost one of their five senses.

Me, Myself, and I

Objectives:

1. Develop an awareness of individual differences and the uniqueness of others.
2. Demonstrate the ability to share materials cooperatively.
3. Respond to a story through art and drama.
4. Identify and express feelings.
5. Learn how to browse, check out, and care for books.
6. Describe the child's role in the family.
7. Practice steps in problem solving: think, predict, and choose.
8. Demonstrate how family members help and care for one another.

Recommended Readings:

Anholt, Catherine, and Anholt, Laurence. *All About You*. Viking, 1992.
Direct questioning and rhyming text elicit the participation of young readers. (Objective 1)

Browne, Anthony. *I Like Books*. Alfred A. Knopf, 1988.
A young chimpanzee demonstrates his love for all kinds of books. (Objectives 1 and 5)

Carson, Jo. *You Hold Me and I'll Hold You*. Illustrated by Annie Cannon. Orchard, 1992.
A young girl discovers that holding and being held can bring comfort. (Objectives 4 and 8)

Kimmel, Eric A. *I Took My Frog to the Library*. Illustrated by Blanche Sims. Viking, 1990.
A young girl's pets, from a frog to an elephant, create hilarious disasters when taken to the library. (Objective 5)

Lasky, Kathryn. *I Have Four Names for My Grandfather*. Illustrated by Christopher G. Knight. Little, Brown, 1976.

Black-and-white photographs extend the simple text of a young boy's loving relationship with his grandfather. (Objective 1)

Mayper, Monica. *Oh Snow*. Illustrated by June Otani. HarperCollins, 1991.
Fresh snowfall beckons a little boy to experience the joys of the winter world. (Objective 3)

Pellegrini, Nina. *Families Are Different*. Holiday House, 1991.
An adopted Korean child realizes that, although there are many different kinds of families, they are all held together by love. (Objective 1)

Russo, Marisabina. *Alex Is My Friend*. Greenwillow, 1992.
A young boy affirms that friends care about each other and can enjoy the same things even though they may be very different. (Objectives 1 and 2)

Williams, Vera B. *Something Special for Me*. Greenwillow, 1983.
Rosa finds it very difficult to choose her own special birthday gift until she hears a man play the accordion. (Objective 7)

Ziefert, Harriet. *Me Too! Me Too!* Harper & Row, 1988.
Two young sisters share the fun of playing in the rain. (Objectives 6 and 8)

Group Introductory Activity:

Before reading aloud *Families Are Different* by Nina Pellegrini, ask the children to listen to the text and look at the illustrations carefully to try to find a family like their own. After completing the book give students time to share their findings. Let the children discuss what Nico meant when she said she wanted to be just like her friends and why she sometimes felt angry, sad, and different. Conclude the discussion by rereading the final two pages of the story. Play for the class Joe Wayman's "I Like Me" from *I Like Me* (Pieces of Learning, n.d.). Encourage children to join in singing the repeated lines.

As a follow-up give each of the children a sheet of paper on which is duplicated a picture frame and the words "I like me because. . . ." Ask the students to draw a picture of themselves in the frame. Enlist the help of older students or volunteers to write the responses as the children complete the sentence telling why each of them is special and likable. Post the completed pages on a "Me, Myself, and I" bulletin board. As a continuous activity for other books in the unit, have the children discuss the characters in each story and list the qualities they like about them.

Follow-Up Activities for Teacher and Students to Share:

1. Lead children to the wonderful world of books by sharing *I Like Books* by Anthony Browne. If children are already familiar with books, have them name titles or types of books they like. Create a class interest list naming

each child's favorite types of books. If children do not have an extensive background in literature, ask them to list some kinds of books they think they might like. Plan with the library media specialist to bring the children to the library to browse and check out books. Share the interest list with the media specialist prior to the visit so each child can be directed to books that will appeal to him or her.

2. Read aloud *You Hold Me and I'll Hold You* by Jo Carson. Urge children to share their reactions to the story. Let the students discuss times they have been hurt or unhappy. Some children may recall how someone hugged or held them to make them feel better. Read Shel Silverstein's poem "Hug O' War" from *Where the Sidewalk Ends* (Harper & Row, 1974, p. 19). Tell the children that "Hug O' War" is about holding each other and feeling good so "everyone wins." Invite the students to act out the poem as it is read again. Repeat the activity on succeeding days, urging the children to join in reciting the poem as they learn it.

3. Read aloud *I Took My Frog to the Library* by Eric Kimmel. Discuss the disastrous events that occurred in the story. Ask the children to name some pets that could live in a library setting (e g. fish, hermit crabs, gerbils). Visit the school library media center or the local public library to see if there are any pets in these facilities. While in the library, take the opportunity to have the library media specialist teach a lesson on how to care for books. Show examples of books that have been ruined from rain, crayon marks, destructive dogs, and other external factors. After returning to the classroom, ask the children to recall the disasters that may befall a book that is mistreated. Point out to the children that being responsible for a book is like being responsible for a pet.

4. After sharing Kathryn Lasky's book *I Have Four Names for My Grandfather*, lead the children in a discussion of the relationship between the boy and his grandfather. Help the children to decide how the two felt about each other. The photographs in the book show many things that young children and older adults can enjoy together. Have the children name activities that they especially enjoy doing with their parents or grandparents. As a follow-up arrange a field trip to a local retirement home or senior citizen's center. At the center present a brief program sharing songs like "I Like Me" from the introductory activity and poems such as "Hug O' War."

5. Share Monica Mayper's *Oh Snow* with the class. Let the children discuss the ways the boy played in the snow. Invite the children to be the little boy and act out the story as it is reread. As a follow-up let children use tempera paint to make a snow scene showing their favorite winter activities. Salt added to liquid white paint will lend texture and sparkle to the finished paintings.

6. Before sharing Marisabina Russo's *Alex Is My Friend*, tell the children that the author's son has a friend like Alex. According to the information on the book jacket, it was their friendship that inspired Russo to write this book. Read the story aloud. Ask the class to recall ways in which the two boys were different and ways they were the same. Have the children judge which list contains things that really matter in a friendship. Remind the children that when the boys played together they shared things they liked. Have the students discuss why sharing is important between friends. Let the group list things friends might share. Alex shared jokes with his friend. Let children tell favorite jokes and riddles as the whole group shares "snacks, like pretzels and apples and juice."

7. *Something Special for Me* by Vera Williams shows a little girl making a decision. Before reading the story aloud, ask the children to listen closely to what Rosa is thinking each time she nearly buys something. After completing the book, ask the children what they think about Rosa's choice. In the end Rosa followed these steps in selecting her gift: think, predict, and choose. As a follow-up use these three steps to teach problem solving. Give children real-life questions to think about such as "You have lost your lunch money. . ." "You tracked mud in the house. . ." or "You didn't clean up your mess. . . ."

8. When reading aloud *Me Too! Me Too!* by Harriet Ziefert, urge the children to join in the "Me too!" lines of the little sister. Have the class discuss the older child's role in the family and how children care for one another. As an extension of the story read *Rainy Rainy Saturday* by Jack Prelutsky (Greenwillow, 1990). Let the children perform some of the ideas from this poetry book, including somersaults, whistling, and making clay creatures.

Closure:

Read Catherine and Laurence Anholt's *All About You* to the children, beginning with the rhyme on the copyright page. Encourage students to respond to the questions in the book. Let the students make "All About Me" books inspired by the text. Prepare booklets in advance with the following text duplicated on each page:

> All About Me; Everyone is different / No one's quite the same. / This book is all about ME / And this is my name. /_____; When I wake up in the morning this is how I feel; And whenever I get hungry, this is my favorite meal; This is what I like to wear when I get dressed each day; And this is what I like to do when I am ready to play; When I look out the window this is what I see; And when you're looking at my house this is what it will be; Here's my favorite animal, I really

think it's neat; And when I think about my friends, this one can't be beat!; When I take a special trip, here's where I like to be; And when I'm only here at home I'm in this family. Everyone is different, / Even special friends. / This book is all about me / Now it's time to say . . . / THE END

During several class sessions distribute the booklets and let children draw appropriate pictures to accompany the rhyme on each page. Tell the children to be sure the pictures tell the right answers so the reader will know all about each of them. Display the completed books before sending them home.

Rhyme Time

Objectives:

1. Listen and identify rhyming words.
2. Discuss the dedication page of a book.
3. Express personal identification with a character in literature.
4. Organize characters and/or events in chronological sequence.
5. Memorize and recite rhyming lines.
6. Develop visual discrimination.
7. Predict an outcome.
8. Recognize that repetition creates patterns.

Recommended Readings:

Barasch, Marc Ian.*No Plain Pets!* Illustrated by Henrik Drescher. HarperCollins, 1991.
In a rhyming text a young boy uses his imagination to express his desire for an unusual pet. (Objective 8)

Blos, Joan W.*A Seed, a Flower, a Minute, an Hour.* Illustrated by Hans Poppel. Simon & Schuster, 1992.
The beauty and mystery of change is depicted in brief text and colorful illustrations. (Objectives 1, 7,and 8)

Cauley, Lorinda Bryan. *Clap Your Hands.* G.P. Putnam's Sons, 1992.
The rhyming text is an open invitation for children to become actively involved in each action described. (Objective 1)

Florian, Douglas. *Vegetable Garden.* Harcourt Brace Jovanovich, 1991.
A family harvests the bounty of the seeds they have sown. (Objectives 1 and 6)

Lindbergh, Reeve. *The Day the Goose Got Loose*. Illustrated by Steven Kellogg. Dial, 1990.
When the wild geese fly over a farm the goose gets loose and wreaks havoc on the farm. (Objectives 1 and 6)

————. A young boy and his mother explore secrets of the farm at midnight. (Objectives 1 and 6)

Lindgren, Barbra. *The Wild Baby*. Adapted from the Swedish by Jack Prelutsky. Illustrated by Eva Eriksson. Greenwillow, 1980.
When Baby Ben disobeys his mother he tumbles from one adventure to another. (Objectives 1 and 3)

Lyon, George Ella. *The Outside Inn*. Illustrated by Vera Rosenberry. Orchard, 1991.
A day's menu of "taste-tempting treats" from the outdoor world is proposed in rhyme. (Objectives 1, 5, and 7)

Marzollo, Jean. *Uproar on Hollercat Hill*. Illustrated by Steven Kellogg. Dial, 1980.
Family members learn that fighting is sometimes acceptable, as long as they make up afterward. (Objectives 1, 2, 3, 5, and 6)

Van Laan, Nancy. *Possum Come a-Knockin'*. Illustrated by George Booth. Alfred A. Knopf, 1990.
Possum's knocking disrupts a family's activities in this rhythmical cumulative tale. (Objectives 1, 4, and 5)

Group Introductory Activity:

Introduce the concept of rhyme by sharing the nursery rhyme "Humpty Dumpty" with the children. Recite "Humpty Dumpty sat on a wall, Humpty Dumpty had a great," then pause and allow the children to supply the rhyming word for the line. Complete the poem in the same manner. Ask the students how they knew what word to use. If no one suggests that "fall" rhymes with or sounds like "wall," then suggest that idea to them. Explain that words that end with the same sounds are said to rhyme with each other. Show the children several items and ask them to choose any two whose names rhyme. Articles could include a star and a car, a truck and a duck, a teddy bear and a chair, and other concrete pairs. Explain to the children that stories are often told in rhyme. Remind them how the rhyming words in "Humpty Dumpty" were found at the end of the lines. Ask them to listen carefully as Nancy Van Laan's *Possum Come a-Knockin'* is read aloud and try to find lines that rhyme. Children will enjoy reciting the repetitive "When a possum come a-knockin' at the door, at the door," as the lines are read.

After reading the story ask the children to recall rhyming lines they discovered in the book. Give the students the opportunity to share these lines. Write the rhyming words on a rhyme chart to be used throughout the unit (add rhyming words as children discover them in each book). Follow up by letting children discuss the different family members who were upset by the opossum's visit. Ask the children to identify the sequence in which the characters appeared. If the children need help, turn to the first page and have them try to recall who will appear next. Continue to identify and list the characters on the chalkboard. Leave the list of characters on the board for a few days. As a daily exercise point to a character name, read it aloud, and ask the children to chant the action words associated with that character in Van Laan's tale (e.g., "Tom-cat started sniffin' and a-spittin' and a-hissin' when a possum come a-knockin' at the door"). By the end of the unit the children will be able to act out their interpretation of the story.

Follow-Up Activities for Teacher and Students to Share:

1. Explain to the class that *A Seed, a Flower, a Minute, an Hour* by Joan W. Blos is an illustrated poem that talks about changes. Discuss the changes mentioned in the book's title. When children grasp the relationship between paired lines that show changes, tell them to listen to the title again and try to find words that rhyme. Number the brief lines as one, two, three, and four. Use extended fingers to count the lines as the title is repeated. The children should hear that lines two and four rhyme. Explain to the class that the same rhyme pattern (ABCB) is used throughout the book. Ask children to listen carefully as the book is read and try to predict what will be on the back of each page based on their knowledge of how things change and the rhyme pattern Blos used.
2. Remind children of the ABCB rhyme pattern they found in Joan W. Blos's *A Seed, a Flower, a Minute, an Hour* if that book has already been shared. If not, introduce the ABCB rhyming pattern, explaining that in this form the second and fourth lines rhyme. Invite the children to join in reciting the rhyme as they read Marc Ian Barasch's book *No Plain Pets!* As a follow-up the children can illustrate or sculpt from clay their own imaginary pet.
3. Share Lorinda Bryan Cauley's book, *Clap Your Hands*, urging the children to act out each rhyming line as the book is read. If space is limited, you may need to divide the class into groups and select one group to act out each separate line. Ask the children to recall the rhyming sound they heard. Offer a further extension of the book by placing it in a center where children can read the pictures and do the activities.

4. Read aloud Douglas Florian's *Vegetable Garden*. Encourage the children to join in on the rhymes. After reading the story, refer to the illustrations. Point out the plants that are not named and have the children identify them (e.g., tomatoes, watermelons, and pumpkins). Let the children discuss what a gardener does and why. Have small groups act out the steps in gardening, demonstrating an understanding of the concept.

5. Introduce *The Day the Goose Got Loose* by Reeve Lindbergh by pointing out that the illustration on the title page actually begins the story. Before reading the first lines, urge the children to read the pictures on the following page and identify different actions that take place. Children will need time to see all that is occurring in Steven Kellogg's action-packed illustrations on each page. Read the story aloud at least once for pure pleasure. Ask the children to listen as the book is reread and to identify the rhyming sounds.

6. Ask children to count the animals on the pages, one through ten, as they listen to *The Midnight Farm* by Reeve Lindbergh. Students will especially enjoy searching for the ten field mice. Discuss how the midnight farm is different from a farm by day. Let the class speculate about what they might find if they explored their home by night. Ask the children to identify the rhyming words as the story is reread.

7. After reading *The Wild Baby* by Barbra Lindgren, ask the children if they have any personal experiences similar to those in the book that they would like to share. Lead the children into a discussion of personal safety. Refer to the story and have the children consider each reckless activity of Baby Ben. Ask children to think very hard and decide what Ben's mother must have told him not to do in each case. Urge the children to share rhyming words they found in the story.

8. Before sharing George Ella Lyon's *The Outside Inn*, prepare a menu insert using some of the food items Lyon lists in the book. Duplicate a copy for each student. Ask the group to listen for rhyming words in the text as the book is shared. Read *The Outside Inn* aloud, pausing before reading the answer to each question so the students have an opportunity to predict the rhyming lines. After completing the story, allow children to share rhymes they heard. Let the class discuss reactions to the menus Lyon suggests.

As a follow-up have children design individual menu covers for "The Outside Inn" on a folded piece of construction paper. Staple a menu insert inside each cover. Let the children order from the menu and eat in the classroom "Outside Inn." It would be wise to limit orders to the "Specialty of the Day." Use real food items to represent Lyon's foods, such as cocoa for "puddle ink," cooked pasta noodles for "slugs in a sack," and granola for "gravel crunch." As a special treat serve "worms and dirt" from the following recipe.

Dirt Cake

1 16-oz. package of crushed
   chocolate sandwich cookies
8 oz. non-dairy whipped topping
candy
3 c. cold milk

2 4-oz. packages chocolate
   instant pudding mix
4-oz. "gummy" worm

Press half the crushed cookies into the bottom of a 9" × 13" baking dish or new, large terra cotta flower pot (plug the drain hole). Prepare pudding according to package directions using 3 c. milk instead of 4. Fold in whipped topping and candy worms. Spoon into prepared pan and sprinkle with remaining cookie crumbs to resemble loose soil. Chill for one hour or overnight. If served in a flower pot, decorate by inserting a stem of plastic flowers and serve with a new gardening trowel.

9. While reading aloud Jean Marzollo's *Uproar on Hollercat Hill*, pause briefly on each page to allow the children to view the facial expressions of the characters and the illustrated action. Repeat the two recurring rhymes beginning with "Strawberry shortcake, huckleberry pie," having the children join in until they can repeat the rhymes from memory. Follow the reading with a discussion about families and why brothers and sisters might fight or disagree. Give the children an opportunity to identify with the book characters by letting them repeat the two rhymes and demonstrate the feelings of each character through their facial expressions.

    If the children do not already know the roles of the author and illustrator, explain that the author writes the words and the illustrator creates the pictures for a book or story. Turn to the dedication page and read the dedication from author Jean Marzollo. Ask the children to think about the words of the story and speculate about why she dedicated the book as she did. Conclude by reading the dedication made by Steven Kellogg, the illustrator, and let children decide why he may have used those words (e.g., the book characters are represented as cats).

Closure:

    Allow the children to explore rhyming words in a learning center. Refer children to the rhyme chart that they have been compiling from books throughout the unit. Ask the children if they can see some similarities in the way the rhyming words look. Some child will notice that many of the words end with the same letters. Tell the children that the rhyme chart will be cut into cards with single words on them. Place the cards in a rhyme center where children may attempt to find rhyming pairs. Reread Lorinda Bryan Cauley's *Clap Your Hands*, allowing the children to read or chant the poem as they dramatize the rhyme.

It's as Easy as ABC

Objectives:

1. Express ideas and emotions through sounds.
2. Verbalize or demonstrate the action represented by illustrations and/or words.
3. Recognize sign language as a means of communication.
4. Select pictures and words that correspond to the letters of the alphabet.
5. Classify foods by fruits or vegetables.
6. Recognize the shapes of the letters of the alphabet.
7. Develop visual discrimination.

Recommended Readings:

Berger, Terry. *Ben's ABC Day.* Illustrated by Alice Kandell. Lothrop, Lee & Shepard, 1982.
Black-and-white photographs and action words describe Ben's day from awakening to yawning and "Z-z-z-z-z-z" (sleeping). (Objective 2)

Chaplin, Susan Gibbons. *I Can Sign My ABC's.* Illustrated by Laura McCaul. Gallaudet University, 1986.
Colorful illustrations depict both the manual letter signs and a sign for the object pictured with each letter of the alphabet. (Objectives 2 and 3)

Cox, Lynn. *Crazy Alphabet.* Illustrated by Rodney McRae. Orchard, 1990.
Bright graphics illustrate this cumulative alphabet story depicting the trouble that comes from eating an apple. (Objectives 1 and 7)

Doubilet, Anne. *Under the Sea from A to Z.* Illustrated by David Doubilet. Crown, 1991.
Brilliantly colored photographs of unusual marine life are extended by detailed text and large-print, single-sentence captions. (Objective 4)

Ehlert, Lois. *Eating the Alphabet: Fruits and Vegetables from A to Z.* Harcourt, Brace, Jovanovich, 1989.
Graphic illustrations in vivid colors delight the palette in this eating alphabet. (Objectives 5 and 7)

Elting, Mary, and Folsom, Michael, *Q Is for Duck.* Illustrated by Jack Kent. Clarion, 1980.
This alphabet guessing game encourages divergent thinking in young readers. (Objective 4)

Feldman, Judy. *The Alphabet.* Children's Press, 1991.
Photographs depict alphabet shapes in the natural world. (Objectives 6 and 7)

Hoguet, Susan Ramsey. *I Unpacked My Grandmother's Trunk*. E.P. Dutton, 1983.
Grandmother's trunk holds an alphabet of visual adventures in this book that contains directions for playing the word game upon which the book was based. (Objective 2)

MacDonald, Suse. *Alphabatics*. Bradbury, 1986.
Through twists, turns, and acrobatics each letter of the alphabet gradually changes into an illustration of its corresponding noun. (Objective 7)

Shelby, Anne. *Potluck*. Illustrated by Irene Trivas. Orchard, 1991.
A multicultural feast furnishes food and fun for all in this alliterative ABC book. (Objective 4)

Snow, Alan. *The Monster Book of A-B-C Sounds*. Dial, 1991.
Monsters play hide-and-seek with each other and make an alphabet of sounds. (Objective 1)

Group Introductory Activity:

While reading *Q Is for Duck* by Mary Elting and Michael Folsom, give children time to speculate about possible answers to each riddle. As a follow-up produce a one-act play based upon the text. "Letter A" may walk across the stage as a narrator or group reads the question and children representing zoo animals can follow as another narrator or group answers the riddle. The entire staging could follow this format with the letters entering as the question is asked and the corresponding animal character acting out the answer as it is given.

Follow-Up Activities for Teacher and Students to Share:

1. Share aloud *Ben's ABC Day* by Terry Berger, asking the children to demonstrate a few of the activities as the book is read. Have the children name action verbs ending in "-ing" that describe activities they participate in during the day. Ask the music teacher to let the children sing and dramatize some of these action words to the tune of "The Mulberry Bush."

2. Read aloud and demonstrate the letter and word signs in Susan Gibbons Chaplin's *I Can Sign My ABC's*. Teach the children to sign their teacher's name, their school name, or other selected common words.

3. After reading *Crazy Alphabet* by Lynn Cox have the children create the sounds that accompany each character or activity in the book. If a word does not have a corresponding sound (e.g., "vase"), let the children use their bodies to form the word. If desired, write a class language experience story based on a cumulative story rhyme.

4. After having shared Anne Doubilet's *Under the Sea from A to Z*, let children cut pictures of marine life from old magazines and compile them in an "Under the Sea" scrapbook. Have children dictate sentence captions for their selections.

5. Before reading Lois Ehlert's *Eating the Alphabet: Fruits and Vegetables from A to Z* aloud, ask parents or teachers to bring samples of the various fruits and vegetables mentioned in the text. After sharing the book with children have them sample some of the foods available. Let each child draw a picture of his or her favorite sample. Display these pictures on a bulletin board captioned "We Are What We Eat." Another way to extend this activity is to have the children cut out pictures of fruits and vegetables from magazines. Have the children classify these foods by placing them under the headings of fruits or vegetables.

    Another way to eat the alphabet is to have each child use colored milk (tinted with food coloring) to paint his or her initials on a slice of white bread. Toast the bread slices, serve them with honey or butter, and eat the alphabet.

6. Before reading *The Alphabet* by Judy Feldman, explain to the children that the photographs do not show things that begin with each letter of the alphabet. Instead each letter shape is contained in the photographs (e.g., the letter *S* in the flamingo's neck on the cover). Share the book aloud, giving the children time to locate each letter shape in the picture. As a follow-up allow the children to demonstrate the shapes of the letters with their bodies. For further reference on how children may use their bodies to make shapes, see Rachel Carr's *Be a Frog, Be a Bird, Be a Tree* (Doubleday, 1973).

7. While sharing Susan Ramsey Hoguet's *I Unpacked My Grandmother's Trunk*, give the children time to verbalize the action shown in each illustration. After completing the story, play the game with the class according to Hoguet's directions.

8. Share Suse MacDonald's *Alphabatics* with the children. The sequential transformations in the book lend themselves to the video format. It is recommended that children view the video (Random House/Miller Brody, 1989) if it is available. After the children have experienced *Alphabatics* in its print or nonprint format, place the book in a learning center equipped with large, cutout or die-punched alphabet letters; paper; glue; and pencils or crayons. Let the children use center time to select a letter, glue it onto paper, and add details with pencil or crayons to transform the letter into an object.

9. Children will love to make the sounds of the creatures in Alan Snow's *The Monster Book of A-B-C Sounds*. As the book is read aloud, indicate to the children the appropriate time to vocalize the sounds. After completing the book, share Maurice Sendak's *Where the Wild Things Are* (Harper & Row, 1963), letting the children use their new vocabulary of monster sounds to depict the wild rumpus from Max's adventure.

Closure:

Review the ABC books by looking at all of the foods mentioned. Emphasize foods that begin with the first letter of each student's name. Read aloud Anne Shelby's *Potluck.* Let the children discuss the events in the book. Plan with the students and parent volunteers to have a class potluck lunch or snack. Request that each child bring a food item whose name begins with the first letter of the student's first name.

The Antics of David McPhail's Characters

Objectives:

1. Identify the purpose of a field trip.
2. Use globes or maps to develop geographic skills.
3. Develop awareness of individual differences and the uniqueness of others.
4. Arrange events in sequence.
5. Exchange ideas through discussion.
6. Engage in a creative visual art process.
7. List or graph differences.
8. Communicate name, address, and telephone number orally or in writing.
9. Express ideas in oral and written language.

Recommended Readings:

McPhail, David. *Andrew's Bath*. Little, Brown, 1984.
Andrew's imagination adds excitement to his first solo bath. (Objective 6)

———. *The Dream Child*. E.P. Dutton, 1985.
Throughout the night a dreaming child and her Tame Bear help make the world a better place to live. (Objective 4)

———. *Emma's Pet*. E.P. Dutton, 1985.
Emma's search for a big, soft, cuddly pet frustrates her until she finds the perfect solution. (Objectives 4 and 9)

———. *Farm Morning*. Harcourt Brace Jovanovich, 1985.
A young girl and her father work together to finish the early morning farm chores. (Objectives 4 and 9)

———. *Farmboy's Year*. Atheneum, 1992.
Gentle illustrations and journal-like text highlight meaningful moments in a young nineteenth-century New England boy's life. (Objectives 7 and 9)

————. *First Flight*. Little, Brown, 1987.

A young boy behaves well on his first airplane flight but his teddy bear has some difficulties. (Objective 8)

————. *Fix-It*. E.P. Dutton, 1984.

In an attempt to entertain Emma, her mother reads her a story that captures her desire to read it again and again, even though the television is now fixed. (Objective 5)

————. *Lost!* Little, Brown, 1990.

A bear lost in the city becomes an imaginary friend for a little boy. (Objectives 1 and 2)

————. *Pig Pig Grows Up*. E.P. Dutton, 1980.

Pig Pig loves being a baby so much that, for a time, he refuses to grow up. (Objective 9)

————. *Something Special*. Little, Brown, 1988.

Sam, the youngest member of a talented family, searches until he finds his own special gift. (Objective 3)

————. *The Train*. Little, Brown, 1977.

Imagination transforms a boy into a mechanic and his toy train into a real locomotive. (Objectives 2 and 9)

Biographical Sources:

For information on David McPhail see *Something about the Author*, vol. 47, pages 150–65 and *Fifth Book of Junior Authors & Illustrators*, pages 213–14.

Group Introductory Activity:

Lost! by David McPhail is an effective tool to introduce the library as a room filled with information. After the book is read in the library media center, have the library media specialist help the children locate a globe or map. Assist the children in interpreting the map and finding the location of their state and town. If a local map is available, help the children locate the school and other important places in their community. "Books played a . . . significant role in my childhood," says McPhail, "and I still have fond memories of the public library" (*Fifth Book of Junior Authors & Illustrators*, p. 213). A field trip to the local public library for the purpose of gathering facts and learning the location is an appropriate follow-up activity.

Follow-Up Activities for Teacher and Students to Share:

1. Read aloud *Andrew's Bath* by David McPhail. As a follow-up let the children make soap-suds art. Squirt a mound of canned shaving foam on each child's desk and let the students use their hands to smooth it so they can write their names and draw in the foam. After the free expression art time have the children use the remains of the foam to scrub their desks and wash their hands.

2. David McPhail's *The Dream Child* is an effective tool to help children settle down after play time. Explain that McPhail used his daughter Jaime as the model for the Dream Child (*Something about the Author*, vol. 47, p. 161). To establish a dreamy mood play Peter, Paul & Mary's "All through the Night" (*Peter, Paul & Mommy*, Warner Brothers, WB M5 1785) or other quiet music as a background to the reading or use the sound filmstrip of *The Dream Child* (Random House, 1985) to share the story. Ask the children to listen for all the situations the Dream Child and her Tame Bear become involved in during the story. After sharing the story, ask the children to list and describe the events that happened in sequential order. Encourage the class to think of real situations that could be made better through the help of children. Look at the children's list and let the group choose one suggestion to undertake as a class project. Possibilities include adopting an animal at the local zoo, helping with animal care or pet adoption through a local humane society, or practicing good ecology and recycling.

3. After reading David McPhail's *Emma's Pet*, share with the class Steven Kellogg's *Can I Keep Him?* (Dial, 1971). Compare and contrast the two books with the children. Conduct a search for a classroom pet. Let children propose a variety of animals so they can examine the positive and negative characteristics of each animal. Children may select a few of the suggestions and use them to write a class book in the following format: "Mr./Ms. _____'s class wanted a pet. They tried a _____, but it was too _____. They found a _____, but it was _____. They caught a _____, but it was _____." After proposing several unsuitable pets, conclude with, "Finally they brought a _____ and it was just right." After children illustrate the lines, they may place the pages in the proper sequence and compile them into a book titled *Our Class Pet*. If possible, complete the activity by bringing the selected animal to school and keeping it in a science center as a class pet.

4. Practice reading *Farm Morning* by David McPhail prior to reading it aloud to the class so that the proper inflection can be used in the reading of the text. Be aware that the whole story is told by the father, who often repeats the girl's questions and comments. Invite the students to make appropriate animal sounds as the animals are named in the book. After sharing the story

aloud, ask the children if they know who was telling the story. If desired, ask the children to recall the order of feeding to reinforce sequential skills. Reread the book, stopping after each comment by the father. Ask the children to speculate about what the little girl said that caused her father to answer as he did.

5. Share David McPhail's *Farmboy's Year* with the children. After the reading ask the children to think about ways the boy's life was different from their own. If necessary review portions of the text and illustrations to jog the children's memories. List the responses on the board. Let the group classify the completed list into differences caused by where they live and those caused by the time in which they live. If the students are sufficiently advanced, the teacher may prepare sequencing cards with the names of the months of the year and let children practice identifying the names and placing them in proper order.

6. David McPhail likes to use animals in his books for many reasons but especially because they can do "all sorts of silly antics that for an actual child would be very dangerous. . . . They can have human characteristics, and I can even endow them with bad qualities without reflecting on a particular kind of person" (*Something about the Author*, vol. 47, p. 161). Share his comments with the children. Then read McPhail's book *First Flight* aloud.

   Follow up by creating an airline center where children may play pilot, passenger, and flight attendant. Include tickets, plastic or paper wings, and luggage tags. Ask each child to communicate, orally or written, his or her name, address, and telephone number to be placed on the luggage tag. Attach these tags to treat bags prepared by the teacher, media specialist, or parent volunteer. Visit the library, where the media specialist may share transportation books, and conclude by having the children go to an area designated as "Baggage Claims." Here the children may sort through the prepared treat bags to find and claim their bag.

7. For a share-and-tell session ask the children to bring something from home that was special to them as a baby or toddler. As they share these items ask them to tell why each thing is special. Tell the class that David McPhail has written several books about a character named Pig Pig, who loved all of his baby things. Share the story *Pig Pig Grows Up* with the group. As a follow-up review the first six pages of illustrated situations and have the children describe how each event could change now that Pig Pig is grown up. In a class discussion have children share ideas for helping at home as they grow up.

8. After sharing David McPhail's *Something Special*, point out that, like Sam, everyone has a special talent even though he or she might not have yet discovered it. Discuss activities at which the individual students excel.

Plan a talent show in which children may perform or exhibit samples of their talents. Prepare a choral reading of a favorite poem such as Margaret Hiller's "Just Me" (*Random House Book of Poetry for Children*, Random House, 1983, p. 120) so that all of the children are included in the performance and celebrated for their diversity.

9.   Read aloud *The Train* by David McPhail. Let children discuss the jobs Matthew did on the train. Use a state or city map to help the children identify places they could visit. Have them draw a picture of where they would go and what kind of transportation they would use. If possible, contact the public library to find a local club for miniature railroad enthusiasts. Invite a member of the club to visit the class and tell the children about his or her hobby. Teach the children to sing what was probably Matthew's favorite song, "I've Been Working on the Railroad."

Closure:

When Emma, in David McPhail's *Fix-It*, discovers the story her mother reads, she wants to hear it again and again. Read this book aloud and then ask the children to describe all the activities they could do if they did not watch television. In celebration of Emma's delight in reading have a class or school "TV Turn-Off" for one night.

Chapter 2
First Grade/Second Grade

A Pet Project

Objectives:

1. Create a graph of pets that students own or would like to own.
2. Engage in creative drawing, constructing, and/or sculpting.
3. Be aware of the concepts of chapter books and the table of contents.
4. Discuss problems and solutions.
5. Understand and demonstrate responsibility by caring for a pet in the classroom.
6. Compose an original poem or story.

Recommended Readings:

Brown, Marc. *Arthur's Pet Business*. Little, Brown, 1990.
   Arthur demonstrates how responsible he can be when he opens his pet care business. (Objectives 1 and 5)

Coffelt, Nancy. *Goodnight, Sigmund*. Harcourt Brace Jovanovich, 1992.
   A young boy's pet cat, Sigmund, is always there to be loved. (Objectives 2 and 6)

Ernst, Lisa Campbell. *Walter's Tail*. Bradbury, 1992.
   Walter's wagging tail creates constant mishaps until his owner can no longer take him downhill to town. (Objective 4)

Kamen, Gloria. *Second-Hand Cat*. Atheneum, 1992.
   After a visit to the veterinarian Nathan's cat shows his indignation by running away. (Objective 6)

Kroll, Virginia L. *Helen the Fish*. Illustrated by Teri Weidner. Albert Whitman, 1992.
   Hannah's older brother offers her consolation after her pet goldfish dies. (Objective 5)

Lockwood, Primrose. *Cat Boy!* Illustrated by Clara Vulliamy. Clarion, 1990.
A young boy shares virtually all his daily activities with his beloved cat. (Objective 6)

Schertle, Alice. *Little Frog's Song.* Illustrated by Leonard Everett Fisher. HarperCollins, 1992.
After Little Frog is washed away from his pond, a young boy saves him and returns the creature to his home. (Objective 4)

Stolz, Mary. *King Emmett the Second.* Illustrated by Garth Williams, Greenwillow, 1991.
After the death of his pet pig and a move to Ohio, Emmett is determined to be miserable but gradually learns that changes are not all bad. (Objectives 1 and 3)

Group Introductory Activity:

Introduce Mary Stolz's *King Emmett the Second* by explaining that Emmett, the boy in the story, has a very unusual pet. Allow the children to speculate about what type of animal might bear the name "King Emmett." Show the children the Garth Williams illustration on the cover to identify Emmett's pet as a pig. Explain to the children that this is a long read-aloud story that will take more than one day to complete. Share the table of contents with the children. Point out that Mary Stolz divided the story into parts called chapters. These are listed on the contents page with the page number where each begins. Share the book aloud, reading one or more chapters daily. After completing the book, tell the children that there is another book about Emmett and his first pet. Have multiple copies of Mary Stolz's "I Can Read" book *Emmett's Pig* (Harper & Brothers, 1959) available for individual reading during the unit.

As a further extension read "Hot Dog" from Shel Silverstein's *A Light in the Attic* (Harper & Row, 1981, p. 69). Let the children draw assumptions from the poem and illustration to guess what the boy really would have liked for a pet. Ask the students to speculate about why he substituted a hot dog. Discuss and graph types of pets the class members own or hope to own someday.

Follow-Up Activities for Teacher and Students to Share:

1.   Ask the children to listen carefully to *Arthur's Pet Business* by Marc Brown to discover all of the different pets Arthur cares for in his business. List the pets on the chalkboard as the group recalls them. Refer to the list of pets and ask what is involved in the care of each one (e.g., dog, canary, ant farm, frog, and trained boa constrictor). Make a chart of some of the common steps in pet care. If the students do not know how to care for a variety of pets or would like to learn more about other animals, refer to *Your First Pet and*

How to Take Care of It by Carla Stevens (Macmillan, 1974) or *Pets* (Eye Openers series, Macmillan, 1991). These books may be placed in a reading center along with other books on pets.

As a further extension the students will enjoy searching for the names of Marc Brown's sons, Tucker and Tolon, which are hidden in most of his books, including *Arthur's Pet Business.*

2. Read aloud Nancy Coffelt's *Goodnight, Sigmund.* Ask the children to compare their day's activities to those of the little boy in the story. The book follows a pattern, the first part of which reads: "When Mother reads me a story, I sit on her lap to listen . . . Hello, Sigmund." Use the same writing style in a class collaboration to incorporate the children's ideas into a story or to extend the story of Sigmund.

   Follow up with the children reproducing a scene in which they can imagine Sigmund appearing. Using color crayons or oil pastels on black construction paper, draw and heavily color in the scene to create an effect similar to the book's illustrations.

3. Share *Walter's Tail* by Lisa Campbell Ernst with the children. After reading let the children discuss the problems caused by Walter's tail. To extend the discussion ask the students to think about the problems a new puppy could cause in a home. List the children's ideas on one side of a chart. On the other side or on another chart list children's suggestions of positive things about puppy ownership. Let the children compare the good aspects with the bad. Follow by reading Jack Prelutsky's poem "My Dog, He Is an Ugly Dog" to the children (*The New Kid on the Block*, Greenwillow, 1984, pp. 62–63) to emphasize that loving a pet can make up for many bad qualities the animal may have.

4. Explain to the children that many "sound" words are included in Gloria Kamen's *Second-Hand Cat* (e.g., "splash," "barking," "howled," and "screeched"). Have the children listen as the book is shared to find words that represent sounds. After reading the story write the sound words on the board as students recall and demonstrate them. Discuss when and where each sound might be heard. Remind students that Nathan's cat did not want to ride in the car so he howled and yowled. Let the children speculate on how the cat felt in the veterinarian's office. Have the students mimic the sounds the cat may have made while there.

   Arrange to visit the library media center, where the media specialist may share other books about sounds with the children such as Peter Spier's *Gobble, Growl, Grunt* (Doubleday, 1988), *Crash! Bang! Boom!* (Doubleday, 1990), or Alan Snow's *Monster Book of A-B-C Sounds* (Dial, 1991). Team up with the media specialist to explain to the children that using sound words makes a story more interesting and suggest they write a sound story of their own to share with the class.

5. Read aloud *Helen the Fish* by Virginia L. Kroll. Let the boys and girls share their own experiences with the death of a pet. Remind the children that Seth told Hannah that Helen lived longer than most fish because Hannah took such good care of her pet. Let the students discuss things a good pet owner does for his or her animal and what might happen if those things are not done. As a follow-up obtain from the library media center a nonfiction book about goldfish or aquarium fishes. Place the book in a learning center where children may browse through it to learn about proper care for pet fish. After the children have explored the information book, discuss their findings and list rules for fish care on a chart. Post the chart near a goldfish bowl and let students take turns sharing the responsibility for the care and feeding of a goldfish.

6. After reading to the class *Cat Boy!* by Primrose Lockwood, explain that there are some activities which may be shared with a pet while others are better done alone. Reexamine the illustrations by Clara Vulliamy, asking the children to judge whether each scene shows an activity which the boy would have been wiser to do alone or one which is appropriate to share with a pet.

    Extend the activity with another point of view using the poem "What If?" from Beatrice Schenk de Regniers's *The Way I Feel . . . Sometimes* (Clarion, 1988, pp. 32–33). In this poem the little girl wonders, "What if my cat could talk? . . . What if my goldfish could learn? . . ." and "What if my dog were smart?" Have the children apply the "What if . . ." phrase to their own pets, real or imaginary. Have them write a paragraph or poem explaining what they wish their pets could do.

7. Read aloud *Little Frog's Song* by Alice Schertle. Let students discuss why some animals need to live in the wild and should not be kept as pets. Let the children brainstorm a list of animals that belong in the wild, not in houses as pets. Have the students suggest problems that could arise from trying to keep one of those animals as a pet. Let the group offer possible solutions to those problems. If possible, invite a naturalist or someone from the State Wildlife Department to talk with the class about caring for injured animals and returning them to the wild. Suggest to the music teacher that the children learn "Gatgoon" from *Sharon, Lois, and Bram Sing A to Z* (Crown, 1991) or other songs about frogs and pets.

Closure:

Create a display in the library media center showcasing the puppets and exotic clay pets the children have made. Ask the library media specialist to show students how to look up subject headings on pets, dogs, cats, and other animals so that they may continue to read about pets on their own.

Talent A to Z: Amy SchwartZ

Objectives:

1. Be exposed to a foreign language (German).
2. Use context clues in reading and listening.
3. Explain how to demonstrate respect for another person.
4. Respond to a story through writing, performing, and art.
5. Identify feelings and actions in oneself and in book characters.
6. Describe ways family members can resolve problems.
7. Demonstrate how to measure, using manipulatives.
8. Identify and role play jobs, careers, and related tasks.
9. Construct a basic family tree.

Recommended Readings:

Calmenson, Stephanie. *Wanted: Warm, Furry Friend.* Illustrated by Amy Schwartz. Macmillan, 1990.
It is disgust at first sight for two rabbits who later begin a pen-pal relationship that develops into true friendship. (Objectives 3 and 4)

Carlstrom, Nancy White. *Blow Me a Kiss, Miss Lilly.* Illustrated by Amy Schwartz. Harper & Row, 1990.
After the death of elderly Miss Lilly, her best friend, Sara, learns that memories are always alive. (Objective 5)

Hest, Amy. *The Crack-of-Dawn Walkers.* Illustrated by Amy Schwartz. Macmillan, 1984.
Sadie thoroughly enjoys her early Sunday morning walk, mainly because she has her beloved grandfather entirely to herself. (Objectives 4, 5, and 6)

———. *The Purple Coat.* Illustrated by Amy Schwartz. Macmillan, 1986.
Grampa and Gabby affirm that, "Once in a while it's good to try something new," as Gabby chooses and Grampa tailors her new purple coat. (Objective 7)

King, Larry L. *Because of Lozo Brown.* Illustrated by Amy Schwartz. Viking, 1988.
A young boy imagines his new neighbor to be a larger-than-life bully until he is forced to meet him. (Objective 2)

Schwartz, Amy. *Annabelle Swift, Kindergartner.* Orchard, 1988.
Annabelle's elder sister tries to prepare her for the first day of kindergarten, but most of her teaching misses the mark. (Objectives 4 and 5)

————. *Bea and Mr. Jones.* Bradbury, 1982.
Mr. Jones, advertising executive, and Bea, kindergartner, trade places with surprisingly happy results. (Objectives 4 and 8)

————. *Begin at the Beginning.* HarperCollins, 1983.
Sara is honored to be chosen to paint a picture for the second-grade art show but has difficulty finding where to begin. (Objectives 4 and 5)

————. *Her Majesty, Aunt Essie.* Bradbury, 1984.
Ruthie must find a way to prove to her doubting friend that imperious Aunt Essie is a real queen. (Objectives 5, 8, and 9)

————. *Oma and Bobo.* Bradbury, 1987.
Alice takes her new dog, Bobo, to obedience school, but it is still up to Grandma Oma to save the day. (Objective 1)

Biographical Sources:

For information on Amy Schwartz see *Something about the Author*, vol. 47, pages 190–92 and the *Sixth Book of Junior Authors & Illustrators*, pages 268–70.

Group Introductory Activity:

Introduce author and illustrator Amy Schwartz to the children by telling the children that she was raised in a very close Jewish family. "Some of my strongest memories from my childhood involve books. . . . I remember looking forward each year to the annual ritual of receiving a book from my grandmother on my birthday" (*Something about the Author*, vol. 47, p. 191). Schwartz was especially close to her grandmother and has said she usually "shows up in one way or another in several of her books" (*Sixth Book of Junior Authors & Illustrators*, p. 269). Before reading aloud Schwartz's book *Oma and Bobo*, it is important to learn the correct pronunciations of the German words Grandmother Oma speaks. Consult a German dictionary or foreign language instructor for help if necessary. Share the book with the children. If any class members are bilingual, let them describe and discuss experiences they have had with another language being spoken in the home. As a follow-up to the book, learn greetings or numbers in German or another appropriate language. Play excerpts from Ernst Wolff's *German Children's Songs*, vol. 1 (Smithsonian Folkways, 7271) for the children. With the help of the music teacher, select one of the children's favorites and learn to sing it in German.

As a further extension ask the children to share their experiences with dog training. Invite a guest to bring a well-trained dog to the class and demonstrate commands.

Follow-Up Activities for Teacher and Students to Share:

1. After reading Stephanie Calmenson's *Wanted: Warm, Furry Friend* to the class discuss the dangers of judging people by appearances. Ask the children if they think Ralph and Alice would have ever become friends if they had not been pen pals. Urge the students to choose details in the story that support their ideas. Refer to the magazine *Children's Album* (E.G.W., monthly) for current lists of pen pals so that each student may choose and correspond with a child in another location.

    As a follow-up read Shel Silverstein's poem "No Difference" from *Where the Sidewalk Ends* (Harper & Row, 1974, p. 81). Let the children discuss what the poem means to them. Ask the students to decide on ways they could "turn off the light" in order to see the real person inside others instead of judging by appearances. Make a "Turn Off the Light" poster with the children's suggestions that can be displayed in the room to help the children remember not to judge newcomers unfairly.

2. Read Nancy White Carlstrom's *Blow Me a Kiss, Miss Lilly* aloud to the group. After reading let the children share their reactions to the book. Lead the discussion into the affective domain by asking children how the story made them feel. Many of the children will probably express sorrow at Miss Lilly's death. Ask the children to judge whether the story would be better or more satisfying if Miss Lilly had not died. Then have the students decide if the book would have been as realistic if she had not died. Let the children list and discuss the things Sara did to help herself feel better after Miss Lilly died. Make a chart labeled "When I am sad I . . ." at the top and ". . . and then I feel better!" at the bottom. Let the students suggest actions that can bridge the gap between the emotions.

3. Introduce Amy Hest's *The Crack-of-Dawn Walkers* by asking the children if they have ever wished they could spend time alone with a parent or special adult without anyone else along. Show the children the cover of the book and explain that Sadie and her younger brother Ben both love being with their grandfather and do not want to share him. Tell the class to listen carefully as the story is read to discover how Sadie and Ben solve the problem and how Sadie and her grandfather feel about the solution. After reading the book, let the children suggest other solutions that Sadie and Ben might have chosen. Follow the discussion by sharing red rope licorice with the students. As a follow-up let children play out *The Crack-of-Dawn Walkers* and later perform their product for special guests during a "Just You and Me Day" at the end of the unit.

4. Before sharing *The Purple Coat* by Amy Hest obtain a large spool of string and several yardsticks for later use. Read the story aloud. Let the children discuss why Gabby hated the fittings. Let children discuss why it was important that Grampa have the right measurements for Gabby's coat. As

a follow-up have the children take each other's measurements and record them. Note that Grampa used a flexible tailor's measuring tape. Let the children speculate about the advantages of a flexible tape. Begin to measure using rulers or yardsticks so the children can see the difficulty of measuring around the waist with an inflexible instrument. Show the class the spool of string and ask the children how they might use it to take their measurements. If no one suggests that they could stretch the string down or around the areas to be measured, cut it, then measure it with a ruler, lead the discussion to that conclusion. Let pairs of students measure each other with the string and record their results, taking each of the measurements Grampa used. The strings may be labeled with students' names and displayed on a bulletin board, "This Class Really Measures Up!" with columns for "Arm," "Leg," "Waist," and "Chest." Let students make a list of other things that can be measured.

5. Before reading Larry L. King's *Because of Lozo Brown* to the class, ask the children to pay special attention to Amy Schwartz's illustrations. After completing the poem let the children speculate about why Amy Schwartz drew Lozo Brown as a giant. Let the children list some of the things the boy imagined about Lozo Brown and then contrast them with what he found when he got to know his new neighbor. Let the class discuss the difference between real and imagined. As a follow-up reread the poem, leaving out words. Children must use context clues to supply words that could logically fill the blanks.

6. Before reading Amy Schwartz's *Annabelle Swift, Kindergartner*, share the information about the origin of the story from the author's acknowledgment on the copyright page. Explain that authors often get their ideas from their family experiences. Amy Schwartz has said most of her ideas come from her memories of her family. Introduce the book by reading "Helping" from Shel Silverstein's *Where the Sidewalk Ends* (Harper & Row, 1974, p. 101). Tell the children that in this story Lucy, Annabelle's older sister, tries to help her get ready for kindergarten, but sometimes her help is the kind of help Annabelle can do without. Share the story aloud with the class. Follow up by counting nickels and pennies. As a further extension let each child write a sentence that tells kindergartners how to get ready for first grade. Illustrate and compile these into a "How to Succeed in First Grade" booklet.

7. After reading aloud *Bea and Mr. Jones* by Amy Schwartz, let the children share what their fathers, mothers, or other relatives do for a living. Have the children write a list of five or more activities they would perform if they traded jobs with a relative. Read the lists aloud or have each student select a job or task from his or her list to act out or role play. Let the rest of the class try to guess each occupation from the listed or enacted activities.

8.   Amy Schwartz says, "I usually write humorous and, I hope, warm picture books. They all come out of some sort of personal experience" (*Something about the Author*, vol. 47, p. 192). Tell the children that her book *Begin at the Beginning* grew out of her experience of finding it hard to begin writing. Share the story aloud. Reread the advice Sara's mother gave her on page 22: "You can only begin at the beginning. The universe is only people like you and me, and your desk and this room, and those houses. . . ." Ask the students to think about where they would choose as their "beginning place." Give the children the opportunity to paint their own "beginning" scenes, the things they know and care about. Display the paintings on a board labeled "Where We Begin."

9.   Share Amy Schwartz's *Her Majesty, Aunt Essie* with the children. After reading let the children discuss the character of Aunt Essie. Have the children recall details in the story about how Aunt Essie acted. Ask the group if they believe she would be easy to live with. Have them describe actions that would make her easy or difficult to get along with.

As a follow-up remind the children of the family tree Ruthie drew. Let the children draw individual family trees like that in the book showing parent(s) or guardians as well as other family members. Ruthie drew crowns on the heads of the kings and queens in her family tree. Tell the children to draw the people in their family tree dressed in the type of clothing they wear at work, for example, hard hats, business suits, or uniforms. Label each person in the family tree with name, relationship, and occupation, as dictated or written by the children. Display these on a "We're Branches on the Human Family Tree" bulletin board.

Closure:

The books Amy Schwartz has written and/or illustrated depict emotions and problems encountered in life. Celebrate her books by having a "Just You and Me Day" with the children. Have each child invite a special adult to visit the classroom. Share lunch and other special activities with the children and guests during the afternoon. At the close of the school day suggest that the child and adult go home together as in *The Crack-of-Dawn Walkers*. As a special activity children could perform the *Crack-of-Dawn Walkers* play they developed, give book talks on each book in this unit, or share their writings.

The Art and Language of Audrey and Don Wood

Objectives:

1. Define the following terms: *author, illustrator, Caldecott Award.*
2. Recognize visual cues in illustrations.
3. Predict an outcome.
4. Generate ideas using the arts.
5. Pretend to be a book character.
6. Demonstrate imagery through body movement and visual arts.
7. Discover how an author's stories are related to real life.
8. Increase vocabulary.

Recommended Readings:

Wood, Audrey. *Detective Valentine*. HarperCollins, 1987.
> The Old North Wind leaves no clues as Detective Valentine searches for the missing hats. (Objectives 3, 4, and 6)

———. *Elbert's Bad Word*. Illustrated by Audrey and Don Wood. Harcourt Brace Jovanovich, 1988.
> A clever concoction from the wizard's kitchen overcomes Elbert's bad word. (Objectives 4 and 8)

———. *Heckedy Peg*. Illustrated by Don Wood. Harcourt Brace Jovanovich, 1987.
> A mother must save her seven children when they are changed into foods by a wicked witch. (Objectives 3 and 8)

———. *King Bidgood's in the Bathtub*. Illustrated by Don Wood. Harcourt Brace Jovanovich, 1985.
> Nothing can coax King Bidgood to leave the bathtub until a logical young page solves the problem. (Objectives 1,3, 5, and 6)

———. *Little Penguin's Tale*. Harcourt Brace Jovanovich, 1989.
> Six little penguins listen as Grand Nanny tells a tale of penguin adventure while the seventh penguin chooses to experience her own story. (Objectives 3 and 6)

———. *The Napping House*. Illustrated by Don Wood. Harcourt Brace Jovanovich, 1984.
> A wakeful flea causes a series of incidents in this cumulative tale of the napping house where almost everyone is sleeping. (Objectives 1, 2, and 3)

———. *Silly Sally*. Harcourt Brace Jovanovich, 1992.
> Silly Sally travels to town backwards and upside down. (Objectives 5 and 6)

————. *The Three Sisters*. Illustrated by Rose Krans Hoffman. Dial, 1986.
Three sisters dance and laugh their way through three short stories. (Objectives 6 and 7)

————. *Weird Parents*. Dial, 1990.
A young boy shows how embarrassing and yet special it is to have weird parents. (Objective 4)

Wood, Don. *The Little Mouse, the Red Ripe Strawberry, and the Big Hungry Bear*. Child's Play, 1990.
A little mouse is thrilled with his beautiful strawberry, but how can he hide it from the big hungry bear? (Objectives 2 and 5)

Biographical Sources:

For information on Audrey Wood see *Something about the Author*, vol. 50, pages 218–24 and *Sixth Book of Junior Authors & Illustrators*, pages 320–21.   Information on Don Wood may be found in *Something about the Author*, vol. 50, pages 224–31 and *Sixth Book of Junior Authors & Illustrators*, pages 322–23.

Group Introductory Activity:

Audrey and Don Wood collaborated in writing and illustrating *The Napping House*. Review with the children the terms *author* and *illustrator*. Audrey says that rhythm is terribly important to her in a picture book. As she wrote *The Napping House* she actually sang the words to herself. Don says that he had trouble illustrating the book until Audrey made a simple change that turned the whole story around. "She had everyone in the house fall asleep stacked in a pile, one atop the other. Suddenly the comic and cozy possibilities seemed endless" (*Something about the Author*, vol. 50, p. 231). Don also says, "Most characters in our books are people we know. Audrey has done a lot of posing for me, and so has our son, Bruce. For the mouse in *The Napping House*, I worked for weeks with one crawling all over my drawing table!" (*Something about the Author*, vol. 50, p. 230).

Before reading *The Napping House* to the children tell them to study the characters in each illustration carefully and try to predict action on the next page. Share the book, giving the students time to examine and comment on what they see in each scene. Reread the story so the children may find the rhythm of the lines and join in the telling. Before reading explain to the children that every character in the story is included in every scene of the bedroom. The group will enjoy searching for the mouse and the flea in each illustration.

Follow-Up Activities for Teacher and Students to Share:

1. Read aloud *Elbert's Bad Word* by Audrey Wood. Tell the children that this time Audrey and Don shared the job of illustrating. Discuss with the children, as the wizard did, words that can be appropriate to describe how we feel. Elbert's word is described as ugly and covered with dark, bristly hairs. Before continuing, ask the children to draw or create their versions of the bad word. Have children listen to the language of the story as the wizard "pulled out a drawer filled with words that crackled and sparkled." Audrey Wood says that she works from an "idea box" filled with ideas that have come to her mind (*Something about the Author*, vol. 50, p. 222). Suggest that the class construct a "Wood Box." After reading books by the Woods, children can write suggestions for creative dramatics, movement, music, writing, storytelling, or other activities and place them in the box. Once a week examine the ideas and select one or more to do in the classroom.

   Extend *Elbert's Bad Word* by baking a cake like the wizard did with flour, honey, raisins, milk, and eggs. Cut the cooled cake into bars. Tape words on toothpicks and insert each toothpick into a piece of cake. Let the children learn new words in the same way Elbert did.

Honey Spice Cake

1½ c. flour (preferably whole wheat)	2 eggs
1 t. baking soda	2 t. vanilla
2 t. ground cinnamon	¼ c. honey
1 t. ground nutmeg	¾ c. milk
½ t. ground cloves	1/3 c. sugar
½ t. ground allspice	1½ c. raisins
1/3 c. margarine	

Preheat oven to 350°. In a medium bowl combine flour, baking soda, and spices, mixing well. Add margarine. Using a fork or pastry blender, mix until mixture resembles coarse crumbs. In a large bowl combine remaining ingredients, *except* raisins. Beat on low speed with an electric mixer until smooth. Add dry ingredients and beat one minute. Stir in raisins. Pour batter in an 8" square pan that has been sprayed with nonstick cooking spray. Bake 25 minutes. Cool in pan 10 minutes, then invert onto rack or plate to finish cooling. Cut into bars and serve.

2. Read aloud *Heckedy Peg* by Audrey Wood. Before reading the page where the mother guesses the foods, ask the children to predict what foods the children have been turned into. After completing the story, let the students

discuss the method used to identify the children while they were food. Ask the children to list other food combinations, for example, peanut butter wants jelly, salt wants pepper, strawberries want whipped cream, and hamburger wants french fries.

3. Audrey Wood, who frequently appears in her husband's illustrations says, "We 'cast' the book, much as if it were a stage play" (*Something about the Author*, vol. 50, p. 224). For his illustrations in *King Bidgood's in the Bathtub* Don Wood was named runner-up for the Caldecott Award. (There might be a silver medallion on the cover of the book to indicate the award.) Tell the children that this award goes to an illustrator for outstanding pictures. Before reading the book aloud, explain to the children what is meant by staging a play. Ask them to imagine this story as a play. Point out that Audrey Wood plays the role of the queen and their son Bruce is the clever page. Children can join the story each time the King cries with a "boom boom boom" or a "yum yum yum." At this point have the children predict what will happen in the next scene. If time allows, extend the story to group and individual roles and have the class act out the story or perform a choral reading.

4. Share *The Little Mouse, the Red Ripe Strawberry, and the Big Hungry Bear* by Don Wood with the students. Have the children speculate as to who is telling the story. Before sharing strawberries, if available, with the children, reexamine the pages showing the little mouse and the many different emotions he demonstrates. Ask the children to express the feelings of the little mouse and reflect these feelings through their facial expressions. Now act on the book by creating "Groucho Marx" glasses. To do this cut out pairs of connecting rings from plastic six-pack can holders. Punch a hole on opposing sides of each pair of glasses. Attach pipe cleaners for ear pieces. To make the nose cut a large teardrop shape from construction paper and attach it with tape on the bridge of the glasses. While the children wear the glasses, serve the strawberries and eat "incognito."

5. When Audrey Wood was growing up, she says,

   As the eldest of three sisters, I quite naturally fell into the role of storyteller. I would open one of my parents' lavishly illustrated art books and make up stories about paintings. The nature encyclopedia was also one of our favorites, especially the section on reptiles and amphibians. I remember these story sessions as idyllic but recall my youngest sister's cries of alarm: 'Mommy! Mommy! Audrey's making the snakes crawl off the page again!' (*Something about the Author*, vol. 50, p. 219).

   While reading *Little Penguin's Tale*, written and illustrated by Audrey Wood, ask the children to identify illustrations that show characters moving and dancing right off the pages. Children can also predict what will happen to the little penguin in each episode. If the children do not catch the humor in the last line of the story, explain the meaning and use of the homonyms "tale" and "tail." Children will enjoy pretending to walk like a penguin as Sergei Prokofiev's "March" from *Love for Three Oranges* (*Fiedler's Favorite Marches*, Boston Pops, RCA [CS 60700-4-RC]) is played.

Divide the class into a group of dancers and a group of artists. Secretly tell the dancers to select an animal movement, (e.g., a penguin walking, a goony bird dancing, a whale swimming, or a bird flying). Ask the dancers to think about how they can use their bodies to show that movement. Give the artists markers and art paper. Have the artist group watch the dancers and move their markers in the same way the dancers are moving their bodies. Artists' marks on paper should form a contour or line that reflects the dancers' motions. After the dancers have had ample time to demonstrate the movement, ask the artists to share their drawings and guess what animal movement the dancers were performing. Reverse the roles and repeat.

6. Read aloud Audrey Wood's *Silly Sally*. Children can act on this rhyming story in one of several ways. Re-create this story with the children by using a transparency marker to draw a happy face to represent Silly Sally on each child's index finger. Pretend the other fingers become the characters in the story and act it out accordingly. If room space allows movement, the children could be Silly Sally upside down by bending forward and holding their ankles. In this position they can pretend to walk backwards upside down as the teacher rereads *Silly Sally*.

7. Share Audrey Wood's *The Three Sisters* with the students. Make sure the children are aware that neither Audrey nor Don Wood illustrated the book. Remind the children that Audrey was the eldest of the three sisters. She said that at the age of three she could read voraciously in English and Spanish (*Something about the Author*, vol. 50, p. 219). What can the children deduce about Audrey's life and her stories? If no one suggests that her stories are often based on her real life, suggest that idea to the group. Audrey goes on to say, "My parents had all of us involved in the arts. We took dance lessons, drama lessons, and classes in sculpture and painting. We would put on plays of our own creation . . ." (*Something about the Author*, vol. 50, p. 219). Give small groups of children the opportunity to act out the stories and situations in the book *The Three Sisters*.

8. After reading *Weird Parents* by Audrey Wood, the children may wish to share imagined stories about "weird" parents, aunts, uncles, and others. Tell the children this is their chance to imagine funny, made-up stories. The more artistic child might prefer to draw his or her version. Let the students help prepare a recipe from *Mudworks* by MaryAnn Kohl (Bright Ring, 1989) such as "Peanut Butter Play Dough" (p. 117). The children can use this dough to sculpt their own weird creation and then eat it. On another day

team with the library media specialist to dress weirdly and serve "weird" food to the students. The media specialist might share food stories or books about eccentric personalities like *Amelia Bedelia* by Peggy Parish (Harper & Row, 1963).

Closure:

As Audrey Wood's *Detective Valentine* is being read aloud, give the children time to recall the clues and predict what has happened to the lost crown and hat. Salute Audrey and Don Wood with "Hats Off to Audrey and Don Wood Day." Ask the children to bring hats from home and pretend to be different characters when wearing the hats.

Grandparents: A Family Album

Objectives:

1. Show sensitivity to human needs and feelings.
2. Understand the value of photographs.
3. Re-create characters or events through creative dramatics, art, storytelling, and/or writing.
4. Predict a story outcome.
5. Recognize rhymes and patterns in reading.
6. Participate in a problem-solving discussion.
7. Recall events in a story.

Recommended Readings:

Bunting, Eve. *The Wednesday Surprise*. Illustrated by Donald Carrick. Clarion, 1989.
Young Anna works with Grandma every Wednesday night on a birthday surprise for her dad. (Objectives 1 and 4)

Cech, John. *My Grandmother's Journey*. Illustrated by Sharon McGinley-Nally. Bradbury, 1991.
Gramma tells the story of when she was a little girl. (Objective 7)

Dionette, Michelle. *Coal Mine Peaches*. Illustrated by Anita Riggio. Orchard, 1991.
Family traditions and memories are passed down as a young girl listens to her grandfather's stories. (Objectives 1 and 2)

George, William T. *Fishing at the Pond*. Illustrated by Lindsay Barrett George. Greenwillow, 1991.
Young Katie and her Grampy spend a day fishing and observing the sights of nature. (Objectives 3 and 7)

Hirschi, Ron. *Harvest Song*. Illustrated by Deborah Haffele. Cobblehill, 1991.
Family stories help a young boy imagine what his grandmother's childhood must have been like. (Objectives 5 and 7)

Lasky, Kathryn. *My Island Grandma*. Illustrated by Amy Schwartz. Morrow, 1993.
The island offers a summer home where Abbey and her grandmother can explore nature, swim, and tell stories. (Objectives 3 and 7)

Lindbergh, Reeve. *Grandfather's Lovesong*. Illustrated by Rachel Isadora. Viking, 1993.
Grandfather expresses his love for his grandson through metaphorical descriptions of the seasons. (Objectives 1, 5, and 7)

McCully, Emily Arnold. *Grandmas at the Lake*. Harper & Row, 1990.
Two grandmothers with decidedly different opinions ruin the boys' vacation until they take matters into their own hands. (Objectives 1 and 3)

Moore, Elaine. *Grandma's Promise*. Illustrated by Elise Primavera. Lothrop, Lee & Shepard, 1988.
Kim enjoys sharing time with Grandma during a winter week together and looks forward to the promise of summer. (Objectives 3 and 6)

Waddell, Martin. *Grandma's Bill*. Illustrated by Jane Johnson. Orchard, 1991.
Little Bill learns about his grandfather Bill through the pictures in Grandma's photo album. (Objectives 1 and 2)

Group Introductory Activity:

To introduce the unit on grandparents the teacher may choose to bring a picture, item, or food (e.g., chocolate chip cookies) that reminds him or her of grandparents. Share the object and a personal memory, if possible, with the children. Follow up by reading *Coal Mine Peaches* by Michelle Dionette. Give the children an opportunity to share thoughts about the story before returning to the page where the little girl and her grandfather are looking at a picture on the mantle. Begin reading with, "I loved the things in my grandfather's house." End with, "Other babies came. . . ." Discuss the meaning of a family tree with the children. Make a bulletin board where the children can display pictures of themselves and their grandparents. Each day as the teacher reads a story in the unit, the children may wish to bring pictures or objects related to their grandparents to share with the class. Ask the children to speculate on the value or meaning that photographs have for families.

Follow-Up Activities for Teacher and Students to Share:

1. Read aloud *The Wednesday Surprise* by Eve Bunting, stopping the reading with the page that ends, "It's a special surprise. . . ." Have the children predict the ending before continuing. Let the children discuss the possible reasons why Grandma never learned to read when she was young. Allow the students to speculate about how Grandma felt before and after learning to read. To share the importance of reading, have "reading buddies" in class or invite elderly people to visit the classroom to discuss reading or share a story with the group.

2. Before sharing *My Grandmother's Journey* by John Cech aloud, the teacher will gain a better understanding of the grandmother by reading "A Note on the Story" from the back of the book. Explain to the children that the grandmother in the book is the mother of the author's wife. Ask the children to recall parts of the story they remember best. Then have the children connect those parts, retelling the story beginning with Gramma's question, "How does it start?" The students can sequence the middle events and retell the ending in their own words.

   As an extension ask other teachers in the building to bring a variety of shoes to display. Use the shoes in a center where children can imagine where these shoes have been, who wore them, what they did in the shoes, and what problems the person may have faced. In conclusion have the students team up to make up a story about one of the pairs of shoes. Ask the music teacher to sing a song about feet or shoes with the children, such as "Put Your Little Foot Right Out" by Larry Spier (*The Reader's Digest Children's Songbook*, Reader's Digest, 1985, pp. 208–10).

3. Read aloud to the class *Fishing at the Pond* by William T. George. List scenes from the story that the children recall. Have the students discuss what they like about the various scenes. Ask the children to think about grandparents, real or imaginary. Use the question, "If you could spend a day with _____, what can you imagine doing together?" As an extension the teacher might ask a senior citizen or other guest to demonstrate some fishing techniques.

4. Before reading aloud Ron Hirschi's story *Harvest Song*, serve potato cakes (frozen or home-made) to the children and have them learn the rhyme from the book:

   > One potato for the morning
   > two for the noonday sun.
   > One potato for suppertime,
   > then our day is done.

Explain to the children that this rhyme comes from the book *Harvest Song* by Ron Hirschi and that the book, like Cech's *My Grandmother's Journey*, is based on stories told to the author by his grandmother. Read the story aloud. Ask the children to recall some of the stories about nature found in the book. The book ends with a rhyme that the children can learn.

5. Before reading *My Island Grandma* by Kathryn Lasky, ask the children to imagine a place where they would like to spend their summers. Ask them what things they would do there. Read aloud Abbey's story about her summer with the children. Have the group listen for the summer things Abbey does, then have them recall these activities in order. List them on the board. Later, after the children have had an opportunity to complete an art activity, have them refer to this list and write three to five sentences telling what they'd like to do during the summer (real or imagined).

    If the children do not recognize the story Abbey pretends to be a part of, locate and read Robert McCloskey's *Blueberries for Sal* (Viking, 1948) or show the filmstrip of that title (Weston Woods, N041). If possible, take the children outside so they can lie on the ground and watch the cloud formations as Abbey did. Other follow-up activities could include finger-painting, sculpting clouds from cotton balls, making individual terrariums or moss gardens, or baking moon and star cookies.

6. Read aloud Reeve Lindbergh's *Grandfather's Lovesong*, asking the children to listen for a pattern to the words or a cycle to the story. The students might note the repetitive beginnings, the seasonal references, or the rhyming pattern ABCB. To truly appreciate Rachel Isadora's illustrations, turn to any one of the pages and ask the children to imagine what the boy and his grandfather might be thinking or doing. As a class write a poem about the feelings the children have for their grandparents. Use the pattern in the book for the style and format. Once students learn this pattern, encourage them to write individual love songs to a favorite person. Artistic children may choose to show their feelings by drawing scenes where they would like to be with a grandparent.

7. Read aloud Emily Arnold McCully's *Grandmas at the Lake*. Discuss with the children the differences in the two grandmas. Let the class predict what each grandmother would do or say in various new situations. As a follow-up activity the children may role play the story characters to retell McCully's story or another plot of their choice.

8. Before reading aloud *Grandma's Promise* by Elaine Moore, discuss the meaning of the word *promise* with the children. Share the book aloud and then have them explain what the word *promise* means in this story. Initiate a discussion by asking students to compare what the different families in this unit did instead of watching television. Make a class list of all the activities the children could do with their families instead of watching television. As a follow-up establish an activity center with dress-up clothes in a trunk. Give the children center time to dress up and pretend.

9. Before reading *Grandma's Bill* by Martin Waddell, refer to the bulletin board and discuss how pictures bring back memories. Read the story aloud. In this story Bill and his grandmother enjoy looking at family photographs in her album. Emphasize the variety of family types by showing the video *Free to Be . . . A Family* by Marlo Thomas and Friends (Children's Video Library, 1974). If possible, have the children bring a family photo album to share.

    To help the children understand a family album or scrapbook, have them draw family pictures. The teacher can draw a frame on a piece of paper and photocopy it for the children's use. Students may draw family members of their choice within the frame. When each child has drawn at least four pictures, ask an older student or book buddy to label each picture as the child artist dictates the person's name and relationship. Staple these pages together to make individual picture albums.

Closure:

Have a "Goodies for Grandparents" day in the classroom. Ask the children for suggestions on foods such as the ones they've read about in the books in this unit (e.g., apple slices, cheese, potato cakes, and apple cider) that may be served. Display the pictures, artwork, and books in the unit for everyone to enjoy. The children could perform their love songs, inspired by Lindbergh's *Grandfather's Lovesong,* at this time.

Presenting Information with Gail Gibbons

Objectives:

1. Collect, classify, draw, and/or graph information.
2. Compose letters.
3. Demonstrate a concept or object through creative movement, drawing, or constructing.
4. Extract main ideas from selected information sources.
5. Research a problem or concept.
6. Locate factual books in the library media center.
7. Portray various job roles.

Recommended Readings:

Gibbons, Gail. *Clocks and How They Go*. Thomas Y. Crowell, 1979.
Simple illustrations and brief text show how people keep time. (Objective 1)

————. *Department Store*. Thomas Y. Crowell, 1984.
The variety of merchandise and services provided in a department store is examined. (Objective 7)

————. *Fire! Fire!* Thomas Y. Crowell, 1984.
Simple illustrations capture the tasks of fire fighters in the city, country, forest, and on the waterfront. (Objectives 3 and 5)

————. *From Seed to Plant*. Holiday House, 1991.
The complex cyclical relationship between plants and seeds is examined through illustrations, diagrams, and text. (Objective 1)

————. *How a House Is Built*. Holiday House, 1990.
Brief text describes how a house is built, identifying the many skills of the construction crew. (Objectives 3 and 7)

————. *New Road: (Trains, Trucks, Fill It Up)*. Thomas Y. Crowell, 1983.
The building of a road from planning to construction is described. (Objectives 3 and 7)

————. *The Post Office Book*. Thomas Y. Crowell, 1982.
Modern-day steps in mail delivery are described. (Objectives 2 and 7)

————. *Sharks*. Holiday House, 1992.
Clear illustrations, concise captions, and text identify various kinds of sharks. (Objectives 4, 5, and 6)

————. *Weather Words and What They Mean*. Holiday House, 1990.
Four major weather concepts are introduced. (Objectives 1, 3, and 5)

————. *Whales*. Holiday House, 1991.
Captioned illustrations with pronunciation guides extend the simple text of this introduction to whales of the world. (Objectives 3 and 4)

Biographical Sources:

For information on Gail Gibbons see *Something about the Author*, vol. 23, pages 77–78; vol. 72, pages 76–80; *Something about the Author Autobiographical Series*, vol. 12, pages 71–82; and *Sixth Book of Junior Authors & Illustrators*, pages 96–97.

Group Introductory Activity:

Gail Gibbons has written more than 25 nonfiction books for children. She says that she writes nonfiction books because while writing she learns a lot about the world in which she lives (*Something about the Author Autobiographical Series*, vol. 12, p. 81). In 1987 she received the *Washington Post* Children's Book Guild Award for her contributions of nonfiction books for children. Because her works are varied, this unit concentrates on books dealing with science concepts, nature, and jobs.

Sharks by Gail Gibbons may awaken children's curiosity about the world. Ask the students to listen to the book and be able to recall at least one fact that fascinates them. After completing the reading ask individual students to recall the facts they have learned about sharks in this book. Let the children discuss the information and select facts they found most interesting.

Follow-Up Activities for Teacher and Students to Share:

1. Before sharing *Clocks and How They Go* by Gail Gibbons, set up a clock observation center. Ask students and friends to loan clocks to the classroom for a day or two. Use pictures if real clocks are not available. Once a variety of clocks are displayed, read the book aloud. After reading, point to each clock in the display and ask the students to classify it as either a weight clock, spring clock, or digital clock. A local jeweler would be a good resource person to demonstrate how clocks work. As an extension activity, select a small group of students to do a survey and graph of alarm clocks. Ask the children for input on selecting questions for the survey. Suggest that it would be fun to find out what noises teachers and support staff wake up to: buzzes, bells, music, or recorded voices.

   When using books by Gail Gibbons dealing with jobs, set up a "clock-in" station for the children. With each of the different jobs portrayed in Gibbons's books have the children clock in and clock out during the activity time. Use a handless clock dial stamp, if available, and stamp pad. Each child should have his or her own card. When he or she begins a job-centered activity, have the child stamp the card with the clock face and draw in the location of the hands as shown on the classroom clock. Each student should repeat the procedure when the activity is completed.

2. Read aloud Gail Gibbons's *Department Store* and show the time clock on the back of the title page. Use this page as an explanation of how and why time clocks are used on the job. Children can follow up in activity time by pretending to be any of the people working in the department store. Return to the page in *Department Store* that shows customers making purchases. Let the children speculate about the reasons people buy certain products and talk about different payment methods.

3. Before reading *Fire! Fire!* by Gail Gibbons, check with the local fire department to arrange a field trip to the station or a demonstration at the school site. Read aloud the book, then provide time for the children to act out what to do if there is a fire or if their clothes should catch on fire. A small group of children might want to research how or why the dalmatian became the mascot of fire departments all over the country. The library media specialist can assist students in defining the problem; seeking and locating information; and extracting, organizing, and presenting the information.

4. After reading aloud Gail Gibbons's *From Seed to Plant*, follow up by completing the seed project described in the book. If possible, ask a florist to donate some wilted flowers for the students to examine. Large blossoms like gladioli are easier for children to dissect. The students can study the illustrations near the end of the book showing the foods we eat. Ask the group to distinguish between foods that are seeds and those that are not. A chart could be displayed showing this information. Use old seed catalogs to cut out pictures of foods we eat. Label these pictures on a chart and refer to these words when children do daily writing activities. If possible bring some of the illustrated foods to school for the children to sample.

5. *How a House Is Built* by Gail Gibbons is filled with information on jobs and skills required to build a house. After reading the book aloud, turn back to the page on which all of the workers are assembled. Write the name of each job on a "Job Chart." As each job is listed, ask the students to recall what that person does.

    For an art activity let the children use MaryAnn Kohl's recipe for sawdust dough (*Mudworks*, Bright Ring, 1989, p. 52) to mold houses or simple shelters from the past as illustrated on the last page of Gibbons's book.

Sawdust Dough

1 c. sawdust
½ c. wallpaper paste
water
paint (optional)

Mix sawdust with wallpaper paste in a medium bowl. Add enough water to make a mixture like soft putty. Squeeze and pat the modeling mixture to the desired shape. Allow to air dry. Paint when dry if desired.

6. Read aloud *New Road* by Gail Gibbons. Have the students discuss the physical labor involved in building a road. Let the children share ideas about how specific machines help humans. Follow up by using creative movement to pretend to build a road. Divide the students into work groups of machines and people based on the work crews in Gibbons's book.

Children will enjoy pretending to be a bulldozer or dump truck. Let each small group decide how to act out their part in the road building. Give the children time to plan and practice building a "new road" in the hallway or outside.

7. After sharing *The Post Office Book* by Gail Gibbons, have the students write letters to friends or family members. Select different forms of letter writing for the children to experience: informal or friendly letters, informative letters, invitations, and thank you letters. Set up a mini-post office in the classroom. Teach children how to address a letter, stamp it with a pretend stamp, and mail it. Ask children to volunteer for various job roles in the post office. Contact the local post office for information on the Wee Deliver School Starter Kits for In-School Postal Service.

8. Gail Gibbons divides *Weather Words and What They Mean* into four parts. Post the words *temperature*, *air pressure*, *moisture*, and *wind* on four large poster boards. Read the book aloud to the class. Return to each section and discuss the weather concepts, being sure the students identify the main idea in each section. Divide the class into four groups and assign each group to one of the four concepts. Ask each group to take turns using their bodies to illustrate the concept they learned. Allow each group to use art materials to illustrate their concept on the labeled poster board. Display the posters for future discussions. Encourage the children to further research a concept of special interest such as tornadoes, hurricanes, blizzards, or floods. Depending on the season, follow up with art activities depicting clouds, rainbows, wind, sunshine, or snow.

9. Read aloud Gail Gibbons's *Whales*. Tell the students to listen and study the pictures as the book is read to learn a new fact about whales. Some students may draw a picture of the whale they remember while others orally share information they learned. After both *Whales* and *Sharks* have been read, select several artistic children to draw whales and sharks on butcher paper. These can be 12–36 inches in size. Let the children cut out each one and use it as a pattern to cut out an identical shape. Have other children color these shapes before stapling them together, adding light stuffing to give depth to the artwork. Hang the sea creatures from the ceiling. Ask a parent volunteer or upper-grade students to draw or trace several of the whale and shark shapes onto prepunched puzzle forms for the students to use in a center.

Closure:

Work with a teacher in a neighboring school to establish a pen pal program with his or her students so that the children can demonstrate their letter writing skills. Give the children the opportunity to share letters they receive in reply.

Developing Character through the Works of Lillian Hoban

Objectives:

1. Identify books by author and/or illustrator.
2. Listen and/or read to identify the main idea and summarize the story.
3. Predict the meaning of unknown words.
4. Identify positive qualities in self and others.
5. Discuss conflict and emotions between characters in books and real life.
6. Engage in creative drawing, sculpting, constructing, and movement.
7. Note the title page and/or table of contents.
8. Memorize a rhyme.

Recommended Readings:

Cohen, Miriam. *First Grade Takes a Test.* Illustrated by Lillian Hoban. Greenwillow, 1980.
> The children learn that a written test does not measure all the things they can do. (Objectives 1, 3, 4, and 5)

Delton, Judy. *I'm Telling You Now.* Illustrated by Lillian Hoban. E. P. Dutton, 1983.
> Artie's experiences teach him that many things he does have rules he did not know. (Objectives 1, 2, 3, and 5)

Hoban, Lillian. *Arthur's Christmas Cookies.* Harper & Row, 1972.
> Arthur makes a surprise present for his parents when his sugar cookies turn out to be clay cookies. (Objectives 1, 2, 3, and 6)

———. *Arthur's Halloween Costume.* Harper & Row, 1984.
> Arthur's attempt to make a scary costume fails, but his originality wins him a prize. (Objectives 1, 2, 3, and 6)

———. *Arthur's Pen Pal.* Harper & Row, 1976.
> Arthur's wish is to be a big brother to his pen pal until a picture from his pen pal helps him appreciate his own little sister, Violet. (Objectives 1, 2, 3, and 4)

———. *Arthur's Prize Reader.* Harper & Row, 1978.
> Thanks to big brother Arthur, Violet learns to read hard words and wins the first-grade reading contest. (Objectives 2 and 3)

———. *It's Really Christmas.* Greenwillow, 1982.
> A young attic mouse discovers that, no matter what, giving to others is really the spirit of Christmas. (Objectives 2, 6, and 7)

Hoban, Russell. *Best Friends for Frances.* Illustrated by Lillian Hoban. Harper & Row, 1969.
Frances learns that even a sister can be a best friend. (Objectives 1, 2, 3, and 4)

————. *Bread and Jam for Frances.* Illustrated by Lillian Hoban. Harper & Row, 1964.
Young Frances learns that, although there is nothing better to eat than bread and jam, she does like other foods sometimes. (Objectives 1, 2, 3, and 8)

Rabe, Bernice. *The Balancing Girl.* Illustrated by Lillian Hoban. E.P. Dutton, 1981.
Margaret can balance blocks, books, cones, and dominoes, even though she is in a wheelchair. (Objectives 1, 2, 3, 5, and 6)

Biographical Sources:

For information on Lillian Hoban see *Something about the Author,* vol. 69, pages 106–9 and *Third Book of Junior Authors,* pages 128–29.

Group Introductory Activity:

Lillian Hoban has written and/or illustrated more than 100 books for children. Her badgers and chimps have become the friends of many young readers. Raising four children of her own has given Hoban many real-life experiences and observations about which to write. As her books are read aloud, refer to the different dedications in them. Have the children look for the names of her children—Phoebe, Brom, Esmé, and Julia—in the dedication messages.

As a basis for this unit introduce "Author News" each day on the chalkboard. Note the difference in "author," the writer and "Arthur," the character name, because some children may become confused by the similarity between the two words. The news may take the following format, which can be left on the chalkboard to be used daily. Simply substitute appropriate words for the blanks each day:

> Today is _____. We will read _____, written by _____ and illustrated by _____. We will listen for these new words: _____, _____, _____, _____, and _____. The main characters are _____ and _____. The story is about. . . .

Explain to the students that the last line will be completed after the story has been read. They will need to listen for the main idea and details of the story. As the story is read encourage the children to use context clues and pictures to predict the meaning of unknown words.

Read aloud *Arthur's Prize Reader* to the class. Ask the children to speculate about Lillian Hoban's family after reading the story and dedication. Have the children identify the main idea of the story and discuss the events. Then ask someone to summarize the story in one or two sentences. Let the group recall and discuss the new words they heard in the story.

Several children may be able to extend *Arthur's Prize Reader* and other books in this unit by keeping a book character journal each day. The journals may include a sentence or two plus illustrations of the main characters, setting, and main ideas of the stories read.

Follow-Up Activities for Teacher and Students to Share:

1. Read aloud Miriam Cohen's *First Grade Takes a Test* and complete the "Author News." Have the students recall the roles of the author and illustrator. If the children have taken aptitude tests, discuss how their feelings about the test compared with those of the children in the book. Ask the children to name or write down one thing they can do well and one thing another classmate can do well. Those children who need more kinesthetic expression should be allowed to demonstrate what they can do.

2. Use the "Author News" to introduce Judy Delton's *I'm Telling You Now*. After reading the book, ask the children to recall all the "don'ts" that Artie's mother told him. Have the children explain the need for obeying safety rules at home, school, and play, based on what they heard in the story and their previous knowledge.

3. Introduce Lillian Hoban's *Arthur's Christmas Cookies* with the "Author News." Before reading the book aloud be sure the children note the dedication. After completing the reading, follow up the story by making "clay cookies" or sugar cookies. A basic art dough recipe can be found on page 28 of *Mudworks* by MaryAnn Kohl (Bright Ring Publishing, 1989). The book contains many other clay ideas that are great for the classroom.

Art Dough

Materials: 4 c. flour
1 c. iodized salt
1 ¾ c. warm water
Large bowl

Mix all ingredients in the bowl. Knead for 10 minutes. Mold to desired shape and bake at 300° until hard or air dry for a few days.

4. Be sure to include the word *original* when introducing Lillian Hoban's *Arthur's Halloween Costume* in the "Author News." Read the book aloud. Return to page 20 and reread what *original* means. Encourage the children

to discuss times or situations when it is important to be original. If it is near Halloween, ask the children to suggest different original homemade costumes. If costumes are not appropriate, use paper sacks to create original masks. Suggest that the children create a room mascot out of boxes to make the classroom "unique."

5. If several of Lillian Hoban's "Arthur" books have been shared with the children, complete the "Author News" and discuss positive and negative qualities of Arthur in those stories. Read *Arthur's Pen Pal* aloud. Let the children identify ways in which Arthur and Violet demonstrate positive self-concepts. Place a "message box" in the classroom. Encourage the children to write positive remarks about each other as Arthur and Sandy did, addressing and delivering them via the message box. During recess time ask the children to demonstrate the jump rope rhymes that Violet knew.

6. Use the "Author News" to introduce the chapter book *It's Really Christmas* by Lillian Hoban. Point out the table of contents page, explaining that the book is divided into four chapters. Name the chapters and write each one on the board. Read one chapter at a time to the group. At the end of each chapter ask students to recall what Gamey Joe learned about Christmas. Write these statements on the chalkboard under each chapter heading. When the story is completed, ask the children what conclusions they can make about the statement on page 20: "If you give, you will have, and it truly will be Christmas."

    Follow up the story by having the children draw what they imagine the tree made of roses looked like. If desired read the descriptive paragraph on page 39. Several students might prefer to construct or draw a diagram of the attic. In a puppet center children can act out their own attic mice children stories. Mice finger puppets are easy to construct from paper or cloth scraps. (See *Puppets for Dreaming and Scheming* by Judy Sims [Learning Works, 1988] for more puppetry ideas and patterns.)

7. After reading *Best Friends for Frances* by Russell Hoban and completing the "Author News," ask the children to recall some of the games and activities that were mentioned in the story. List these on the chalkboard and have the children select those activities they would like to do at recess. Later, let the children discuss what qualities it takes to have and to be a best friend. As a follow-up introduce Arnold Lobel's amphibian friends, Frog and Toad. Ask the children to listen carefully to the ups and downs of the relationship between Frog and Toad in *Frog and Toad Are Friends* (Harper & Row, 1970). Have the students discuss and compare the behavior of Frog and Toad with that of Frances and her sister.

8. When using "Author News" with Russell Hoban's "Frances" books, explain that Russell and Lillian were married and that she began her career by illustrating his books when they were expecting their fourth child. They

are now divorced. Share *Bread and Jam for Frances* with the children, then serve jam on toast. Frances loved jam so much she even jumped rope to her jam rhyme (p. 10). Take time for the children to learn and demonstrate her jump rope rhymes. Ask the children to share other jump rope rhymes they can recite. Refer to Joanna Cole's *Miss Mary Mack and Other Children's Street Rhymes* (William Morrow, 1990) for other rope rhymes.

9. Complete the "Author News" and read aloud *The Balancing Girl* by Bernice Rabe. As books written by different authors and illustrated by Lillian Hoban are read, ask the children to observe the illustrations in the various books, looking for similarities in style of the artwork. After the story has been read, let the children discuss the conflict between Margaret and Tommy and how it was resolved.

Clear a space for a balancing center. Allow the children individual and team time to use blocks, cans, boxes, or whatever is available to build and balance imaginative structures. If this becomes routine, challenge the students to build bridges or structures with hidden passages. Children can also learn to walk or participate in a relay race with erasers balanced on their heads. Ask the physical education teacher to work with the students to demonstrate momentary stillness while balancing shapes on a variety of body parts. Gross motor skills such as balancing on one foot or hopping forward on one foot can also be incorporated.

Closure:

Have an advanced group of students reread *Best Friends for Frances*. Ask them to organize a "Best Friends Outing" based on the foods and games listed in the story. Each child is to choose a book character as a best friend. Give the children an opportunity to go to the library media center and check out a favorite book to bring to the outing. While enjoying food and games, have the children tell why they selected that book character as a friend.

Family Fun with Marc and Laurie Brown

Objectives:

1. Use vocabulary words from a story in speaking and/or writing activities.
2. Role play personal problems and solutions.
3. Participate in a physical activity.
4. Demonstrate how family members care for, instruct, and help one another.
5. Identify with feelings and actions of book characters.

6. Identify feelings that result from participation in physical activity.
7. Tell a personal story.
8. Interview family members for information.
9. Use the steps think, predict, and choose to solve a problem.

Recommended Readings:

Brown, Laurie K. *Baby Time*. Illustrated by Marc Brown. Alfred A. Knopf, 1989.
This handbook to use with babies gives special emphasis to developing the child's five senses. (Objective 4)

————. *Dinosaurs Alive and Well: A Guide to Good Health*. Illustrated by Marc Brown. Little, Brown, 1990.
This guide shows the importance of physical, mental, and spiritual well-being. (Objectives 2 and 3)

————. *Toddler Time*. Illustrated by Marc Brown. Little, Brown, 1990.
Nursery rhymes and humor combine with informative hints to help parents relax and enjoy their toddler's days. (Objectives 3 and 4)

Brown, Laurie Krasny, and Brown, Marc. *Dinosaurs to the Rescue: A Guide to Protecting Our Planet*. Little, Brown, 1992.
Illustrations and captioned text on recycled paper show how saving our planet begins with each individual. (Objective 1)

Brown, Marc. *Arthur's Baby*. Little, Brown, 1987.
Arthur's friends and sister offer all kinds of advice on what to do with a new baby. (Objectives 4 and 5)

————. *Arthur's Christmas*. Little, Brown, 1984.
Santa and Arthur both receive special gifts at Christmas. (Objectives 5 and 9)

————. *Arthur's Eyes*. Little, Brown, 1979.
Arthur is teased by his friends when he wears his new glasses. (Objectives 2 and 5)

————. *Arthur's Tooth*. Little, Brown, 1985.
Arthur discovers that it is painful being the last one in the class to lose his baby teeth. (Objectives 7 and 8)

————. *D. W. Flips*. Little, Brown, 1987.
D. W. learns the importance of practicing a new skill. (Objectives 3 and 6)

Biographical Sources:

For information on Marc Brown see *Something about the Author*, vol. 53, pages 9–18 and *Fifth Book of Junior Authors & Illustrators*, pages 54–55. For information on Laurie Krasny Brown see *Something about the Author*, vol. 54, page 6.

Group Introductory Activity:

Marc Brown, illustrator and author, said in an article for *Something about the Author*, vol. 53, that he discovered the work of Marc Chagall through art books and was so impressed that he changed the spelling of his name from Mark to Marc. His appreciation for art is evident in *Arthur's Teacher Trouble* (in which the school displays artwork of Picasso) and in *Arthur's Tooth* (where a picture by Matisse is hanging in the house).

Marc Brown and his wife, Laurie Krasny Brown, who has an Ed.D. from Harvard, have collaborated on several nonfiction books. Marc considers Laurie to be the expert nonfiction writer, researcher, and organizer. As for his writing style, Marc says, "I depend on an idea drawer full of scraps of stories, bits of dialogue, quick drawings, title, and concepts" (*Something about the Author*, vol. 53, page 14).

Because many young families have toddlers and school-age children, include the family while teaching the unit on Marc and Laurie Brown. Send a bibliography of Marc and Laurie Brown's books home with the children so parents will know what is available from the school and local public libraries. Teach the children a song and dance from page 2 of the Browns' *Toddler Time* that they can share with young brothers or sisters. Present the information on pages 28–29 about familiarizing toddlers with the alphabet, numbers, shapes, and colors. Children will feel they are an important part of the family if they can help teach simple concepts to their younger siblings. Another book that contains rhymes and activities appropriate for school-age children to share with younger brothers and sisters is *Finger Rhymes*, selected and illustrated by Marc Brown (E.P. Dutton, 1980).

Follow-Up Activities for Teacher and Students to Share:

1. Use *Baby Time* by Laurie K. Brown in conjunction with her book *Toddler Time*. Take classroom time to review the five senses and then have the students select an activity they can teach or demonstrate to younger brothers and sisters, day-care children, or a kindergarten class.
2. Ask the physical education teacher or school nurse to read aloud Laurie Brown's *Dinosaurs Alive and Well: A Guide to Good Health*. Many of the physical exercises in the book can be performed during physical education class or recess. Challenge the class to learn a new game that is healthy but noncompetitive. For ideas on appropriate games refer to the *New Games Book* by Andrew Fluegelman (Doubleday, 1976). Much attention is given

by health professionals to emotions and stress. Allow children to role play resolutions to feelings or problems. To keep the family involved in learning, ask an adult to demonstrate how to give back rubs. Each child can learn by practicing on one another and then surprising their families with a new skill. If desired, follow by letting the children discuss how safety practices contribute to good health and share *Dinosaurs Beware: A Safety Guide* by Marc Brown and Stephen Krensky (Little, Brown, 1982).

3. Celebrate the planet Earth with a "Go Green" day. Ask the children to wear green that day. Begin the day by reading Laurie Krasny Brown and Marc Brown's collaboration *Dinosaurs to the Rescue: A Guide to Protecting Our Planet*. After reading the story, select words from the students that have to do with saving the earth, for example, *reduce*, *reuse*, *recycle*, *resources*, and *pollution*. Each time a students uses one of the words correctly, add a marble to a party jar. When the jar is full, celebrate with a popcorn party and let the children perform one of the environmentally conscious ideas from the book.

   As an extension of the book have the children describe ways and means of learning to use less, reuse, and recycle to save the planet. Let the students discuss ways they can help promote an environmentally safe school and community. Suggest that either the dinosaurs or school mascot be used as part of the symbol for a "Go Green Club" whose members may plan and carry out monthly ideas for saving the environment.

4. Before reading aloud Marc Brown's *Arthur's Baby* to the class, share the dedication with the children. Throughout the "Arthur" books Marc Brown has hidden the names of Tucker and Tolon, his sons, as well as that of his wife, Laurie. In *Arthur's Baby* he adds the name of his daughter Eliza, giving the children another name to locate on the pages. Be sure to have all available "Arthur" books in a reading corner so children may search for the hidden family names, book titles, and funny foods.

   After reading *Arthur's Baby,* return to the pages that show Arthur's mother sharing the family photograph album. Ask the children to speculate as to why she might do this. Let the students determine what value this would have for Arthur and D. W. Ask the children to describe or demonstrate the activities Arthur and D. W. could do for the family now that there is a new baby. Children can share experiences or discuss feelings they've had with a new baby. Ask them to select a family scene to illustrate in which they could draw hidden names and have classmates look for them.

5. Share the dedication in *Arthur's Christmas* and ask the children to speculate on what it means. Read aloud Marc Brown's story, then ask the children to recall their favorite parts. Have the children identify how D. W. demonstrated the gift of giving. Ask the children to define Arthur's problem in the story. Write the problem on the board. Using the steps think,

predict, and choose as examples of problem-solving strategy, ask the children to describe what steps Arthur took and the results achieved. Ask students what Arthur could have done differently. Children may compare Arthur's problems to difficulties they may have experienced. If other "Arthur" books about the holidays are available, read them for fun and problem-solving activities.

6. Before reading aloud *Arthur's Eyes* by Marc Brown, set the scene for the children by projecting a page of text from a book on an unfocused opaque projector or use an unfocused overhead transparency to project a blurred image. Ask the children to try to read what they see. Then have the children place cotton balls in their ears and listen as a selected poem is read very quietly. Let students discuss the problems created in these situations. Ask the children to name some of the symptoms they might experience if they really did have vision or hearing problems. Have the group identify steps they could follow to receive help with such problems.

   Read aloud *Arthur's Eyes*, stopping at the page where the principal takes Arthur to his office. Have the children discuss how Arthur feels about not being able to see clearly and what solutions might be available. Finish reading the story. Ask the students to share their feelings and thoughts about Francine's act of friendship, about being embarrassed, and about the emotions expressed in the picture of Mr. Mario's class on the last page of the book. Enlist the assistance of the school counselor for a role-play activity in which small groups of children enact various "friendship" conflicts that occur to Arthur and/or to children in real life.

7. After sharing *Arthur's Tooth* by Marc Brown, briefly discuss the cycle of losing teeth. Just like Arthur, everyone has different experiences when it comes to losing the "first tooth." Take advantage of this unique experience to allow every child the opportunity to tell his or her story. Because this is a family unit, ask students to interview members of their families to see how old they were or where they were when they lost their first tooth. Allow children to share this information orally, in written sentences, or graph it by ages or locations (e.g., school, home, or car).

8. In Marc Brown's *D. W. Flips*, Arthur's little sister gets her own book. After reading the story aloud, let the children suggest appropriate and inappropriate places to practice forward rolls and other physical exercises. Have a leader assume the role of the book character Miss Morgan and have the children participate as if in the story with warm-ups, skipping in a circle, forward rolls, and backward rolls. After the activity have the children suggest other important physical skills to practice. Ask the group to identify feelings that result from participation in physical activity. (For further adventures of D. W. read *D. W. All Wet* by Marc Brown [Little, Brown, 1988].)

Closure:

Plan an "Author Party for Marc and Laurie Brown." Before the party, review the various books in the unit by asking the children to recall the main idea of each and to justify their ideas with a description of an event in the story. List each book title with the children's comments. When the list is complete, ask the students to categorize the books by their main ideas into the headings "friendship," "family," and "giving/sharing." Ask the children what conclusions they can make about the stories Marc and Laurie Brown have written.

Rhythms and Rhymes

Objectives:

1. Predict story outcomes.
2. Act on a story through movement, singing, or oral expression.
3. Recognize and use rhyming words and sounds.
4. Compare two versions of the same counting rhyme.
5. Create musical rhythms or instruments.
6. Retell a story.
7. Use subject headings in the card catalog to locate books in the library media center.

Recommended Readings:

Cauley, Lorinda Bryan. *Clap Your Hands.* G. P. Putnam's Sons, 1992.
Children are invited to join the action in this rhyming poem by rubbing their stomachs, wiggling their noses, and jumping up and down. (Objectives 2 and 5)

de Regniers, Beatrice Schenk. *The Way I Feel . . . Sometimes.* Illustrated by Susan Meddaugh. Clarion, 1988.
A full range of emotions is rhythmically expressed in this collection of poetry. (Objectives 2 and 3)

Ehlert, Lois. *Feathers for Lunch.* Harcourt Brace Jovanovich, 1990.
When the door is left open, a house cat runs out but fails in his attempt to have a bird for lunch. (Objectives 2 and 3)

Garne, S. T. *One White Sail.* Illustrated by Lisa Etre. Green Tiger, 1992.
Images of the Caribbean demonstrate the numbers one through ten in bold watercolors. (Objective 6)

Langstaff, John. *Over in the Meadow.* Illustrated by Feodor Rojankovsky. Harcourt, Brace & World, 1957.
The inhabitants of the meadow are depicted in colorful illustrations that extend the lyrics of the old folk song. (Objective 4)

Lobel, Arnold. *Whiskers & Rhymes.* Greenwillow, 1985.
Thirty-five original poems in the Mother Goose style are illustrated with cats as characters. (Objective 7)

Merriam, Eve. *Blackberry Ink.* Illustrated by Hans Wilhelm. William Morrow, 1985.
The five senses are stimulated through humorous rhymes in this delightful collection of original poems. (Objectives 2 and 3)

Moss, Marissa. *Knick Knack Paddywack.* Houghton Mifflin, 1992.
In this variant of the familiar folk song the old man acquires materials to build a spaceship. (Objectives 1 and 2)

O'Donnell, Elizabeth Lee. *The Twelve Days of Summer.* Illustrated by Karen Lee Schmidt. William Morrow, 1991.
Sights at the beach are enumerated in this cumulative counting tale of a young girl's vacation experiences at the seashore. (Objective 2)

Rossetti, Christina. *Color.* Illustrated by Mary Trichman. HarperCollins, 1992.
Rossetti's poem "What Is Pink?," first published in 1871, is now available as a single illustrated volume introducing poetry and color. (Objectives 2 and 3)

Group Introductory Activity:

Many of the poems in Eve Merriam's *Blackberry Ink* lend themselves to movement. When reading "Latch, catch / Come in free. / Catch a ball but you can't catch me," have the children stand. Have the children use the movements "step right, step left, clap, clap" with a beat of four as the rhyme is repeated. Other movements may also be appropriate. Repeat over several days until the children know the rhyme by heart. Let students participate in "Five little monsters . . ." by doing a finger play or teaching the single lines to five students who may recite the memorized lines while the remainder of the class recites the group lines.

Poems such as "Swish, swash, Washing machine" give children the opportunity to hear onomatopoeia as the sounds suggest the movement. The end rhyme is easily distinguished in "Night light" and "I'm sweet says the beet." What other rhyming food connections can the children suggest after hearing "I'm sweet says the beet?" Eve Merriam makes use of the five senses throughout her poetry. Treat the children by letting them listen to the rhythms, see the illustrations, imagine the touch of a cat's tongue, smell dirty Bertie, and taste "Gooseberry, Juice berry, Loose berry jam."

Follow-Up Activities for Teacher and Students to Share:

1. The first time *Clap Your Hands* by Lorinda Bryan Cauley is read aloud, ask the children to join in the action in the first stanza: "Clap your hands, stomp your feet. / Shake your arms, then take a seat." Continue reading aloud, asking the children to listen and join in with the rhyming words. All actions in the story can be performed by a class or small group. The teacher may want to select a certain action and then, pretending to be a conductor, ask the children to participate when the signal is given. A small group of children may wish to create musical rhythms to go with the verses.

2. The poems found in *The Way I Feel . . . Sometimes* by Beatrice Schenk de Regniers are best read aloud when feelings have surfaced in the classroom. Several can be acted out or read as a group. "Queen of the World" (pages 34–38) is a fun poem to share through a transparency. As the poem is displayed on the screen, divide the class with the girls in one group and the boys in another. Ask the children in each group to all read together with the boys substituting "king" for "queen."

    Although children may not recall the literary term *alliteration*, they will learn to hear it and use it after it is pointed out in "The Churlish Child's Week" (p. 14). After reading the poem aloud, ask the children for other sound combinations that form alliterative phrases. Each poem in the book reflects different feelings. Share the poems, letting the children discuss the emotions expressed in each, and identify alliterative phrases.

3. Children will quickly catch on to the end rhyme scheme in *Feathers for Lunch* by Lois Ehlert. As the story is read aloud, have the children use their hands as cat paws silently stepping to the rhythm of the poem. Children should pounce loudly on their laps or desks after the line, "but all he catches." Reread the book, asking small groups of children to act out the story by moving their bodies in rhythm. Every plant and bird pictured in the book is identified on the pages of this story. After the book is completed, turn back to each page and ask the children to name the plants and birds shown before the answer is given. Have the children make a chart like the one in Ehlert's book showing birds common to their location. Pictures of birds may be cut out and glued onto the chart or drawn by the students.

4. Before reading to the class *One White Sail* by S. T. Garne, help the children locate the Caribbean Sea and its islands on a map or globe. Tell the children that the author is a retired scientist who now lives in the Caribbean and that the illustrator, Lisa Etre, grew up and lives there, too. The scenes they use in *One White Sail* are images they see in their everyday lives. Read the book aloud as a recording of steel drum music is played in the background (*Steel Band Music of the Caribbean*, Olympic, 6168). Allow time during or after the reading for children to discuss unusual images such as women balancing baskets on their heads and curtains blowing in the breeze at shuttered

windows. As a follow-up remind the children that the author and illustrator used images they saw around them each day. Let the students think about everyday sights they see and prepare a counting book *One* _____ _____ (e.g., *One Tall Tree* or *One Steel Skyscraper)* based upon their community. Have the children illustrate the book with original drawings or with pictures cut out from old magazines.

5. Share John Langstaff's version of *Over in the Meadow* with the class. Work with the music teacher or media specialist to teach the song from the back of the book. Children can make stick puppets of the various animals named in the song and perform a puppet play as the song is sung. Have the children compare Langstaff's book to Olive A. Wadsworth's *Over in the Meadow: An Old Counting Rhyme,* illustrated by David A. Carter (Scholastic, 1991). Children will notice the stylized, almost cartoonlike quality of Carter's collage illustrations as opposed to the realistic look of Feodor Rojankovsky's work.

6. Prior to sharing Arnold Lobel's *Whiskers & Rhymes,* plan with the library media specialist to introduce the card catalog or computerized catalog to the class. Share the title of the book aloud while displaying the cover. Ask the children to use those clues to predict the subject of the book. Read the book aloud. Children will discover that, although the illustrations all depict cats, the poems cover a variety of subjects. Visit the library media center with the class and team teach a lesson on the card catalog or computerized catalog. Introduce the students to subject headings and call numbers on cards or listings. At the close of the activity have the children use the catalog to locate books about cats that they may wish to check out.

7. Tell the children to look carefully at the illustrations in Marissa Moss's book *Knick Knack Paddywack* to try to predict what the old man is building in the story. Teach the class the melody and motions of the folk song "This Old Man" *(The Reader's Digest Children's Songbook,* 1985, p. 218). Tell the children that the tune may be used to sing the words of *Knick Knack Paddywack* as well as the old rhyme. Sing the song together as the book is shared again, using the original "Knick knack paddywack" line in each verse rather than the inventive line Moss substituted. This will make both the words and motions much easier for the children to follow.

8. Use Christina Rossetti's *Color* as the foundation to create a bulletin board. Read the poem aloud to the children. On following days celebrate each color through dress, the writing of original rhymes, monochromatic painting, and sampling of appropriate colored foods. Culminate the poem by allowing the children to paint a country scene reflecting the mood and content of Rossetti's poem.

   If *Roses Are Red. Are Violets Blue?* by Alice and Martin Provensen (Random House, 1973) is available, read aloud "Two Tone Poems" (pp. 31–32) and discuss the moods that are associated with various colors.

Extend this activity by sharing Mary Serfozo's *Who Said Red?* (Macmillan, 1988). Use this book as an antiphonal reading between the teacher or a student leader and the large group. Children can use their hands and feet to tap out rhythms or use their bodies to demonstrate emotions associated with various colors.

Closure:

Read Elizabeth Lee O'Donnell's *The Twelve Days of Summer,* allowing time on each page for the children to count the sights the narrator sees. After reading let the children use their bodies to demonstrate the action of each creature the girl saw. If desired, reread the text, letting the children add the character motions as they are enumerated. As a further extension teach students the melody of "The Twelve Days of Christmas." Prepare sequencing cards with the animals the children see in the story. Place the cards on display and use them as a visual aid to enable the group to sing "The Twelve Days of Summer." Once the children have learned the musical version, work with them to use their rhyming skills in creating their own class story. Let the children choose a seasonal theme and compose a story to match the five days of the school week. Perform the story for another class or a school assembly.

The Many Faces of Tony Johnston

Objectives:

1. Extend a story through creative drawing, constructing, music, and/or physical activity.
2. Locate folktales in the library media center.
3. Identify and express feelings.
4. Express personal identification with a book character.
5. Apply problem-solving skills to book character situations and real life.
6. Realize that music is an important part of everyday life.
7. Demonstrate recognition of vocabulary words from a story through discussion, writing, or creative dramatics.

Recommended Readings:

Johnston, Tony. *The Badger and the Magic Fan: A Japanese Folktale.* Illustrated by Tomie dePaola. G. P. Putnam's Sons, 1990.

A trickster badger steals a magic fan and uses it to make a rich young girl's nose grow and grow and grow. (Objectives 1 and 2)

————. *Farmer Mack Measures His Pig*. Illustrated by Megan Lloyd. Harper & Row, 1986.
Two pigs, Goldie and Hugh, wreak havoc on the farm when the farmers try to determine which is fatter. (Objectives 1 and 6)

————. *Goblin Walk*. Illustrated by Bruce Degen. G. P. Putnam's Sons, 1991.
Gentle forest creatures frighten a young goblin on his way to Grandma's. (Objectives 1, 3, and 4)

————. *Grandpa's Song*. Illustrated by Brad Sneed. Dial, 1991.
Memory loss takes away Grandpa's boisterous exuberance until the children restore his spirits by singing their favorite song. (Objectives 1, 4, and 6)

————. *Little Bear Sleeping*. Illustrated by Lillian Hoban. G. P. Putnam's Sons, 1991.
A reluctant young bear proposes several alternatives to going to bed until his patient mother lulls him to sleep. (Objectives 1 and 7)

————. *Pages of Music*. Illustrated by Tomie dePaola. G. P. Putnam's Sons, 1988.
Paolo's childhood experiences on the island of Sardinia instilled within him a love for music that eventually brings joy to everyone. (Objectives 1 and 6)

————. *The Quilt Story*. Illustrated by Tomie dePaola. G.P. Putnam's Sons, 1984.
A patchwork quilt makes a little girl feel at home in her new surroundings. (Objectives 3, 4, and 5)

————. *Slither McCreep and His Brother Joe*. Illustrated by Victoria Chess. Harcourt Brace Jovanovich, 1992.
A young boa constrictor turns nasty when his brother refuses to share, but he finds getting even makes him feel worse. (Objectives 1 and 5)

————. *Whale Song*. Illustrated by Ed Young. G. P. Putnam's Sons, 1987.
Are the great whales merely singing or are they counting each other with their calls? (Objectives 1 and 7)

————. *Yonder*. Illustrated by Lloyd Bloom. Dial, 1988.
The growth and change of a plum tree accompanies the changes in three generations of a farm family. (Objectives 1 and 3)

Biographical Sources:

For information on Tony Johnston see *Something about the Author*, vol. 8, page 94 and *Sixth Book of Junior Authors & Illustrators*, pages 151–52.

Group Introductory Activity:

Tony Johnston writes in a variety of styles, and children will notice the sharp contrasts among her books. Explain that the illustrations in a book must reflect the mood of the text. Display several of Johnston's books illustrated by different artists. Ask the students to study the cover illustrations carefully to try to predict the mood of the stories. Focus the children's attention on *Slither McCreep and His Brother Joe*. Students will probably predict from Victoria Chess's cover that the book will be humorous.

Share Slither's tale with the group. Stop reading with the line "'The Sultan of Stingies,' said Slither." Use the situation in the book to review problem-solving skills. Remind the children of the three steps in problem solving: think, predict, and choose. Apply those steps to the plot by letting the children pretend to be Slither in order to define the problem and suggest possible actions he could take. List the actions on the board and have students predict what would happen as a result of each choice. Allow the children to choose which alternative Slither should take. Continue reading so the group can discover Slither's choice and its consequences.

Remind students of their prediction about the humorous mood of Slither McCreep's story. Explain that even funny stories can contain serious points. As a follow-up let the children discuss the conclusion of the story to determine whether it would have changed if Slither had acted differently. Point out that "getting even" only made Slither feel worse, and allow the students to respond with instances when they have been upset with friends or family and how they handled the situation.

Tony Johnston enjoys many hobbies in addition to writing, including cooking, tennis, archaeology, and collecting dance masks (*Sixth Book of Junior Authors & Illustrators*, p. 151). Tell the children that they will make masks of the characters in the Tony Johnston books that they experience for a "Many Faces of Tony Johnston" collection. Locate illustrations of ornamental masks or photographs of dance masks. Obtain thin, flexible paper plates which may be used as the base for the masks. Cut eye holes in several plates to be used as patterns. Place the masks, plates, and a variety of fabric scraps, natural items, and art materials in a center where children may create ornamental masks of Johnston's characters as each of her books is shared. Show the students how to nest a plate with the eye pattern inside another plate, mark the position for the eye holes, and cut them out. Let the children choose the media they feel best represents each character. Display the completed masks on a wall or bulletin board.

Follow-Up Activities for Teacher and Students to Share:

1. Ask the library media specialist to read aloud Tony Johnston's *The Badger and the Magic Fan: A Japanese Folktale* and show the students where they can find many other folktales such as this one in the 398.2 section of the library. Have paper plates, colored markers, staplers, and dowel rods or craft sticks available so the students can make their own magic fans. Remind the students to illustrate one side with the sun and the other with a moonlit scene.

2. After sharing *Farmer Mack Measures His Pig* by Tony Johnston, hold a hog-calling contest, giving the children the opportunity to give their best pig calls. Award a prize such as a pig eraser or a package of pork rinds to the student or students whose calls are judged to be the most original, loudest, or most outstanding. After the contest serve Goldie's favorites, cornflakes and "donuts in a spoon (honey-nut o-shaped cereal)." Teach the children to sing the farmer's song to the tune of "Old MacDonald Had a Farm."

3. Before sharing Tony Johnston's *Goblin Walk,* ask the children if anyone remembers a folktale about a child who walks through the forest to her grandma's house. If no one suggests "Little Red Riding Hood," remind the children of the story. Explain that the story *Goblin Walk* is about a little goblin and the things that scare him as he travels through the woods. Let the children speculate about things that might scare a little goblin. Read the book aloud. Follow up by listing the things that frightened the goblin. Were those creatures frightened as well? Have the class discuss things that might scare children. Children may wish to tell about a time they might have felt like the little goblin.

    Ask the students to stand in a circle and clap a short, rhythmic pattern to accompany the story as it is reread. If desired, alternate with other motions (e.g., patting thighs or head, stomping feet, snapping fingers, or blinking eyes) while keeping the same rhythm. Just before dismissing the class for the day, eat cookies together like he and his grandma did. Bid the children farewell with the lines from the book: "And they gobbled some, one, two, three. Then it was time to go home. . . . And now and then he skipped . . . and the whole wood jiggled. And he giggled, he felt so good."

4. After reading Tony Johnston's *Grandpa's Song,* enlist the aid of the music teacher or library media specialist to teach the children some of Grandpa's favorite songs like "Home on the Range," "Red River Valley," or the ice cream chant. Children can describe the role that music plays in Grandpa's life and in their lives as well. If possible, arrange for a local bass or baritone to visit the classroom and sing for the children, demonstrating the low male voice. Share ice cream and "cracked cake" with the guest.

5. Before sharing with the group *Little Bear Sleeping* by Tony Johnston, ask the children to listen carefully to find action words in the story that end with "-ing." After completing the book, let the children recall and list the "-ing" words on the board. Have them act out each verb and then write sentences using the action words. As a class project, write an additional verse for Little Bear's story using the four-line pattern Johnston followed with identical first and fourth lines.

6. Before sharing Tony Johnston's *Pages of Music* with the children, read aloud the dedication, "For Tomie dePaola, an artist who 'makes paint sing.'" Have the children speculate about what the author meant by that phrase. Read the story aloud. Some children may notice the similarity between the protagonist's name and Tomie dePaola, to whom the book is dedicated.

   After reading ask the music teacher to work with the class to select a piece of music that seems pastoral. When the music has been chosen, select an art medium for the children to use to paint, draw, or create a country scene as the music is played. If possible serve olives, cheese, and *fogli di musica* to the children so they may experience the music, art, and food in Paolo's life. The thin, hard bread may be made from one of several recipes in MaryAnn Kohl's *Mudworks* (Bright Ring, 1989). Good choices are Pâté Briseé (p. 106) or Frozen Bread Dough (p. 60). Roll the dough into very thin sheets and bake as directed. Cooking time will decrease due to the thinness of the bread.

7. After reading Tony Johnston's *The Quilt Story*, let the children discuss how each child in the story felt in a new home. Give the children the opportunity to share personal experiences with moving and the lonely feelings of separation and isolation it can bring. The quilt was the single item that said "home" to the girls in Johnston's story. Let children discuss the meaning of the proverb "Home is where the heart is." Ask the children to suggest one item that would make each of them feel more comfortable if they were to move to a new home. The students may wish to bring these items from home to display in an arrangement labeled "Home Is Where the Heart Is."

8. Read Tony Johnston's *Whale Song* aloud, singing each of the numbers in a resonant voice. Invite the children to join in the whale count as the book is read. Share whale trivia with the class, noting that the humpbacks "stand on their heads" as they sing. Point out that Johnston was born and raised in California near where the whales migrate up and down the coast. Perhaps she has watched as the gentle giants swim to and from their summer homes in the northern waters.

   In the text the author refers to "a pod of uncle whales / (just like a pod of peas if you please)." Introduce the collective noun "pod." Show the class a pea pod if they are in season, break it open, and display the peas inside. Explain that a pod is the shell that holds a group of peas together and a pod is also the name for a group of whales. The whales in a pod swim and travel together just like "peas in a pod." As an extension arrange with the media specialist for the students to research collective nouns and find other unusual names for groups of animals or objects. An excellent resource is Ruth Heller's *A Cache of Jewels* (G.P. Putnam's Sons, 1989).

9.   Before sharing Tony Johnston's *Yonder*, explain that the story was inspired by a tradition in the author's life. Like the family in the story Johnston's family plants a fruit tree to commemorate each birth or death in their family. Through the years they have planted an entire orchard of fruit trees, each of which is associated with a special family memory (*Sixth Book of Junior Authors & Illustrators*, p. 152). Ask if any of the children's families do special things to mark a baby's birth or other special event in their lives. Read the story to the class. Ask the children to identify feelings expressed or implied in the story. Explain that having and expressing feelings is natural. Allow the students to relate the story to real-life experiences they may have had. If possible, show the class the video version of *Yonder* (Random House/Miller-Brody, 1990). Ask them to compare the different versions of the story. Let the children choose which version they prefer and explain why they chose it.

Closure:

If possible, obtain permission to plant a tree or other perennial plant on the school grounds. Let the children help plan and participate in a commemorative celebration. Activities might include singing a song from one of Johnston's books or wearing the character masks in a Johnston parade.

Chapter 3
Second Grade/Third Grade

Feelings Shared by Cynthia Rylant

Objectives:

1. Express emotions through writing.
2. Recognize how the author uses real-life experiences in writing.
3. Respond to literature through art, writing, and music.
4. Show empathy for a book character.
5. Recall important events in a story.
6. Identify the sequential order of a story.
7. Distinguish between the beginning, middle, and end of a story.
8. Develop letter-writing skills.

Recommended Readings:

Rylant, Cynthia. *All I See*. Illustrated by Peter Catalanotto. Orchard, 1988.
   A young boy is fascinated by the artist who gazes at the inland lake while painting nothing but whales. (Objective 3)

———. *An Angel for Solomon Singer*. Illustrated by Peter Catalanotto. Orchard, 1992.
A lonely old man discovers that dreams can come true. (Objectives 3 and 4)

———. *Birthday Presents*. Illustrated by Suçie Stevenson. Orchard, 1987.
A six-year-old girl's parents delight in telling her about the memorable experiences of her birth and each succeeding birthday. (Objective 1)

———. *Henry and Mudge*. Illustrated by Suçie Stevenson. Bradbury, 1987.
Henry, an only child, is no longer lonely after his parents give him Mudge, a puppy of his very own. (Objectives 5, 6, and 7)

———. *Henry and Mudge and the Wild Wind: The Twelfth Book of Their Adventures*. Illustrated by Suçie Stevenson. Bradbury, 1993.

Henry, his family, and his huge dog must face their fears and find new pastimes when an electrical storm causes a power outage. (Objectives 1 and 3)

————. *Miss Maggie*. Illustrated by Thomas DiGrazia. E.P. Dutton, 1983.
Nat is afraid of his elderly neighbor, Miss Maggie, until her loneliness and his concern form a bridge between their generations. (Objectives 2 and 7)

————. *Mr. Griggs' Work*. Illustrated by Julie Downing. Orchard, 1989.
Mr. Griggs' whole life revolves around his work at his beloved post office. (Objective 8)

————. *Night in the Country*. Illustrated by Mary Szilagyi. Bradbury, 1986.
Bold illustrations and gentle text evoke images of the rural night. (Objective 3)

————. *The Relatives Came*. Illustrated by Stephen Gammell. Bradbury, 1985.
Everyone has a wonderful time "hugging and eating and breathing together" when the relatives from Virginia come to visit. (Objective 2)

————. *When I Was Young in the Mountains*. Illustrated by Diane Goode. E.P. Dutton, 1982.
The author's tender memories of her childhood are enhanced by gentle illustrations, dominated by blues and browns. (Objectives 1 and 2)

Biographical Sources:

For information on Cynthia Rylant see *Something about the Author*, vol. 50, pages 182–88; *Something about the Author Autobiographical Series*, vol. 13, pages 155–63; and *Sixth Book of Junior Authors & Illustrators*, pages 255–56.

Group Introductory Activity:

Introduce Cynthia Rylant and her books by explaining that the author lived with her grandparents in the mountains of West Virginia when she was a young child. Several of her books are about that time which she says "seems to have sunk thickest into my brain and my heart" (*Sixth Book of Junior Authors & Illustrators*, p. 255). Rylant has stated that it was difficult for her to be away from her parents, and perhaps she felt emotions more strongly during that time. She believes that when someone writes stories it is the most intense feelings that come out (*Sixth Book of Junior Authors & Illustrators*, p. 255).

After sharing Cynthia Rylant's *When I Was Young in the Mountains*, reread the book, pausing on each page so the children can tell what each page is basically about; for example, the first page tells what the writer's grandfather did for a living and how he greeted her each night while the second tells what the family ate for supper. List student responses on the chalkboard. Use the list as a guide for the group to rewrite the story in a new setting, that of the children's home. Tell the children that Cynthia Rylant has said that people mostly long for the same things, fear the same things, and want someone to write about those things so "we won't feel too crazy or alone" (*Sixth Book of Junior Authors & Illustrators*, p. 256). Encourage students to put common feelings and events in their retelling so other people can identify with them. Let the students illustrate and compile a class book *When I Was Young in* _____, filling the blank with the name of the community or area.

Follow-Up Activities for Teacher and Students to Share:

1. After sharing *All I See* by Cynthia Rylant, let the children discuss what Gregory may have meant when he told Charlie that whales were all he saw. If they were to choose something to be "all they saw," what would it be? Set up an easel in an art center where students may use tempera paint to paint "all they see." Display the completed paintings in the hallway with an appropriate label.

2. After *An Angel for Solomon Singer* is read aloud to the class, let the children discuss Solomon's feelings. Ask them to speculate on what caused Solomon to wander the streets. Let the students list the attributes exhibited by Solomon and Angel. Suggest some "what if . . ." questions for the children to consider (e.g., "What might have happened if Solomon became very ill?" or "What could have happened if Solomon had grandchildren who came to stay with him?").

   The students can also learn to express emotions through line art. Select four vocabulary words such as *lonely, sad, happy,* and *excited.* Have the children fold drawing paper into fourths. Demonstrate how to draw bold, fine, or textured lines to depict one of the emotions. On each of the four panels children may draw lines expressing that feeling. As a further art follow-up, ask the children to illustrate Solomon's dreams of balconies and purple walls.

3. After reading aloud Cynthia Rylant's *Birthday Presents,* ask the class members to interview a parent or other adult to learn an amusing or interesting anecdote about the student's birth or a birthday celebration. Let the students write these short stories in booklets made by folding a 6-by-12-inch rectangle of wrapping paper in half to form a 6-inch square. Insert a square of lined paper inside and staple along the fold. If desired the fronts of the booklets could be decorated with bows and gift tags. Display these "birthday presents" in a writing center or on a bulletin board. As an alternative activity let children make "Birthday Timelines" showing highlights of their lives from birth to the present.

4. Share *Henry and Mudge* by Cynthia Rylant. Let the students recall and list on the chalkboard the important events in the story. Use the list to lead into a discussion of story structure. Explain to the students that all good stories

have a beginning, a middle, and an end. Have the students examine their list of story events from *Henry and Mudge* to try to decide which events belong in which section of the story. Point out that the beginning of the story lets them meet the characters and find out where and when the story takes place, the middle presents exciting action or a problem, and the ending solves the problem or wraps up the loose ends. Have the children place the story events on their list in sequence. Ask the group to find the event in the list that is the high point or turning point of the story. Tell the group that this turning point is called the climax. Explain that the ending of the story is determined by what the characters do in the climax.

After children have selected Mudge getting lost as the turning point, let the students discuss what other actions Henry could have taken instead of looking for his dog. Ask how these actions might have changed the ending. As a group rewrite the story from the climax, choosing a different solution and following it to its logical ending.

5. After sharing Cynthia Rylant's *Henry and Mudge and the Wild Wind: The Twelfth Book of Their Adventures,* read Mary Stolz's *Storm in the Night* (HarperCollins, 1988). Lead the children to compare the reactions of the families to the storm. Ask the students to write paragraphs telling about their own feelings and actions during storms. Set the mood for the children by playing a thunderstorm sound effects recording (*In Harmony with Nature,* vol. 2, "Stormy Night," Madacy, C4-5628-2) as they think and write.

6. Before reading Cynthia Rylant's *Miss Maggie,* remind the students that the author has said many of her books stem from the years she spent with her grandparents in Appalachia. Explain that as a child Rylant knew a real Miss Maggie and that the book character was modeled after her. Ask the students to listen carefully as *Miss Maggie* is read aloud and find things about the old lady that make her character interesting and different. Share the book and then ask students to recall the unusual aspects of Miss Maggie's character. Urge the students to choose someone in their own lives who would make a good book character. Have each child make a list of things about that person that would make him or her an interesting character. If appropriate, have the students write individual stories about the characters described, being sure to have a well-defined beginning, middle, and end.

This book may be used to introduce a discussion about prejudice. Ask the children to speculate about why Nat initially disliked Miss Maggie. Children's responses should include the observation that Nat feared her because she was different. Ultimately the students should note that, once Nat overcame his fear and got to know her, his feelings changed.

7. After reading *Mr. Griggs' Work* by Cynthia Rylant, arrange a field trip to the post office so the children can observe how a modern facility operates. As a further follow-up contact the local post office for information on obtaining the Wee Deliver School Starter Kits for In-School Postal Service

available through the U.S. Postal Service or set up an original post office where students can mail notes to classmates or school staff. Let the children take turns acting as mail carrier, sorting the mail, placing it in individual mailboxes, or delivering it to the addressees. Use this as an activity to teach the essentials of letter writing and how to address an envelope.

8. Share Cynthia Rylant's *Night in the Country* with the children. As an extending activity let the students use crayons to create a rural scene or a scene near their home as it might look at night. Tell the children to leave the sky blank. After the crayon illustrations are complete, the children may use thin dark blue or black tempera paint to wash over the entire scene, creating the night sky and darkening the entire scene. Display the illustrations on a bulletin board or wall labeled "Night in Our Country."

Closure:

Extended families are very important in Cynthia Rylant's stories. Remind the children that Rylant lived with her grandparents in the West Virginia mountains for four years when she was quite young. After hearing *The Relatives Came,* ask the children if they can draw any conclusions about the author's life. If available, let the children view *Meet the Picture Book Author: Cynthia Rylant* (Random House/Miller-Brody, 1990). Give the children time to reflect on her other stories. Ask the children to describe attributes of Rylant's book characters that reflect Rylant's own life and experiences. Have the children interview or invite older family members to school. Ask these adults to share a story or anecdote from their childhood. Lead-in questions might include: "How did you travel when you visited other relatives?" "What holiday event is most vivid in your memory?" "What were your favorite foods, music, movies, clothes, or friends?"

Mirrored Feelings in the Books of Elizabeth Winthrop

Objectives:

1. Identify positive and negative characteristics and feelings in book characters, self, and others.
2. Use the "Think, Predict, Choose" method to solve a problem.
3. Participate in games.
4. Describe or demonstrate sequential directions for playing a game.

5. Create puppets and/or other original art.
6. Express empathy for a book character.
7. Explore and demonstrate the subtle ways people communicate with words and tone of voice.
8. Identify figurative language.
9. Role play a scene from a book or act out a play.

Recommended Readings:

Winthrop, Elizabeth. *Bear and Mrs. Duck.* Illustrated by Patience Brewster. Holiday House, 1988.
Bear discovers that his babysitter, Mrs. Duck, is really quite clever. (Objectives 3 and 5)

————. *Bear's Christmas Surprise.* Illustrated by Patience Brewster. Holiday House, 1991.
Bear feels terribly guilty after he peeks and sees his Christmas present from Nora. (Objectives 1 and 6)

————. *Belinda's Hurricane.* Illustrated by Wendy Watson. E.P. Dutton, 1984.
During a fierce hurricane Belinda gets to know the better side of her grandmother's grouchy neighbor. (Objectives 5 and 8)

————. *The Best Friends Club.* Illustrated by Martha Weston. Lothrop, Lee & Shepard, 1989.
Lizzie learns that rules don't make or keep friendships. (Objectives 1, 3, and 4)

————. *Katharine's Doll.* Illustrated by Marylin Hafner. E.P. Dutton, 1983.
Katharine's new doll, Charlotte, causes problems between Katharine and her friend, Molly. (Objectives 1 and 9)

————. *Lizzie and Harold.* Illustrated by Martha Weston. Lothrop, Lee & Shepard, 1986.
Lizzie and Harold become best friends when they realize that best friends are not planned, but just happen. (Objectives 1, 3, and 4)

————. *Luke's Bully.* Illustrated by Pat Grant Porter. Viking, 1990.
A third-grade boy bullies Luke day after day until Luke is finally forced to solve his own problem. (Objectives 2, 6, and 9)

————. *Tough Eddie.* Illustrated by Lillian Hoban. E.P. Dutton, 1985.
It takes a real act of courage for Eddie to finally share his dollhouse with his friends. (Objectives 1, 6, and 7)

————. *Vasilissa the Beautiful.* Illustrated by Alexander Koshkin. HarperCollins, 1991.
Thanks to the blessings of her mother, Vasilissa is able to outwit her stepmother and Baba Yaga. (Objectives 1 and 7)

————. *A Very Noisy Girl.* Illustrated by Ellen Weiss. Holiday House, 1991.
When noisy Elizabeth pretends to be a very quiet dog, she discovers that her mother really loves her, even when she is noisy. (Objectives 6 and 7)

Biographical Sources:

For information on Elizabeth Winthrop see *Something about the Author*, vol. 8, pages 124–25 and *Fifth Book of Junior Authors & Illustrators*, pages 330–31.

Group Introductory Activity:

Introduce this unit on Elizabeth Winthrop by explaining to the class that she believes that young readers want to see their own feelings reflected in the mirror of a book. She goes on to say that as a writer she takes all of her loves and fear, worries and angers and puts them inside her characters (*Something about the Author*, vol. 8, p. 125). As the different characters are introduced in this unit, help the children identify the feelings expressed in the stories. Throughout the unit ask the students to think about what the author believes.

Read aloud Elizabeth Winthrop's *Tough Eddie*, asking the children to listen closely to the conversations that Eddie has and the tone of voice he uses. After the story has been read, have the students identify the problem or conflict in the story and the positive and negative qualities of the book characters. Let the children note Eddie's feelings in various situations. Take this opportunity to demonstrate and have the students practice the mechanics of speech through dialogue. As an example read the line "What are you doing?" First change the tone of voice in several readings to indicate different moods, for example, anger, dismay, or surprise. Then read the sentence four more times, first stressing "what," then "are," then "you," and lastly "doing." Let the students discuss what meaning they attach to the way the line is read. Other lines that could be used for this activity include "Eddie, put away that gun," "Do you really have a dollhouse?" and "I'm not going to talk to you."

For a continuous activity throughout the unit, divide the students into two groups. Allow the groups to construct their versions of Eddie's dollhouse during activity time. If possible, an adult member of a local miniatures club could be invited to visit the class and share his or her hobby with the children.

Follow-Up Activities for Teacher and Students to Share:

1. After reading *Bear and Mrs. Duck,* have the children discuss activities they can do at home with a babysitter. If many of the students are latchkey children, it may be desirable to discuss games they can play alone. Students

may wish to teach others in the class how to play the games. Let the children discuss what rules they need to know and follow in order to be safe at home. Compile the children's ideas and have a group of children write a puppet play using some of the student suggestions. Let the children make paper sack puppets, sock puppets, or body puppets to use in the puppet show. Refer to *Puppetry in Early Childhood Education* by Tamara Hunt and Nancy Renfro (Nancy Renfro Studios, 1982) for more ideas.

2. Read aloud *Bear's Christmas Surprise* by Elizabeth Winthrop. After completing the reading, have the children draw a picture of the train or hat that Bear and Mrs. Duck wanted for Christmas. Frame the picture like Patience Brewster framed her book illustrations. Ask the students to explain Bear's feelings and why he felt sick when he peeked at the Christmas presents. Lead the children in discussing how or why baking cookies with an adult or sharing hot chocolate might make them feel better when they are upset.

3. *Belinda's Hurricane* by Elizabeth Winthrop is filled with colorful descriptive language. After reading the first chapter, reread the sentence on page 2: "They fit together like the two old armchairs that sat on either side of the fireplace." Explain that authors use descriptive language to help the reader imagine or picture what is being said. Tell the children that, as they begin to read longer books with fewer illustrations, descriptive or figurative language will help them make mental pictures of the characters and actions. Ask the children to listen as the rest of the book is shared for phrases that make comparisons between unlike things, using words such as *like* or *as*. At the end of each chapter, list any lines the students noted. After completing the book, let the children discuss the changes in Belinda. Follow up by allowing each child to select a favorite figurative language phrase from the list and illustrate the scene.

4. After reading aloud *The Best Friends Club* by Elizabeth Winthrop, have the group discuss the positive and negative characteristics of the book's characters. Let the class find ways in which Lizzie and Harold are like real people. Take the class outside to learn and play Lizzie's version of running bases. Have the children list other games that two to four friends can play.

    Extend this activity by having students write out or draw directions for playing a game. The directions can be checked for proper sequence by handing each set of directions to another person to perform exactly as the directions read.

5. List the following words on separate sheets of butcher paper: *Sharing, Caring, Loving, Playing, Worrying, Arguing, Fighting, Tattling.* Have the children discuss what each word means. Read aloud *Katharine's Doll* by Elizabeth Winthrop. Ask the children to listen to see which of these feelings and actions are reflected in the story. During the follow-up discussion ask the students to identify feelings that were demonstrated in

the book and how they were shown. Write the title of the book under the appropriate feeling. As other books by Elizabeth Winthrop are read, those titles can be added to the list. Other feelings the children note in the books may be added as well. As an extension activity have small groups of students act out or role play several of the scenes in *Katharine's Doll*.

6. Read aloud Elizabeth Winthrop's *Lizzie and Harold*. Follow the reading with a class discussion on what it takes to be a friend. Be sure children bring out the positive characteristics they look for in a friend. Have several pieces of string, approximately 24-inches in length. If there are older children in the school who know how to make the "Cat's Cradle" invite them to demonstrate this string game. Otherwise follow the directions in the book to learn how to play it. Refer to *Cat's Cradle, Owl's Eyes: A Book of String Games* by Camilla Gryski (Morrow, 1984) or to *Super String Games* by Camilla Gryski (Morrow, 1988) for instructions on other string games children may enjoy. As a further extension activity ask the music instructor to teach the children to sing Carmen Ravosa and Margaret Jones's "Best Friends" (*Silver Burdett Music, Book 2*, 1974).

7. Read aloud *Luke's Bully* by Elizabeth Winthrop. Stop reading after Luke and Arthur trade parts for the class play (page 30) and have students predict the outcome. Luke, a real thinker, tells Mr. Robbins that he has an idea (page 42). Stop reading here and have the students pretend to be Luke and use the "Think, Predict, Choose" method to come up with their own idea for solving the problem. After the class offers several ideas, complete the story and compare the students' ideas to Luke's. Let the children discuss other ways they can apply the problem-solving method to their lives or the lives of book characters. Lead the children to discover ways they can identify with Luke and/or Arthur.

8. Before sharing Elizabeth Winthrop's *Vasilissa the Beautiful* with the children, read "About the Tale" on the last page. Have the children listen as the story is read aloud for parts that sound like other folktales. Before Baba Yaga gives Vasilissa the answers to her three questions ask the children to predict what the men symbolize. Urge the group to consider why the doll and the words "Morning is wiser than the evening" comfort Vasilissa. Ask the students what words of comfort they or people they know use to help others.

   Advanced readers will enjoy comparing *Vasilissa the Beautiful* to *Oom Razoom*, a Russian tale retold by Diane Wolkstein (Morrow, 1991); Ernest Small and Blair Lent's version of *Baba Yaga* (Houghton Mifflin, 1966); and/or Eric Kimmel's retelling of *Baba Yaga* (Holiday House, 1991).

9. After the students have heard or read Elizabeth Winthrop's *A Very Noisy Girl*, give them the opportunity to share qualities of Elizabeth that help them to identify with her. Noisy Elizabeth may very well be like some

students in the classroom who are kinesthetic learners. Sounds and actions are important to these learners. Follow the reading by playing sound charades. Divide the class into groups of two or three. Explain that students are to create sounds that describe a scene. They are to use only sounds that can be made by voices, bodies, or objects in the room. They are not to use recognizable words, action, or pantomime. Each group will receive a scene card. Tell the groups to keep the scene a secret so that their classmates can guess the scene they portray. Allow five to ten minutes for the students to create sound scenes. This activity may be performed outside if desired. Several suggestions for sound scenes include a bus or subway ride, an airport, a train station, a circus, a thunderstorm, a zoo, a quarrel, or a scary movie.

Closure:

Have the children write a booklet to be published in the classroom on one of the following topics: games to play with friends, games to play alone, rules to follow when home alone, or how to be a friend. Have Elizabeth Winthrop's books in a center so children may refer to them for ideas and inspiration.

Eve Bunting: A Bit o' the Irish

Objectives:

1. Become acquainted with a wide variety of music including diverse musical styles and genres.
2. Apply problem-solving skills to real-life event.
3. Draw inferences from words or pictures to predict an outcome or event.
4. Identify emotions and mood expressed in a story, music, or illustrations.
5. Define the role of the author and illustrator.
6. Recognize and use figurative language in writing.
7. Illustrate a description in a story.
8. State the point of view in a story.
9. Relate and compare story events to real life.

Recommended Readings:

Bunting, Eve. *Fly Away Home*. Illustrated by Ronald Himler. Clarion, 1991.
The airport becomes home to a boy and his father. (Objectives 2 and 9)

————. *Ghost's Hour, Spook's Hour*. Illustrated by Donald Carrick. Clarion, 1987.

A stormy night gives a young boy and his dog every reason to be scared. (Objectives 3 and 4)

————. *Happy Birthday, Dear Duck*. Illustrated by Jan Brett. Clarion, 1988.

Hugs, squeezes, and a day filled with friends were the very best gifts Duck received for his birthday. (Objectives 3 and 6)

————. *In the Haunted House*. Illustrated by Susan Meddaugh. Clarion, 1990.

A brave little girl takes her father through the haunted house. (Objectives 6 and 7)

————. *The Mother's Day Mice*. Illustrated by Jan Brett. Clarion, 1986.

The little mice give their mother the gifts of love and music. (Objectives 3 and 5)

————. *St. Patrick's Day in the Morning*. Illustrated by Jan Brett. Clarion, 1980.

Young Jamie sets out to prove to himself that he's not too small to walk in the parade. (Objectives 1, 3, 5, and 7)

————. *Scary, Scary Halloween*. Illustrated by Jan Brett. Clarion, 1986.

Halloween is a very scary night when seen through the eyes of a mother cat. (Objectives 5 and 8)

————. *Summer Wheels*. Illustrated by Thomas B. Allen. Harcourt Brace Jovanovich, 1992.

Trust and friendships are built through the efforts of the neighborhood Bicycle Man. (Objectives 3 and 9)

————. *The Traveling Men of Ballycoo*. Illustrated by Kaethe Zemach. Harcourt Brace Jovanovich, 1983.

Three men spend their lives traveling and bringing music to their listeners. (Objectives 1, 6, and 7)

————. *The Wall*. Illustrated by Ronald Himler. Clarion, 1990.

A young boy and his father search for the name of the boy's grandfather on the wall at Vietnam Veteran's Memorial. (Objective 4)

Biographical Sources:

For information on Eve Bunting see *Something about the Author*, vol. 64, pages 60–68 and *Fifth Book of Junior Authors & Illustrators*, pages 60–61.

Group Introductory Activity:

Plan with the library media specialist and the music teacher to introduce the life and work of Eve Bunting to the class. The media specialist may wish to share biographical information with the students, pointing out that the author was born in Ireland and spent the first 30 years of her life in that country. It was not until she married that she came to the United States and became a naturalized citizen (*Fifth Book of Junior Authors & Illustrators*, pp. 60–61). Let the music teacher introduce the three musical instruments played in Eve Bunting's book *The Traveling Men of Ballycoo* and the terminology she uses to describe the music. Read the story aloud. Ask the music teacher to assist in guiding the follow-up discussion concerning the role the three men played in Irish society.

Bunting uses figurative language extensively in descriptions (e.g., "resin . . .hung like a mist around his head," "eyes, big and shiny as two licked stones," and "a back as wide as the valleys"). If the students have already completed the unit "Under the Poet Tree," remind them that this type of figurative language is called a simile. Introduce the term if it is not familiar to the group. Explain that similes appeal to the senses by using sensory words to help create visual images for the reader. Read again some of the similes used by Bunting in her text. Urge the children to share the visual images the lines paint in their minds. Again work with the music teacher to select a recording of Irish folk music, such as *James Galway and the Chieftains in Ireland* (RCA, 5798-4-RC). Play the recording for the children and ask them to complete the simile "The music makes me feel like. . . ." Record the descriptions on the chalkboard or use a tape recorder. Follow up with an art activity allowing the children to paint a picture that shows how the music makes them feel.

Follow-Up Activities for Teacher and Students to Share:

1. Read aloud *Fly Away Home* by Eve Bunting. After completing the book let the children discuss and compare their feelings about homelessness to the feelings the boy and father experienced in the story. Let the children speculate about how it would feel to dress and look like "nobody at all." Ask the students to identify the problems homeless people face and possible solutions. Let the students generate ideas for helping homeless people in their community. Use the following strategy to help students focus on the problems of the homeless: What do we know? What do we want to learn? How can we find the answers?

    Read the title again. Ask the children to think about the story itself and then decide what the title might mean. Introduce cause and effect by having the students speculate on the events that may have led the man and boy into the situation that exists in the story.

    Develop a thematic spelling list from the airport terminology in the book. Include words such as *passengers, pilots, flight attendants, luggage, escalators,* and *jets.* Have the children use a dictionary to define the words and use them in complete sentences.

2. Eve Bunting says a writer needs to have "the feeling for words, the driving need to tell a story, the love of the characters who constantly inhabit your mind" (*Something about the Author*, vol. 64, p. 65). Ask the children to listen for ways Bunting used words in *Ghost's Hour, Spook's Hour* to add suspense to the story or to create a mood of being afraid. Read the story aloud. Encourage children to make the sounds written in italics. Reread the book, asking the students to listen for and identify verbs that show action and descriptive words. Help the group to classify these words into the three categories of hearing, touching, and seeing.

3. Read aloud *Happy Birthday, Dear Duck* by Eve Bunting. When Hen explains that the last guest is usually late, ask the children to predict who the last guest will be and what gift he or she will bring. Complete the reading and allow the children to review their prediction of the last guest's identity. Ask what clues in the story pointed to the identity of the final guest.

   Let the children identify the animals in the story. Have the students research these animals in the media center to determine which of them actually live in the desert. Have children describe the habitat of the animals they researched.

   Have students recall rhyming pairs from the text. Use these pairs in a spelling list. Include brim/him, beak/squeak, such/much, rudeness/goodness, wrap/map, splashed/dashed, cakes/shakes, wing/sing, and lot/got. Work with the music teacher to let the children plan, practice, and perform a birthday dance for Duck, using Mexican folk instruments for accompaniment.

4. Ask the students to listen for the rhyming words and imagine the scenes as Eve Bunting's *In the Haunted House* is read aloud. Have the children speculate about who is saying the lines in italics. After the reading, list the rhyming words as the children recall them. Use these words for spelling, dictation, or an activity in which the students write their own haunted house story.

   Select a line such as "The roof space is creeping crawling with things" to use on a bulletin board and have the children draw what they imagine the line describes. If possible, use pencil and watercolor as the medium for the illustrations just as illustrator Susan Meddaugh did.

5. When reading aloud *The Mother's Day Mice* by Eve Bunting, stop at the point where Little Mouse makes up his mind about a gift and says, "Something I kept hidden." Ask the children to predict what the gift will be. Finish the story. Let the students discuss what gifts they could share with people they love. Have the children sing Little Mouse's song.

   Refer to the student predictions. If no one guessed the gift, explain that the author gave the reader clues in the story. Ask the group to name any clues they may recall. Reread the story with the children listening specifically for clues to the gift. As they recognize these clues, write them on the board. Explain that these clues indicate an outcome and are called "foreshadowing." Urge children to note this technique in other stories they read or hear.

As a further extension let children compare the illustrations in the book to those in *Happy Birthday, Dear Duck; Scary, Scary Halloween;* and *St. Patrick's Day in the Morning.* Children should see the marked similarities in the style of the artwork in all four books. Students will probably deduce that all four books were illustrated by the same artist.

6. Remind the children that Eve Bunting was born and raised in Ireland, so it is natural that many of her books would be set in that country. Share *St. Patrick's Day in the Morning* by Eve Bunting with the class. After hearing the book, ask the children to explain the main idea of the story and then to summarize it.

   An an extension play additional selections from *James Galway and the Chieftains in Ireland* or other Celtic music. Explain to the children that Jan Brett's illustrations in *St. Patrick's Day in the Morning* give clues in pictures just as the author gives clues or foreshadowing in the words. Tell the children to listen to the music as they illustrate a scene from the story, trying to include visual clues to later happenings. Ask the students to use only an outline color such as black and the three colors of the Irish flag. If desired, students may be sent to the media center to research the Irish flag prior to the activity.

7. Ask the children to listen as Eve Bunting's *Scary, Scary Halloween* is read aloud and identify who is telling the story. Share the book with the group. When the children have identified the mother cat as the one who is telling the story, explain that Eve Bunting chose to tell the story from the cat's point of view to trick the reader. Let the students discuss how the story might be changed if it were told from a different viewpoint.

8. Eve Bunting's *Summer Wheels* is a chapter book and should be read over a period of several days. Take the opportunity while reading to stop after chapters 2, 4, and 5 and allow the children to predict what they think will occur. Predictions can be made orally or in student journals.

   Have the children discuss the role of responsibility, trust, and friendship in the story. Urge the group to retell the main events in the story and compare them to real life. Let children use information from the story to infer the reason for the Bicycle Man's actions.

9. Display a time line of 1900 through 2000. Show the division of decades with a different color of paper or line for every 10 years. Mark the decades and the present school year. Explain to the students that the time line will be used throughout the year to help them understand when events in history actually occurred. Follow by reading Eve Bunting's *The Wall.* Send a

group of children to the library media center to research the dates of the Vietnam conflict and help them mark that era on the time line. Through discussion help the students to identify the emotions expressed in the story.

Have the children use a globe or map to locate Washington, D.C., and Vietnam. Extend the story by having children ask their parents and grandparents to recall their memories of the Vietnam War, then compile a class booklet of these memories.

Closure:

To review Eve Bunting's books, have the children reexamine the three stories about Halloween, *Ghost's Hour, Spook's Hour; In the Haunted House;* and *Scary, Scary Halloween.* Ask the children to explain three ways the stories are alike and three ways they are different. Eve Bunting says, "There used to be Shanachies in the Ireland of long ago. The Shanachie was the storyteller who went from house to house telling his tales. . . . Maybe I'm a bit of a Shanachie myself, telling my stories. . . " (*Something about the Author,* vol. 64, p. 65). Encourage the children to tell about the Eve Bunting stories they remember. Several students may want to become class Shanachies. Arrange for the media specialist to work with those children to develop their storytelling ability.

Janet Stevens's Characters in Costumes

Objectives:

1. Recognize the parts of a folktale.
2. Perceive and interpret mood and feeling in illustrations.
3. Understand homonyms and the use of hyperbole in writing.
4. Draw inferences from reading by predicting outcomes.
5. Express personal ideas and opinions in class discussions and simple reports.
6. Identify differences in point of view.
7. Organize and tell or act out a story in sequence.
8. Restate the moral of a fable.
9. Respond to literature through a variety of art forms.

Recommended Readings:

Kimmel, Eric. A. *Anansi and the Moss-Covered Rock.* Illustrated by Janet

Stevens. Holiday House, 1988.
Anansi the trickster spider gets caught in his own scheme. (Objectives 1, 7, and 9)

―――. *Anansi Goes Fishing.* Illustrated by Janet Stevens. Holiday House, 1992.
Wise old Turtle tricks Anansi into doing all of the work to catch the fish. (Objectives 1, 7, and 9)

―――. *Nanny Goat and the Seven Little Kids.* Illustrated by Janet Stevens. Holiday House, 1990.
The clever Nanny Goat outwits the big bad wolf and saves her family. (Objective 5)

Lear, Edward. *The Owl and the Pussycat.* Illustrated by Janet Stevens. Holiday House, 1983.
The well-known nonsense poem about an unlikely animal romance is enhanced by humorous illustrations. (Objective 9)

―――. *The Quangle Wangle's Hat.* Illustrated by Janet Stevens. Harcourt Brace Jovanovich, 1988.
Various imaginative creatures decorate the Quangle Wangle's hat atop the Crumpetty Tree. (Objectives 6 and 9)

Stevens, Janet. *Androcles and the Lion.* Holiday House, 1989.
An act of kindness to a wounded animal later saves Androcles's life. (Objective 8)

―――. *How the Manx Cat Lost Its Tail.* Harcourt Brace Jovanovich, 1990.
A tale is born when the Manx cat loses his tail on Noah's ark. (Objectives 3, 4, 5, and 9)

―――. *It's Perfectly True!* Holiday House, 1988.
The statement made by one chick grows and changes out of all proportion as it is retold again and again. (Objectives 3, 7, and 9)

―――. *The Princess and the Pea.* Holiday House, 1982.
The real princess cannot be fooled by a clever queen who hides a pea under 20 mattresses and 20 feather beds. (Objective 2)

―――. *The Three Billy Goats Gruff.* Harcourt Brace Jovanovich, 1987.
The mountain troll finds he is no match for the clever billy goats as they cross his bridge. (Objectives 1 and 2)

Biographical Sources:

For information on Janet Stevens see *Sixth Book of Junior Authors & Illustrators,* pages 288–89.

Group Introductory Activity:

Read aloud Janet Stevens's retelling of *The Three Billy Goats Gruff* so students may hear the story. Ask the children if they noticed anything special or different about the animals in the book. Explain to the children that, in her personal appearances, Janet Stevens has said that she loves to draw animals, especially animals in human clothing. Reread the story and allow time for the children to view the illustrations. Let the children speculate about why Janet Stevens chose the particular clothing she placed on each goat. Give the children the opportunity to discuss what image the clothes project for each character. Ask the children to study the faces of the characters and discuss the emotions they show. Children may also notice the changes in the faces on the riverbank and the mood of the toad as the story moves along.

When Janet Stevens retold this story she added an important line, "What to do?" This simple device introduces the problem/solution relationship. Help the children begin to recognize the parts of a folktale (e.g., introduction, setting, good and evil characters, problem, action, and solution).

Follow-Up Activities for Teacher and Students to Share:

1. Before reading Eric Kimmel's *Anansi and the Moss-Covered Rock,* write the words *introduction, setting, characters, problem, action,* and *solution* on the chalkboard. Ask the children to listen carefully and identify these parts of the folktale when the story is completed. As the book is read aloud, have the children join in chanting the trickster spider's line. Refer to the words on the chalkboard and ask the children to recall the parts of the story.

    For a follow-up art activity use green powdered tempera to tint sawdust or pencil shavings. Let each child spread the top of a rock with glue. The children may then sprinkle the colored wood shavings on the glue to create "moss-covered" rocks of their own. Anansi models can be made out of small stuffed paper bags with accordion-folded spider legs attached. The trickster spiders may be hung from the ceiling or arranged around the students' rocks.

2. After having shared *Anansi and the Moss-Covered Rock,* ask the children to characterize Anansi (e.g., lazy, trickster). After the children have described the clever spider, read Eric Kimmel's *Anansi Goes Fishing* to the group. Stop reading after the first two pages to have the children establish the folktale characters, setting, and problem and to predict the outcome. Before resuming the story, remind the children to listen closely for the trick line. When the story is complete, allow the students to discuss the ending. Ask them how this story explains how spider webs came to be. Children will enjoy acting out the events of this folktale as a follow-up. As a further extension children could design spider webs. Have them draw a picture of

a web on paper. Cover the paper with a scrap piece of laminating film. Then let children use white glue to trace the web on the film. After the webs are dry they may be carefully peeled from the film and displayed on windows or smooth walls. One corner of the classroom could be decorated with a large hand-tied yarn web.

3. Prior to sharing Eric Kimmel's *Nanny Goat and the Seven Little Kids,* explain that the problem or conflict in this folktale is between personified animals, that is, animals that talk and have human characteristics. Ask the children to listen and identify how the animals and the problems they face are similar to problems the children might encounter. Read the story aloud. After completing the book, let the children share their ideas. Lead a discussion on choices children must make for personal safety.

4. Read aloud the Janet Stevens illustrated version of Edward Lear's *The Owl and the Pussycat.* As a follow-up a small group of children can construct a "beautiful pea-green boat." Other students might enjoy illustrating the "land where the Bong-tree grows." Send a small group of students to the library media center to locate, if available, other versions of Lear's poem, such as Jan Brett's illustrated edition (G.P. Putnam's Sons, 1991) and compare the illustrations to those of Stevens. As a further follow-up let the children listen to Carly Simon's rendition of "The Owl and the Pussycat" from *Lobster Quadrille* (Columbia Book and Record Library) or "The Owl and the Pussycat" performed by Lou Rawls and Deniece Williams on *In Harmony 2* (Columbia, 1981).

5. Share with the children Edward Lear's *The Quangle Wangle's Hat* as illustrated by Janet Stevens. After reading the nonsense poem, plan with the music teacher and the library media specialist to develop and perform a play based on the story. On a smaller scale students could make and decorate the quangle wangle's hat in the classroom. Serve the quangle wangle's favorite foods, jam jelly and bread, to the children. Ask the library media specialist to locate other versions of Lear's poem and share the different illustrators' viewpoint and style with the group. Children can then follow up with an art activity expressing their own interpretation of the hat. They might want to use clay to sculpt the strange animals that are mentioned in the poem.

6. Tell the children that Janet Stevens often retells and illustrates fables. Define a fable as a story that teaches a lesson. Tell the children that the sentence moral at the end of a fable might be called the "theme" of the story because it is what the story is about. Read aloud Stevens's version of *Androcles and the Lion.* Write the fable's moral on the board and follow by having the children summarize the events of the story that led to the fable's ending. Ask the students to work in small groups to restate their own moral for the fable. The children may wish to reflect on how the fable relates to their lives.

7. As the story *How the Manx Cat Lost Its Tail* by Janet Stevens is read aloud, urge the children to join the text when Noah calls the kitty and when the sons cry, "Let us close the door. . . ." Stop on the page where all four men call for the kitty. Have the children predict the end of the story before completing the tale. Ask the students to identify the various animals Janet Stevens has shown in the story. Let the children determine which of those animals appear in other books Stevens has illustrated. Children will enjoy completing the pets list after the line which reads, "every other pet you can think of." If show-and-tell is still a part of class activities, have the students tell something that a favorite pet did. Have other students listen and identify characters, problems, and solutions as children share their stories.

   Take the opportunity to introduce the homonyms *tail* and *tale* with this story. Keep a chart of homonyms in the room and add to it throughout the year. Children may wish to create a homonyms booklet which could be illustrated with animals similar to those Janet Stevens uses in her books.

8. Read aloud *It's Perfectly True!* by Janet Stevens. Ask the children to discuss the lesson to be learned in this story. Have the children retell and act out the story in sequence. A small group of children may choose to go to the library media center to read Verna Aardema's *Why Mosquitoes Buzz in People's Ears* (Dial, 1975), if it is available, and compare it to Stevens's book.

   Set up a situation where children can create their own gossip story beginning with lines such as "After the alarm went off I . . ." or "When the sun went down she. . . ." To aid figurative language development, note the line in the beginning of *It's Perfectly True!* that starts "It was so scary. . ." Explain that when authors stretch or exaggerate a comparison, it is called hyperbole. Ask the students to discuss and then write their own hyperboles based on an experience in the story they just created. To help them get started ask the question "How funny (scary, sad, silly) was it?"

9. Tell the children that, as *The Princess and the Pea* by Janet Stevens is read aloud, they are to interpret the mood of the story from the illustrations. After completing the book, let the children discuss the mood of the story and the attitude or characteristics of the princess, prince, and the queen. Urge the children to speculate about whether or not the queen really wanted the prince to find a suitable princess.

Closure:

Now that the students have read some of the books written and/or illustrated by Janet Stevens have the children prepare illustrated riddles about Stevens's books which may be published in a class book. Show an example of a riddle and have the students illustrate it on one page and write the riddle on the bottom. One example might be "The pea under her mattress kept her from sleeping. Who was she?" The answer, of course, is "The princess from *The Princess and the Pea.*" If the children have had much experience with rhyme and poetry, they might wish to try to make their riddles in rhyme form (e.g., "He was saved from the lion's jaw / Because he'd pulled a thorn from his paw." The answer, "Androcles," should be written on the back of the sheet with the illustrated riddle if the individual riddles are not to be compiled into a book. If the riddles are compiled, put all the answers together on the final page).

Winter Times and Tales

Objectives:

1. Recognize figurative language.
2. Increase oral and written vocabulary.
3. Compare the cultural heritage of another country to the student's own locale.
4. Research and report information in oral, written, and art forms.
5. Describe ways families can work together to resolve problems and conflicts.
6. Identify logical relationships such as problem and solution, compare and contrast, cause and effect, and sequential order.
7. Respond to literature through choral reading, dramatization, art activities, and discussion.
8. Interpret a story from illustrations.
9. Recognize various forms of literature including folktales, poetry, fiction, and nonfiction.

Recommended Readings:

Brett, Jan. *The Mitten.* G.P. Putnam, 1989.
> A young boy's lost mitten becomes a home to a host of animals on a snowy day. (Objectives 1, 8, and 9)

Carlstrom, Nancy White. *Northern Lullaby.* Illustrated by Leo and Diane Dillon. Philomel, 1992.
> This quiet goodnight story salutes the beauty of nature through its words and illustrations. (Objectives 3, 4, 8, and 9)

Delton, Judy. *A Walk on a Snowy Night.* Illustrated by Ruth Rosner. Harper & Row, 1982.
> A little girl and her father see, hear, and feel the beauty of the snowy night as they walk together. (Objectives 1, 2, 5, and 6)

Dragonwagon, Crescent. *Winter Holding Spring.* Illustrated by Ronald Himler. Macmillan, 1990.
The circle of life unfolds as Sarah deals with the death of her mother. (Objectives 5 and 6)

Frost, Robert. *Stopping by Woods on a Snowy Evening.* Illustrated by Susan Jeffers. E.P. Dutton, 1978.
The classic poem and illustrations combine to depict the beauty of nature on a snowy evening. (Objectives 7 and 9)

Haarhoff, Dorian. *Desert December.* Illustrated by Leon Vermeulen. Clarion, 1992.
In order to reach his parents on Christmas Day, a young South African boy makes his way across the land through the night and day of the desert. (Objectives 1, 3, and 7)

Hughes, Shirley. *The Snow Lady: A Tale of Trotter Street.* Lothrop, Lee & Shepard, 1990.
Sam and Barney create a snow lady that bears a remarkable resemblance to mean Mrs. Dean. (Objectives 3 and 7)

Say, Allen. *Tree of Cranes.* Houghton Mifflin, 1991.
A young Japanese boy learns the meaning of Christmas from his American-born mother. (Objectives 3 and 7)

Selsam, Millicent, and Hunt, Joyce. *Keep Looking!* Illustrated by Normand Chartier. Macmillan, 1989.
A wildlife watch on a winter's day shows many animals feeding. (Objectives 4, 6, and 9)

Wild, Margaret. *Thank You, Santa.* Illustrated by Kerry Argent. Scholastic, 1991.
A young Australian girl corresponds with Santa in his North Pole home throughout the year. (Objectives 2, 3, and 7)

Group Introductory Activity:

Judy Delton's *A Walk on a Snowy Night* provides a tool to introduce how one experiences things through the senses and how winter and snow can heighten these experiences. After reading the story aloud, have the students recall words and phrases from Judy Delton's story and prepare a wall chart of those winter words and phrases that they can refer to in their writing experiences. Have the children add to this list phrases and words from other books they read and hear in this unit. To help the students recognize figurative language used in the story, have them select a comparative line using *like* or *as* to illustrate.

Follow-Up Activities for Teacher and Students to Share:

1. The adaptor/illustrator Jan Brett has researched Ukrainian customs and architecture to make her story *The Mitten* more authentic. She has also included her favorite animal, the hedgehog, an animal not found in the United States. Individual students may want to visit the library media center to learn more about this animal. Before reading the book, explain that Jan Brett tells the story in pictures that can be interpreted to tell the story. Read aloud to the point where Baba instructs Nicki to return with his mittens. Now have the children study the pictures in the frame of the mittens to predict the events of the story before reading ahead.

    This folktale relies on repetition to build to the climax, so it is an easy story for children to learn and tell aloud. Reread the story aloud several times to demonstrate the importance of voice projection and animation in telling. Follow by encouraging children to learn to tell this tale. If Alvin Tresselt's *The Mitten* (Lothrop, Lee & Shepard, 1966) is available, a small group of children may wish to read it and compare the two versions of the story and illustrations.

2. Have the children examine the art on the inside cover of Nancy White Carlstrom's *Northern Lullaby*. Children should notice the repeating pattern in the border. Ask the students to study the illustrations as the book is read aloud and note the repeating figures. Background music can be a very effective addition to the reading of this book. A possible selection is George Winston's *A Winter's Solstice* (Windham Hill, 1985).

    Ask the students to recall the animals' names in the lullaby. Send a group of children to the library media center to locate pictures of these northern animals, as well as the northern lights and the Alaskan landscape. Another group can research the weather of Alaska in the winter and the different names the Eskimos have for snow. Ask the children how the lullaby would differ if it told about their area.

3. Throughout the book *Winter Holding Spring* Crescent Dragonwagon has indicated the circle of life in lines such as "In the middle of summer, there's always fall" (p. 3) and "nothing just ends without beginning the next thing at the same time . . ." (p. 11). Stop reading aloud after these lines to give the children time to reflect and discuss what these lines mean to them and to the book's character, Sarah. Ask how these lines and thoughts help Sarah come to terms with the death of her mother. Let the children discuss how families can work together to resolve other problems and conflicts. Students can follow the reading and discussion by writing a journal entry as if they were Sarah. If the book *First Snow* by Helen Coutant (Alfred A. Knopf, 1974) is available, have a small group of students read and compare the two stories.

4. Before reading aloud Robert Frost's poem *Stopping by Woods on a Snowy Evening,* explain that this story is a famous poem written many years ago. Susan Jeffers, the illustrator, says on the jacket cover, "I wanted the pictures to tell about the patterns of winter trees in the sky and the textures of feathers and fur and branches and the spaces around and between them." Have the children study the illustrations for textures and patterns as they listen to the poem being read aloud. Duplicate the poem and let children share it as a choral reading.

   As a follow-up allow the children to participate in a textured art activity. Collect a variety of materials with differing textures (e.g., sandpaper, foil, and scraps of velvet, corduroy, satin, fur, or other cloth). Place these in a bag. Allow the children to reach into the bag, choose an object and, without removing it from the bag, try to identify it from its texture. After the children have had a tactile experience with texture, place the items in an art center where students may use them with other media to create a textured collage.

5. After reading *Desert December* by Dorian Haarhoff, have the children speculate about the winter weather of the Namibian desert in Africa. Discuss the differences between the boy's life in Africa and the life the children in the classroom experience. Reread the story, asking the children to listen for and identify figurative language.

   In the story the boy carved a wooden figure for his mother. As an art activity have the children experience carving in soft wood, soap, sponges, cork, or styrofoam. Display the students' sculptures in the classroom or media center.

6. Before reading *The Snow Lady: A Tale of Trotter Street* by Shirley Hughes, explain the meaning of the English words defined on the copyright page. After the students have heard the story, have them respond through discussion of the winter events and dramatization of a scene from the book. Paper bag puppets can be created and dialogue added to prepare a puppet show about the snow lady.

7. Read aloud Allen Say's story *Tree of Cranes.* Ask the children to recall what memory of Christmas the boy's mother stressed. Let the students compare and contrast their lives to that of the boy in the story. As a follow-up place a book on origami or paper folding such as *Origami* by Hideaki Sakata (Harper & Row, 1984) in an art center with paper squares so the children can learn how to fold and create an object using this traditional Japanese technique.

8. Ask the students whether they would read fiction or nonfiction to learn facts on animals. After listening to Millicent Selsam and Joyce Hunt's *Keep Looking!,* ask them to decide what kind of book it is (fiction or nonfiction). Check the call number to verify their answer. Have small groups of children research animal tracks using Millicent Selsam's *How to*

Be a Nature Detective(Harper & Row, 1966) or other appropriate resource. Each group can then draw or press in clay the tracks of the animals they have selected and challenge classmates to guess which animals make such tracks. Let the children discuss how animals in their state survive during winter. Students could follow up by creating dioramas of animals in winter.

9.   Locate Australia, Antarctica, and the North Pole on the globe. Ask the children to listen closely to Margaret Wild's *Thank You, Santa* to discover the difference in seasons in Australia and the United States. Read the story aloud. Let the children share their observations of the seasons. Most students will notice that while it is summer in the United States, it is winter in Australia. Have the children locate both countries on a globe. Show students that, during July and August, the northern hemisphere is tilted toward the sun and that, during December and January, the tilt reverses so that the southern hemisphere is tilted toward the sun. Individual students may wish to select an animal from the story to research more fully. If this book is shared shortly after the Christmas holiday, the children may write thank-you notes to Santa as Samantha did in the book.

Ask an adult to visit the class and show the students how to knit or crochet. Follow the visit by establishing a center where students may knit or crochet simple stitches when their assigned work is completed.

Closure:

Review each of the winter books in this unit and have the students recall the events and/or characters in each story and area of the world. As a final activity have the students write original wintertime tales from their own point of view or that of a character in one of the stories. Bind the completed stories into a book called *Winter Views*.

Adventures in Science with Joanna Cole

Objectives:

1.   Report information in a variety of oral, written, and visual formats and through creative movement.
2.   Listen and read for information and main ideas.
3.   Recognize that books with facts are located by call numbers in the library.
4.   Respond to a story through oral discussion and/or writing.

5. Distinguish between statements of fact and statements of opinion.
6. Express empathy with book characters or life experiences of others.

Recommended Readings:

————. *How You Were Born*. Illustrated by Hella Hammid, et al. William Morrow, 1984.
Black-and-white photographs highlight the text that explains how a baby is conceived, grows, and is born. (Objectives 3 and 4)

————. *The Magic School Bus at the Waterworks*. Illustrated by Bruce Degen. Scholastic, 1986.
The strangest teacher of all, Miss Frizzle, takes her students on a field trip to a water purification plant. (Objectives 1, 2, and 5)

————. *The Magic School Bus Inside the Earth*. Illustrated by Bruce Degen. Scholastic, 1987.
An imaginative teacher introduces her students to types of rocks and other features of the earth. (Objectives 1, 2, and 5)

————. *The Magic School Bus Inside the Human Body*. Illustrated by Bruce Degen. Scholastic, 1989.
Miss Frizzle takes her class on a field trip inside the human body. (Objectives 1, 2, 3, and 5)

————. *The Magic School Bus Lost in the Solar System*. Illustrated by Bruce Degen. Scholastic, 1990.
Miss Frizzle and her class take a colorful voyage to each planet in the solar system. (Objectives 1 and 2)

————. *The Magic School Bus on the Ocean Floor*. Illustrated by Bruce Degen. Scholastic, 1992.
A journey to the ocean floor reveals new discoveries about life in the ocean. (Objectives 1 and 2)

Cole, Joanna, and Calmenson, Stephanie. *Miss Mary Mack and Other Children's Street Rhymes*. Illustrated by Alan Tiegreen. William Morrow, 1990.
This collection of "just-for-fun" activities includes hand clapping, ball bouncing, counting out rhymes, and more. (Objective 1)

————. *My Puppy Is Born*. Illustrated by Margaret Miller. William Morrow, 1991.
Colorful photographs depict a Norfolk terrier puppy from birth through the first eight weeks of life. (Objective 4)

————. *The New Baby at Your House*. Illustrated by Hella Hammid. William Morrow, 1985.

Many family experiences in welcoming a new baby are expressed in photographs and text. (Objectives 3 and 7)

————.*A Snake's Body.* Illustrated by Jerome Wexler. William Morrow, 1981. The anatomy of the Indian python is examined through text and photographs. (Objective 1)

Biographical Sources:

For information on Joanna Cole see *Something about the Author*, vol. 49, pages 68–74 and *Fifth Book of Junior Authors & Illustrators*, pages 77–78.

Group Introductory Activity:

Joanna Cole has said that when she was a child she loved to do science experiments and write them up as reports. She recalled, "I was also interested in the plants and animals I found in my backyard . . . Much of my childhood was spent watching insects—ants, praying mantises, crickets, wasps, bees" (*Fifth Book of Junior Authors & Illustrators*, p. 77). The addition of humor and imagination helps her books flow smoothly rather than merely list facts. Explain that Joanna Cole does not draw the pictures that appear in her books. Consequently, she has teamed up with Bruce Degen, photographer Jerome Wexler, and other illustrators.

Introduce the class to Joanna Cole through her book *The Magic School Bus Inside the Human Body.* The book begins with a science experiment. Conduct the experiment on seeing your own cells before reading further. Convert the one-sentence reports in the book to questions. Read aloud and post these questions so students will know what information to listen for as the story is shared. As the story is read, be sure to call attention to the use of the dialogue balloons for conversation. Help the students distinguish facts from opinion. After reading the book, ask the children to tell about any part of the story that makes them curious to learn more. Use this book as a springboard for a one- to three-sentence factual report.

To help students locate more information on the subject of the human body and other Joanna Cole books, make bookmarks out of 3" × 11" construction paper. Put the title of each Joanna Cole book and its call number on the bookmarks. Laminate the bookmarks and let the children use the call numbers to locate other nonfiction books on the same subject. Use discussion to help children deduce that books with facts are arranged by subject and call number. Have the class decorate a cardboard school bus as a creative lead-in to the classroom presentation of reports.

Follow-Up Activities for Teacher and Students to Share:

1. After sharing Joanna Cole's *How You Were Born* with the children, allow time for questions and concerns the children may have. Ask the children to bring in baby pictures of themselves. Explain that each student is to write out a description of something they did beginning with the phrase "When I was a baby I. . . ." The description can be attached to the photograph and posted on the wall without names given. Let the children guess who belongs to which picture.

    Have the children examine the various call numbers of books by Joanna Cole. Students should try to deduce what subject is represented by each call number based on the book to which that number is assigned. Let the students visit the library media center to confirm or refute their conclusions.

2. Assign a group of children to read and report on *The Magic School Bus at the Waterworks* by Joanna Cole. Students may want to dress like Miss Frizzle and her students to act out or demonstrate their reports. Reports could be done as scenery or backdrops, diagrams, or charts showing how water gets to homes and buildings. Bruce Degen's illustrations show this process on pages 34–35. Use a field trip or a guest speaker to find out the source of the water used in the local community.

3. Allow a group of children to read and report on *The Magic School Bus Inside the Earth* by Joanna Cole. Reports may take the form of word balloons like Cole and Degen used in the book, displays of identified rocks, or paragraphs extending the information given in the book.

4. One group of children may be assigned to read and report the information obtained from Joanna Cole's *The Magic School Bus Lost in the Solar System.* As a follow-up each individual in the group should select one planet to research further. The group members may collect and report solar system data on a chart like the one in the book.

5. In order to share Joanna Cole's *The Magic School Bus on the Ocean Floor*, ask fourth- or fifth-grade volunteers to select various roles or sections of the book to read aloud to the class (e.g., Miss Frizzle, a narrator, lifeguard, reports, or dialogue). Divide the class into cooperative groups. One group may develop a food chain of life on the ocean floor and compare it to a second group's food chain from the earth's surface. A third group can set up displays of seashells or other marine life. Another group may be responsible for caring for live sea creatures (e.g., hermit crabs or aquarium fish). Yet another group could create paper dolls or body puppets of Miss Frizzle, being sure to dress them appropriately.

6. Introduce *Miss Mary Mack and Other Children's Street Rhymes* by Joanna Cole and Stephanie Calmenson by sharing the title rhyme from the book. Explain that this rhyme is often used as a jump rope game. Have pairs of

students select and learn one or two rhymes of their choice from the book. When the students know their rhymes, allow time for them to teach them to the class. Ask the physical education teacher to let the children use appropriate rhymes from the book to accompany jump rope activities.

7. Read aloud Joanna Cole's *My Puppy Is Born.* Give the students time to tell their favorite pet stories. Let the children discuss how to care for and train a puppy. They may wish to create a dog collage of pictures from magazines. Ask the students to research the dogs they place in the collage in order to identify the breeds included. Children may mention other types of pets they own. If so, allow the group to discuss ways in which all of the pet types are alike and ways in which they are different. Refer to other Joanna Cole books such as *A Cat's Body* (William Morrow, 1992) or *A Dog's Body* (William Morrow, 1986).

8. After reading Joanna Cole's *The New Baby at Your House,* ask the students to respond to the first question in the book, "Is there a new baby at your house?" If some children have experienced having a new baby at home, invite them to share that experience in words, photographs, or by acting out a scene from their lives. Let the students identify the emotions they expressed that are also described in the book. Help the children increase their vocabulary by letting them identify and define unfamiliar words found in the book (e.g., *pregnant, womb, diaper,* and *attention*). If possible, invite a family to bring their infant to visit the classroom.

    Note that this book carries the call number of 305.2. Children can visit the library media center to see if they can locate other books about families in the 305.2 section. Several students may wish to locate, read, and compare the feelings expressed in these nonfiction books with those in picture books such as Ezra Jack Keats's *Peter's Chair* (Harper, 1967), Kathryn Lasky's *A Baby for Max* (Charles Scribner, 1984), and Martha Alexander's *Nobody Asked Me If I Wanted a Baby Sister* (Dial, 1971).

9. Read aloud Joanna Cole's *A Snake's Body.* Refer to the diagram on page 7, explaining that it represents the snake's body. Students may respond by selecting an animal to study and diagram for a report. Encourage interested students to do research to discover other animals that rely on one or two main senses for survival and to find out about which senses they are dependent upon.

Closure:

Let the children pretend to be different cartoon-type characters from Joanna Cole's "Magic School Bus" series, for example, Arnold or Miss Frizzle. Work with the children to combine the information gathered in this unit with what the students know about the author's writing style in that series to produce a play for the whole school. Videotape the production to share with future classes.

Under the Poet Tree

Objectives:

1. Recognize the use of the Dewey Decimal system for the organization of materials.
2. Use the card catalog to locate books by an author's surname.
3. Locate on a map a city or state mentioned in literature.
4. Form and correctly use compound words.
5. Develop oral reading skills.
6. Use reference books.
7. Recognize and use figurative language.
8. Respond to poetry through art, written expression, or movement.

Recommended Readings:

Merriam, Eve. *Fighting Words.* Illustrated by David Small. William Morrow, 1992.
A quick-witted word fight between two friends ends when their voices tire and they agree to a handshake. (Objectives 6 and 7)

———. *A Poem for a Pickle.* Illustrated by Sheila Hamanaka. William Morrow, 1989.
Funny, imaginative words and activities are described in poetic form. (Objective 7)

———. *Where Is Everybody?* Illustrated by Diane de Groat. Simon and Schuster, 1989.
Animals of the alphabet are engaged in everyday activities. (Objective 7)

———. *You Be Good and I'll Be Night.* Illustrated by Karen Lee Schmidt. William Morrow, 1988.
This collection of poems is filled with bounce, rhythm, rhyme, and imaginative actions. (Objectives 4, 5, and 7)

Prelutsky, Jack. *Beneath a Blue Umbrella.* Illustrated by Garth Williams. Greenwillow, 1990.
Nonsense rhymes about people, places, and things are collected in this slim volume. (Objectives 3 and 8)

———. *Ride a Purple Pelican.* Illustrated by Garth Williams. Greenwillow, 1986.
This collection of nonsense rhymes takes the reader from Seattle to New York and many places in between. (Objectives 3, 6, and 8)

————. *Something Big Has Been Here*. Illustrated by James Stevenson. Greenwillow, 1990.
> Poetry about food, friends, and fun fill the pages of this volume. (Objectives 1, 2, 5, and 8)

Biographical Sources:

For information on Eve Merriam see *Something about the Author,* vol. 40, pages 141–49 and *Third Book of Junior Authors*, pages 193–94. For information on Jack Prelutsky see *Something about the Author,* vol. 22, pages 195–97 and vol. 66, pages 180–84; and *Fifth Book of Junior Authors & Illustrators*, pages 251–52.

Group Introductory Activity:

Prepare for this unit by constructing a Poet Tree center in the classroom. Possible construction methods include using a tree branch supported in a large container by a plaster of paris base or placing a flat tree on a bulletin board. Under this tree display the books for the unit and biographical material on each poet. Write to the publishers to request photographs and current information on the featured poets: Eve Merriam and Jack Prelutsky.

Team with the library media specialist to introduce each poet and the location of poetry books according to the Dewey Decimal system. These books will be located in the 811 section. Send small groups of children to the media center to learn how to use the card catalog to look up a poet's name and find his or her books on the shelf.

Jack Prelutsky's poetry reflects his interests and views on life. Children will notice that many of his poems are about food and feelings. Almost all of his poems are funny. Introduce Prelutsky's book *Something Big Has Been Here* by reading a selection of "feeling" poems such as "I Am Tired of Being Little," "You're Nasty and You're Loud," and "Life's Not Been the Same in My Family." Allow time to identify the different feelings expressed in the poems.

Follow up the reading by explaining that the students are to read *Something Big Has Been Here* while sitting under the poet tree. Give each child a booklet entitled "The 3F's of Jack Prelutsky: Food, Feelings, and Fun." Have the children copy and illustrate in this booklet at least one poem for each subject. They should label each page with the subject, written in capital letters (e.g., FOOD, FEELINGS, or FUN), followed by the poem title in quotation marks. If students will be reading several Prelutsky books, they will need to also note the book title. If the group contains children with severe reading disabilities, pair those children with other students who can read the poems aloud in the center. When the disabled child hears a poem about one of the subjects, the reader should stop and allow the other student to illustrate the poem and label the subject. Read aloud funny poems from *Something Big Has Been Here* frequently during the unit, asking the group to listen for the subject.

Follow-Up Activities for Teacher and Students to Share:

1. Read aloud *Fighting Words* by Eve Merriam. Students will note that this is not a poetry book. However, because author Eve Merriam is a poet her writing reflects many of the skills of a poet (e.g., colorful language, extensive vocabulary, and comparisons in metaphors and similes). Work with the fighting words by placing the book in the hands of the children, asking each child to read a word aloud while the teacher writes it on a chart. When the list is complete ask each child to select two to five words to define. After the words have been defined, let the children read and discuss the various meanings.

    Reread the book, asking the children to listen for comparisons beginning with the word *like*. List these on the board as students recall them. Note that figurative language using the words *like* or *as* is called a simile. Encourage pairs of students to write original similes. As a follow-up have the class use the information gathered from Eve Merriam's book to compose an original poem about Lida and Dale or their classmates, including at least one simile.

2. Read aloud the poems in the collection *A Poem for a Pickle* by Eve Merriam. Copy and display the title poem on a large piece of poster board. Before rereading it, serve dill pickles to the children. Ask the class to read the poem together. Have the children speculate on the meaning of the term *couplet*. Guide the discussion so children may discover that a couplet is two successive lines that usually rhyme and have the same beat. Compose several class collaborative couplets. Urge the children to listen as the book is shared to discover other poems that use couplets.

    Ask for volunteers to jump rope to the "Skip Rope Rhyme" as it is read to the group. After reading aloud "The Ice Cream Fountain Mountain," copy and distribute the poem to the children. During free time have the children select two lines of the poem and draw a double-decker ice-cream cone picture to illustrate the lines.

3. While reading aloud Eve Merriam's *Where Is Everybody?*, give the children time to find the mole in each illustration as he photographs everyone. After reading the story brainstorm two lists: a list of places in the neighborhood or community where people or animals could be and a second list of various animals by alphabet letters. Send a student to the library media center to use the card catalog and check out other alphabet books naming animals A through Z so the children can have a choice of

animals for the difficult letters *I, Q, U, V, X, Y,* and *Z.* When the two lists are complete, compose a class "Where Is Everybody?" story. Have children illustrate the completed story, bind it, and display it in the library media center.

4. Make an overhead transparency of the poem "Ten Little Apples on Ten Apple Trees" from Eve Merriam's *You Be Good and I'll Be Night.* During art time have the children illustrate the first set of rhyming lines from the poem, "Ten little apples on ten apple trees / nine little beehives with nine buzzing bees." Continue illustrating one rhyme each day for several days until the poem is entirely illustrated, ending with a picture from their own imaginations.

   Read "Lunch box, lunch box, / what's for lunch?" Introduce the basic food groups and the essentials of a healthy diet. Let the students discuss what they enjoy eating and make a list of lunch box menus that would be healthy. Children might enjoy preparing some tasty, healthy snacks that can be carried in a lunch box. A good reference for simple nutritious recipes is Vicki Lansky's *The Taming of the C.A.N.D.Y.* Monster: *Continuously Advertised, Nutritionally Deficient Yummies!* (Meadowbrook, 1978). After reading another food poem in the collection, "Crusty corn bread," share a pan of corn bread so the students can experience "crumbly crumbs, / mumbly muffins, / buttery thumbs."

   In her book *Everybody Needs a Rock* (Macmillan, 1974) Byrd Baylor describes the importance of having a personal rock. This idea is reiterated in Merriam's poem "I found a little stone" from *You Be Good and I'll Be Night.* Let children search for and find their own smooth round stone to keep at school.

   After reading "You're my turtle," point out that the final two lines of each verse refer to the two words that end the first two lines (e.g., turtledoves coo and are a symbol of love, safety pins fasten and hold materials, and jumping jacks are a repetitive exercise). Introduce the concept of compound words by writing the words individually and then combining them to make new words on the board. Let the students think of other compound words or double word combinations that could be used to create additional verses for the poem. Have students use each compound word in a sentence. Share the sentences orally. Using the ideas generated in the children's sentences, write several class collaborative verses to add to Merriam's poem.

5. Read aloud several poems from Jack Prelutsky's *Beneath a Blue Umbrella* that use nonsense language such as "Rickety Pickety Percival Peake" (p. 10), "Jiggity jumpity jog" (p. 20), or "Patter Pitter Caterpillar" (p. 34). Team with the music teacher to introduce creative movement. Have the children demonstrate a movement to accompany the nonsense rhymes. Follow up by having the children create original nonsense lines or rhymes.

6. Introduce *Ride a Purple Pelican* by Jack Prelutsky by reading aloud the last poem in the book (p. 62). Be sure to have a large map of North America displayed in the room. Locate Seattle and New York on the map. Ask the children what they might see if they flew like the poem suggests. As other poems are read, locate each city or state mentioned in the poem. The library media specialist could introduce advanced children to the world atlas as a means of finding cities and states.

Each child may select a state or city mentioned in one of the poems to research. Students may prepare a brief report of what might be seen as someone flew over that city or state. Use pins to mark and label each location found on the map.

Closure:

Ask the children to identify the kind of poem they each liked best in this unit and explain why. Was it on a subject they liked? Was it the way it was written? The sounds? A favorite poet's style? Have the children select a favorite poem or stanza from a poem by one of the three poets to memorize and recite. Ask the library media specialist to videotape the children reciting the poems under the poet tree. The video might be played at a PTA meeting or in a waiting area on parent conference day.

Mem Fox and Margaret Mahy: Readings from Down Under

Objectives:

1. Recognize literature as an essential base of cultural and practical knowledge.
2. Judge the effects of an event.
3. Research animals and/or food native to a country.
4. Act creatively with visual arts, movement, music, and/or oral and written expression.
5. Recall the sequential order of a story.
6. Identify problems and solutions (conflict) in a story.
7. Relate to the actions and feelings of a book character.
8. Use a map to locate story events.

Recommended Readings:

Fox, Mem. *Koala Lou.* Illustrated by Pamela Lofts. Harcourt Brace Jovanovich, 1988.
A young koala demonstrates how important it is to hear the words "I do love you" when she enters the Bush Olympics. (Objectives 1, 2, and 3)

————. *Night Noises.* Illustrated by Terry Denton. Harcourt Brace Jovanovich, 1989.
The night noises bring a pleasant surprise for 90-year-old Lily Laceby. (Objective 5)

————. *Possum Magic.* Illustrated by Julie Vivas. Abingdon, 1987.
When Grandma Poss's bush magic makes Hush invisible, it takes a food-eating tour of Australia to make the young opossum reappear. (Objectives 1, 3, and 8)

————. *Shoes from Grandpa.* Illustrated by Patricia Mullins. Orchard, 1990.
Grandpa's gift of shoes begins a cumulative rhyme story about clothes. (Objectives 4 and 5)

————. *Wilfred Gordon McDonald Partridge.* Illustrated by Julie Vivas. Kane/Miller, 1983.
By sharing objects from his childhood, a young boy shows his love and concern for an elderly lady who has lost her memory. (Objectives 4, 6, and 7)

Mahy, Margaret. *17 Kings and 42 Elephants.* Illustrated by Patricia MacCarthy. Dial, 1987.
In this nonsense rhyme, the kings take readers through an imaginative jungle. (Objective 4)

————. *The Boy with Two Shadows.* Illustrated by Jenny Williams. J. B. Lippincott, 1987.
A young boy discovers that babysitting a witch's shadow can create some unexpected problems. (Objectives 4 and 6)

————. *The Great White Man-Eating Shark: A Cautionary Tale.* Illustrated by Jonathan Allen. Dial, 1990.
It takes a great white shark to teach Norvin a lesson about being too greedy. (Objectives 4 and 6)

————. *Making Friends.* Illustrated by Wendy Smith. Macmillan, 1990.
With the help of two very clever dogs, two lonely people meet and become friends. (Objectives 4, 6, and 7)

Biographical Sources:

For information on Mem (Merrion Frances) Fox see *Something about the Author*, vol. 51, pages 65–70; *Sixth Book of Junior Authors & Illustrators*, pages 88–89; and *Trumpet Video Visits: Mem Fox* (Trumpet Video, 1992). For information on Margaret Mahy see *Something about the Author*, vol. 69, pages 140–46, and *Fourth Book of Junior Authors & Illustrators*, pages 248–50.

Group Introductory Activity:

Introduce authors Mem Fox and Margaret Mahy by turning to the map in the back of Fox's book *Possum Magic* or by using a large map to locate Australia and New Zealand. Explain that Mem Fox lives in Australia and that Margaret Mahy lives in New Zealand. Tell the children that each author writes about her native land.

Mem Fox says that all of her ideas for books come from her life. She also says that as a child she was quite a tomboy but loved to read. When she discovered that there was no Australian children's literature she wrote *Possum Magic* to help children around the world learn about her homeland (*Something about the Author*, vol. 51, p. 68). Before reading any stories ask the children to free write for three minutes everything they may know about Australia. Have the students sign and date their papers and keep them in a folder.

Read aloud *Possum Magic* by Mem Fox. Then refer to the glossary of Australian terms and the map at the end of the book to explain what Hush and Grandma Poss ate. As a further follow-up students may wish to prepare some food from the story to share with the group, such as lamington, squares of sponge cake dipped in thin chocolate icing and rolled in coconut.

As another extension activity students may wish to take a food tour of the United States. Let a small group of students use such library media center resources as cookbooks and encyclopedias to research regional foods and place them on a map.

To help children recognize literature as an essential base of cultural knowledge hand each child a folder. Ask the students to decorate the front with a picture that indicates something they have learned about Australia. As the unit continues, place all writing and art in the individual folders.

Follow-Up Activities for Teacher and Students to Share:

1. Before sharing *Koala Lou* by Mem Fox, bring a stuffed koala toy or puppet to the classroom that children may hold and read to during the unit. Read the book aloud. Have the children discuss Koala Lou's feelings about competition. Ask the students to speculate what might have happened if Koala Lou had won the event in which she participated. Encourage a small group of children to research other animals native to Australia and report to the class.

   Ask the children to judge, if the story took place in America, what animal would best represent the United States. Let children brainstorm, list possible answers, and then vote for the animal of their choice. A mini-debate could develop before the voting. Let a team research the facts and conduct a short debate on the merits of the different suggestions.

2. Ask the children to listen and participate by making the appropriate sounds of the night as Mem Fox's *Night Noises* is read aloud. Stop reading on the page when fists beat upon the door and ask the students to predict the next series of events. After completing the story, ask the students to recall the sequence of events in Lily Laceby's dream. Ask a small group of children to figure how many guests actually came to the party

3. Read *Shoes from Grandpa* by Mem Fox aloud to the children, inviting them to join in the rhyme. After hearing the story, ask the children to recall sequentially the items of clothing that Jessie received. Point out that the illustrations are done in torn paper collage. Demonstrate how to tear and apply tissue paper to construction paper to create a collage. Refer to the page showing the mittens and have the students create their own collage mittens. Artistic children may want to follow by making a flannel board story out of the rhyme. If material other than wool felt is used, attach Velcro or sandpaper to the back of each piece so the item will adhere to the flannel board. Let children use the flannel board characters to retell the story.

4. Read aloud to the group Mem Fox's *Wilfred Gordon McDonald Partridge*. Present Wilfred's question, "What is memory?" to the class for response and discussion. Discuss with the children their concerns about elderly people and the problems they face. If possible adopt a nearby care home. Take field trips seasonally to the care home to meet the people and share stories.

   To help the children identify with Wilfred and Miss Nancy, ask each child to bring an object from home that evokes a memory. As in show-and-tell, ask the children to share their objects and memories. Invite other teachers to brings objects and share their memories with the class. Follow up by having each child write a brief story about a favorite memory. When the stories are complete, add a title and title page to each story. Ask the library media specialist to work with the class on the parts of a title page and a dedication.

5. After reading the rhymed text in Margaret Mahy's *17 Kings and 42 Elephants,* plan with the music teacher to have the children use various musical instruments to play the steady beat and/or the rhythm patterns as the poem is reread. If desired plan with the art teacher to have students do batik paintings on cloth or paper to simulate the artwork in the book.

6. Read aloud Margaret Mahy's *The Boy with Two Shadows* and encourage the children to discuss the problems the boy faced in the story. As a movement activity have the children play outside to cast their imaginative shadows on the ground. For art have the children work in pairs to create shadow silhouettes. Instruct one child in each pair to move freely until

hearing the teacher say, "1, 2, 3, freeze." At that point tell the students to remain in that "frozen" position while the partner uses colored chalk to trace the shadow on butcher paper. Repeat the activity as the students exchange roles. Display the imaginative shadows around the room.

As an alternative activity students can produce shadow shows. Tautly stretch a white sheet from floor to ceiling and use an overhead projector to cast a light from behind the sheet. Allow the students to create shadow plays of their favorite stories by moving between the sheet and the light source.

7. Before reading aloud *The Great White Man-Eating Shark: A Cautionary Tale* by Margaret Mahy, ask the children to explain what they think the phrase "a cautionary tale" means. After hearing the story, have the students describe the problems Norvin created. Have the students summarize in one sentence a lesson to be learned from this story. Select a list of fable morals or proverbs, (e.g., "Look before you leap" or "A bird in the hand is worth two in the bush") and then have each child choose one and explain its meaning. As a follow-up let the students create a better solution to the problem than the one Norvin chose in the story.

8. Explain to the students that, as the story *Making Friends* by Margaret Mahy is being read aloud, they are to listen for the problem and be able to suggest a solution. Read the story aloud, pausing after Mr. Derry finds a dog. Allow the children to discuss the problem that Mr. Derry and Mrs. deVere had and predict possible solutions. Complete the reading and compare the book solution to those the children proposed. In this story the author describes the main characters and their actions with words such as "lonely," "moodily," "shy," and "cheerfully." Have the students define what the words mean, then act out the word meaning through body language. These words can then be used in a spelling list.

Closure:

Celebrate literature "from Down Under" by decorating the library media center or the classroom with maps and artwork that the children have completed in this unit. Obtain parent volunteers to help prepare and serve Australian and New Zealand foods. Locate a copy of the tape *Citizens of the World* by Seona McDowell (Wallaby Records, 1990) which may be played in the center. Ask the children to think about the characters they have met in the "Down Under" stories in this unit. Let the students discuss the actions of and feelings displayed by the book characters. Encourage the group to apply the characters' emotions and actions in a role-play situation. As a class, briefly compare the cultural heritage found in these books with those in books by favorite American authors such as Cynthia Rylant and Elizabeth Winthrop.

Let the children free write for five to ten minutes everything they know about Australia and New Zealand. Compare these writings to those done on the first day of the unit to determine student growth.

Viewing Nature with Joanne Ryder

Objectives:

1. Recognize that the author's background influences the content of his or her work.
2. Demonstrate comprehension by acting out a story.
3. Write in second person.
4. Present information pictorially through illustrations and other media forms.
5. Identify figurative language, similes, and alliterations.
6. Write a story based on a formula or pattern.
7. Demonstrate the use of texture and/or symmetry in an art project.
8. Select musical instruments to represent sounds from nature.
9. Compose an original poem.

Recommended Readings:

Ryder, Joanne. *Hello, Tree!* Illustrated by Michael Hays. E.P. Dutton, 1991.
Basic characteristics of a tree are explored through the eyes of children. (Objectives 1 and 4)

————. *Lizard in the Sun.* Illustrated by Michael Rothman. William Morrow, 1990.
Figurative language allows the reader to imagine what life would be like as a green anole lizard. (Objectives 2 and 3)

————. *Mockingbird Morning.* Illustrated by Dennis Nolan. Macmillan, 1989.
A clear, crisp morning leads the reader to become a part of the world all around. (Objectives 1 and 5)

————. *Step Into the Night.* Illustrated by Dennis Nolan. Four Winds, 1988.
As a young girl listens and watches in the darkness of night, she imagines becoming the nocturnal creatures she observes. (Objective 2)

————. *Under the Moon.* Illustrated by Cheryl Harness. Random House, 1989.
Mama Mouse teaches her youngest child about life and survival through the use of the five senses. (Objective 6)

———. *Under Your Feet.* Illustrated by Dennis Nolan. Four Winds, 1990.
Figurative language encourages the reader to sense the life of the creatures beneath the earth's surface. (Objectives 4 and 7)

———. *When the Woods Hum.* Illustrated by Catherine Stock. William Morrow, 1991.
The reader experiences the life cycle of the cicada through the eyes of a young girl. (Objectives 1 and 8)

———. *Where Butterflies Grow.* Illustrated by Lynne Cherry. E.P. Dutton, 1989.
Figurative language highlights the mystery of metamorphosis in this story, followed by suggestions for attracting butterflies to a home garden. (Objectives 5 and 7)

———. *White Bear, Ice Bear.* Illustrated by Michael Rothman. William Morrow, 1989.
Descriptive language invites the reader to imagine a day in the life of a polar bear. (Objectives 3 and 6)

———. *Winter Whale.* Illustrated by Michael Rothman. William Morrow, 1991.
Imagery transforms the reader into a humpback whale for a day. (Objectives 4, 5, and 9)

Biographical Sources:

For information on Joanne Ryder see *Something about the Author*, vol. 65, pages 181–86 and *Sixth Book of Junior Authors & Illustrators*, pages 253–55.

Group Introductory Activity:

In personal appearances Joanne Ryder says that as a child she was fascinated by the small creatures her father would find in their garden. She always knew when she looked in her father's cupped hands that she would find something wonderful, perhaps a cicada that hummed loudly or a snail that would slide across her palm like "warm Jell-o." As an adult she became a poet and a book editor. Eventually she combined her three loves—nature, poetry, and books—into her work as an author. Ryder's strong reliance on second-person point of view makes her writing distinctive. Have children listen carefully as Joanne Ryder's *Mockingbird Morning* is read aloud so they can hear how she uses poetic phrases and figurative language to describe animals and the natural world. After completing the book, list phrases the students recall on the chalkboard.

As a follow-up begin construction of Ryder Park. Use art paper to decorate a wall or corner of the classroom or library media center as if it were a scenic park. If desired, build trees or add benches. Have the children draw animals from Ryder's books to place in the park. As each new book in the unit is shared, children may wish to add more characters to Ryder Park.

Follow-Up Activities for Teacher and Students to Share:

1. After the children have experienced Joanne Ryder's *Hello, Tree!* ask them to bring leaves from local trees to identify and display if the season is appropriate. Ask the children to speculate on how the author's background might have influenced the content of this story. Ryder suggests that a tree is a home to other animals. Have children share observations about the different birds and animals that live in the trees in their region. Follow up by allowing the students to build bird nests out of tree bark, grass, and other natural materials. These may be placed in Ryder Park or used to create a habitat diorama.

    As an extension invite a naturalist, bird-watcher, or wildlife expert to visit the class to share his or her knowledge and experiences with the children. The state wildlife department and local Audubon Society are good sources for locating speakers.

2. Share Joanne Ryder's *Lizard in the Sun* with the children. Extend the reading by asking them to imagine what animal they would like to be. Have the students wear the colors of that animal one day and describe what that animal can do. The other students may try to discover the animal each child has chosen from the color and behavior clues. Ask the children to write five sentences in second person, using "you" as the subject. Each sentence should tell different actions and feelings one might experience if he or she became the animal selected.

3. Share aloud *Step Into the Night* by Joanne Ryder. Invite children to become "shape changers" as the book is reread. Children may use their bodies to dramatize the text as they listen and become each nocturnal animal mentioned. If desired, play instrumental music as a background to the reading to help establish the contemplative mood of the night. A good selection is Richard Wagner's "Liebestod," from *Tristan und Isolde* on the recording *Classical Nature* (NorthWord, 1992, NSAC 22024), which blends authentic nature sounds with orchestral music.

4. After reading *Under the Moon,* have the children discuss the sensory experiences of the little mouse. Have the group complete the following sensory text:

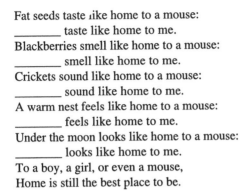

Fat seeds taste like home to a mouse:
_____ taste like home to me.
Blackberries smell like home to a mouse:
_____ smell like home to me.
Crickets sound like home to a mouse:
_____ sound like home to me.
A warm nest feels like home to a mouse:
_____ feels like home to me.
Under the moon looks like home to a mouse:
_____ looks like home to me.
To a boy, a girl, or even a mouse,
Home is still the best place to be.

Have the children illustrate individual lines on separate pages and compile the completed poem into a class book. Remind the children that all books need a title. Let the group decide on an appropriate title for their story. As a follow-up allow individual students to write stories and titles based on this formula.

5. After sharing *Under Your Feet* by Joanne Ryder, cover a bulletin board with earth-tone paper. Coat the paper with spray adhesive, sprinkle the entire paper with sand, and allow it to dry. Reread the book and let the children discuss the animal images found in the illustrations on the page that begins "From year to year / you live and grow / between earth and sky." Have children use blunt instruments (e.g. craft sticks or spoons) to scrape animal images into the sand. Display the finished product on an "Under our Feet" bulletin board.

6. Encourage the children to listen for and identify figurative language in Joanne Ryder's *Where Butterflies Grow*. After the book is read, the children may choose to experiment with patterns and symmetry in a learning center. Duplicate a symmetrical outline of a butterfly with wings extended onto construction paper. Place the butterfly outlines, tissue paper in various colors, scissors, and glue in the center. Assist the children in folding the paper in half and cutting shapes to be used to create a symmetrical pattern on the butterfly's wings. Students may explore patterns for the butterfly. When symmetry has been achieved, children may glue the pattern onto the outline. The finished butterflies may be cut out and hung from the ceiling or displayed on a bulletin board. This activity may be simplified by precutting the tissue shapes.

7. After sharing Joanne Ryder's *White Bear, Ice Bear* with the class, have the children create dioramas of the polar bear's world. Scraps of styrofoam make an excellent "ice and snow" base for the display. As a further extension share other books in the "Just for a Day" series: *Catching the Wind* (William Morrow, 1989), *Lizard in the Sun* (William Morrow, 1990), and *Sea Elf* (William Morrow, 1993). Help the children to analyze

the books, discovering the common pattern in them (e.g., second-person point of view, weather phenomenon that stimulates a change, habitat exploration, and closure with evening and a sensory experience). Use the pattern to develop a "Just for a Day" story based upon an animal of the students' choice.

8. After sharing *Winter Whale,* create a three-dimensional mural depicting creatures that share the humpback whale's environment. This can be built in a large appliance box. After the artwork is complete reread *Winter Whale*. Ask the children to listen specifically for figurative language (e.g., "long, long flippers / crashing and splashing" or "soar through the sea / graceful whale"). Encourage the children to raise their hands when they hear flowing phrases and repeat the descriptive passages they hear. Write a class collaborative poem about the winter whale.

Closure:

Read aloud Joanne Ryder's *When the Woods Hum.* Urge the children to speculate on how the author's background influenced this story. Coordinate with the music teacher to let the children choose available musical instruments to represent the natural sounds of the woods. As an alternative, children may develop sound sources from natural objects, for example, dry leaves rubbed together, sand shaken in a jar, or sticks beaten together. When the children are able to produce sound effects (like Foley artists do for motion pictures) have groups of children select favorite Joanne Ryder books. One member of a group may read a scene from the book while other group members make appropriate sound effects.

Chapter 4
Third Grade/Fourth Grade

Bridges to the Past: Biographies by David Adler

Objectives:

1. Re-create experiences in the lives of famous people.
2. Formulate questions.
3. Research events in history and the lives or quotes of famous people.
4. Determine ways to foster better relations between people of different races, cultures, religions, and countries.
5. Write from another person's point of view.
6. Identify characteristics of effective leadership.
7. Develop a time line of events.
8. Use a Venn diagram to compare lives and events in history.

Recommended Readings:

Adler, David A. *Jackie Robinson: He Was the First.* Illustrated by Robert Casilla. Holiday House, 1989.
  The courage of the first African-American player in major league baseball is clearly defined in this concise biography. (Objectives 1 and 4)

———. *Martin Luther King, Jr.: Free at Last.* Illustrated by Robert Casilla. Holiday House, 1986.
  Black-and-white illustrations extend the text in this biography and index of the prominent American civil rights leader. (Objective 4)

———. *A Picture Book of Abraham Lincoln.* Illustrated by John and Alexandra Wallner. Holiday House, 1989.
  Simple text chronicles major events in the life of the Great Emancipator. (Objectives 2, 5, and 6)

———. *A Picture Book of Eleanor Roosevelt.* Illustrated by Robert Casilla. Holiday House, 1991.

The values of dedication to a just cause and the betterment of humanity are exemplified in the life of Eleanor Roosevelt, "First Lady of the World." (Objectives 3 and 6)

————. *A Picture Book of George Washington.* Illustrated by John and Alexandra Wallner. Holiday House, 1989.
The life of the "Father of Our Country" is described in brief text and illustrations. (Objectives 2 and 7)

————. *A Picture Book of Helen Keller.* Illustrated by John and Alexandra Wallner. Holiday House, 1990.
This simple biography relates how blind, deaf, and mute Helen Keller overcame her disabilities through her own determination and the help of a dedicated teacher. (Objective 1)

————.*A Picture Book of Jesse Owens.* Illustrated by Robert Casilla. Holiday House, 1992.
Jesse Owens, one of the greatest track-and-field athletes of all time, is recognized for his accomplishments both on and off the athletic field. (Objectives 1 and 3)

————.*A Picture Book of Martin Luther King, Jr.* Illustrated by Robert Casilla. Holiday House, 1989.
Simple text and illustrations chronicle Martin Luther King, Jr.'s commitment to the struggle for civil rights. (Objectives 3 and 6)

————. *A Picture Book of Simón Bolívar.* Illustrated by Robert Casilla. Holiday House, 1992.
The life and times of the Latin American liberator are explained in simple terms and illustrations. (Objectives 7 and 8)

Biographical Sources:

For information on David A. Adler see *Something about the Author*, vol. 70, pages 1–4 and *Sixth Book of Junior Authors & Illustrators*, pages 6–7.

Group Introductory Activity:

Introduce this unit on biographies to the class by letting children discover the meaning of the word *biography* for themselves. Write the words *biology*, *biosphere, biodegradable,* and *biorhythm* on the chalkboard. Explain that these words literally mean "the study of life," "the circle of life," "breaking down through life," and "rhythm of life," respectively. Ask the students to look at the words and meanings to find parts that are similar. Let the children discuss the terms until they make the connection that "bio" means "life." List on the chalkboard the words *photography, telegraphy, geography,* and *bibliography.* Tell students that the literal meanings of these words are, respectively, "light picture," "distant picture," "earth picture," and "book picture." Follow the earlier process to help the children determine that "graphy" means "picture." Now write the word *biography* on the board. Have the children combine what they learned from the two previous word lists to form a definition of this term. Explain that a biography is indeed a picture of a life, a picture formed by the words in a book about the life of a real person.

Ask the group if anyone knows who George Washington is. Allow the children time to share the information they may know about the first president of the United States. Some child may share the stories about young George chopping down the cherry tree or the adult Washington throwing a silver dollar across the Potomac River. If so, point out that these two stories are legends, but as far as anyone knows, they did not happen. Show children the cover of David A. Adler's *A Picture Book of George Washington*. Explain that this book is a simple biography. Point out that biographies should contain only information that is true and can be verified. A story like chopping down the cherry tree will not be presented as truth in a biography because no one can prove the event happened. Tell the children to listen carefully as the book is read aloud to find at least two facts about George Washington they did not know before. Ask a small group of students to construct a time line from 1700 to the present. Explain that their responsibility will be to note on the time line the birth and death of each person discussed in this unit. Color coding each person's life would allow for the students to then note important historic events that occurred during the lives of those people.

As another small group follow-up activity, let the children create an original board game, "Biography Bits," by writing questions and answers about George Washington. Each question should be copied on one side of a card labeled with a large "Q" and the answer copied on the reverse side, labeled "A." Children must be able to verify their question and answer if challenged. As the unit progresses the students may add cards for each biography shared aloud or read individually.

Follow-Up Activities for Teacher and Students to Share:

1. Read *Jackie Robinson: He Was the First* by David A. Adler to the class. Compare the efforts of Jackie Robinson and those of other leaders such as Martin Luther King, Jr. to advance the cause of black civil rights. Branch Rickey, president of the Brooklyn Dodgers, said he did not want a man who was afraid to fight back, but one who had the courage *not* to fight (p. 30). Allow the group time to discuss why it sometimes takes courage not to fight. Let children discuss problem-solving skills that make it possible to avoid violence in conflicts. Allow the children to role play situations in which students must choose whether or not to fight.

2. Share David A. Adler's *A Picture Book of Abraham Lincoln* aloud. Let the children discuss why Abraham Lincoln is considered to be a great man. The discussion should include the characteristics he possessed that made him a great leader. In small groups formulate questions and answers about Lincoln to add to "Biography Bits." As a further follow-up have students imagine that Abraham Lincoln returned to the modern-day United States. Ask the children to speculate on what might please him the most and what might be the most upsetting to him. Tell the students to pretend to be Abraham Lincoln and write a short speech he might give to the people of the United States today.

3. Eleanor Roosevelt's motto was "Tomorrow is now." After sharing David A. Adler's *A Picture Book of Eleanor Roosevelt* with the group, have the students each write a paragraph that explains what that phrase means to them. Let the children discuss the leadership characteristics Eleanor Roosevelt exhibited. Instruct the students to read the newspaper, magazines, or watch the evening news on television to find out about women who are currently in leadership positions and report to the class. Ask them to analyze the strengths and leadership qualities of each woman.

4. After reading *A Picture Book of Helen Keller* by David A. Adler to the class, discuss how it must feel to be unable to communicate with anyone. To experience the problems encountered by Helen Keller, plan with the library media specialist to have the class visit the library media center to browse, research, or check out books without speaking. Lap chalkboards can be of great assistance in this activity because students will be allowed to communicate only through writing or sign language. If this experience can be extended to a physical education class and the lunchroom, it will become more significant and will give students an opportunity to compare experiences. Add to this experience during the week by dividing the class into teams in which one person at a time is blindfolded during a certain activity. The role of the partner is to protect the blindfolded teammate from accidents or injury. Culminate the experiences by sharing each child's perspective on the event. Ask them to imagine how much more intense or difficult Helen Keller's life must have been because of her multiple disabilities. As a further follow-up some readers may wish to read Paul Fleischman's fantasy novel *The Half-a-Moon Inn* (Harper & Row, 1980) in which the protagonist is a mute. Ask the media specialist to help readers create a skit or reader's theater script based on Fleischman's novel to share with the rest of the class.

5. Read aloud *A Picture Book of Jesse Owens* by David A. Adler. Ask the physical education teacher to assist in planning a class track-and-field day to include the events at which Jesse Owens excelled. Mark distances of 100 and 200 yards on the playground or track. Explain to the class that Jesse Owens ran the 100 in 10.3 seconds. Challenge the group to see how much of that distance they can cover in the same period of time. Use a stopwatch to

determine the time accurately. Tell the students to start and stop at a given signal. Compare the students' distances to the marked 100 yards. Repeat with the 200 if desired. Following the long jump competition, use a tape measure to show the children Jesse Owens' mark of 26' 5 5/16".

6. Prior to sharing David A. Adler's *A Picture Book of Martin Luther King, Jr.,* meet with the library media specialist to obtain a recording of one of King's speeches, preferably the "I Have a Dream" speech. Ask the children how many of them recognize the name Martin Luther King, Jr. Give the students time to share information they know about the civil rights leader. Explain to the students that King was one of America's most powerful speakers. As the biography is read aloud, ask students to listen for the characteristics and skills King possessed that made him a powerful speaker and leader. If using a recording of his "I Have a Dream" speech, stop reading on the page of the text that refers to it and play the excerpt so the group can hear King's powerful voice. As a follow-up send a few students to the library media center to find some of Martin Luther King, Jr.'s most memorable quotes. Let the group share these quotes with the class by writing them on 9-inch-by-18-inch sheets of construction paper and posting them around the room. If a computer printing program is available (such as *Super Print* by Scholastic) let students make signs or posters on the computer, adding appropriate graphics. Ask the group to speculate about the responses different groups or individuals (e.g., an African American, a Ku Klux Klan member, or a politician) may have had to King's speeches.

7. After reading *A Picture Book of Simón Bolívar* by David A. Adler, construct a time line on a classroom wall marking Simón Bolívar's struggle for freedom in South America. Use library resources to develop a comparative chronology of that same struggle in the United States. Include dates ranging from declared independence through the abolition of slavery for both countries, noting each major event and date. Use contrasting colors for the two countries on the time line. Let children compare the time spans between independence and the abolition of slavery in each country. Demonstrate how to construct and use a Venn diagram as a visual device for comparisons. (See Regie Routman's *Invitations* [Heinemann, 1991, p. 95] for details on Venn diagrams.) Ask the students to speculate about why the South Americans managed to end slavery much sooner than the United States even though their War of Independence was much longer.

Follow-Up Activities for Individual Students:

1. After having shared David A. Adler's *A Picture Book of Eleanor Roosevelt* in class, ask the library media specialist to help you locate a biography about another individual. Read the biography and report to the class on what contribution that person has made.

2. After reading *A Picture Book of Jesse Owens* by David A. Adler, visit the library media center to research current Olympic records. See if any of Jesse Owens's records still stand. If not, record the new distance or time and determine the difference between the current record and the record Owens set in 1936.

3. Simón Bolívar has been called the "George Washington of South America." After hearing *A Picture Book of Simón Bolívar* by David A. Adler, decide whether or not you believe he deserves that name. Give details from Bolívar's life and comparisons to America's first president to support your answer. Develop a Venn diagram to show the facts.

4. After sharing *Jackie Robinson: He Was the First* by David A. Adler, read Peter Golonbock's *Teammates* (Harcourt, Brace, Jovanovich, 1990). Although the information in this book is also true, it is considered an information book about baseball rather than a biography. After reading *Teammates*, answer the following questions: How do the two stories compare? Which style of writing do you prefer and why? What did you learn about ways to foster better relations between people of different races? Visit the library media center and use the card catalog to create a bibliography of at least five other baseball books or biographies of athletes.

5. After hearing David A. Adler's *A Picture Book of Martin Luther King, Jr.* in class, read Adler's *Martin Luther King, Jr.: Free at Last.* Choose facts from the book to be made into questions for "Biography Bits." Create a display with the caption "I Have a Dream" and post it along with ideas of ways people can foster better relations between different groups, especially races, religions, and countries. Share your ideas with the class and encourage others in the group to add suggestions of their own.

Closure:

To complete the biography study have a "Biography Day" in which students may dress in costume as a biographical figure. Each student may give two or three verbal clues to his or her identity and see if the rest of the class can guess who is being impersonated. Arrange for the library media specialist to videotape each student in an interview format for a "Lifelines of the Rich and Famous" show which may be shown at a school event. Divide the class into teams and play "Biography Bits."

Caldecott Connections

Objectives:

1. Identify books and illustrators who have received the Caldecott Award.
2. Understand the significance of the Caldecott Award.
3. Interpret a story from the illustrations.
4. Recognize various art formats used to illustrate literature.
5. Recognize connections between stories and illustrations, styles, and methods.
6. Create original artwork similar in style and method to Caldecott-winning illustrations.
7. Retell a story through art, puppetry, or creative dramatics.

Recommended Readings:

Aardema, Verna. *Why Mosquitoes Buzz in People's Ears: A West African Tale.* Illustrated by Leo and Diane Dillon. Dial, 1975.
This cumulative tale recounts how Mosquito wreaks havoc in the jungle and suffers the consequences. (Objectives 1, 6, and 7)

Ackerman, Karen. *Song and Dance Man.* Illustrated by Stephen Gammell. Alfred A. Knopf, 1988.
Vaudeville lives on in the memory of a former song-and-dance man who shares his old routine with an appreciative audience of grandchildren. (Objectives 1, 4, 5, and 6)

Goble, Paul. *The Girl Who Loved Wild Horses.* Bradbury, 1978.
A young Native American girl's love for and understanding of horses grows into a legend among her people. (Objectives 1, 4, 5, and 6)

Hodges, Margaret. *Saint George and the Dragon.* Illustrated by Trina Schart Hyman. Little, Brown, 1984.
Striking bordered illustrations highlight this retelling of how George, the Red Cross Knight, slays the evil dragon and restores harmony to the land. (Objectives 1, 4, 5, and 6)

Macaulay, David. *Black and White.* Houghton Mifflin, 1990.
Double-page illustrations are divided into four quadrants, each telling a separate story, or perhaps four viewpoints, of a larger overall tale. (Objectives 1, 2, and 5)

McCully, Emily Arnold. *Mirette on the High Wire.* G.P. Putnam's Sons, 1992.
A determined young girl learns the art of tightrope walking. (Objectives 1, 4, and 6)

Wiesner, David. *Tuesday*. Clarion, 1991.
The night sky changes as frogs from a lily pad take flight and explore their surroundings in an almost wordless book. (Objectives 1, 3, and 6)

Yolen, Jane. *Owl Moon*. Illustrated by John Schoenherr. Philomel, 1987.
A young girl and her father trek deep into the woods on a cold, quiet winter night to see and hear the great horned owl. (Objectives 1 and 6)

Young, Ed. *Lon Po Po: A Red Riding Hood Story from China*. Philomel, 1989.
A hungry wolf disguises himself as a grandmother in the hope of obtaining an easy meal. (Objectives 1, 5, and 7)

Group Introductory Activity:

Introduce the children to the Caldecott Award by explaining that the award is given each year by the American Library Association. It is the most prestigious award for illustrators in this country. Point out that the award is named for Randolph Caldecott, an early illustrator of children's books, and that the medal features a reproduction of some of his most famous artwork. Ask the library media specialist to show children a replica of the Caldecott Medal, explain the scenes depicted on it, and book talk some Caldecott winners for the class.

Explain that when artists illustrate picture books, they must be careful to connect their pictures to the story. Each illustration must agree with and extend the text that accompanies it. During this unit children will see a variety of art styles and methods used in illustrations that have received the Caldecott medal. Urge the children to compare the illustrations in the various books and speculate on why certain styles were chosen for particular stories.

Show the class David Macaulay's *Black and White*. Tell the students that Macaulay received the Caldecott Award in 1991 for his imaginative illustrations in this book. Explain that the Caldecott Medal is presented each year to the artist who is judged to have created the most outstanding picture book for children published in the United States during the previous year. Display the title page and read the "warning" notice Macaulay placed there. Turn the page to show the four titles of the subplots Macaulay uses and ask the children if the illustrations are alike or different in style. Let the children speculate about whether or not the use of such diverse styles as cartoons and realism helped to win the award.

In his Caldecott acceptance speech David Macaulay said *Black and White* "is designed to be viewed in its entirety, having its surface read all over. It is a book of and about connections—between pictures and between words and pictures" (*Horn Book*, vol. 67, no. 4, July/August 1991, p. 411). Ask the children if they can find any ways in which the illustrations are similar or any common elements among the illustrations in the different subplots. Children may note the train and train station, the boy's and the convict's striped shirts, and the mask on the dog and the convict.

Tell the children that this book is far too complex to make a good read-aloud story but that it will be available in the reading center for them to examine during their free time. Urge the students to complete the individual activity for *Black and White*. In a center set out half sheets of paper labeled "Black and White Connections." Instruct the students to write down the connections they find in David Macaulay's book (e.g., the train station that appears in one subplot as the setting and as a toy in another), being sure to include their name and the date. Slip each finished connection sheet into a shoe box covered with newspaper. At the conclusion of the unit a prize may be awarded to the student who finds the most connections between the four subplots. Possible prizes could be a paperback copy of a favorite Caldecott book or a package of "black-and-white" sandwich cookies.

Follow-Up Activities for Teacher and Students to Share:

1. Read aloud or share the filmstrip of the 1976 Caldecott Award winner *Why Mosquitoes Buzz in People's Ears* (Weston Woods, 199) by Verna Aardema. Explain that the Dillons used cut paper to create the artwork for this book. Select an African animal, such as a lizard or python, to illustrate in a style similar to the Dillons'. Let children draw the character on colored construction paper, then draw, paint, or stamp a repeated pattern on the paper to create an effect similar to African batik. Point out to the children how the Dillons used white outlines to highlight each character. Simulate this effect by having the children cut the drawing apart along major detail lines (e.g., separating the head and legs from the body and the ears from the head). Let the students glue the figure parts onto white paper, expanding the parts to leave white outlines.

   In their Caldecott Award acceptance speech Leo and Diane Dillon said they felt as illustrators they were free to go beyond the text or to pick out elements of it upon which to build. An example of this freedom is the little red bird in the book. The bird never appears in the text at all. The Dillons put her in one illustration and began to think of her as the observer or reader and so added her to the other illustrations as well. She watches as the events take place and flies away when the story ends. The Dillons say, "For us she is like the storyteller, gathering information, then passing it on to the next generation" (*Newbery and Caldecott Medal Books, 1976–1985,* Horn Book, 1986, p. 172).

2. Prior to sharing Karen Ackerman's *Song and Dance Man,* tell the children that Stephen Gammell's illustrations for this book won the Caldecott Award in 1989. Gammell has said that this book deserves a long life for all grandpas everywhere and kids who have them (*Horn Book,* vol. 65, July/August 1989, p. 459). When Ackerman saw the sketches of Grandpa she said that he even

looked a bit like her own father, for whom the book was written (*Horn Book*,vol. 65, no. 4, July/August 1989, p. 459). Allow time for the children to share a memory about a grandparent.

Have the children study the illustrations carefully as they listen to the story. Read the book aloud, then ask the children what quality in the illustrations they noticed or enjoyed most. Some children will point out the artist's bold use of color. Point out to the children how the slashing lines of color simulate the stage lights of a theater. If the school has an auditorium with stage lights, take the students there so they may see the effect of the footlights and spotlights. Some students who take dance lessons may wish to perform for the class while there.

As a further extension show a clip from the video of *Yankee Doodle Dandy* (Warner Brothers, 1942) in which James Cagney performs a song-and-dance routine to George M. Cohan's title song. Explain that this is the song Grandpa sang in his routine. Ask the music teacher or a senior citizens group to teach the class to sing the song and perhaps do a simple soft-shoe dance.

3. Explain that Paul Goble received the Caldecott Award in 1979 for his book *The Girl Who Loved Wild Horses*. Goble has often been asked how he, an Englishman, came to write Native American tales. He has answered that when he was a child his mother read him the books of Gray Owl and Earnest Thompson Seton, both of whom wrote about Indians. The world they wrote about was so different from his crowded island home that he was fascinated by everything Indian. He has great respect for the Native American rapport with nature. In his Caldecott acceptance speech he said that Native Americans' knowledge of their "relationship with the universe gives them confidence. They have no thought to reorganize nature in a way other than that in which the Great Spirit made it" (*Newbery and Caldecott Medal Books, 1976–1985,* Horn Book, 1986, p. 206).

Read aloud *The Girl Who Loved Wild Horses* by Paul Goble. Let the children speculate on whether or not the girl did become a horse. Tell them Goble says, "perhaps she becomes one. If we think about something long enough, maybe we will become like that thing" (*Newbery and Caldecott Medal Books, 1976–1985,* Horn Book, 1986, p. 206). Have students study the illustrations in the book to discover elements of the artist's style (e.g., the use of warm colors, flat figures that have little sense of depth or texture, and repetition). Let the group use stencils of various horse shapes, without manes or tails, to create a scene similar to the one in the book. The children may outline each stencil in pencil and then use watercolors to color the shapes. Simple details, manes, and tails may be added with black marker or pen and ink. Let the students compare and contrast Goble's stylized illustrations with the equally stylized, but very different, illustrations done by the Dillons for *Why Mosquitoes Buzz in People's Ears.*

4. Before sharing *Saint George and the Dragon* by Margaret Hodges, tell the class that Trina Schart Hyman won the Caldecott Medal in 1985 for her work on this book. In her acceptance speech she said, "Books and illustrations are a part of me: They're not just what I do; they're what I *am*" (*Newbery and Caldecott Medal Books, 1976–1985,* Horn Book, 1986, p. 267). Tell the children to study the illustrations carefully as the book is read. After reading, ask the students if they noticed anything special or unusual about the illustrations. Someone will probably mention the borders on each page that often resemble a stained-glass window. If not, point these out to the children and tell them that Trina Schart Hyman often works in this style.

Hyman has said that she learned a great deal while working on *Saint George and the Dragon.* "I learned about herb-lore and ancient roses and wild flowers when I decided to decorate my borders with whatever grew in the fields and hedgerows of fourth-century England . . ." and that "the Romans named England 'Alba,' for the many wild white roses that grew there" (*Newbery and Caldecott Medal Books, 1976–1985,* Horn Book, 1986, p. 273). All of these images can be found in Hyman's illustrations and borders, thus connecting her artwork to the reality of the past.

Let the children examine some of the borders in Hyman's other books such as *Little Red Riding Hood* (Holiday House, 1983). Children should note that the borders contain elements from the text or scene. As a follow-up ask each child to visit the library media center and choose a favorite picture book. Have the students examine the illustrations carefully. Give each child a sheet of paper and instruct him or her to design a border that would be appropriate to use with a scene from the book selected. Remind the students that the borders do not need to be elaborate but should contain references to the story.

5. Before sharing Emily Arnold McCully's *Mirette on the High Wire,* work with the art teacher to select and share with the class several impressionistic paintings such as Monet's *Water Lilies* or Van Gogh's *The Starry Night,* available from Shorewood Fine Art Reproductions. Let the children examine the prints closely to see how the images are made of small dabs of color that do not look like an object when viewed closely but, at a distance, give the desired impression. Explain that this technique was used by McCully in *Mirette on the High Wire,* which received the 1993 Caldecott Award. Tell the class that this book was first begun as a biography of the real-life daredevil Blondin. On the book jacket McCully says she changed the concept to connect the story to her own life experiences as a tree-climbing child and risk-taking adult.

Read the book aloud. Let the children discuss the personal strengths of Mirette and Bellini. Allow the students to speculate on the causes for Bellini's fear of the wire. Discuss and compare the various talents and skills it would take to be an acrobat, juggler, mime, artist, musician, or singer. List the children's responses on the chalkboard. Have the group examine the list to determine what qualities these talented performers have in common.

As a follow-up work with the physical education teacher to develop a basic gymnastics unit featuring the balance beam. Explain to students that walking on the narrow beam is similar to Mirette's high wire. Children may wish to simply walk the beam or practice simple gymnastic feats that may be performed upon it.

6.   David Wiesner has said that a commission to draw a cover for the March 1979 issue of *Cricket* magazine was the inspiration for his 1992 Caldecott Award-winning book *Tuesday*. The issue featured stories about St. Patrick's Day and frogs

> the link there being green, I think. St. Patrick's Day didn't strike a chord—but frogs, they had potential. . . . Frogs were great fun to draw—soft, round, lumpy, and really goofy-looking. But what could I do with them? I drew one on a lily pad. That shape . . . the round blob with the saucerlike bottom. . . . Together the frog and lily pad looked like a fifties B-movie flying saucer! (*Horn Book*, vol. LXVIII, no. 4, July/August 1992, p. 419)

Several years later Wiesner returned to that idea, carefully plotting the story, connecting illustrations, and developing details in order to "move the story forward as logically as possible, from the full moon that rises slowly in the sky that first Tuesday night to the gibbous moon that appears a week later at the end" (*Horn Book*, vol. 68, no. 4, July/August 1992, p. 421). Share David Wiesner's *Tuesday,* beginning with the first illustration. Allow students time to study the details and the humor in each scene. Explain that everyone will have an opportunity to read the pictures again and verbalize the action. Tell the children that David Wiesner believes readers do not connect with wordless stories in the same way they do to stories with text. He says, "There is no author's voice telling the story. Each viewer reads the book in his or her own way. The reader is an integral part of the storytelling process. As a result, there are as many versions of what happened that Tuesday night as there are readers" (*Horn Book*, vol. 68, no. 4, July/August 1992, p. 421). As a further follow-up let the students write individual stories about the pigs' adventures that might happen after the final scene in the book. Because Wiesner used watercolors in the 1992 Caldecott-winning illustrations, have the children use watercolors to create a series of paintings that tell the stories they have written.

7.   Ed Young has said, "I have been given to find ways to play out storytelling in picture books" (*Horn Book*, vol. 66, no. 4, July/August, 1990, p. 429). Ask the children to study the illustrations as Young's 1990 Caldecott Award-winning book is read aloud to see how they extend or add to the story. Do not share the subtitle, *A Red Riding Hood Story from China,* with the group.

After reading, let the children identify similarities between it and other folktales they know. The class will recognize this variant of the "Red Riding Hood" tale. Ask the children to speculate about the country from which this version of the story came. Then read the subtitle aloud.

Discuss with the class the style Ed Young used in his art. No doubt the children will note the dividing panels in each illustration. Point out that Oriental art is often done on long vertical panels like these, frequently in groups of three called a triptych. As a follow-up ask the music teacher to introduce the children to a musical wolf story with some similarities to *Lon Po Po*, Sergei Prokofiev's *Peter and the Wolf* (illustrated by Jorg Muller; Alfred A. Knopf, 1986. With accompanying cassette, ISBN 0-394-88418-3). After the children have shared the story, ask them to compare and contrast the two wolf tales. Let the children act out *Peter and the Wolf* as the music is played.

Follow-Up Activities for Individual Students:

1. Reread the West African folktale *Why Mosquitoes Buzz in People's Ears* by Verna Aardema. Because this is a cumulative tale, it is easy to tell. Like the little red bird in the illustrations, be a storyteller. Learn to tell the story without using the book and present it to the class.

2. After sharing *Song and Dance Man* in class, create an illustration similar to those in the book. Draw a central figure and use colored pencils to add color, highlights, and shadows as a "frame."

3. Read the Caldecott-winning book *Black and White* by David Macaulay. Examine the illustrations carefully to find ways in which the stories within the book overlap or interact. Try to discover at least two ways in which each story or a character from the story blends with each of the other three. List your findings on a sheet of paper. Put your name on the paper, fold it in half, staple it closed, and place it in the box in the reading center. At the close of the unit the papers will be opened and a prize will be awarded to the student finding the most connections.

4. After sharing Emily Arnold McCully's *Mirette on the High Wire* in class, use watercolors to illustrate a scene from the viewpoint of a tightrope walker. In the painting use short brush strokes or dots of color as impressionist painters do to give the impression or idea of the desired shape instead of painting the entire shape.

5. After sharing *Tuesday* by David Wiesner in class, write a newspaper article based on the illustration where the police and reporters appear. Use imaginative headlines. Ask the library media specialist to help you conduct a live television (video) interview with someone pretending to be the man who saw the flying frogs.

6. In the Caldecott Award book *Owl Moon,* illustrator John Schoenherr brings the words of Jane Yolen to life. Patricia Lee Gauch has written, *"Owl Moon . . .* slows the world down, allowing us to be a part of an experience of the most quiet sort . . . if we, like John Schoenherr, can only 'see what we see'" (*Horn Book,* vol. 64, no. 4, July/August 1988, p. 463). Read *Owl Moon.* Imagine the cold, still beauty of the night. Lines like the following help one imagine what nature can offer: "trees stood still as giant statues"; "a line of pine trees, black and pointy against the sky"; "the owl pumped its great wings." Select a scene such as those described above to paint with watercolors. Leave a white space on the picture to write in the descriptive words. For more information on the great horned owl read *Tiger with Wings* by Barbara Esbensen (Orchard, 1991).
7. After sharing Ed Young's *Lon Po Po* in class, use watercolors on three tall paper panels to create scenes illustrating the beginning, middle, and end of the story. Write a one-sentence summary of each story part on the back of each painting. Tape the panels together sequentially to form a triptych.

Closure:

Let the children discuss the connections between the artwork and the text of the books they experienced in this unit. Have them recall the various art styles represented and speculate upon why specific styles were selected for certain stories. Conclude by displaying a chart labeled "Connections—They're All There in *Black and White,*" David Macaulay's *Black and White,* and a newspaper. Ask the students what connection exists between the book and the newspaper. Children will recall that the newspaper was read, shredded, folded, and worn by characters in the four subplots of the book. Teach the children to fold paper hats like those in Macaulay's book. Hats may be folded by following the first three steps on pages 17–18 of H.A. Rey's *Curious George Rides a Bike* (Houghton Mifflin, 1952). Open the "Black and White Connections" sheets from the reading center shoebox one at a time and list the children's answers on the chart. As each succeeding sheet is read, place a check mark beside repeated answers. After all the sheets have been shared, total the check marks to see which connections were noticed most often. Count the connections on individual students' papers. Award a prize and two paper feathers, one black and one white, for the cap of the child who discovered the most similarities between the subplots.

Story Mapping with Johanna Hurwitz

Objectives:

1. Verbalize emotions and attributes of a book character.
2. Demonstrate how to count and exchange money.
3. Identify the importance and value of names.
4. Establish criteria for evaluating a book.
5. Sequence events through picture mapping and/or comic strips.
6. Examine qualities of effective leadership.
7. Respond to a book through art, cooking, storytelling, movement, and/or demonstrations.
8. Summarize a story.

Recommended Readings:

Hurwitz, Johanna. *The Adventures of Ali Baba Bernstein*. Illustrated by Gail Owens. William Morrow, 1985.
There are three other Davids in David Bernstein's third-grade class so he adopts a new name, Ali Baba, a name as unique as David himself. (Objectives 1 and 3)

————.*Aldo Applesauce*. Illustrated by John Wallner. William Morrow, 1979.
Moving to a new school in the middle of the year is trying for young Aldo Sossi who quickly receives the embarrassing nickname "Applesauce." (Objectives 1 and 4)

————. *Aldo Ice Cream*. Illustrated by John Wallner. William Morrow, 1981.
Aldo tries to earn money to buy his sister an ice-cream freezer. (Objectives 2 and 5)

————. *Baseball Fever*. Illustrated by Ray Cruz. William Morrow, 1981.
Even though Ezra loves baseball and his dad does not, Ezra learns it is more important to try to understand each other. (Objectives 1 and 8)

————.*Busybody Nora*. Illustrated by Susan Jeschke. William Morrow, 1976.
Inquisitive young Nora has many adventures living in a New York City apartment house. (Objective 8)

————.*Class Clown*. Illustrated by Sheila Hamanaka. William Morrow, 1987.
Lucas Cott tries to be the perfect third grader, but things always seem to take an unexpected twist. (Objective 5)

————. *Class President*. Illustrated by Sheila Hamanaka. William Morrow, 1990.
Julio offers to help his best friend run for class president, even though Julio is the one with leadership qualities. (Objective 6)

————. *Hurray for Ali Baba Bernstein.* Illustrated by Gail Owens. William Morrow, 1984.
Nine-year-old David Bernstein, who calls himself Ali Baba, finds surprises all around him. (Objectives 4 and 5)

————.*Nora and Mrs. Mind-Your-Own-Business.* Illustrated by Lillian Hoban. William Morrow, 1977.
Finding privacy in a crowded apartment and busy complex is sometimes difficult for Nora. (Objectives 5 and 8)

————. *Russell Rides Again.* Illustrated by Lillian Hoban. William Morrow, 1985.
Russell's expectations for his sixth birthday lead to a big disappointment and hurt feelings. (Objectives 1, 8, and 9)

Biographical Sources:

For information on Johanna Hurwitz see *Something about the Author*, vol. 71, pages 97–101 and *Sixth Book of Junior Authors & Illustrators*, pages 144–46.

Group Introductory Activity:

Introduce Johanna Hurwitz to the class by telling the children Hurwitz has said that one of her earliest memories is of taking a book from a low shelf and knowing that reading was a wonderful thing that she wanted to be able to do by herself. When Johanna was 12 she received a check for 50 cents for her first published work, a poem: "For me to read a book is still / And always will be quite a thrill . . . / And what is more, I'll read until I'm grown / And then I'll write books of my own" (*Sixth Book of Junior Authors & Illustrators*, p. 146). Sure enough, Johanna Hurwitz grew up to become a writer.

Hurwitz says that all her fiction seems to grow out of real experiences (*Something about the Author*, vol. 71, p. 99). The adventures of Aldo Sossi and his family are based on her life in Great Neck, New York. Read aloud *Aldo Applesauce*, Hurwitz's first book about the Sossi family. Help students learn to establish their own criteria for evaluating a book. For instance, if they think*Aldo Applesauce* is a funny book, have them list reasons and passages from the book, or if they feel like they can relate to Aldo's life have them state their feelings and justify their response. A form for stating their opinions might look like this: In _____ I especially liked or understood the part where _____. It had meaning for me because _____.

Tell the children that they will create and decorate "Hurwitz Hall" as a tribute to Johanna Hurwitz and all of her realistic characters. As the different books in this unit are experienced by students, urge the children to draw a mural on butcher paper depicting favorite scenes and characters.

Further encourage the students to read more books by Johanna Hurwitz by having a "Read a Sundae" campaign. Draw the shape of an ice cream cone, sundae dish, or banana split tray on construction paper. Draw three to five scoops of ice cream, a layer of whipped cream, and a cherry on another piece of paper. Duplicate a copy of each paper for every student. Have the children keep track by coloring, cutting out, and adding a scoop of ice cream or a topping to their page for each book by Hurwitz they read and report on. The criteria format is one way to keep a record of what they have read. Set a goal for the number of books to read and respond to by a certain deadline. All students who have reached the goal will receive real ice cream sundaes at the close of the unit while students who did not complete the goal will not receive a sundae.

Follow-Up Activities for Teacher and Students to Share:

1. Read the opening chapter of *The Adventures of Ali Baba Bernstein* by Johanna Hurwitz to the class. After completing the episode let the children discuss the importance of names. Ask the students to think about what name they would choose if they were to give themselves new names. Let each child write his or her chosen name on an index card. Place the cards on a bulletin board. Let the children try to guess which classmate chose which name. If desired, the children may affix their new names onto the front of their desks.

2. After reading aloud *Aldo Ice Cream* by Johanna Hurwitz, allow the children to discuss ways they might earn money and how the money could be used. Connect this with a math lesson where the students demonstrate how to count and exchange money. Because Hurwitz's books so closely relate to the lives of children, help the students develop comprehension skills by showing them how to do picture mapping. Write the title of the book on the chalkboard and draw a circle under it. Invite a child to draw, at the the twelve o'clock position on the clock, an image of the first important event in *Aldo Ice Cream*. Then, moving clockwise around the circle, draw the order of the other major events in the story. Once the children have the idea, erase the circle. Have the children create picture maps, reminding them to plan ahead with their drawings so that they complete a balanced circle of no more than 10–12 pictures. The children need to be able to defend or explain their pictures. This format reinforces their sense of sequential order and will provide a record of student reading. The picture mapping activity can be used with other books throughout the unit, if desired.

3. Read aloud Johanna Hurwitz's *Baseball Fever* or let a small group of students read it for a book discussion. (A paperback edition is available for purchase if multiple copies are desired for a discussion group.) Have the

students identify reasons why it is important to learn to compromise. As a follow-up, invite a baseball card collector (student or adult) to set up a baseball card display in the library. Decorate the library media center or classroom as a sports museum for a day. If a baseball card display is not possible, compromise with other collection options (e.g., stamps, butterflies, etc.). As a further extension, establish a chess club. Ask the children how Mrs. Feldman's belief, "The important thing is that you try to understand and respect each other" (p. 127), had meaning for Ezra and his dad. Urge the children to extend that idea and apply it to themselves and to others.

4. After reading Johanna Hurwitz's *Class Clown,* let students look up the word *rambunctious* in a dictionary to discover its true meaning. Because the main character, Lucas Cott, is so funny, children will enjoy sequencing his episodes in a comic strip format. Show the students how to fold paper into six sections. After hearing Lucas's story, have the students draw the most important episodes in the comic strip. Using the bubble for conversation will provide a means of showing students the importance of quotation marks. As a follow-up, plan and present a class circus. Work with the physical education teacher to develop tumbling routines for acrobats and others. The music teacher may wish to help with music for various acts. Hold a picture contest to promote the class circus. Let students draw and color original pictures showing favorite circus acts. Display the pictures in the hallway as promotional materials designed to publicize the event.

5. After reading *Class President* by Johanna Hurwitz, allow the children to discuss the qualities that make a good leader. List the main characteristics on the chalkboard. Give the students a few days to think about class members who display those qualities. Hold a mock class election, using the nomination and election procedure described in Hurwitz's novel.

6. If multiple copies are available, use Johanna Hurwitz's *Russell Rides Again* for a book discussion. Tell the class the author says Russell and his friends came from her experiences while living in a Manhattan apartment house (*Sixth Book of Junior Authors & Illustrators,* p. 145). After completing the book or hearing it read aloud, let the children discuss Russell's expectations for his birthday and his reactions when reality did not meet his expectations. Encourage the students to describe problems they had learning to ride a bicycle or learning some other feat that takes practice. Ask the children to identify the rewards it yielded. As a follow-up let children use the recipe in MaryAnn Kohl's *Mudworks* (Bright Ring Publishing, 1989, p. 135) to make soap balls or create original bubble bath or soap art.

Follow-Up Activities for Individual Students:

1. Read Johanna Hurwitz's *Busybody Nora*. Select one of the following events from the story to share with the class: make "stone soup" based on the book of that title by Marcia Brown (Charles Scribner's Sons, 1947), read and tell a version of *Jack and the Beanstalk*, construct a birthday tower, or draw an original picture. Explain to the class how the event ties in with the book.

2. After hearing *The Adventures of Ali Baba Bernstein* by Johanna Hurwitz, read the sequel, *Hurray for Ali Baba Bernstein*. Ali Baba helped Mr. Salmon with his diet and exercise program. Complete one of the following activities to present in class: draw a picture map of the main episodes, evaluate the book based on your own criteria, show the sequence of events and dialogue in a four- to six-frame comic strip, or write a newspaper article telling about Ali Baba's experiences.

3. After reading Johanna Hurwitz's *Hurray for Ali Baba Bernstein* follow-up by consulting the physical education teacher or the school nurse about proper diet and daily exercise for elementary students. Share the information with the class, demonstrating the exercises.

4. After reading Johanna Hurwitz's *Nora and Mrs. Mind-Your-Own-Business*, plan with the teacher or the library media specialist to construct a private reading area. Explain how this idea relates to Nora. Give this private reading area an imaginative title or name.

5. Draw a picture map or comic strip of Nora's problems after reading *Nora and Mrs. Mind-Your-Own-Business*.

6. In *Russell Rides Again* by Johanna Hurwitz, Russell spoke "Spinanch"—because he was exposed to Hebrew, Spanish, and French. Write a brief explanation of the role foreign language plays in Russell's life and a summary of the story. Then conduct a survey to discover what languages are spoken by families in your school. Present your report to the class. Visit the media center to check out a book on secret languages such as Alvin Schwartz's *Cat's Elbow* (Farrar, Straus & Giroux, 1982). Select one language and practice it with friends.

Closure:

When the children have completed the "Hurwitz Hall" mural, have each student select a scene on the mural to tell about. Share the "Hurwitz Hall" stories with other classes. Ask a homeroom mother to help set up the "Read a Sundae" celebration in the school cafeteria while the children are sharing their stories. After the students have completed their sharing close the unit by building and eating the sundaes the children earned during the unit. Local grocers or dairies may be willing to donate ingredients so students may prepare the sundaes they have earned.

A Variety of Verses

Objectives:

1. Compose original poetry.
2. Design an original bookmark.
3. Compare cultural heritages through poetry and rhymes.
4. Respond to poetry through discussion, dramatization, music, and art.
5. Recite from memory.
6. Demonstrate speaking skills.
7. Understand how poetry books are classified in the Dewey Decimal system.
8. Communicate through a variety of written forms.

Recommended Readings:

Chandra, Deborah. *Balloons and Other Poems*. Illustrated by Leslie Bowman. Farrar, Straus, & Giroux, 1990.
Original poems present a unique perspective on the world. (Objectives 1 and 4)

Dakos, Kalli. *If You're Not Here, Please Raise Your Hand: Poems about School*. Illustrated by G. Brian Karas. Four Winds, 1990.
Thirty-eight poems illuminate the variety of experiences, moods, and emotions in an elementary classroom, from exuberance to grief. (Objectives 4 and 6)

Feelings, Tom, and Greenfield, Eloise. *Daydreamers*. Dial, 1981.
The illustrations of children's faces reflect their thoughts and dreams in this insightful poetry collection. (Objectives 1, 3, and 4)

Hopkins, Lee Bennett, ed. *Good Books, Good Times!* Illustrated by Harry Stevenson. HarperCollins, 1990.
Poems celebrate the imaginative times and places that can be experienced through reading. (Objectives 2 and 4)

————. *Munching Poems about Eating*. Illustrated by Nelle Davis. Little, Brown, 1985.
A collection of poems that describes the delights of eating. (Objectives 4, 7, and 8)

Prelutsky, Jack. *Poems of A. Nonny Mouse*. Illustrated by Henrik Drescher. Alfred A. Knopf, 1989.
The action-packed illustrations are as humorous as the lighthearted poetry found in this collection. (Objectives 4, 6, and 8)

Yolen, Jane. *All Those Secrets of the World*. Illustrated by Leslie Baker. Little, Brown, 1992.
Two young children recollect a memory of childhood secrets. (Objective 4)

————, ed. *Street Rhymes Around the World*. Illustrated by 17 international artists. Wordsong, 1992.

Illustrations in a variety of styles highlight this colorful collection of action rhymes from around the world. (Objectives 3, 5, 6, and 8)

Group Introductory Activity:

Introduce this unit by reading Lee Bennett Hopkins's poem "Good Books, Good Times!" from the collection of poems by the same title. Generate a list of books, events, stories, and rhymes that the children remember after reading this poem. Once the list is posted on the chalkboard, have each child select his or her favorite story, event, or rhyme, then design an original bookmark based on that subject to use in this unit. Additional bookmarks may be made and donated to the library media center. Link the idea of a variety of books and ideas to the variety of verses the students will be reading and writing in this unit.

Encourage the children to make a connection with good books or poems and good times through a learning center where poetry books are available. Allow each child to select one special book from the library media center which will remain in the learning center throughout the unit. Have the children decorate poetry notebooks or folders to hold their writing. For each week of the unit celebrate poetry by having a new tape or recording of poetry available for listening in the center, for example, Jack Prelutsky's *The New Kid on the Block* (Listening Library, FTR 115C, 1986) or Shel Silverstein's *Where the Sidewalk Ends* (Columbia, FCT39412, 1984).

After reading "There Is a Land" by Leland Jacobs or "I Met a Dragon Face to Face" by Jack Prelutsky, have the children paint a wall mural of the variety of places people visit in books. Students may read aloud all the poems in this collection so they become acquainted with the different types of verse.

Follow-Up Activities for Teacher and Students to Share:

1. Ask the children to listen for fun and descriptions as "Fireworks" from Deborah Chandra's *Balloons and Other Poems* is read aloud. Use this poem as an example of how students can take an idea or a vision and brainstorm a list of examples of descriptive language. Select other ideas such as the ones Chandra used in her book to create a class list of descriptors, words that describe another thing. When the list is sufficiently complete, let the children write free flowing poetry of their own.

2. Children may identify with many of the experiences reflected in the poems from Kalli Dakos's *If You're Not Here, Please Raise Your Hand: Poems about School*. Ask the children to select poems to read aloud over several days. Follow up the poem "Teacher, Could You?" (p. 21) by having a "Mute Day" in which no one, teacher or students, may speak while in the classroom.

All communication must be accomplished through writing or sign or body language. Discuss the experience the next day. If possible invite a mime to the class to demonstrate how a mime uses his or her body to communicate with the audience.

A serious class discussion about feelings and emotions may follow the sensitive poem "Were You Ever Fat Like Me?" (p. 52). Remind the children of the chant "Sticks and stones may break my bones, but words can never hurt me." Ask the group to decide if the cliché is true or if words hurt somewhere inside each of us.

In another poem "I Have No Time to Visit with King Arthur" (p. 47), the poet vows, "Nouns and verbs and compound words / Are sad and dull and stale, / Unless they're fired with the spark / Of a mighty, wondrous tale." As a follow-up share a "mighty, wondrous tale" such as one of the Arthurian legends in Robin Lister's *The Legend of King Arthur* (Doubleday, 1990) with the children, asking them to listen to find several nouns, verbs, and compound words. Let the children share the words they heard and classify them into the appropriate groups.

3. Before reading Tom Feelings and Eloise Greenfield's *Daydreamers* to the class, explain that, according to the book jacket, Tom Feelings drew the portraits of the African-American children before the poems were written. The touching, often haunting portraits inspired writer Eloise Greenfield to depict the children's feelings in poetry. Allow the children time to study each portrait and discuss the emotion each expresses before the poem is read. After reading, let the children decide whether their interpretations of the faces matched Greenfield's. As a writing follow-up have the students use old magazines to find photographs showing a range of emotions on people's faces. Working in pairs they can select a picture and write a poem or statement that can serve as a caption for the photograph.

4. Read aloud several poems from *Munching Poems about Eating*, edited by Lee Bennett Hopkins. Send a small group of children to the library media center to use the poetry index or card catalog to locate poems on food they can copy for a booklet. Be sure the source of each is noted. Each group member should have a specific responsibility. Decisions should be made as a group regarding the appropriateness of poems, designs, and illustrations for the booklet. As a class, read Lee Bennett Hopkins's poem "Questions" from *Munching Poems about Eating*. Have the children discuss what food items they have eaten that have been cooked in an oven. Ask them to collect a favorite recipe of a food or meal that has to be cooked or baked in the oven. Help the class produce a recipe book called "Oven Delights."

5. Read aloud the introduction to *Poems of A. Nonny Mouse* by Jack Prelutsky. Ask the children to suggest the significance of the word *anonymous*. Have the children find the word in the dictionary to confirm the definition. Challenge students to work individually or in pairs to read

aloud to the class the poems in this collection. Ask the children to play detective as they listen and try to find any of the four original Jack Prelutsky poems in the collection. As they discover a Prelutsky poem, they are to copy the first line of the poem on a sheet of paper. Direct the children to follow the recorded line with a sentence giving their reasons for believing the poem to be one of Prelutsky's. After all children have participated, use the note on the copyright page to discover the correct four.

6. Read aloud Jane Yolen's *All Those Secrets of the World*. Let the children discuss the differences between peace and war. Have the students recall the experiences of the book characters with war and peace. Follow the discussion by having students in the class describe experiences they remember with pleasure. Emphasize the use of descriptive words related to the five senses. Children should express smells, sounds, tastes, feelings, or sights they recall. Direct the children to write sensory poems about their experiences. Let each line detail one specific sense and title the poem with the name of the pleasurable situation, for example, the lines "Happy faces around a table / Warmth of candles on my face / Smell of chocolate cake in the air /Voices singing a bit off-key / Cool, sweet taste of homemade ice cream /Not a happier feeling anywhere" all point to the title "Happy Birthday."

Follow-Up Activities for Individual Students:

1. Deborah Chandra's language in *Balloons and Other Poems* paints vivid scenes. After hearing "Fireworks" in class, select another poem in this collection. Read the descriptive poem and respond to it by drawing the scene it describes. Color the scene first with warm colors (reds, oranges, and yellows), then do the same scene again in cool colors (blues, greens, and violets). Choose your favorite of the two scenes and justify your choice.

2. Read the note to readers on the back of the book jacket for *If You're Not Here, Please Raise Your Hand: Poems about School* by Kalli Dakos. Dakos speaks about a pair of magic glasses that lets stories pop up everywhere. Accept the challenge to "try on a pair of these special glasses." Tell the story of your life either in a poem or a paragraph. You may choose one particular incident or write a general biographical sketch.

3. Read "Surprise" by Beverly McLoughland in the collection *Good Books, Good Times!* Think of a book character or a book adventure that reminds you of yourself. Write a free-verse poem based on that similarity.

4. After hearing *Poems of A. Nonny Mouse* in class, you may wish to learn more about poet Jack Prelutsky, whom A. Nonny Mouse trusted, and what other types of poetry he writes. Ask the library media specialist to help you write to one of the publishers of Prelutsky's poetry, asking for a biographical sketch about him. If *Something about the Author* or the *Junior Book of*

Authors & Illustrators series is available in the library media center or public library, look up biographical information on Prelutsky. Use the card or computer catalog to find other books Jack Prelutsky has written. After reading several of these books, select six or more favorite Prelutsky poems to copy into your own "Prelutsky Poetry" booklet.

5. Read *Street Rhymes Around the World*, edited by Jane Yolen. Select a rhyme from a country and practice to perform it for the class. You may present the poem individually or with a friend. Be prepared to tell the class what country the poem comes from and locate that country on a map or globe.

6. Read *Street Rhymes Around the World*, edited by Jane Yolen, to discover common elements between the cultures of different countries contained in the verses. List some of these common factors. Then select one rhyme and write a short paragraph explaining how it is unique to the country of its origin.

Closure:

Ask each child to memorize a favorite verse. Perform the memorized poems for another class. Assign a small group of students to plan a "munching party" to celebrate. Foods might include several items from Lee Bennett Hopkins's collection *Munching Poems about Eating*. Ask the library media specialist to visit the class during the celebration and share selections from Arnold Adoff's *Eats* (Lothrop, Lee & Shepard, 1979) with the children, being sure to include the poem that begins with "Eats / are on my mind from early morning / to late at night," and concludes two pages later with "my tongue says / we are / full today / but / teeth just / grin / and / say / come in / i am always hungry." Conclude the party by serving broccoli florets with dip and "Twinkies" as the media specialist shares the poem about "the giant Twinkie . . . on the White House lawn."

Inventive Thoughts

Objectives:

1. Discuss and recognize how inventions meet humans' needs.
2. Dramatize or re-create an inventive moment in history.
3. Develop a time line of American inventions.
4. Attempt to invent a new machine or gadget.
5. Demonstrate a selected experiment or how a machine works.
6. Increase science vocabulary.

7. Research and report on various scientific principles and/or famous inventors.
8. Develop rational powers of thinking.
9. Locate books by using call numbers.

Recommended Readings:

Allison, Linda, and Katz, David. *Gee, Wiz! How to Mix Art and Science or the Art of Thinking Scientifically*. Illustrated by Linda Allison. Little, Brown, 1983.
Gee Wiz and Smart Art lead children through a series of discoveries involving science and art. (Objectives 2, 5, and 8)

Caney, Steven. *Steven Caney's Invention Book*. Workman, 1985.
Stories, suggestions, and plans for being an inventor fill the pages of this volume. (Objectives 4, 6, and 8)

Cobb, Vicki. *Fun and Games: Stories Science Photos Tell*. Lothrop, Lee & Shepard, 1991.
Explicit photographs help explain a variety of scientific principles. (Objectives 6 and 7)

Cobb, Vicki, and Darling, Kathy. *Bet You Can't! Science Impossibilities to Fool You*. Illustrated by Martha Weston. Lothrop, Lee & Shepard, 1980.
Scientific principles are demonstrated in many forms with a humorous approach. (Objectives 5 and 8)

Konigsburg, E.L. *Samuel Todd's Book of Great Inventions*. Atheneum, 1991.
Samuel Todd tells why he thinks certain inventions are great. (Objective 1)

Murphy, Jim. *Guess Again: More Weird and Wacky Inventions*. Bradbury, 1986.
Clues and drawings invite the reader to guess the purpose for each of the 45 included inventions before the book reveals the answers. (Objectives 1, 2, 3, and 4)

———. *Weird and Wacky Inventions*. Crown, 1978.
Many of the unusual inventions submitted to the U.S. Patent and Trademark Office are described in this witty volume. (Objectives 2, 4, 5, and 7)

Wyler, Rose. *Science Fun with Toy Cars and Trucks*. Illustrated by Pat Stewart. Julian Messner, 1988.
Simple activities using toys demonstrate various scientific principles. (Objectives 1, 5, 8, and 9)

Zubrowski, Bernie. *Messing around with Drinking Straw Construction*. Illustrated by Stephanie Fleischer. Little, Brown, 1981.
Basic principles of construction are demonstrated using straws as the framework. (Objectives 4, 5, and 8)

Group Introductory Activity:

The human spirit of inventiveness, imagination, and willingness to keep trying is the basis for this unit. As Jim Murphy says in his book *Guess Again: More Weird and Wacky Inventions*, "Inventiveness . . . coupled with our willingness to laugh at ourselves . . . truly unites us even today" (p. 3). Read aloud the introduction, which emphasizes the humor and attempts to make life easier. Stress with the students that we often learn more from our mistakes than from our successes. Open with the invention on page 37. Let the students discuss the advances human beings have made since the time this invention was built. Ask the children to speculate upon the need that created this idea. After reading the chapter "Fun and Games" (pp. 41–56), have the students discuss the various needs, desires, or emotions that triggered these inventions. Direct the children to keep an open mind and brainstorm needs they have that could benefit from an inventive thought. Post this list in the classroom where students may add to it during the unit and may refer to it as a source of ideas. As a follow-up set up a time line in the classroom so children may note the dates when certain inventions occurred.

Follow-Up Activities for Teacher and Students to Share:

1. Science is not only inventive and fun but it is also an art. Share with the class Linda Allison and David Katz's *Gee, Wiz! How to Mix Art and Science or the Art of Thinking Scientifically*. As an art extension select a couple of children to demonstrate "Dippy Designs" from page 34 and "An Absorbing Challenge" from page 35. The last activity challenges students to experiment and figure out how to duplicate the designs. Have the children predict how to fold the paper before actually doing so. Complete the activity and display the final dried artwork. Ask the children to share their experiences with the experiment. Lead the group to analyze the results and then introduce "capillary action" as the name of that process. Urge the children to complete the individual activity and tell them they may examine the book throughout this unit to find other discoveries that can be made using the experiments it contains.

2. In *Steven Caney's Invention Book* the author suggests that to be an inventor you must learn to let your mind search and then think of many possible solutions to each invention problem you encounter. Use Caney's suggestion and hang the following sign in a designated area of the room where students may play at experimenting, creating, and inventing: "Invention in progress. Do not criticize." Refer to the materials suggestions on page 27 to set up a workshop area in the classroom. To help students become better thinkers place these phrases around the room: "Imagine what might happen if . . .," "Predict what will happen when . . .," "Analyze the results," "Compare what happens when . . .," and "Evaluate the product or the process."

Connect science to language arts by having the students submit new words from the science books for spelling and vocabulary extension. A few suggestions include *inventor, thinking, experiment, concentrate, tinker, craft, design, solution, materials,* and *tools.*

3. After viewing the photographs in Vicki Cobb's book *Fun and Games: Stories Science Photos Tell,* have the students keep a science journal or inventor's notebook. Keep old magazines in the room for children to cut out photographs to glue in their journals. At the back of the notebook children will need to make a glossary of new words as Vicki Cobb did.

4. Many scientific principles can really fool the observer. To find out how much fun one can have with science, read Vicki Cobb and Kathy Darling's *Bet You Can't: Science Impossibilities to Fool You* to the class. Use the brain teasers on pages 115–20 to stretch the imaginative thinking powers of the children. If possible team with a fifth- or sixth-grade class to demonstrate the tricks in this book. Have cross-grade level pairs of students (one third grader and one fifth grader) work as teams to select and demonstrate one of the concepts. Have each team explain the scientific concept involved. Encourage the children to use Vicki Cobb and Kathy Darling's *Bet You Can!* (Avon, 1983) for further science fun.

5. After sharing E. L. Konigsburg's *Samuel Todd's Book of Great Inventions* with the children, let them write a class collaboration book of what they would choose as really great inventions and justify each choice. Begin by having the group brainstorm a list of modern conveniences. Ask the children to speculate how these things came to be and what people would do without them. After the list is generated and discussion is complete, continue the writing process of prewriting, drafting, revising, editing, and publishing. Let children illustrate the text, compile, and display their book in the library media center.

6. Read Rose Wyler's book *Science Fun with Toy Cars and Trucks* aloud, asking the children to listen for ideas about different experiments to demonstrate using toy cars. Allow children to test some or all of the experiments as they are read. Urge them to think about inventions as they listen. Wyler has said that the ramp is a "great invention." Let students discuss and list various inventions or discoveries that needed to occur in order to develop modern vehicles. Students can work in teams to demonstrate ideas expressed in the book. Urge the children to draw deductions and generalizations from their experiments.

If the children are intrigued with Wyler's book, encourage them to look for other books under the author's name in the library media center's card catalog. Have the students make a bibliography of books by Ruth Wyler or a specific subject. Libraries are filled with books on science and inventions. Show the children and explain that the call number of a book is found on the spine of the book and on the upper left-hand corner of the cards in the card catalog. If the media center has a computerized catalog, plan with the library media specialist to teach the children how to use it. Have the children name the call numbers on the books in this unit. Ask them to speculate on why some of the books have Dewey Decimal numbers of 502, 507, 607, and 608. Explain that the 500's represent pure science and the 600's represent applied science or technology. Encourage the children to think analytically and decide how it helps to have books organized by subjects. Select small groups of students to locate other science books using the card catalog. Generate a list of subject headings to look up (e.g., "inventions," "science," or "experiments").

Follow-Up Activities for Individual Students:

1. After sharing in class *Gee, Wiz? How to Mix Art and Science or the Art of Thinking Scientifically* by Linda Allison and David Katz, pretend to be Smart Art or Gee Wiz from the book. As that character, demonstrate a selected experiment for the class.
2. Follow the directions on page 38 of *Steven Caney's Invention Book* to create a "Rube Goldberg" (making a simple task incredibly complicated).
3. Vicki Cobb's *Fun and Games: Stories Science Photos Tell* can help you better understand phenomena, using certain scientific principles. Select one photograph and explanation to study. Share the photograph with the class and explain what they are seeing.
4. Read one of the five stories in chapter 7 of Jim Murphy's *Guess Again: More Weird and Wacky Inventions*. Dress up and act as one of the characters. Pretending to be that character, explain or demonstrate what he or she invented. Be sure to use the first person "I" in your presentation.
5. In *Weird and Wacky Inventions* Jim Murphy names seven famous inventors: Benjamin Franklin, Eli Whitney, Cyrus McCormick, Charles Goodyear, Alexander Graham Bell, George Eastman, and Thomas Edison. Select one of these men to learn more about. Read a biography or other factual information on the selected inventor. Give an oral or written report to the class. Be sure to include some of the funnier inventions or ideas these men came up with.
6. Select one of the inventions in Jim Murphy's *Weird and Wacky Inventions* to demonstrate for the class.
7. After reading either of Jim Murphy's books, *Weird and Wacky Inventions* or *Guess Again: More Weird and Wacky Inventions*, dream, create, and invent something new. If it doesn't work, remember to laugh and share that experience of inventing with the class.

8. Read Bernie Zubrowski's book *Messing around with Drinking Straw Construction*. Then follow the author's directions, beginning with the basic structures and concepts. Complete several structures and then become inventive. What other structures can be invented using the triangle? What can be deduced about the use of the triangle in construction?

Closure:

Team with an upper-grade class to hold or host an "Invention Fair." Set up the guidelines according to time and availability of materials. It may be desirable to make the fair noncompetitive so that the children are encouraged to complete their own projects with a minimum of adult input. Explain to the students that demonstrating the processes of scientific thinking and inventiveness is the goal of the "Invention Fair."

Examining Theme in Jane Yolen's Books

Objectives:

1. Explore theme in stories.
2. Write an original story based on a model.
3. Present information in oral and/or written formats.
4. Retell a story orally through puppetry or creative dramatics.
5. Conduct research for specific information.
6. Chart comparative information.
7. Use the card catalog to locate materials in the library media center.
8. Increase awareness of disabilities and coping mechanisms.

Recommended Readings:

Yolen, Jane. *The Acorn Quest.* Illustrated by Susanna Natti. Thomas Y. Crowell, 1981.
King Earthor sends four trusted knights in search of the Golden Acorn in this animal parody of the quest for the Holy Grail. (Objectives 1, 3, 5, and 6)

———. *Dove Isabeau.* Illustrated by Dennis Nolan. Harcourt Brace Jovanovich, 1989.
The theme of overcoming evil through kindness is repeated in a strong fantasy tale. (Objectives 1, 6, and 7)

————. *The Dragon's Boy*. Harper & Row, 1990.
The mysterious dragon that guides young Artos toward his destiny adds a twist to this retelling of Arthurian legend. (Objectives 1, 3, and 6)

————. *Greyling*. Illustrated by David Ray. Philomel, 1991.
The foundling child Greyling is actually a "selkie," a seal in human form, who returns to the sea to save his foster father. (Objectives 1, 6, and 7)

————. *Mouse's Birthday*. Illustrated by Bruce Degen. G. P. Putnam's Sons, 1993.
Unexpected results surprise everyone when Mouse's friends all squeeze into his tiny house to celebrate his birthday. (Objective 2)

————. *The Seeing Stick*. Illustrated by Remy Charlip and Demetra Maraslis. Thomas Y. Crowell, 1977.
No one can give sight to the blind young princess until an old man arrives with his magical seeing stick. (Objectives 1 and 8)

————. *Sleeping Ugly*. Illustrated by Diane Stanley. Coward, McCann, 1981.
A wise prince recognizes that beauty is more than skin deep in this variation on the Sleeping Beauty story. (Objectives 1, 4, and 6)

————. *Welcome to the Green House*. Illustrated by Laura Regan. G. P. Putnam's Sons, 1993.
Quiet poetry and luminous gouache paintings present the tropical rain forest and its inhabitants. (Objectives 1, 2, and 3)

————. *Wings*. Illustrated by Dennis Nolan. Harcourt Brace Jovanovich, 1991.
The Greek legend of Daedalus warns of the danger in hubris or human pride. (Objectives 1, 4, and 6)

Biographical Sources:

For information on Jane Yolen see *Something about the Author*, vol. 40, pages 217–30; *Something about the Author Autobiographical Series*, vol. 1, pages 327–46; and *Fourth Book of Junior Authors & Illustrators*, pages 356–58.

Group Introductory Activity:

Introduce the children to Jane Yolen, a very prolific reader and writer who has published more than 100 books and won multiple awards for her work. She writes in a wide variety of styles and genres from poetry to novels, but she is especially well known for creating modern stories that resemble classic folktales. Like all good books Jane Yolen's works have deep meanings or truths, called themes, that lie beneath the stories. These themes may be interpreted differently by different readers. Yolen has said, "I just tell stories. I hope my stories amuse and entertain and move people. But in truth, I'm just telling a story and what happens between the story and the listener is between the story and the listener" (*Something about the Author*, vol. 40, p. 223). For more information on theme see Charlotte Huck et al.'s *Children's Literature in the Elementary School*, 5th ed. (Harcourt Brace Jovanovich, 1993) or Rebecca Lukens' *A Critical Handbook of Children's Literature*, 4th edition (HarperCollins, 1990). Explain to the children that they will have the opportunity to share many of Jane Yolen's books in this unit.

Ask the children to listen carefully for the main idea they think the author is trying to convey in her book *Sleeping Ugly*. After completing the story, let the children discuss the sequence of the plot. Lead the discussion into speculation about why the prince did not awaken the beautiful princess. Brainstorm a single sentence statement of the theme as the culmination of the discussion. Remind students of the old sayings "Beauty is only skin deep" and "Pretty is as pretty does." Ask the children to relate these clichés to the theme in *Sleeping Ugly*. If the children are not familiar with the Sleeping Beauty tales, read Trina Schart Hyman's retelling, *Sleeping Beauty* (Little, Brown, 1974), or other versions of the folktale. Help the children to compare this story to Yolen's tale. As a follow-up let the children use puppets to act out the story of *Sleeping Ugly*. Allow time for the students to practice the puppet play thoroughly and then present it to another class.

As each book in the unit is completed, let the students select and draw an appropriate shape relating to the book's theme or title on construction paper, cut it out, and write the book title and theme on the shape. These theme statements may be posted on a bulletin board labeled "Theme Is What It's All About." Ask the music teacher to help you and the children learn a "theme song" for the unit that may be sung to the tune of "The Hokey Pokey." The lyrics might be similar to: "You put the setting here, / You put a hero there, / You put a problem here, / And some action everywhere. / You give the story meaning that will really give it clout —/ Theme is what it's all about!"

Follow-Up Activities for Teacher and Students to Share:

1. *The Acorn Quest* by Jane Yolen is a parody of the King Arthur legends that Yolen has called "the greatest story ever told." After reading the book aloud, divide the class into four cooperative groups. Let the groups visit the library media center to research the Arthurian legend. Assign each group to research one of four assignments:

   - Which of Arthur's knights may have been Yolen's models for Belliful, Tarryhere, Gimmemore, and Runsalot? Who was Arthur's magician?
   - King Arthur's knights went in quest of what object and why was it important to them?

- What is the parallel in the Arthurian legend of the "Large and Beautiful Paw" and what item was obtained from it?
- One of the themes of the Arthurian legend involves respect for the rights of others. Research the Round Table and stories of Arthur's knights (e.g., Selina Hastings's *Sir Gawain and the Green Knight* [Lothrop, Lee & Shepard, 1981] or Rosemary Sutcliffe's *The Sword and the Circle: King Arthur and the Knights of the Round Table* [E.P. Dutton, 1981]) to find events that demonstrate that theme. Lerner and Lowe phrased this ethic in their musical *Camelot* as "Might for right." Compose a paragraph explaining what that motto or theme means to your group.

   When the students have completed their research, let the groups share their information with the class. Have the children work as a large cooperative group to synthesize the information into a brief retelling of the Arthurian legend. Urge children who read on a higher level to read and complete the individual activity on Jane Yolen's *The Dragon's Boy* as a further follow-up.

2. Share Jane Yolen's *Greyling* with the class. Let the children speculate about why Greyling's mother always tried to keep him from the sea. Some children may believe that she was afraid he might drown while others may conclude that she suspected his true nature. Ask the children why Greyling longed for the sea. Share the Shakespearean adage "To thine own self be true" (*Hamlet*, I, iii, 78). Let the children relate the statement to Greyling. Help the students formulate a theme statement relevant to their own lives.

3. Prior to reading Jane Yolen's *The Seeing Stick* aloud, ask the group how people see. Discuss if there are other ways of "seeing" besides with eyes. Some child will probably mention that blind people "see" with their hands. Read the story to the class. Let the students discuss how the author foreshadowed the surprise ending. Encourage the students to speculate about why the old man bothered to teach the princess and why she in turn taught other blind children. This discussion can lead logically into formulation of a theme statement. As a follow-up to help children identify with visual disabilities play a variation of "Blind Man's Bluff" on the playground, in the gymnasium, or in another open area. Blindfold one child. Allow the other students to move about the room, selecting a spot on which to stand or crouch. When the "Blind Man" finds a child, he or she must use fingertips to "see" and identify that person. After the "Blind Man" has correctly identified three children, another child may assume the role and continue the game.

4. Ask the children to listen carefully for the plants, animals, and sounds that fill the tropical rain forest in Jane Yolen's *Welcome to the Green House*. After the book is read, record student responses on the chalkboard. Let the children discuss the things that the animals and plants on the list need in order

to survive. Lead into a discussion of the theme or underlying meaning of the story. Children should be able to recognize Yolen's message of the importance of preserving the rain forest.

As a follow-up write a class cumulative story patterned after "The House that Jack Built." Begin with "This is the rain forest, house of green." Build the story by adding plants and animals from the list on the board, for example, "This is the tree that grows in the rain forest, house of green. This is the sloth who creeps through trees / that grow in the rain forest, house of green. This is the capuchin, quick and fleet / who leaps past the sloth / that creeps through the trees / that grow in the rain forest, house of green. . . ." When the class story is near completion, read aloud the final page of *Welcome to the Green House* headed "Did You Know?" Urge the children to add a final stanza to their cumulative tale similar to "These are the children who vow to save the . . . rain forest, house of green." Let the children illustrate the individual verses and compile a class book titled "This Is the Rain Forest, House of Green."

5. Before sharing Jane Yolen's *Wings* with the class, explain that in this myth the illustrator has placed the Greek gods in the clouds. They watch the action almost like an audience watching a play. Tell the children to observe the expressions of the gods carefully as the story is read to see the different emotions they express. Read the story aloud. Have the children discuss the feelings the illustrator depicted. Ask them to speculate about why the gods reacted as they did. This leads into a discussion of the book's theme. Children should mention the gods' displeasure with the pride and arrogance of Daedalus. Review the final lines on the first and last pages of text: "The gods always punish such a man." Urge the children to relate those lines to the theme.

    Read aloud "About the Story" from the copyright page. As a follow-up have the children locate Athens, Greece; Crete; and the Icarian Sea on a map. Let the group retell the story in an abbreviated form with creative dramatics. Have a small group of children take the role of the Greek gods, reacting to events but not interfering, while another group acts as a Greek chorus to read together the italicized text telling of the gods' reactions.

Follow-Up Activities for Individual Students:

1. After sharing *The Acorn Quest* by Jane Yolen in class, select a book on King Arthur from the library media center. Read the book and select one adventure not included in Jane Yolen's book to share with the group.
2. Read Jane Yolen's *Dove Isabeau*. Think about the courage Kemp Owain showed when he threw away his sword and knife. Isabeau, in dragon form, had already killed and devoured 99 young men. Later Isabeau showed great

strength of character when she refused to kill her stepmother, flinging away the knife instead. These actions all support the theme "Evil can be overcome through kindness." Although the witch died, Isabeau did not kill her; she fell from the window after the knife hit her shoulder. Do you think the spell on Kemp Owain could have been broken if Isabeau had chosen to *deliberately* kill the witch? Why or why not? Yolen tells readers that as the dragon Isabeau wept, she licked the bones of the young men she had slain. What does this tell you about Isabeau and how does it relate to the theme of the story?

3. Jane Yolen's *Dove Isabeau* has many similarities to traditional folktales. After reading this book use the card catalog to locate and read a copy of the Snow White tale such as Paul Heins's retelling, *Snow White*, illustrated by Trina Schart Hyman (Little, Brown, 1974). Make a chart to list the similarities between the stories.

4. After having shared *The Acorn Quest* in class, you may wish to follow another quest. Read Jane Yolen's *The Dragon's Boy* to find how young Artos quests for knowledge and wisdom. After completing the story, think about the dragon's words to Artos: "In order to gain wisdom, you must learn to read *inter linea*, between the lines," and his promise that Artos would one day "read *inter linea* in people as well." Write a paragraph explaining what you think the dragon meant, especially by the last promise. How can one read between the lines in people? How might this be helpful to a ruler or leader? Read *inter linea* to discover the theme of Yolen's fantasy novel and write it in one sentence.

5. After hearing Jane Yolen's *Greyling* in class, use the card catalog or computerized catalog to locate other "selkie" stories in the library media center, such as Susan Cooper's *The Selkie Girl* (Macmillan, 1986). SELKIES or SEALS—FICTION are two subject headings you may find helpful. Read one or more of these books and compare the similarities and differences in the story. As a follow-up select your favorite of the selkie stories and prepare a shadow box or other visual display of your favorite scene from the book.

6. After experiencing *Welcome to the Green House* and writing a story based on that model, read Jane Yolen's *Mouse's Birthday*. This short, simple book offers a clear model for writing. Think about another animal who might have a very small house, such as a hummingbird, a mole, or an insect. Write and illustrate an original friendship story using the animal of your choice and others who might visit him or her. Think about how the visitors would arrive (e.g., birds on the wing or on the fly; bugs on tiny feet, tiny legs, or fairy wings). Try to include a surprise at the end such as Yolen did when Mouse's house exploded and he moved to the big barn. Place your completed book in the reading center for others to share.

7. After sharing Jane Yolen's *Welcome to the Green House* in class, write the Earth Island Institute at the address Yolen gives in her book to learn more about what you and your friends can do to save the rain forests. Share the information with your class in an oral report.
8. After experiencing Jane Yolen's *Wings* in class, read Gerald McDermott's version of the same myth, *Sun Flight* (Four Winds, 1980). Compare and contrast the two versions. Write a paragraph in which you explain and justify which of the two versions you prefer.

Closure:

Let the children play "Theme Concentration." When students have completed the "Theme Is What It's All About" bulletin board, write the theme statement for each book on a 5-inch-by-8-inch index card. Make a corresponding title card for each theme. Lay the cards, face down, in a floor grid. Label the rows (x-axis) with letters and the columns (y-axis) with numbers. Divide the class into two teams and let members take turns to name coordinate points calling for two cards; for example, "A-3" would indicate the first row, third card. In order to make a match the student must find a title and its corresponding theme card. Matching pairs are pulled from the grid and awarded to the team selecting them. Close the game and the unit by singing "Theme Is What It's All About."

Jerry Pinkney's Illustrations: Reflections of Life and Character

Objectives:

1. Identify the elements of a folktale.
2. Compare stories with similar themes.
3. Discuss ways the illustrations support the story line.
4. Respond to literature through art, writing, and/or storytelling.
5. Expand speaking and spelling vocabulary.
6. Compare cultural heritages through literature.
7. Relate real-life stories to those of fictional characters.

Recommended Readings:

Dragonwagon, Crescent. *Home Place*. Illustrated by Jerry Pinkney. Macmillan, 1990.
Only the flowers and foundation remain to mark the location of the old home place. (Objectives 2, 4, and 7)

Fields, Julia. *The Green Lion of Zion Street*. Illustrated by Jerry Pinkney. Macmillan, 1988.
Crouched above a city lane, a stern stone lion claims his territory. (Objectives 4 and 5)

Flournoy, Valerie. *The Patchwork Quilt*. Illustrated by Jerry Pinkney. Dial, 1985.
Each patch of material in Tanya's quilt tells a story about her loving family. (Objectives 6 and 7)

Hamilton, Virginia. *Drylongso*. Illustrated by Jerry Pinkney. Harcourt Brace Jovanovich, 1992.
The folk hero, Drylongso, shows that where he goes crops will grow. (Objective 3)

Lester, Julius. *The Tales of Uncle Remus: The Adventures of Brer Rabbit*. Illustrated by Jerry Pinkney. Dial, 1987.
The wit, humor, and wisdom of Brer Rabbit comes to life in these stories and illustrations. (Objective 4)

Levitin, Sonia. *The Man Who Kept His Heart in a Bucket*. Illustrated by Jerry Pinkney. Dial, 1991.
Brokenhearted Jack has no reason to experience the joys of life until a young maiden presents him with a challenge. (Objective 1)

McKissack, Patricia C. *Mirandy and Brother Wind*. Illustrated by Jerry Pinkney. Alfred A. Knopf, 1988.
Mirandy, with the help of Brother Wind, is sure to win the Junior cakewalk. (Objectives 3 and 4)

Pinkney, Gloria Jean. *Back Home*. Illustrated by Jerry Pinkney. Dial, 1992.
Ernestine's trip back home to the country and the house in which she was born provides lasting memories. (Objectives 2, 3, 4, 6, and 7)

San Souci, Robert D. *The Talking Eggs: A Folktale from the American South*. Illustrated by Jerry Pinkney. Dial, 1989.
Sweet, kind Blanche and her mean, cross sister remain true to their nature and receive their just reward. (Objectives 1, 2, 3, and 4)

Biographical Sources:

For information on Jerry Pinkney see *Something about the Author*, vol. 41, pages 164–74; *Something about the Author Autobiographical Series*, vol. 12, pages 249–66; *Sixth Book of Junior Authors & Illustrators*, pages 225–27; and *Talking with Artists: Conversations with Victoria Chess, Pat Cummings, Leo and Diane Dillon, Richard Egielski, Lois Ehlert, Lisa Campbell Ernst, Tom Feelings, Steven Kellogg, Jerry Pinkney, Amy Schwartz, Lane Smith, Chris Van Allsburg, and David Wiesner*, pages 60–65.

Group Introductory Activity:

Jerry Pinkney, the illustrator of *The Patchwork Quilt* by Valerie Flournoy, has said that he felt fortunate to illustrate a story that summed up some of the feelings that he had about embracing and celebrating African American culture. Not only is it a story about the strength of an African American family, it is a story about the relationship between a grandmother and granddaughter. With this book he "needed models who responded to the text and at the same time knew and cared for each other . . . I began to realize that this was an interesting way of approaching text—getting models actually involved in the story" (*Something about the Author Autobiographical Series*, vol. 12, p. 263).

Read aloud *The Patchwork Quilt* and then let the children discuss how the illustrations support the story line. Let the students compare the way the family in the story celebrates life to their own families and experiences. Allow the children to share memories or memorabilia they have of their grandparents. As a unit project make a patchwork quilt of favorite scenes from books illustrated by Jerry Pinkney. Use men's handkerchiefs as the basic squares. Allow about one inch for seams. On the four outside edges use a permanent marker or crayon to either draw a frame or write the title, author, illustrator, and the student artist's name around the edge as a frame (one on each side of the square). Use straight pins or masking tape to firmly attach the handkerchief to a square of cardboard. Children should then draw the scene with pencil in the center of the handkerchief. Use this as a base to color the scene with crayon or markers. After the children have completed all the squares, sew them together or ask a parent volunteer to do so. Use a sheet as backing and colorful material for a border. When the unit is complete celebrate by sharing the quilt with the children and displaying it in the media center.

Follow-Up Activities for Teacher and Students to Share:

1. Read aloud *Home Place* by Crescent Dragonwagon. Suggest that the students think of old homes and foundations that might exist in their area. Have them bring to school old bottles, coins, or other items they may have

found. Brainstorm story ideas that the objects suggest. If possible, invite a curator or docent from a local museum to share artifacts and stories about the area. During art time have students use pencil and watercolors to create a daffodil scene similar to the one Jerry Pinkney included in *Home Place*.

2. Before reading *The Green Lion of Zion Street* by Julia Fields, ask the children to have crayons and paper on their desks. Because this is a unit of study about an illustrator, the students will need to think and imagine like artists. Explain that as the story is read they are to listen for the description of the lion and draw what they imagine it to look like. Stop reading with the line "disdainful head of imperturbable hair." Encourage the children to look up the definitions of the unfamiliar words. When the drawings are complete, finish reading the story and share Jerry Pinkney's illustration of the lion and those of the children.

    Take advantage of the opportunity to expand the children's vocabulary through Fields's descriptive language. Reread the story, asking the students to quietly raise their hand each time they hear a new word or a phrase that begins with the word *like* or *as*. Write these words and phrases on the chalkboard. Let the children select five to ten words from the list to use in a spelling unit and have them use these words orally in class discussions. Possible words include: *arrogant, stern, stolid, haughty, snide, fierce, mighty, proud, smirky, vain, snooty, crouched, scowl,* and *reigning*.

3. Rather than read the words to *Drylongso* to the children, begin by introducing the title, author, and illustrator. Ask the students to tell what is happening in each scene by presenting only the illustrations in sequential order. Instruct the children to describe the setting as Pinkney has illustrated it. Urge the children to also notice the mood that is set in each scene. Once the illustrations have been "read," go back and read Virginia Hamilton's words. Follow the reading by having the children analyze the role specific illustrations play in gaining insight into the story.

4. Tell the children to listen as the author describes how Jack feels when he carries his heart in the bucket and compare that to the description of how he feels as he solves the riddle in Sonia Levitin's *The Man Who Kept His Heart in a Bucket*. Make a chart to help the students realize how the figurative language in the tale relies on the five senses. Challenge several students to go to the library media center and locate folktales that have a riddle to be solved. Let the children speculate on the role of the riddle in these folktales.

5. Read aloud the author's note in Patricia McKissack's *Mirandy and Brother Wind* and then ask the students to predict what they think the book will be about. This book was selected as a Caldecott honor book because of the quality of Jerry Pinkney's illustrations. Ask the children to study the illustrations as the story is read aloud and be able to identify specific illustrations that support the story line. Have the group compare the content

of the story to the children's predictions. As a follow-up have the children assume the role of the illustrator and draw their interpretations of Brother Wind.

6. *Back Home* was written by Jerry Pinkney's wife, Gloria Jean. Explain to the students that her own experiences provided the inspiration for the book. This is the first book the Pinkneys have worked on together. After reading the story, have the children share their observations about how the illustrations reflect the story line.

   List on the chalkboard all of the states and cities where the children were born. Urge class members to interview family members to determine their place of birth and add those locations to the list. Select several students to do a survey of the faculty to find out and list their birthplaces. Have the children use atlases to locate each place. Mount a wall map on a bulletin board. Let the children write each name on a small tag, attach the tags to map tacks, and mark each birthplace on the map. As a further extension students may want to interview family members or neighbors about their childhood memories. These stories can then be retold or written down as in *Back Home*.

7. *The Talking Eggs: A Folktale from the American South* by Robert D. San Souci is the retelling of a Creole folktale. To help the children identify the elements of a folktale and to compare folktales, construct a chart with space across the top for at least three folktale titles. On the left side make a column down with the following categories: setting (where and when), main characters, plot development, magical element, and recurring images or rhymes. Laminate the chart so it may be erased and reused. Share the chart with the class and explain that after *The Talking Eggs* is read aloud they will need to fill in the chart. Read aloud *The Talking Eggs*. Complete the section of the chart on that book. After the parts of the folktale are identified, ask what similarities the students have begun to notice in Jerry Pinkney's illustrations for different books such as *The Talking Eggs* and *Back Home*. When the chart has been completely filled in by individual students, select a small group of children to act as illustrators and draw the different scenes described on the chart. Students can then tape the scenes together sequentially so that the stories can be compared visually.

Follow-Up Activities for Individual Students:

1. After hearing Valerie Flournoy's *The Patchwork Quilt* in class, read Sharon Bell Mathis's *The Hundred Penny Box* (Viking, 1975) or Eth Clifford's *The Remembering Box* (Houghton Mifflin, 1985) and compare the stories. Consider these elements in your comparisons: the settings, the relationships between the two main characters, and the family stories

involved. Graph what is alike and different about the stories. How do the young children change as a result of the relationship with the older person in each story? In your opinion why did the authors write each book?

2. After having shared Crescent Dragonwagon's *Home Place* and Gloria Jean Pinkney's *Back Home* in class, think about the two stories. Ernestine's story takes place about 40 to 50 years ago. Pretend that the old house in which she was born has now fallen down. All that remains is a foundation, insects, and flowers. Use thoughts from Crescent Dragonwagon's *Home Place* such as "And if there was a house, there was a family. . . . Listen . . . look, you can almost see them" to help you write a story about Ernestine's old home.

3. Reread Julia Fields's *The Green Lion of Zion Street*. Think about a park near where you live. What type of statue can you imagine as being appropriate for that park? Use clay to mold a scaled-down version of the statue you would like to see there. Write a brief statement or poem showing its value to the community and your purpose in creating what you did.

4. Select three to five stories in Julius Lester's *The Tales of Uncle Remus: The Adventures of Brer Rabbit* to read. Respond to the stories in one of the following ways: illustrate in pencil the scene that best describes the story, explain what elements the stories have in common (refer to the classroom chart for help), learn one of the tales and retell it for the class, or work with a small group and act out one of the stories.

5. Read at least three selections from Julius Lester's *Tales of Uncle Remus: The Adventures of Brer Rabbit*. Write down the three stories you have read along with the following explanation. Explain the role of Brer Rabbit, the trickster, in the story and his positive qualities and how he demonstrates them.

6. After hearing Robert D. San Souci's *The Talking Eggs* in class, ask the library media specialist to help you find two other versions of the Cinderella tale and compare them to the Creole version San Souci retold. Use a chart similar to the one in the classroom. Share the information with the rest of the class.

Closure:

Celebrate the illustrations of Jerry Pinkney by planning with homeroom parents and the physical education and music teachers a cakewalk like the one in which Mirandy might have danced. Serve foods and tell stories from the African American tradition. Present the completed quilt to the class during the celebration.

Wild Voices: Mysteries of Animal Communication

Objectives:

1. Memorize descriptive lines.
2. Research habitats and animals calls, reporting orally or in writing.
3. Mimic or imitate the sounds of animals.
4. Respond to information through various art forms.
5. Locate books by using the card or computer catalog and noting the Dewey Decimal number.
6. Compare the life cycle and/or characteristics of different animals.
7. Understand the different ways people and animals communicate.
8. Track the migration patterns of animals.

Recommended Readings:

Ashby, Ruth. *Tigers*. Atheneum, 1990.
Color photographs assist the reader in understanding the life of tigers. (Objective 4)

Esbensen, Barbara Juster. *Tiger with Wings: The Great Horned Owl*. Illustrated by Mary Barrett Brown. Orchard, 1991.
The great horned owl's characteristics, habits, and life are described. (Objectives 3 and 6)

Facklam, Margery. *Bees • Dance • and • Whales • Sing: The Mysteries of Animal Communication*. Illustrated by Pamela Johnson. Sierra Club, 1992.
The mysteries of how animals communicate are described. (Objectives 2, 3, and 5)

Horton, Tom. *Snowfall: Journey of the Tundra Swans*. Illustrated by David Hays. Walker, 1991.
The text and colored photographs trace the journey of the tundra swans through an entire year. (Objectives 3, 4, and 8)

Melville, Herman. *Catskill Eagle*. Illustrated by Thomas Locker. Philomel, 1991.
Luminous paintings illustrate the eagle, drawn to the mountains for the sunny spaces, the gorge, and the waterfalls. (Objectives 1, 2, and 4)

Nelson, Drew. *Wild Voices*. Illustrated by John Schoenherr. Philomel, 1991.
The voices of the wild animals are heard as they roam the countryside. (Objectives 4 and 6)

Patterson, Dr. Francine. *Koko's Story.* Illustrated by Ronald H. Cohn. Scholastic, 1987.
A gorilla named Koko learns to use sign language to communicate. (Objective 7)

Powzyk, Joyce. *Wallaby Creek.* Lothrop, Lee & Shepard, 1985.
The life rhythms of Australian animals are presented through their comings and goings at Wallaby Creek. (Objectives 2, 3, 4, and 6)

Schoenherr, John. *Bear.* Philomel, 1991.
A young bear learns to survive without the protection of his mother. (Objectives 2, 3, and 4)

Group Introductory Activity:

In the book *Bees • Dance • and • Whales • Sing: The Mysteries of Animal Communication,* author Margery Facklam writes, "Hardly an animal on earth doesn't make a sound. But seldom are the sounds just noise. Most are a matter of life or death" (p. 26). Read aloud chapter 4 (pp. 23–28) of Facklam's book, "Barks, Chirps, and Melodies." Have the students listen closely for information on how various animals communicate. Ask the students to list the animals that are described in this chapter, including the vervet monkey, robin, goldfinch, ducks, and other birds. When the children hear how each animal sounds, they are to write it beside the proper animal on their list. Follow up by allowing the students to mimic these sounds.

Continue reading the book aloud, giving the class an opportunity to discuss the various ways animals communicate. Ask each child to select one animal not mentioned in Facklam's book to study to learn how it communicates. Divide the class into small groups for the follow-up activity. Assign the teams to use the subject headings in the card or computer catalog to locate other nonfiction books about animals. Add structure to the children's search by specifying that books selected must have the Dewey Decimal classification of the sciences or applied sciences (500's or 600's).

Follow-Up Activities for Teacher and Students to Share:

1. Before sharing Barbara Juster Esbensen's book *Tiger with Wings,* label the great horned owl and the tiger on a chart on which to enter comparative data. Direct the students to listen carefully as the book is read aloud to identify skills each animal has. As the children respond after the book is read, write the skills on the chart. Discuss and compare the similarities of the two great animals. Take the comparison a step farther by allowing the children to mimic the sounds, shrieks, wails, growls, and roars of the two creatures. Follow up this factual account of the great horned owl by reading aloud Eve Bunting's *The Man Who Could Call Down Owls* (Macmillan, 1984) and

Jane Yolen's *Owl Moon* (Philomel, 1987). Even though these are both fictional stories, ask the students what additional information or insights they may have gained from hearing these two books read.

2. Read aloud *Snowfall: Journey of the Tundra Swans* by Tom Horton. On page 4 the author describes the swans' wild voices: "Wild yodeling pierced the frosty air for miles . . . primeval as any wolf's howling." Allow the children time to imagine, comprehend, and mimic the sounds that must bellow from these swans. Have the students track the migration of the swans during the four seasons. As an art follow-up reread the description of the tundra on page 40. Have the children use colored chalk to create the scene they imagine.

3. The descriptive language in Herman Melville's *Catskill Eagle* is an excellent tool to introduce memory work. Tell the children that the text for this book was taken from a much longer work, the famous adult novel *Moby Dick*. Read aloud the story and share the elegant paintings of Thomas Locker. Input the story on a computer using a large print font. If this is not available, take the input story to a copy shop to have it enlarged. Mount the large type on poster board. Work with the students to memorize some of the lines in the book. Refer to the illustrations to help the students visualize the scene. As an art follow-up allow the students to use finger paint to draw an eagle and show the texture of his wings.

4. Explain to the class that even though Drew Nelson's *Wild Voices* is a fiction book, it is based on facts about wild animals. Ask the students to listen for references to the animals' senses of sight, sound, and smell. As each chapter is read aloud, have students write down the chapter heading (e.g., PUMA) and list the responses the animal makes because of its reliance on the five senses (e.g., on page 58 the puma is alerted by the scent of a dog). When references are made to other animals and their use of the senses, the students may be able to record these as well. Discuss what the students heard at the close of each chapter. As a follow-up the students may create a mountain scene mural depicting the animals and scenes in *Wild Voices*. Refer to this mural later in the unit to help the children compare and contrast this habitat and its creatures with that in Joyce Powzyk's *Wallaby Creek*.

5. After sharing *Koko's Story* by Dr. Francine Patterson, let the children discuss the different life-style Koko would lead if she lived in the wild. Ask the children to think about some of the natural means of gorilla communication that Koko used. Urge the children to determine an important advantage of sign language for Koko. Follow up by having the children demonstrate how humans communicate with body language alone. Ask the group to share sounds people make to communicate sorrow, joy, and other emotions. If possible, ask someone to teach the class some basics of American Sign Language. Students may wish to learn more about Koko by reading Dr. Francine Patterson's *Koko's Kitten* (Scholastic, 1985).

6. Before reading Joyce Powzyk's *Wallaby Creek,* line one portion of a classroom wall with paper. Indicate to the students that this will become a mural of life at Wallaby Creek. After the book is read aloud, have the students divide into teams to reread and research in the library media center selected animals from the book. Members of each team may then draw or paint the animals described and illustrated in Powzyk's book. Work with the teams to see what comparisons they can make between the animals in *Wallaby Creek* and those in *Wild Voices.* Allow the children to mimic the wild voices of the animals they depict. As a class follow-up play a kangaroo relay game. Use regular relay instructions with the addition that students must place a ball between their knees during the relay. The children must jump the desired distance without dropping the ball. If the ball falls, that member of the relay must start over. As a further follow-up ask the music teacher to teach the children an Australian folksong such as the "Kookaburra" round (*Silver Burdett Centennial Songbook*, Silver Burdett, 1985, p. 38).

Follow-Up Activities for Individual Students:

1. Read Ruth Ashby's *Tigers.* Select a description to illustrate. Imagine the actual animal and mimic the sounds it might make in the scene. For example, on page 20 the forest is filled "with the shrieks and calls of peacocks, mynahs, and parakeets welcoming a new day. . . . The tigress gives a huge yawn and grunts at her cubs to follow." After drawing the scene ask two or three friends to help you imitate the noise that would accompany the picture.

2. Select one chapter of *Tigers* to read in detail and report on to the class. Use clay to make a model of a tiger. Use this model as a visual aid when giving your report.

3. After sharing *Tiger with Wings: The Great Horned Owl* in class, measure a string or strip of paper to represent the wing span of the great horned owl (50 inches). Use this visual aid to compare the arm span of fellow students to the wing span of the owl. A comparison can also be made to other birds' wing spans. Research in the media center to find at least two birds with larger spans and two with smaller spans.

4. After hearing Tom Horton's *Snowfall: Journey of the Tundra Swans* in class, read Hans Christian Andersen's *The Ugly Duckling* (Macmillan, 1987, or Putnam, 1990). Write a paragraph about the characteristics of the swan that appealed to Andersen.

5. After sharing *Snowfall* by Tom Horton in class, read Jennifer O. Dewey's *Birds of Antarctica: The Wandering Albatross* (Little, 1989). Compare the two birds on a chart by showing the seasonal life cycle of each.

6. After sharing Herman Melville's perspective on eagles and Thomas Locker's magnificent paintings in *Catskill Eagle,* research the eagle's habitat and cries. Share your information in an oral report that might close with an imitation of the eagle's cry. If available, refer to Helen Roney Sattler's *The Book of Eagles* (Lothrop, 1989) in your research.

7. After hearing *Wild Voices* by Drew Nelson, read it independently, noting carefully how descriptive words are used, for example, *rumbling, twitched, shrieked.* Create an original story based on an animal, being sure to use descriptive, colorful language as the author did.

8. After reading Joyce Powzyk's *Wallaby Creek,* research facts about the Australian platypus. Write a paragraph discussing the life-style of this strange egg-laying mammal. Speculate on how it has managed to survive the great passages of time.

9. After sharing *Wallaby Creek* by Joyce Powzyk, use encyclopedias to research marsupials. Tell what a marsupial is and how these creatures are unique. List and illustrate at least three marsupials.

10. Read John Schoenherr's *Bear.* Write a paragraph describing how the bear might have felt about being abandoned by his mother or about his feelings of hunger. Follow this description with a factual report on the habitat of bears. Ask for permission to demonstrate the various moans and growls the bear uses to communicate, as you imagine them to sound.

Closure:

Throughout this unit students have had the opportunity to learn how and when animals communicate. There are many other animals that the children may already know communicate, such as crickets, local birds, dogs, and cats. Complete the unit by playing a game called "Sounds in the Night" from Bob Gregson's *The Incredible Indoor Games Book* (Pitman Learning, 1982). Have the students sit in a circle. With eyes closed or the room darkened, each player selects in his or her mind an animal sound to mimic. Give a small sponge ball to the first person who will be "It." This person makes his or her call, followed by the sound of the animal to whom he or she wants to roll the ball. The animal who is called replies with the animal sound, while the first player listens carefully to hear where to aim the ball. If the intended player catches the ball, he or she responds loudly. All of the other "animals" rejoice in unison, calling loudly. If the intended player does not catch the ball, the ball is returned to "It," who must try again.

Story Elements in the Books of Eth Clifford

Objectives:

1. Predict an outcome or conclusion.
2. Identify the elements of a story.
3. Summarize a story.
4. Recognize and arrange items or events in sequential order.
5. Use the five "W's" to write a newspaper article.
6. Create and use descriptive words.
7. Relate to a story through art, creative writing, dramatics, or demonstrations.
8. Recognize point of view in a story.
9. Identify feelings expressed by book characters.

Recommended Readings:

Clifford, Eth. *Flatfoot Fox and the Case of the Missing Eye*. Illustrated by Brian Lies. Houghton Mifflin, 1990.
Flatfoot Fox, the self-proclaimed "world's smartest detective," cleverly solves the case of Fat Cat's stolen eye. (Objectives 2, 4, and 7)

————. *Harvey's Horrible Snake Disaster*. Houghton Mifflin, 1984.
Cousin Nora's curiosity leads to one adventure after another for Harvey. (Objectives 1, 2, 4, 7, and 9)

————. *Harvey's Marvelous Monkey Mystery*. Houghton Mifflin, 1987.
Harvey and cousin Nora come to know each other better while unraveling a mystery. (Objectives 5, 6, and 7)

————. *Harvey's Wacky Parrot Adventure*. Houghton Mifflin, 1990.
Mysterious happenings, hidden treasures, and a parrot named Sinbad lead Harvey and his cousin Nora on an exciting adventure. (Objective 7)

————. *Help! I'm a Prisoner in the Library*. Illustrated by George Hughes. Houghton Mifflin, 1979.
A blizzard forces two young girls to spend the night in a special library. (Objectives 2 and 7)

————. *I Hate Your Guts, Ben Brooster*. Houghton Mifflin, 1989.
When cousin Ben arrives from Japan, a mystery unfolds that helps the cousins become friends. (Objectives 1, 2, and 4)

————. *I Never Wanted to Be Famous*. Houghton Mifflin, 1986.
Goody Tribble has fame thrust upon him by friends and family after he saves an infant from choking. (Objectives 3, 7, and 8)

————. *Just Tell Me When We're Dead!* Illustrated by George Hughes. Houghton Mifflin, 1983.
Two young sisters find adventure when they set out to find their cousin in a supposedly deserted amusement park. (Objectives 7 and 9)

————. *The Man Who Sang in the Dark.* Illustrated by Mary Beth Owens. Houghton Mifflin, 1987.
Young Leah, her mother, and brother must find the courage to make a new life for themselves after the death of Leah's father. (Objectives 2 and 4)

————. *The Summer of the Dancing Horse.* Illustrated by Mary Beth Owens. Houghton Mifflin, 1991.
Bessie will always remember the summer when she danced with the golden palomino, Pegasus. (Objectives 2 and 9)

Biographical Sources:

For information on Eth Clifford see *Something about the Author*, vol. 3, pages 176–77 and *Sixth Book of Junior Authors & Illustrators*, pages 57–59.

Group Introductory Activity:

In the book *I Hate Your Guts, Ben Brooster*, the Andrews's family bookstore always displayed the sign "Your stomach is full now. How about some food for thought? READ A BOOK!" (p. 3). Eth Clifford has said that as a child, teenager, and adult she was "always a reader" (*Sixth Book of Junior Authors & Illustrators*, p. 58). It was reading that gave her the background to be a writer. Let the children select a book theme or slogan that could represent the desire to read to which Eth Clifford refers. With the help of the students design a bulletin board representing this theme or slogan.

Develop a four-column matrix to graph each title by Eth Clifford. On the left side of a poster board number 0 to 9, leaving a blank space beside each number for a book title. Across the top make four columns using these words:*characters*, *setting*, *problems*, and *solutions*. Laminate this matrix for future use. Using an overhead transparency marker write down each book that will be read in this unit. Post the chart on the Eth Clifford bulletin board. As each book is read by the group or individual students, ask the students to fill out the chart, which will be used in the closure activity for this unit.

Read aloud Eth Clifford's *I Hate Your Guts, Ben Brooster*. Let the students discuss the feelings of the characters as the story is read. On page 99 Mr. Andrews removes a plastic fish and a red herring from the buried treasure. One of the characters, Tom, explains that a red herring is a false clue. Stop reading on page 101 and ask the students to recall the clues and predict where the treasure is. Finish the story and compare the solution to the children's predictions. Refer to the matrix and have the students recall the main characters, setting, and the correct sequence of problems and solutions. List these on the chart. Explain that this activity will occur with each book read.

Follow-Up Activities for Teacher and Students to Share:

1. After sharing *Flatfoot Fox and the Case of the Missing Eye* by Eth Clifford, ask the children to recall the events used for the matrix and to name the additional elements of a mystery not found on the matrix. Children should include a crime or puzzle, suspects, and clues. Identify the specifics of each element in this story. List them on a chart labeled "Puzzle (or crime), suspects, and clues." Discuss these elements and why each is important to the story. If desired, let the children write or dictate original mystery stories using the four elements of a mystery. Students can use Flatfoot Fox or create new characters.

2. Read aloud in a book discussion group or whole class setting the first two chapters of Eth Clifford's *Harvey's Horrible Snake Disaster*. Ask the students to write out their predictions for the story. Remind them to include the two main characters, the ensuing problem or problems, and possible solutions. Seal the predictions in envelopes. After the group or class has finished the book, open the envelope. Read the predictions aloud and let students compare their predictions to the book's outcome. Discuss the problems Nora and Harvey encountered in learning simply how to get along. Ask the children to tell about disagreements and problems they have experienced with cousins or brothers and sisters. Refer to the matrix and have students identify the elements of the story.

3. Share aloud chapter 1 of Eth Clifford's *Harvey's Marvelous Monkey Mystery* (pp. 1–5). Use this chapter as a starting point for creative writing. The sentence on page 5, "I'm dreaming all right . . . but I never had a nightmare with sound before," is an excellent lead sentence for creative writing. Write this sentence on the chalkboard and have the students complete a paragraph or page using the dream line as the first sentence. As the book is read aloud, have the students listen for other lines that could be used for extended writing activities.

4. After reading *I Never Wanted to Be Famous* by Eth Clifford, plan with the school nurse or physical education teacher to present a lesson on basic first aid. Be sure to include instructions on the Heimlich maneuver, a better treatment for a blocked airway than the method Goody used. Tell the students that hitting someone on the back may cause the obstruction to become more firmly lodged while the Heimlich maneuver will force the object out of the passageway. Children may be organized in pairs to take turns practicing the maneuver. Encourage students to write personal reactions to this activity in their literature logs.

As a further extension of the book ask the children to summarize the story by explaining what the following sentence from page 129 tells about the story: "Being a page . . . it was a goal I could choose for myself."

5. After sharing aloud Eth Clifford's *The Man Who Sang in the Dark,* arrange for the music teacher to teach the class "The Little White Duck" (*The Reader's Digest Children's Songbook*, p. 92), the song that Gideon Brown sang. Explain to the class that the song depicts a series of events that should be viewed in order. Discuss the importance of arranging items or events in proper sequence. Have the children recall the main events in the story. List the elements on the chalkboard as students recall them. Let the children arrange the listed events in proper sequence. As a follow-up cut newspaper comics into individual frames that students may use to practice sequential order skills.

6. While reading aloud *The Summer of the Dancing Horse* by Eth Clifford, let children look up the meaning of the names of the two horses in the story. Have the students speculate on what their names might symbolize. Send a group of children to research tuberculosis, Pa's illness, in the library media center. Assign the students to discover why, in 1923, people with tuberculosis were placed in a sanatorium. Tell the group to contrast that practice with modern treatment methods.

   Bessie and Ben had several run-ins with the Keefer boys. Let the class discuss possible choices children can make when they are being bullied or teased. Ask the group to evaluate the ways Bessie, Sam, and Ben changed during the course of the story. Call on students to complete the matrix on this book.

Follow-Up Activities for Individual Students:

1. After hearing Eth Clifford's *Harvey's Horrible Snake Disaster* in class, role play a child who wants a snake for a pet. Based on information given in Clifford's book and other sources, act out a scene in which a child tries to convince his or her parents that a snake would make a great pet. Ask a friend to play the part of a parent who doesn't want a snake in the house.

2. While reading *Harvey's Marvelous Monkey Mystery,* make a list of the made-up combination words Harvey used, for example, *splendific* (splendid, terrific), *gi-mendous* (gigantic, tremendous), and *awfibble* (awful, horrible). Using a few of Harvey's made-up words or other invented words, write a newspaper article describing the capture of crocodile man and the importance of the monkey. Be sure to include "who, what, where, when, and why." Follow up by organizing an "Invented Word" contest for the class. Each invented word entry must have the student's name attached and must include a definition and be used in a sentence. Ask the library media specialist to judge the contest.

3. After reading Eth Clifford's *Harvey's Wacky Parrot Adventure,* design a shadow box that is a replica of Captain Corbin's room, his wardrobe, and the secret room. Briefly research the Underground Railroad to find out what its purpose was. Present the shadow box to the class with a brief explanation of how the hidden room was used to hide slaves in the 1850s.

4. Read the first book about Mary Rose and Jo Beth, which was *Help! I'm a Prisoner in the Library* by Eth Clifford. Write a paragraph identifying the events that make this a mystery. Then select 10 descriptive words from the book. Use these words to write a mystery or adventure story about the library.

5. After hearing *I Never Wanted to Be Famous* by Eth Clifford, write a diary entry from Goody's or his sister's point of view for each of the times he was proclaimed a hero (e.g., after saving the baby from choking, after catching Linda as she fell off the ladder, after rescuing an abused gorilla from a circus and having him transferred to the Indianapolis Zoo).

6. After reading Eth Clifford's *Just Tell Me When We're Dead!* in class, use several of these selected words to write an adventure or a mystery story: "zoomed, doomed, amusement, accusing, shuddered, dreadful, slashing, flickering, poisonous, bulging, raging, emergency, collision, cautiously, clutched." Be sure to include the necessary elements of a story (see the matrix for help).

7. After hearing Eth Clifford's *The Man Who Sang in the Dark,* ask the music teacher to help locate some instrumental music that depicts a mood, such as mysterious, lively, or lonely. Listen to the music as Leah might have while you write lines of poetry. Share the music and poetry with the class and explain how the music and poetry helped Leah and Gideon Brown in the book.

Closure:

Refer to the completed matrix of Eth Clifford's books. Briefly review the different titles and what the stories had in common. Individuals or small groups of students may use the matrix to write a short story. Let the children examine the four columns. Assign each child or group to write down the last four digits of a phone number. These digits will determine the characters, setting, problem, and solution. If the digits are 3508 then the characters in the story to be written must be selected from those in the third book in the matrix, the setting must be taken from the fifth book, the problem must come from the tenth book (0), and the solution from the eighth book. When the students have established these four basic elements let individuals or groups write a creative story.

Chapter 5
Fourth Grade/Fifth Grade

Funnybones

Objectives:

1. Recognize various subjects with which fiction books deal.
2. Make inferences and draw conclusions.
3. Increase vocabulary.
4. Respond to a story through creative dramatics, art, and writing.
5. Identify sequential order of events in the plot.
6. Retell a story event from a different point of view.
7. Cite the value of a sense of humor.
8. Write humorous poetry.
9. Identify puns, limericks, and/or devices of sound in poetry and fiction.
10. Recognize theme in a story.

Recommended Readings:

Byars, Betsy. *The Not-Just-Anybody Family*. Illustrated by Jacqueline Rogers. Delacorte, 1986.
   Through thick and thin the Blossom family knows how to stick together. (Objectives 1, 5, 6, and 7)

Giff, Patricia Reilly. *Fourth Grade Celebrity*. Illustrated by Leslie Morrill. Delacorte, 1979.
   Casey's creativity leads to a successful school project. (Objectives 2 and 4)

Hall, Lynn. *In Trouble Again, Zelda Hammersmith?* Harcourt Brace Jovanovich, 1987.
   Zelda's exploits create both trouble and laughter. (Objectives 2, 4, and 7)

Kline, Suzy. *ORP*. G.P. Putnam's Sons, 1989.
   Orville Rudemeyer Pygenski, Jr. discovers he is not the only one who hates his name. (Objectives 2, 9, and 10)

Lowry, Lois. *Your Move, J.P.!* Houghton Mifflin, 1990.
A brief encounter with love changes J.P.'s normally organized and goal-oriented life. (Objectives 3, 4, and 7)

Manes, Stephen. *Be a Perfect Person in Just Three Days!* Illustrated by Tom Huffman. Clarion, 1982.
Milo learns in just three days what it means to be perfect. (Objectives 2, 7, and 10)

————. *Make Four Million Dollars by Next Thursday.* Illustrated by George Ulrich. Bantam, 1991.
Jason experiences several amusing events in his quest to be a millionaire. (Objectives 2, 4, and 7)

Park, Barbara. *The Kid in the Red Jacket.* Alfred A. Knopf, 1987.
Moving and meeting new friends create some humorous moments for 10-year-old Howard Jeeter. (Objectives 1, 2, 3, and 4)

Prelutsky, Jack, ed. *For Laughing Out Loud: Poems to Tickle Your Funnybone.* Illustrated by Marjorie Priceman. Alfred A. Knopf, 1991.
A collection of silly to outrageously funny rhymes is presented. (Objectives 1, 8, and 9)

Scieszka, Jon. *The Not-So-Jolly Roger.* Illustrated by Lane Smith. Viking, 1991.
A mysterious book draws three boys through a wild and funny time warp. (Objective 4)

Group Introductory Activity:

Make a classroom subject card catalog using the Funnybones unit as a basis. Each book in this unit deals with the subject "humor" and several others such as "moving," "friendship," and "feelings," as in Barbara Park's *The Kid in the Red Jacket.* As students read these books and others, have them fill out a 3" × 5" index card for each subject they think the book covers. The library media specialist can demonstrate on a transparency how to write the subject in bold print across the top of the card. In the upper left-hand corner print the call number. The line immediately to the right of the call number is for the author's name (last name first, then first name). On the line below the author's last name indent three spaces and write the title. Follow with the publisher and the copyright date. On the card have the students write a one- to two-sentence description of the story. If a book has other subjects, remind the students to fill out a card for each subject. Keep these cards and add to them so the students will begin to recognize the various subjects that are featured in fiction books. Have them organize the cards alphabetically by subject heading.

While reading *The Kid in the Red Jacket* aloud, let the students collect a list of unfamiliar words from the text for a spelling or word study unit. The following 10 words can serve as a basis: *humiliating, embarrassed, ignore, cafeteria, personalities, frustration, obnoxious, reputation, instinctively,* and *invisible*. Have the children use the dictionary to define the selected words and use them in complete sentences. Let them discuss how these words describe incidents in the story and in real life. Discuss with the students the various subjects with which the story deals. Ask them to draw conclusions about real life versus fiction based on the experiences of Howard Jeeter.

Follow-Up Activities for Teacher and Students to Share:

1. *The Not-Just-Anybody Family* by Betsy Byars is sometimes described as a comedy of errors. Read the story aloud to help the students identify the order of events in the plot. After reading page 88 stop so the children can discuss the series of events that left Maggie alone on the street. Identify the incident that initiated the series of events in the story. As the events unfold, ask the students to identify the rising action and the climax. After finishing the book, ask them to discuss the events or qualities that make the Blossoms the "Not-Just-Anybody" family. Discuss the various subject cards the students will make for this story.

   Offer the students two ways to help recognize the order of events. Students may make a chart with each character's name across the top and, in the columns underneath, write the events that occur to each character in sequential order. Or they can draw a map of events starting with Pap's beer can adventure. The scenes could then be illustrated as the lines connect the order of humorous events. After the climactic courtroom scene ask the children to identify the events that make up the falling action and resolution of the story.

2. To get the class involved with the hilarious episodes of Zelda Hammersmith, read aloud chapter 2, "Zelda and the Awful F" (pp. 31–61) from Lynn Hall's *In Trouble Again, Zelda Hammersmith?* Offer the students a chance to tell a report card story that is funnier than Zelda's. Students may be able to share events in their own lives that might have backfired as Zelda's did. Discuss how a sense of humor helps in real-life situations. Invite individuals or small groups to finish reading Zelda's story.

3. The central idea of a story is called its theme. Theme can be explicit or implied. Explain to the group that explicit themes are stated clearly in the story while implied themes must be deduced from the reading. After reading *ORP* by Suzy Kline, have students respond to the explicit statement "We are what we are. If we change our names we're still the same people" (p. 91). Ask the children to discuss how that thought holds true for ORP. Encourage the children to think about and discuss possible implied themes in the story.

4. Read aloud Lois Lowry's *Your Move, J.P.!* to the class. Initiate an ongoing chess match in the classroom while reading about J.P. After reading to page 51, ask the students to discuss and predict the problems J.P. has created for

himself. Divide the class into teams to play the A–Z game Ralph and J.P. played. Use themes such as foods, song titles, or attributes. Remind the students to consider the various subject headings found in this book.

Your Move, J.P.! can also be used as a group book discussion. Read aloud the humorous description on pages 26–28 to help the students develop empathy with J.P. and to hear and visualize the descriptive language Lowry uses. Ask the group to now keep an index card clipped to the pages of the book. On this card the group members should write down at least five of the descriptive lines read in the book (e.g., "thick, gleaming ponytail"; "gazing rapturously"; or "fearlessly maneuvered"). When the book has been read, these descriptive lines can be used to expand vocabulary, to create a spelling list, or to develop a word list for creative writing.

5. Use the book *Be a Perfect Person in Just Three Days!* by Stephen Manes as a small group read-aloud activity. At the end of chapter 1 ask the students to comment on Milo's concept of perfection. Have the group members use the dictionary to define *perfect*. After chapter 2 ask the students to imagine and describe what it would be like to be a perfect person. Let the group compile a list of qualities or circumstances that the children think embody perfection. Have the students analyze how Dr. Silverfish demonstrates his sense of humor in the story. At the end of chapter 3 have the children discuss and compare Milo's feelings and experiences to those of the group members. In chapter 4 Dr. Silverfish says that courage is a quality of being perfect. Have the children brainstorm ways that courage is a virtue and name times in real life when students may need to conquer fear. Let the children predict what other qualities Dr. Silverfish would expect in perfect people and what the theme of the book is. After chapter 5 discuss the value of willpower. Imagine and then experience doing nothing for 10 minutes. Allow the group to compare their reactions to Milo's. After finishing the book have the children describe the change of attitude Milo experienced. Ask the students to discuss the qualities to look for in "good people," to share conclusions that can be reached about being a perfect person, and to decide what theme is evident (being sure to tell whether it is explicit or implied). As a follow-up the group could wear broccoli necklaces to class and present a brief skit based on the story.

6. The English language can be quite humorous through puns, limericks, and sound devices. Read aloud the following poems from the book *For Laughing Out Loud: Poems to Tickle Your Funnybone*: "An Old Man from Peru" (p. 9); "Friendly Frederick Fuddlestone" (p. 23); "Misnomer" (p. 32); "The Dinosore" (p. 57); ""Raising Frogs for Profit" (p. 70); and "A Big Bare Bear" (p. 77). Ask students to discuss how language adds to the humor of the poems. Let the students illustrate their favorite of the poems.

7. Use various poems in Jack Prelutsky's collection *For Laughing Out Loud: Poems to Tickle Your Funnybone* as a basis for art, creative dramatics, and memory work. "Be Glad Your Nose Is on Your Face" (page 8) can serve as a basis for writing humorous poetry. Using the line "What if..." or "Imagine if..." list the bizarre possibilities the students can name. Let the class write a poem using these ideas.

Follow-Up Activities for Individual Students:

1. After hearing *The Not-Just-Anybody Family by* Betsy Byars in class, visit the library media center. Use the card or computer catalog to locate other stories about the Blossoms. Choose and read one of the books. Then identify the sequence of unique events that make up the rising action, climax, falling action, and resolution in the story.
2. After sharing Betsy Byars's *The Not-Just-Anybody Family* in class, retell a particular event from the point of view of the character involved. For example, what is Junior's version of flying from the barn or Vern's interpretation of breaking into jail? Be sure to write or tell the event in first person.
3. Read *Fourth Grade Celebrity* by Patricia Reilly Giff. Then design a campaign poster that Casey might have made for the school election. Explain how the campaign and election affected the events in the story.
4. In Patricia Reilly Giff's *Fourth Grade Celebrity,* Casey Valentine wrote an imaginative story for the school newspaper. After reading about Casey, write a brief, original story in first person.
5. Read Lynn Hall's *In Trouble Again, Zelda Hammersmith?* Then pretend to be Zelda in one of the five episodes and tell the story to the class.
6. After reading *In Trouble Again, Zelda Hammersmith?* by Lynn Hall, explain how Zelda's mom's wisdom, usually shared in proverbs, created problems for Zelda.
7. After hearing Suzy Kline's *ORP* in class, write a paragraph describing how it might feel to have a name such as Sally Mander or Seymour Clear. Speculate about why parents would give their children names that are puns. Imagine several other examples of puns and names besides the ones listed in the book. List these humorous names.
8. Read *Make Four Million Dollars by Next Thursday* by Stephen Manes. Design a pop-up book, like the glove idea, to get the attention of the class. Include the following in the pop-up book report:

   What did having four million dollars mean to Jason?
   What would it mean to you?
   Cite two examples of humorous word play in the story.
   Explain the steps to becoming a millionaire and why they are necessary.
   What did Jason learn about money?

Refer to Joan Irvine's *How to Make Pop-Ups* (Beech Tree, 1987) in order to construct the pop-up book report.

9. After reading Stephen Manes's *Make Four Million Dollars by Next Thursday,* describe the character Jason and the food he eats. What conclusions can be made about how life is affected by wealth?

10. Read the following poems from *For Laughing Out Loud: Poems to Tickle Your Funnybone*, edited by Jack Prelutsky: "The Alien," p. 16; "Me," p. 31; "Hughbert and the Glue," p. 36; "Mechanical Menagerie," p. 48; and "Help," p. 54. Let these humorous creatures serve as a basis for a junk art model. Use scraps and junk to build or create individual perceptions of what the poems describe.

11. In the book *The Not-So-Jolly Roger* by Jon Scieszka, Joe's uncle tells the boys to "be careful what you wish for. You might get it" (p. 7). Tell or write about a real or imagined time when you wished for something and got it. Rewrite a Mother Goose rhyme to use a magic spell in the story.

12. After reading Jon Scieszka's *The Not-So-Jolly Roger,* illustrate a scene or the description of Blackbeard from the book. Report to the class what action occurred in the story that the picture represents.

13. After reading Jon Scieszka's *The Not-So-Jolly Roger,* locate a book in the library media center on magic tricks. Practice and then present a magic show for the class as Joe might have done. Explain how this activity relates to the book.

Closure:

Ask the children to alphabetically arrange the subject cards that have been made for the books in this unit. Let the students discuss how these subjects relate to the theme of each book. Appoint a committee to plan a "Funnybones Party" or "Spring Fling" similar to the one held in Lois Lowry's *Your Move, J.P.!*

Patricia MacLachlan's Memories and Models

Objectives:

1. Identify with a book character.
2. Recognize the significance of the Newbery Award.
3. Create a glossary.
4. Respond to literature through the arts.
5. Use the writing process to create an original story or book review.

6. Draw conclusions and deductions based upon reading.
7. Use photographs to document experiences.
8. Compare and contrast two versions of or approaches to a subject.

Recommended Readings:

MacLachlan, Patricia. *Arthur for the Very First Time*. Illustrated by Lloyd Bloom. HarperCollins, 1980.
Arthur learns many things about life when he spends the summer on the farm with eccentric Uncle Wrisby, Aunt Elda, and their pet chicken Pauline. (Objectives 1, 3, 4, and 6)

———. *Cassie Binegar*. Harper & Row, 1982.
Cassie, who resists change, longs for a space of her own and a life that always stays the same. (Objective 4)

———. *The Facts and Fictions of Minna Pratt*. Harper & Row, 1988.
Minna, a young cellist, learns to appreciate her eccentric family when she sees them through the eyes of a new friend. (Objectives 3 and 5)

———. *Journey*. Illustrated by Barry Moser. Delacorte, 1991.
Young Journey and his older sister, abandoned by their mother, feel isolated and alone until Grandfather finds the tool to restore their sense of family. (Objectives 6, 7, and 8)

———. *Mama One, Mama Two*. Illustrated by Ruth Lercher Bornstein. Harper & Row, 1982.
Young Maudie helps Katherine tell how she came to stay with a foster family until her mother recovers from depression. (Objectives 4 and 6)

———. *Sarah, Plain and Tall*. Illustrated by Marcia Sewall. Harper & Row, 1985.
Sarah rapidly wins the hearts of Caleb and Anna when she comes to the prairie from the Maine seacoast to consider marrying Papa, a widower. (Objectives 1, 2, 4, 5, and 8)

———. *Seven Kisses in a Row*. Illustrated by Maria Pia Marrella. Harper & Row, 1983.
Young Emma learns to accept differences when her aunt and uncle care for her and her brother while their parents are away. (Objective 4)

———. *Three Names*. Illustrated by Alexander Pertzoff. HarperCollins, 1991.
The child narrator recalls Great-grandfather's stories of attending a one-room prairie school with his dog Three Names. (Objectives 1 and 8)

———. *Through Grandpa's Eyes*. Illustrated by Deborah Ray. Harper & Row, 1979.
A young boy sees the world differently when looking through blind Grandpa's eyes. (Objectives 1 and 4)

————. *Tomorrow's Wizard*. Illustrated by Kathy Jacobi. Harper & Row, 1982.

Tomorrow, who only wants to be a master wizard, finds the patience to teach his apprentice, Murdock, about being a wizard. (Objective 6)

Biographical Sources:

For information on Patricia MacLachlan see *Something about the Author*, vol. 62, pages 115–22 and *Sixth Book of Junior Authors & Illustrators*, pages 183–84.

Group Introductory Activity:

Family, reading, and music have always been important parts of author Patricia MacLachlan's life, as evidenced by her books. She still remembers her parents inviting her into books. "We read them, discussed them, reread them, and acted out the parts. I can still feel the goose bumps as I, in the fur of Peter Rabbit, fled from the garden and Mr. McGregor—played with great ferocity by my father" (*Sixth Book of Junior Authors & Illustrators*, p. 183). Music lessons also played a large role in her childhood. MacLachlan began with the piano and later studied cello. That love for music appears repeatedly in her work. She says, ". . . I write books about brothers and sisters, about what makes up a family, what works and what is nurturing" (*Sixth Book of Junior Authors & Illustrators*, p. 183). Like most writers she freely admits that her own life inspires her work.

In *Through Grandpa's Eyes* the author tells of a very special relationship between a boy and his grandfather. Display a chart labeled with each of the five senses. Tell the children that this book is filled with sensory images. Ask the students to listen carefully as the book is read aloud to find descriptive passages about each of the senses. Share the book with the group. Let the children recall the images and experiences the author described. List each image on the chart under the appropriate sense.

In this story MacLachlan describes how visually impaired people eat. As a follow-up have the students draw Grandpa's breakfast on the plate using the clock-face directions to place each food correctly. As a further extension let the children take turns wearing a blindfold and trying to select a named object from a table by following clock directions that indicate where it is located.

Follow-Up Activities for Teacher and Students to Share:

1. Uncle Wrisby, Aunt Elda, and Arthur speak French to Pauline, their pet chicken in *Arthur for the Very First Time*. As Patricia MacLachlan's book is read aloud, have the students keep a log of foreign and unfamiliar words and phrases (e.g., *comment vas-tu, bonjour, viens, staccato,* and *scatty*).

Teach the children how to make a glossary by writing each word on an index card. Then, after each day's sharing of the book, have the children use a foreign language dictionary and other reference books to define the words. Children should carefully write the definition on each card. Work in a large group to write sentences using each word and let selected students add the sentence to the card, after the definition. Have the students place the cards in alphabetical order in a file box labeled "Patricia MacLachlan Glossary."

Tell the children that Patricia MacLachlan has said "Aunt Elda and Uncle Wrisby in *Arthur for the Very First Time* are my mother and father" (*Sixth Book of Junior Authors & Illustrators*, p. 183). After reading the book aloud, let the children discuss why Arthur started to burn the recorder he wanted so much. At Aunt Elda's suggestion he threw it out the window into a flower bed instead. Ask the students why they think the old woman suggested that alternative. Let the children speculate on whether or not Arthur left the recorder there or later retrieved it. As a follow-up ask the music teacher to demonstrate the recorder to the class. If recorders are available at the school, have the children learn to play simple tunes and the C major scale on that instrument.

2. After reading *Journey* by Patricia MacLachlan, let the children discuss how photography affected Journey's relationship with his grandfather and how photographs form a link with the past. Ask the children to bring favorite photographs from home to create a display. Have students use a camera to document a field trip or a day in the classroom.

3. Tell the students that Patricia MacLachlan once served on the board of a family service agency doing publicity work and interviewing foster mothers. She says, "*Mama One, Mama Two* comes from my experiences with foster mothers and the children they cared for" (*Something about the Author,* vol. 62, p. 118). Read the story aloud. Then ask the children at what point in the book they realized Maudie and Katherine were telling their own story. Let the students share clues from the text and illustrations that helped them reach that conclusion.

4. Before sharing *Sarah, Plain and Tall* by Patricia MacLachlan, ask the children to recall the significance of the John Newbery Medal. If students do not recognize this prestigious award, explain that it is given annually to the author of the most outstanding book for children published in the preceding year. The author must be an American citizen or resident. Tell the children that Patricia MacLachlan received the Newbery Award for *Sarah, Plain and Tall* in 1986.

Remind the children that Patricia MacLachlan has said her stories come from her family experiences. *Sarah, Plain and Tall* was inspired by an incident in her family history (*Sixth Book of Junior Authors & Illustrators*, p. 184). Read the story aloud, then let the children identify the feelings and emotions Caleb and Anna had toward Sarah. Ask the students to use the writing process to create a story about what might have happened to the family after *Sarah, Plain and Tall* ended. Begin the process as a group by brainstorming possible story situations. After a substantial list has been generated, let the children work individually to write, edit, and rewrite their stories. Share with the children that Patricia MacLachlan uses this same process in her writing. She has said, "I feel it is crucial that kids who aspire to write understand that I have to rewrite and revise as they do" (*Something about the Author*, vol. 62, p. 121). Compile the finished works in a booklet titled *Beyond Sarah, Plain and Tall*.

Follow-Up Activities for Individual Students:

1. In *Arthur for the Very First Time* Patricia MacLachlan includes a brief account of Aunt Mag, a mail-order bride. Arthur's Aunt Elda recalls Mag using a prism to cast rainbows around the room as she said, "You won't remember your mother. . .but you will learn that her life touches yours. All of us touch each other. Just like the colors of a prism" (p. 94). Patricia MacLachlan's mother had told her the story of a distant relative who had come to the prairie as a mail-order bride long ago. When she read *Arthur for the Very First Time,* she was surprised and delighted that Patricia had remembered the prism the woman had brought with her to the barren plains. The author recalls her amazement because she had believed she invented that part of the story. "Then I realized that this is the magic. When you write you reach back somewhere in your mind or your heart and pull out things that you never even knew were there" (*Something about the Author*, vol. 62, p. 118).

   MacLachlan's comment about writing parallels the action of a prism that pulls colors from light "that you never even knew were there." Use a prism to create a rainbow of colors in the room. Think about Mag's statement about lives touching others as you look at the colors. Write a paragraph telling what the statement means to you. If you were to draw a comparison between relationships and another thing, what object would you choose and why?

2. Read Patricia MacLachlan's *Cassie Binegar.* Cassie did not want life to change. Gran, however, compared life's "perfect moments" to catching snow. Cassie's best friend, Margaret Mary, likened life to a kaleidoscope pattern, always shifting and changing but always beautiful (pp. 42–43). As an extension of this book follow the directions on pages 64–67 or pages 68–69 of *The Kaleidoscope Book: A Spectrum of Spectacular Scopes to Make* (edited by Thom Boswell; Sterling, 1992) to create a simple kaleidoscope. Share your construction with the class and explain the relationship Cassie's friend saw between the kaleidoscope and life.

3. In Patricia MacLachlan's *Cassie Binegar* the protagonist's eccentric family is very arts oriented. Cassie is a poet, Gran paints, Cassie's mother plays the flute, and the whole family sings. After reading the book, choose which family member's talent appeals most to you. As a follow-up either write a poem about your "space," create an original painting, play a song for the class on an instrument, or teach the group to sing "Dona Nobis Pacem." Share with the class how your activity relates to the book and why you selected it.

4. Read *The Facts and Fictions of Minna Pratt* by Patricia MacLachlan. While reading keep a response journal in which to record your thoughts and reactions to the story. This book is filled with musical terms and other words that you may know. Record these in your journal and prepare glossary entries for the story. Write each term, its definition, and a sentence using it on an index card. Add the cards, in alphabetical order, to the "Patricia MacLachlan Glossary" begun in class so other students may use it as a reference while reading Minna's story.

5. Write a book review of *The Facts and Fictions of Minna Pratt*. Tell what audience you believe would enjoy the book and why. Locate a recording of a Mozart string quartet, such as "Quartets for Strings and Quartetto Italiano" (*The Complete Mozart*, vol. 12, Philips, 422512-1), which contains the piece Minna and her friends played in the competition. Play an excerpt of the music for the class as you share your book review.

6. After hearing Patricia MacLachlan's *Journey,* read Milton Meltzer's *Dorothea Lange: Life through the Camera* (Viking, 1985). Compare and contrast Lange's approach to photography as a way to document social issues and the feelings Journey and his grandfather share about that art.

7. In Patricia MacLachlan's *Mama One, Mama Two* sunsets and yellow birds were joyous scenes Mama One painted and shared with Maudie. Reread the story. Respond to the feelings expressed in the book by using colored pencils and drawing pens to create a scene representing joy to you.

8. After reading both *Sarah, Plain and Tall* and *Arthur for the Very First Time* by Patricia MacLachlan, compare and contrast Sarah with the brief reference to Aunt Mag on pages 92–95 of *Arthur for the Very First Time.*

9. In Patricia MacLachlan's *Sarah, Plain and Tall* Sarah draws charcoal pictures to send to her brother William. The book closes with Sarah bringing home a small package, implying that she will use the blue, gray, and green pencils in it to draw the sea she loved so well. Use colored pencils to create a scene that you would miss if you had to move away from your home. Along with the artwork, describe the character of Sarah and what you liked or did not like about her. Find a passage from the book to defend your statement of character.

10. Read Patricia MacLachlan's *Seven Kisses in a Row*. Select a scene from the book and rewrite it in comic strip form. Your comic strip should be six to eight frames long and should contain both a problem and a solution.
11. Read *Three Names* by Patricia MacLachlan. The book is filled with memories of family and friends in a one-room school on the prairie long ago. Compare Great-grandfather's family and school experiences to your own, compiling a list of at least 10 similarities and differences, including some of each. Beneath your list write a brief paragraph telling whether you prefer experiences of the past or those of today. Justify your answer.
12. After you have read Patricia MacLachlan's *Tomorrow's Wizard*, summarize each of the following episodes in three sentences: Rozelle's story, Three-D's experience, the comely lady, the perfect fiddle, and Murdock's story. Now tell what lesson you could learn from the experience of the book characters. Read the paragraph the author wrote and placed just before the first chapter. In your own words explain what you think Patricia MacLachlan was saying.

Closure:

Patricia MacLachlan has said that "books provide us with models, possibilities, inspiration, and courage" (*Something about the Author*, vol. 62, p. 120). Close the unit on MacLachlan's books by celebrating the possibilities, selecting models, and recognizing the potential of the children. Have each student choose one of Patricia MacLachlan's characters he or she admires. Give the students note cards on which to write and complete one of the following possibility statements: "I want to be like _____ because someday I hope to _____" or "I admire _____ because he or she _____." Let the children make book jackets for the book in which their chosen character appears. Attach the possibility statements to the book jackets and display them on a bulletin board labeled "Patricia MacLachlan: Memories and Models."

Legends and Lore of Earth and Sky

Objectives:

1. Understand how the science of ecology reflects the wisdom found in American Indian stories.
2. Read and compare cycles or patterns in life.
3. Recognize various Native American customs and traditions.
4. Analyze the diversity and commonality among cultures.

5. Develop models, reports, or demonstrations from information collected.
6. Participate in storytelling and other oral activities.
7. Discuss and understand the meaning of symbolism.
8. Respond to a story through an art form.

Recommended Readings:

Bierhorst, John. *The Woman Who Fell from the Sky: The Iroquois Story of Creation.* Illustrated by Robert Andrew Parker. William Morrow, 1993.
The sky woman creates the world in this retelling of the Native American myth. (Objectives 2, 4, and 8)

Bruchac, Joseph, and London, Jonathan. *Thirteen Moons on Turtle's Back.* Illustrated by Thomas Locker. Philomel, 1992.
Poems and a story serve as a reminder that all things are connected through cycles and seasons. (Objectives 2 and 8)

Dixon, Ann. *How Raven Brought Light to People.* Illustrated by James Watts. Macmillan, 1992.
Raven tricks the old chief in order to give the people the stars, moon, and sun. (Objectives 2 and 8)

Goble, Paul. *Buffalo Woman.* Bradbury, 1984.
The deep love and kinship American Indians feel for the buffalo are revealed in this tale. (Objectives 1, 5, and 8)

Highwater, Jamake. *Moonsong Lullaby.* Illustrated by Marcia Keegan. Lothrop, Lee & Shepard, 1981.
The activities of an Indian camp are observed through the night and the moon's cycle. (Objectives 2 and 4)

MacGill-Callahan, Sheila. *And Still the Turtle Watched.* Illustrated by Barry Moser. Dial, 1991.
The great stone turtle watched sadly as the white water turned brown, the stars dimmed, and a different man visited the land. (Objectives 1 and 5)

McDermott, Gerald. *Arrow to the Sun: A Pueblo Indian Tale.* Viking, 1974.
The spirit of the sun is brought to the earth through a young boy's search for his father. (Objectives 5 and 6)

Seattle, Chief. *Brother Eagle, Sister Sky: A Message from Chief Seattle.* Illustrated by Susan Jeffers. Dial, 1991.
Detailed pen-and-ink drawings enhance the emotional impact of this plea for protection of the land. (Objectives 1, 2, and 5)

Steptoe, John. *The Story of Jumping Mouse.* Lothrop, Lee & Shepard, 1984.
A young mouse is able to reach a far-off land because of his determination and unselfish nature. (Objectives 2 and 7)

Yellow Robe, Rosebud. *Tonweya and the Eagles and Other Lakota Tales.*
Illustrated by Jerry Pinkney. Dial, 1979.
The history and the stories of the Lakota people have been preserved in this
collection of animal tales. (Objectives 2, 3, 5, and 6)

Group Introductory Activity:

Create a bulletin board or other visual quoting these lines from *Brother
Eagle, Sister Sky: A Message from Chief Seattle*: "This we know: All things are
connected like the blood that unites us. We did not weave the web of life, we are
merely a strand in it. Whatever we do to the web, we do to ourselves." Let the
children discuss the meaning and the application of these thoughts to ecology and
the future of life on planet Earth. While *Brother Eagle, Sister Sky* is read aloud,
play a selection from Kevin Locke's *Dream Catcher* (Music for Little People,
2696) or another recording of Native American flute songs. Have the group
brainstorm a list of cycles such as food chains, weather, seasons, or life and death.
Ask the children to draw conclusions regarding the environment based on prior
knowledge and the text. As a unit project focusing on the earth and sky, divide
the students into teams. Let each team select a cycle in nature to study and report
on to the class. Besides a written or oral report, students should create a hands-
on demonstration, develop a model, or use an art form to further define their study.

Follow-Up Activities for Teacher and Students to Share:

1. Read aloud John Bierhorst's retelling of *The Woman Who Fell from the Sky:
   The Iroquois Story of Creation*. Have the students identify how nature (e.g.,
   soil, trees, birds, seasons) comes to life through the hands of the woman.
   Locate and read aloud other mythical creation stories so the children can
   compare events and cycles. Have the class analyze the various stories and
   cultures from which they came for diversity and commonality.
2. Locate a calendar that identifies the 13 full moons or new moons. Ask the
   students to describe the weather in their region during each moon (e.g.,
   describe the weather and season experienced in the region during the full
   moon in December). Read aloud Joseph Bruchac and Jonathan London's
   Thirteen Moons on Turtle's Back and compare the local weather to the book.
   Have the students examine the cycles or patterns of nature found in this story.
   As an art extension allow the children to use clay to mold and design a turtle
   shell.
3. After reading *How Raven Brought Light to People* by Ann Dixon, study the
   illustrations for repeated patterns. Examine the scene where the grandson
   opens the box and releases the stars. The background wall shows a design
   depicting bilateral symmetry, in which each side is identical and balanced.
   The character on the front of the boat on the next page also shows bilateral

symmetry. Have the students find other illustrations showing symmetry and other patterns. Discuss with them the significance of the repeating patterns of the artwork in the book. Ask the students what other conclusions they can make about symmetry and the cycles of nature. As an art activity have the students create bilaterally symmetrical totem poles, using 12" × 18" sheets of construction paper. Demonstrate how to fold the paper in half lengthwise and cut a design on the edges away from the fold. Cut into the fold line only for detail. After the students have cut their totem poles, arrange several of the designs, one above the other, to make a class totem pole. For more information on symmetry, view the filmstrip *Connecting* by Jean Morman Unsworth (Reading & O'Reilly).

4. Read the information on the copyright page aloud before sharing Paul Goble's *Buffalo Woman*. Let the students discuss the relationship and the kinship that was formed between the People and the Buffalo nation. After reading *Buffalo Woman*, urge the group to find a connection between this story and other life cycles. Then prioritize significant ecological factors it contains (e.g., the need for food, shelter, and clothing). Help the children to see how this story connects historically with a cultural past, a time when people depended upon the buffalo and the land for survival. Read aloud the "Song of the Buffalo Bulls" from the last page of the book. Have the class perform this passage as a choral reading. Artistic students may want to study Goble's stylized art and then illustrate the ending poem in a style similar to Goble's.

5. In Gerald McDermott's book *Arrow to the Sun: A Pueblo Indian Tale*, the people celebrate the boy's return from the sun with the Dance of Life. Have the group discuss the gifts the sun gives people today. Ask the students to bring examples of or make items that are natural gifts from the cycles of the sun and moon. Let the children brainstorm or research to discover how life is more or less dependent upon the sun today as a source of light and heat than it was for the Pueblo Indians 500 to 1,000 years ago. Set up science stations where students can perform various experiments related to heat and light.

6. In *A Critical Handbook of Children's Literature*, 4th ed., Rebecca Lukens defines a symbol in a story as a person, object, situation, or action that operates on two levels of meaning, the literal and the figurative or suggestive (HarperCollins, 1990, p. 145). After reading aloud *The Story of Jumping Mouse* by John Steptoe, discuss with the students the symbolism in the journey taken by Jumping Mouse and in the gifts he gave. Give the students the opportunity to draw an application from this story for people today. Lead a discussion in which the children explore the symbolic connection between Steptoe's story and the earth and sky. Jumping Mouse had a dream, a hope that helped him endure. Allow the children time to share their hopes and dreams.

Let the children discuss the predators that the bison referred to when he told Jumping Mouse to hop along beneath him so the "shadows of the sky" would not see the small creature. Help the group to recognize the role of predators in the life cycle. Follow up by playing a shadow game on the playground. Create a list of animals and predators. Have the children select an animal to pretend to be. Practice the animal movements on the playground at a time of day when a shadow will be cast. Students may not touch each other. The object of the game is to stay alive by not allowing the animal's shadow to be caught by another shadow.

7. In the epilogue of *Tonweya and the Eagles and Other Lakota Tales* by Rosebud Yellow Robe, the father, Chano, said, "People all over the world have their own way of life, but through their stories we find that we can understand them and live with them. Do not isolate yourselves, you will learn from others" (p. 116). Read aloud the story "The Boy Who Wore Turtle Shell Moccasins" or "The White Fox." Have the students discuss the positive attributes of the Indian characters. Ask the children to recall Chano's words and speculate about how people can come to understand each other through stories. Have the students use pen, pencil, and watercolors to create a scene depicting the spirit of the four winds. Let them discuss and determine how the roles the wind and weather play in people's lives today differ from those of 100 years ago. Other students might prefer to build models of the shelters in which various Native American tribes lived. Have the children use natural articles to build these shelters. The students will need to research various tribes to understand how their homes were constructed, depending on the type of weather they endured.

Follow-Up Activities for Individual Students:

1. In *The Woman Who Fell from the Sky* illustrator Robert Andrew Parker created gouache and pen-and-ink artwork. After hearing the story in class, reread the story. Then use gouache or watercolors to illustrate a creation scene such as the morning when the sun first rose.

2. After having heard in class *Thirteen Moons on Turtle's Back* by Joseph Bruchac and Jonathan London, locate and read any of the books written by Jean Craighead George in the series "The Thirteen Moons." Compare the book or books to the cycle of the moon and the events that occur in *Thirteen Moons on Turtle's Back.*

3. After hearing *How Raven Brought Light to People* by Ann Dixon, study the illustrations of the box that the grandson opened. Design your own box that you would keep treasures in such as the old chief did in the story. Be sure the design in your box is symmetrical. Be able to explain what the connection is between the box you have designed and that of the chief.

4. After reading Paul Goble's *Buffalo Woman,* read "The Passing of the Buffalo" on pages 223–43 of *Keepers of the Animals* by Michael J. Caduto and Joseph Bruchac (Fulcrum, 1991). Prepare a report on the extinction of animals. Select one animal and one reason for its extinction or endangered status on which to focus (e.g., habitat destruction and decimation). Include in the report what can be done to save a species and how animals are important to humankind. Be sure to include an illustration of the animal. You may create an original illustration or use a photograph or magazine picture.

5. After reading Jamake Highwater's *Moonsong Lullaby,* analyze the respect for the cycle of the moon and the differences in cultural viewpoints expressed in the book. Report to the class on how the author, who is of Blackfoot/ Cherokee heritage, views the moon and earth in comparison with people of another culture.

6. In the book *Arrow to the Sun: A Pueblo Indian Tale* by Gerald McDermott, the four trials that the boy endured are illustrated without words. Write a poem or tell a story about the boy's experiences in these trials.

7. Read Sheila MacGill-Callahan's *And Still the Turtle Watched.* Research the land changes that have taken place in your region during the last 200 years. Share your information in the form of relief maps, being sure to include an explanation of the change that occurred in the book compared to the change in your locale.

8. After hearing in class selections from *Tonweya and the Eagles* by Rosebud Yellow Robe, select and read one of the other stories in the book. Prepare to tell the story to the class.

9. Read "Iktomi and the Red-Eyed Ducks" in *Tonweya and the Eagles.* Then locate and read Paul Goble's *Iktomi and the Boulder* (Orchard, 1988). Compare and contrast the two stories.

Closure:

The stories in this unit have a collective theme based on rhythms or cycles and reverence for nature. Ask the students to tell about these themes in the books they have read or heard. Students will reach closure by giving their reports that were initiated during the introduction on various cycles in nature.

Have the students now create musical instruments from nature or simple handmade instruments such as those described in A.S. Wiseman's *Making Musical Things* (Charles Scribner's Sons, 1979). Practice together to create different rhythms and sounds. Have the class divide so that some students create the music while others create movement to the sounds. Remind them that Jumping Mouse hopped to the rhythm of the bison's hooves and the wolf's padding paws. Ask one group of children to pretend to be eagles in flight while the other group plays appropriate rhythm patterns on their instruments. If desired, the group may softly accompany the recording of Native American flute songs used in the introductory activity.

The Surreal World of Chris Van Allsburg

Objectives:

1. Identify landmark sites, states, and countries on a map.
2. Demonstrate divergent thinking through story webbing or chaining.
3. Create an original game.
4. Investigate the need for environmental protection.
5. Respond to literature through art, creative writing, and music.
6. Use a variety of poetic forms and devices in writing.
7. Draw conclusions from story clues.
8. Choose effective strategies for problem solving.

Recommended Readings:

Van Allsburg, Chris. *Ben's Dream*. Houghton Mifflin, 1982.
  A boy falls asleep on a rainy day while studying for his geography test and in his dream floats past various flooded world landmarks. (Objectives 1 and 5)

———. *Jumanji*. Houghton Mifflin, 1981.
  Two children must follow the directions carefully in order to end the amazing and terrifying new board game "Jumanji." (Objectives 2, 3, and 5)

———. *Just a Dream*. Houghton Mifflin, 1990.
  A young boy's devastating dream of a future world inspires him to care for the environment. (Objectives 4, 5, and 8)

———. *The Mysteries of Harris Burdick*. Houghton Mifflin, 1984.
  Fourteen surreal drawings, accompanied by titles and first lines, encourage divergent thinking. (Objectives 2 and 5)

———. *The Polar Express*. Houghton Mifflin, 1985.
  One Christmas Eve a young boy travels aboard the Polar Express and receives the first gift of Christmas from Santa himself. (Objectives 1, 5, and 6)

———. *The Stranger*. Houghton Mifflin, 1986.
  The mysterious stranger whom Farmer Bailey hit with his pickup truck stays with the family and helps on the farm until he regains his memory. (Objectives 6 and 7)

———. *Two Bad Ants*. Houghton Mifflin, 1988.
  Common kitchen items pose life-threatening dangers to two ants who have abandoned the colony. (Objectives 5 and 7)

———. *The Widow's Broom*. Houghton Mifflin, 1992.
  A lonely widow's life is eased and brightened by the companionship and aid of a discarded witch's broom. (Objectives 5 and 8)

————. *The Wreck of the Zephyr.* Houghton Mifflin, 1983.

A boy learns the mysterious art of sailing on air but loses the secret when his pride overcomes caution. (Objectives 5 and 7)

————. *The Wretched Stone.* Houghton Mifflin, 1991.

Startling results occur when a ship's crew becomes enthralled by a strange, glowing stone. (Objectives 5 and 7)

Biographical Sources:

For information on Chris Van Allsburg see *Something about the Author,* vol. 37, pages 204–7; *Fifth Book of Junior Authors & Illustrators,* pages 316–17; and *Talking with Artists: Conversations with Victoria Chess, Pat Cummings, Leo and Diane Dillon, Richard Egielski, Lois Ehlert, Lisa Campbell Ernst, Tom Feelings, Steven Kellogg, Jerry Pinkney, Amy Schwartz, Lane Smith, Chris Van Allsburg, and David Wiesner,* pages 78–83.

Group Introductory Activity:

Chris Van Allsburg has said, "It's not the *thing* that's important to me so much as the *feeling* the picture gives after you've drawn it. I have a favorite kind of mood I like in my art. I like things to be mysterious" (*Talking with Artists,* p. 81). To achieve this sense of mystery and wonder the artist very often works in a style called surrealism. This type of art combines elements that do not normally belong together to create an "other-worldly" sense, an unnatural juxtaposition.

As the children experience Chris Van Allsburg's books in this unit, they will need to listen carefully and examine the illustrations closely to discover the combination of elements that produce the surreal effect, the mystery in the scene or story. Children may use art, personal journals, or other formats to keep a record of the surreal elements in each book they experience.

Van Allsburg has often been asked about the black-and-white Boston bull terrier that appears in every one of his books to date. He says,

It's not a pet that I actually had, but it's a dog that I knew and liked a lot who's now in dog heaven. He was in the first book, so I put him somewhere in other books. It's just a little thing I do to amuse myself, I guess—to always put the dog in the book as a little homage to him. (*Talking with Artists,* p. 82)

Ask the children to look for the dog in each book they read or hear.

Ask the children if anyone can recall the significance of the Caldecott Award. If no one responds correctly, remind the students that this award is presented annually to the illustrator of the best children's picture book published in the United States during the previous year. Point out that the award is a great honor and that Chris Van Allsburg has received the award not once, but twice. *Jumanji* won the Caldecott Award in 1982 and *The Polar Express* received the honor in 1986.

Read aloud Chris Van Allsburg's first Caldecott Award winner, *Jumanji.* Remind the group that, in the story, the children's ability to follow directions allowed them to end the game and the terror it brought. Have the group brainstorm different story possibilities that might have happened if that important detail were changed. Web the children's suggestions on the chalkboard. Have the children create story chains from the webs, outlining the logical progression of events through several possible story lines. They should draw or write the major events in the story, connecting the different events with arrows that show the sequential order, similar to a flowchart.

Follow-Up Activities for Teacher and Students to Share:

1. Read Chris Van Allsburg's *Ben's Dream* to the class in the library media center. Have the children identify each major landmark Ben saw in his dream. Ask the students to use reference materials to locate each place. Because Ben's home site is not mentioned, tell the children to assume that Ben is one of their classmates. Let the students trace Ben's travel route on duplicated individual world maps, plotting and labeling each landmark site with the landmark name, city and state, if applicable, and country.

2. Read aloud the quote from Pogo on the copyright page of *Just a Dream* by Chris Van Allsburg. Let the children discuss what the sentence means to them and then predict what the book might be about. Share the book aloud. As a follow-up begin an environmental awareness project revolving around the three Rs of ecology: reduce, reuse, and recycle.

    To help the children comprehend the amount of garbage people produce, ask the school custodian not to dispose of your classroom's trash for a week. Collect the trash each day in heavy-duty plastic bags. Have the children weigh the week's garbage on a portable scale so they may see both the volume and weight of the trash they produce in their classroom alone. Let them discuss ways they could reduce the amount of garbage they create. Introduce the concept of reducing the volume of trash through compacting. Have each student save his or her empty drink container from lunch. Place all the containers in a bag and have the children weigh the containers. Ask each child to crush one container, then return it to the bag. Have the students compare the volume of the crushed containers to the original amount and then weigh the trash again. The children will comprehend that they have reduced the size of the garbage by compacting it, even though the weight remained the same.

    Let the students brainstorm ideas for reusing classroom or lunchroom waste, (e.g., melt small crayon pieces and pour them into ice cube trays to make chunky crayons for the art center, or tear construction paper scraps into small pieces and use them to create collage maps or illustrations). Explain that reusing materials refers to using it in its existing form for another purpose while recycling means to change waste materials into a new, usable form. Let the children use the recipe on pages 141–142 of Helen Roney Sattler's *Recipes for Art and Craft Materials* (Lothrop, Lee & Shepard, 1973, 1987) to make recycled paper. Students may use their paper to make Earth Day posters or greetings for "Mother Earth."

3. The entry about Chris Van Allsburg in *Something about the Author* mentions a work in progress tentatively called *Harris Burdick's Pictures*. The article states that the work was to be a novel. In Chris Van Allsburg's words,

> It's about an illustrator who brings in fourteen drawings to show an editor and then disappears without a trace. The actual story begins some thirty years after this strange event. I appear in my own persona, having been asked to write an introduction for a book of the drawings. That preface both sets forth the known facts about the mysterious artist, and conjectures, based on clues in the art work, about the probable content of the missing stories. (*Something about the Author*, p. 205)

Read aloud *The Mysteries of Harris Burdick*. Have the children compare the finished book to the projected description. Ask the students to determine how the book is like the projection and how it is different. Tell the students to each write a paragraph speculating upon why the author left the story in this "unfinished" state rather than writing a novel.

4. Read Chris Van Allsburg's *The Polar Express* to the group. As a group, make a story chain to outline the major events in the story. Have the children work from the story chain to rewrite the story as a poem. Children may wish to use Clement Moore's "'Twas the Night Before Christmas" as a model or use other poetic forms such as the limerick or acrostic poem. Share a sample of each to remind children of the forms; for example, "There was a young boy with a bell / Through a hole in his pocket it fell. / Then on Christmas morn / His joy was reborn / With the silvery tones he knew well" and/or:

> "**B** oarding the Polar Express,
> **E** veryone gathered to see the gift given,
> **L** ost the bell from his pocket,
> **L** isten with faith to hear its tones."

5. Before sharing Chris Van Allsburg's *The Stranger,* explain that this story contains clues that foreshadow or give hints to the stranger's identity. Encourage the group to listen carefully for any details that might help them solve the mystery. While reading aloud, pause occasionally and give the children time to share their speculations about the stranger's identity. After completing the story, most of the students will recognize the stranger as Jack Frost. Let the children share the clues that led to that conclusion. Point out the stranger's expression in the third picture from the end. Reread aloud the

text that accompanies that illustration and ask the children to look carefully at the painting to discover what may have caused the stranger to react as he did. If the children do not notice the red leaf he holds, point it out and remind the students that he had pulled a green leaf from the tree and blown on it. Encourage the children to speculate on his expression, that is, is it one of wonder or realization?

Frost on a windowpane sparkles like diamonds. As a follow-up let the children write diamantes (diamond-shaped poems) about *The Stranger*. The poems should take the following form: Line 1: a noun or pronoun; line 2, two adjectives describing the subject in line 1; line 3, three verbs in gerund form (i.e., "-ing" words); line 4, a four-word phrase; line 5, a three-word prepositional phrase; line 6, an adjective and a noun; and line 7, a noun synonym for the subject in line 1. Write a sample diamante on the board (e.g., "Stranger / hurt, lost / wondering, watching, seeking / green leaves strongly beckoned / with his breath / autumn colors / Jack Frost) so the students may see how the form appears. Have the children copy the completed diamantes on gem-shaped cutouts and post them on the wall or hang them from the ceiling.

6. Before sharing Chris Van Allsburg's *Two Bad Ants* with the children, explain that the author limited the text of the story to the experiences and understanding of ants. It is necessary to read the illustrations in order to recognize many of the items or locations in the book. Read the book aloud. When you reach page 10, share only the text and let the children speculate on what the mountain might actually be before showing the illustration of the brick wall. After reading page 11, again give the children the opportunity to predict what the narrow tunnel is (a hole in the window screen) before turning the page. Continue reading in this manner, allowing the students to speculate on each of the following before sharing the illustrations: "glassy, curved wall with crystals below" (p. 11); "giant silver scoop" (p. 16); "boiling brown lake" (p. 17); "cave" (p. 20); "disk with holes" (p. 21); "red glow" (p. 22); "waterfall" (p. 24), "dark chamber" (p. 26); and "long, narrow holes" (p. 28). Ask the children to choose an item in the classroom and describe it from an ant's perspective (e.g., a pencil might be seen as a fallen log).

7. Share aloud *The Wreck of the Zephyr* by Chris Van Allsburg. Let the children discuss the probable identity of the man with the limp. Ask the students to support their ideas with clues from the book. As an art follow-up children may use all-natural materials to create a flying sailboat mobile. Let the children thread a small twig or wooden toothpick through a leaf to resemble a mast and billowed sails. The students may wish to trim the leaf to achieve the desired size and shape and make a ship's flag or pennant that can be attached to the top of the mast. Have the children use quick-drying adhesive or clay to attach the mast to the inside of a peanut-shell hull. When the adhesive is firmly set, the students may carefully tie a 12"–18" piece of

thread to the mast. Tie the threads of the completed boats to wire clothes hangers and hang them from the ceiling. The lightweight boats will move and sail on the slightest breeze.

8. Read aloud Chris Van Allsburg's *The Wretched Stone*. Ask the children to write individual paragraphs speculating about what the wretched stone may have been or why it glowed as it did. Tell the students to cite examples or events in the story that support their ideas.

Follow-Up Activities for Individual Students:

1. After hearing *Ben's Dream* in class, carefully examine the illustrations in the book. Notice how Van Allsburg used lines and cross-hatching to create shading and texture in the drawings. Choose a familiar landmark the author did not include in his book, such as Mount Everest or the Sydney Opera House, and illustrate it with pencil. Use lines and cross-hatching to add appropriate shadows and give the appearance of texture to the picture. Be sure to show the site in a flooded condition like in *Ben's Dream*.

2. After hearing Chris Van Allsburg's *Jumanji* in class, create an original board game with written directions for playing. You might base the game on another Chris Van Allsburg book, such as *Two Bad Ants*. Share the board game with other classmates.

3. After reading either of Chris Van Allsburg's Caldecott Award-winning books, *Jumanji* or *The Polar Express*, imagine that you are a member of the Caldecott Award committee. Write a paragraph explaining why you believe the books' illustrations are worthy of receiving this high honor.

4. After hearing Chris Van Allsburg's *Just a Dream* in class, reread the book and assume the role of Dr. N. Viron Ment. Write a prescription for an ailing patient, Mother Earth. Be sure to include your diagnosis of her problem and exact directions for recovery.

5. After reading *Just a Dream* by Chris Van Allsburg, listen to a recording of "Where Have All the Flowers Gone" (*Peter, Paul, & Mary*, Warner Brothers, M5-1449), a song that was written as a plea for peace. Research ecological concerns in the library media center. Then rewrite the lyrics of the song to create a plea for protecting the environment. If possible, ask the music teacher to help you accompany the song on an Autoharp or other instrument. Teach the melody and your new lyrics to a group of friends and perform the song for the class.

6. Reread Chris Van Allsburg's *The Mysteries of Harris Burdick*. Choose one of the illustrations and write a story about it using Van Allsburg's title and first line. Before writing, focus your thoughts by answering these questions: What are the surreal elements in the picture? What might cause the object or character to be or act in the unusual manner depicted? How might story characters react to the bizarre situation? What situation is suggested by the

combined title, text line, and illustration? Make a web or story chain showing the possibilities, then write your story. Create an original surreal illustration to accompany your story.

7. Chris Van Allsburg is a sculptor as well as an author-illustrator. In fact, in *Talking with Artists* he says, "I liked building things . . . it was sculpture that really made me most enthusiastic about being an artist" (p. 79). In that same interview he also says he sometimes builds models of things he is going to draw so he can see how the shadows fall when the light source changes. After reading *The Mysteries of Harris Burdick,* select one illustration and sculpt or build a model that Van Allsburg might have used in making the drawing.

8. After reading *The Polar Express* in class, imagine you are a passenger on that train. Use an atlas to discover the states and countries you would travel through on a direct route from your home to the North Pole. Create a travelogue booklet illustrating a scene you might see in each state or country. Create the illustrations on drawing paper cut to 3" × 5" dimensions. Write the location at the bottom of each drawing in sequential order, beginning with your home and ending at the North Pole. Ask your teacher or the library media specialist to help you bind the book with staples, rings, or some other tool.

9. After sharing *Two Bad Ants* in class, write a similar story about an ant's adventures after escaping from a class ant farm. Illustrate two or more scenes from the perspective of a tiny insect.

10. Read Chris Van Allsburg's *The Widow's Broom.* Create a newspaper advertisement that an imaginary witch might write to try to sell a used broom that no longer has the power of flight. List all the positive qualities and abilities of the broom. Be sure to include a name and address of a fictional person or business for prospective buyers to contact.

11. After reading Chris Van Allsburg's *The Widow's Broom,* visit the library media center to locate and read Marianna Mayer's version of an old tale about an enchanted broom, *The Sorcerer's Apprentice: A Greek Fable* (Bantam, 1989), or another version of that story. Compare and contrast *The Sorcerer's Apprentice* with *The Widow's Broom.* Consider other possible tasks a magic broom might perform. Evaluate the pros and cons of having the broom do the job and choose whether or not you would like to have a broom's services. Justify your answer.

12. After hearing Chris Van Allsburg's *The Wretched Stone* in class, use clay or other art materials to make a representation of the stone.

Closure:

Play a game to review the Chris Van Allsburg books in this unit. Write each title on a chart and number them from 1 to 10. Label a pair of blank dice with numerals 1–5 on one and 6–10 on another. Since the pair of dice have a total of 12 faces while there are only 10 books in the unit, leave one face blank on each die. This face will serve as "wild card," allowing the children to choose the title of their choice. On a third die write a *P* for plot, *S* for setting, *MC* for main characters, *C* for conflict, *SE* for surreal elements, and *R* for resolution. Let the children play in small groups, rolling the dice to determine what elements and which two books they are to discuss (e.g., if 4, 7, and SE are rolled the player must share the surreal elements in the fourth and the seventh book on the list). After the children have reviewed sufficiently, allow the groups to choose their favorite Chris Van Allsburg book. Record the results on a graph labeled "Van Allsburg's Best."

Investigating Genres with Sid and Paul Fleischman

Objectives:

1. Recognize elements in the genres of poetry, fantasy, historical fiction, and information books.
2. Report information in various formats.
3. Identify with a book character.
4. Recognize the significance of the Newbery Award.
5. Learn to sign individual names and/or phrases in American Sign Language or finger spelling.
6. Write an original poem for two voices.
7. Respond to literature through the arts.
8. Plot a course on a map.

Recommended Readings:

Fleischman, Paul. *The Half-a-Moon Inn.* Illustrated by Kathy Jacobi. Harper & Row, 1980.
    Aaron, a mute, goes into a blizzard to search for his mother and is enslaved by the evil mistress of the Half-a-Moon Inn. (Objectives 2, 3, and 5)

————. *Joyful Noise: Poems for Two Voices.* Illustrated by Eric Beddows. Harper & Row, 1988.
    Poems for two voices reflect the rich variety in the insect world. (Objectives 4 and 6)

—————. *Rondo in C.* Illustrated by Janet Wentworth. Harper & Row, 1988.
The audience reflects on personal experiences as a young girl plays Beethoven's "Rondo in C" at her piano recital. (Objectives 3 and 7)

—————. *The Time Train.* Illustrated by Claire Ewart. HarperCollins, 1991.
A class field trip to Dinosaur National Monument aboard the "Time Train" becomes an opportunity to observe living dinosaurs in their natural habitat. (Objectives 1, 2, and 7)

Fleischman, Sid. *Humbug Mountain.* Illustrated by Eric Von Schmidt. Little, Brown, 1978.
The adventures of a traveling newspaperman are recounted in all seriousness by his son Wiley. (Objectives 1, 2, and 7)

—————. *Jim Ugly.* Illustrated by Jos. A. Smith. Greenwillow, 1992.
Jim Ugly, a wolf-mongrel mix, helps young Jake search for his father, whom most people believe to be dead. (Objective 7)

—————. *The Midnight Horse.* Illustrated by Peter Sis. Greenwillow, 1990.
The ghost of the great magician Chaffalo helps the orphan boy Touch find his fortune, capture a thief, and reveal his great-uncle's treacherous nature. (Objective 7)

—————. *Mr. Mysterious and Company.* Illustrated by Eric Von Schmidt. Little, Brown, 1962.
A family of traveling magicians perform in frontier towns along the way as they make the wagon trip to California. (Objectives 7 and 8)

—————. *The Whipping Boy.* Illustrated by Peter Sis. Greenwillow, 1986.
The quick wits of Jemmy, the whipping boy, save Prince Brat and himself from notorious outlaws. (Objectives 1, 2, 4, and 7)

Biographical Sources:

For information on Paul Fleischman see *Something about the Author*, vol. 72, pages 68–71 and *Fifth Book of Junior Authors & Illustrators*, pages 114–16. For information on Sid Fleischman, see *Something about the Author*, vol. 59, p. 89–95 and *Third Book of Junior Authors*, pages 86–87.

Group Introductory Activity:

Introduce author Sid Fleischman and his son Paul by telling the children that Sid Fleischman won the Newbery Award in 1987 for his book *The Whipping Boy.* The Newbery Award is given each year to the author of the most distinguished children's book published in the United States during the preceding year. Ask if anyone has heard the phrase "Like father, like son." Let children discuss what the phrase means. Explain that Sid and Paul Fleischman exemplify that phrase, for not only is Paul a writer like his father, but he has also received the Newbery Award (in 1989 for *Joyful Noise: Poems for Two Voices*). The works of the Fleischmans span a wide range of styles and genres, "but all are unified by . . . intense attention to sound" (*Something about the Author*, vol. 72, p. 68). Paul has said he would be a musician if he had talent; instead he fills his writing with musical words, alliteration, and rhythm. He credits his father with teaching him the importance of sound in stories saying, "His books brim with the pleasures to be found in the sounds of speech" (*Something about the Author*, vol. 72, p. 69).

Write the terms *poetry*, *historical fiction*, and *fantasy* on the chalkboard. Explain to the children that these are the three genres or types of books they will be reading during this unit. Let the children discuss what they believe each genre may be like, what elements might distinguish each, and how they might be similar. Lead the children to distill the following elements for each genre: poetry *may* have rhythm and rhyme, but it *always* appeals to the emotions; historical fiction is a realistic story set in the past; and fantasy includes at least one element that is not within the realm of possibility.

Create a bulletin board labeled "The Fleischman Spread." As children explore the works of Sid and Paul Fleischman they may complete the board by writing the author, title, genre, and elements that identify the genre on an appropriate shape and posting it on the board.

Share Paul Fleischman's *The Time Train* with the class. Allow time for the children to decide and document the genre in which the story belongs. Complete the bulletin board entry for the book together by writing the author and title, "fantasy" as the genre, and "time travel" as the fantasy element in the story. Affix the information to the board. As a follow-up help the students adapt the picture book into a script for a puppet show. Before beginning the script reexamine the book with the class so the children can focus on the contrast between the reactions of the teacher and her students to their predicament. As a class invent original dialogue and action to extend the book's content. Let the children create puppets and scenes for the script and rehearse throughout the unit so the play will be ready for presentation at the close of the study.

Follow-Up Activities for Teacher and Students to Share:

1. Read aloud *The Half-a-Moon Inn* by Paul Fleischman. Let the children identify the genre and the elements that establish this novel as a fantasy. The students will recognize Miss Grackle's magical powers and the enchanted fireplaces of the inn as fantasy elements. As a follow-up ask the children to write a newspaper article about the strange happenings at the Half-a-Moon Inn and Miss Grackle's death. Remind the children that journalists must always include the five "Ws:" who, what, where, when, and why.

2. Arrange to visit the library media center, where the media specialist will help introduce Paul Fleischman's Newbery Award-winning book *Joyful Noise: Poems for Two Voices*. Remind the children that sound is very important in the Fleischmans' work, then share the title of Paul's Newbery Award-winning poetry collection. The author has said, "If I can please my reader's ears . . . such that a listener who knew no English would enjoy it read aloud purely for its music, so much the better" (*Something about the Author*, vol. 72, p. 70). Ask the group to listen for the music and rhythm of the poetry as well as the sense or meaning of it. Join the library media specialist in reading "Honeybees" (pp. 29–31). Establish the characters of the queen and the worker bee by having one reader wear a crown while the other wears a hard hat, tool belt, or other construction worker attire. Ask the library media specialist to follow the poetry sharing by explaining how two-voice poems work and how they are to be read. As a follow-up urge pairs of children to select a poem from the book to prepare. Encourage the children to establish the character of each insect by using a prop or piece of costuming (e.g., water striders might wear swim fins, whirligig beetles could "hula hoop" before or during the recitation, and fireflies might use small flashlights to punctuate their reading).

3. Play a recording of Beethoven's "Rondo in C," found in *Piano Music of Beethoven, Vol. 1* by Louis Lortie (Chandos, CS ABTD-1305) or other piano music while reading aloud Paul Fleischman's book of the same title. Ask the children to reflect on the poetic text. Let them decide why the music brought forth different memories from each member of the audience. Urge the children to listen attentively as the music is played again, concentrating on the sounds. Ask them to share their responses—the images, memories, or emotions the music evoked. As a follow-up have each child write and illustrate a rhyming couplet about two memories or responses that they experienced while listening.

4. Read Sid Fleischman's *Jim Ugly* to the class. As a follow-up have the children create a roller movie of Jake's story or the story of William Tell. Children may decorate a large box to look like the stage of an Old West theater, cutting out the center for the staging area. Let the children illustrate scenes from the story and tape them together in proper sequence. Affix each end of the pictorial story to an empty paper toweling tube which can be loosely attached behind the stage, one on each side so the story scenes fill the empty stage. When the take-up tube is turned the story will scroll across the stage in filmstrip fashion. Students may wish to occasionally insert text to describe the action as in "silent movies." The children may also select appropriate music to play as the movie is viewed.

5. Before sharing Sid Fleischman's *Mr. Mysterious and Company,* tell the children that the author used to be a professional magician. His son Paul has said that when his father "gave up being a professional magician he became

instead a prestidigitator of words, palming plot elements, making villains vanish, producing solutions out of thin air. He knows how to keep an audience guessing, how to create suspense, how to keep readers reading" (*Horn Book*, vol. 63, no. 4, July/August 1987, p. 432). Ask the children to speculate about the meaning of the word *prestidigitator*, then find the word in the dictionary. Explain that the family members in *Mr. Mysterious and Company* are traveling magicians. Give each child a duplicated copy of a blank United States map and instruct them to track the family's journey to California as the book is read. They may use atlases as references to locate and mark as many towns as possible on the individual maps. As a follow-up have the students list skills and abilities that are necessary to be a successful magician. Interested students may wish to locate a copy of Sid Fleischman's *Mr. Mysterious's Secrets of Magic* (Little, Brown, 1975, o.p.) or another magic book and select one magic trick to study, practice, and perform for the class.

6. Before sharing Sid Fleischman's *The Whipping Boy,* tell the children that the author has said that the idea for this story came while researching another book. He stumbled across the term that later became the title. The idea rumbled around in his mind and typewriter for several years. In 1987 Sid Fleischman was notified that

> a book I had struggled with for almost ten years had won the Newbery Medal. I don't happen to believe in levitation, unless it's done with mirrors, but for the next few days I had to load my pockets with ballast. The Newbery Medal is an enchantment. It's bliss. It should happen to everyone. (*Something about the Author*, vol. 59, p. 94)

Just before beginning the story remind the children of the difference between fantasy and historical fiction. Emphasize that fantasy stories are often set in make-believe kingdoms or worlds. Ask the children to listen closely to Jemmy's story as the book is read aloud, noting elements that mark the story's genre. After reading let the children discuss whether the book should be considered fantasy or historical fiction. The children may not be able to agree on the genre because even literary authorities sometimes place it differently. Allow the children to defend their ideas and select a final genre based on majority rule. As a follow-up have the students discuss the justice or injustice of the "whipping boy" practice. Brainstorm a list of safeguards that could ensure that a ruler cannot abuse power. Develop this list into a statement of "rights" that even royalty must grant to their subjects. Send a group of students to the library media center to research the Magna Carta. Let the group share a brief explanation of this historical document with the class.

7. A group of stronger readers can work with the library media specialist to read and evaluate reviews on children's books. The objective will be to understand the role of the reviewer or critic and to note the criteria used for

judging a book. When students feel at ease with this writing format ask them to write individual reviews on the two Newbery Award-winning books in this unit, *The Whipping Boy* and *Joyful Noise*. If possible, locate the original reviews in professional journals for the students to read and compare.

Follow-Up Activities for Individual Students:

1. After hearing Paul Fleischman's *The Half-a-Moon Inn* in class, think about how the story might have changed if Aaron could have communicated with the illiterate people around him. Experience Aaron's frustrations by arranging with your teachers to spend one day without talking. Carry a lap chalkboard and chalk to use as your only means of communication. Visit the library media center to find a book on American Sign Language or finger spelling such as Laura Rankin's *The Handmade Alphabet* (Dial, 1991) or Leonard G. Lane's *The Gallaudet Survival Guide to Signing* (Gallaudet University, 1987). Learn the signed alphabet or some common word signs. Master the finger spelling of your name. You may wish to learn to sign a favorite song or poem to share while a friend recites the words.

2. After experiencing some of Paul Fleischman's poems from *Joyful Noise: Poems for Two Voices* in class, locate and read his other book of poetry for two voices, *I Am Phoenix: Poems for Two Voices* (Harper & Row, 1985). Select one or more poems from that volume to practice with a friend and share in class.

3. After hearing and reciting poetry from *Joyful Noise: Poems for Two Voices* by Paul Fleischman, select a species of animal and write an antiphonal poem (a poem for two voices) those creatures might voice. Good choices might include animal types in which the male and female or the baby and adult look quite different, such as lions or frogs, or in whose society are distinctly different roles, such as ants.

4. Sid Fleischman said that he

    was lured into writing *Humbug Mountain* by two words—the title. There stands a real Humbug Mountain in the state of Oregon. I can't explain why the look and sound of those words excited my imagination, but they did. *Humbug* suggested to me a mountain that wasn't really there. And *that* suggested . . . my locale, a sense of place.
    (*Something about the Author*, vol. 59, p. 94)

   Read Sid Fleischman's *Humbug Mountain,* noting the setting the author chose and how it differs from the location of the real Humbug Mountain. Determine to which genre this story belongs and complete the matrix entries for it on the classroom chart. This story moves rapidly with many outlandish happenings. Create a diorama, shadow box, or other visual display to represent your favorite episode from the book.

5. Sid Fleischman makes a point about the gullibility of people in *Humbug Mountain*. Gullible people are often said to "believe anything," and Fleischman has said that this story "expresses the universal interplay of illusion and reality in our lives" (*Something about the Author*, vol. 59, p. 94). After reading *Humbug Mountain*, you may wish to read some of Sid Fleischman's more outrageous stories in the tall tales about McBroom and his family. Visit the library media center to locate *Here Comes McBroom* (Greenwillow, 1976, 1992), *McBroom's Wonderful One-Acre Farm* (Greenwillow, 1972, 1992), or another book in that series. Read the book and list ways the truth is stretched to create the fantasy in the story. If you wish, choose a brief section of the tall tale to practice and tell to the class.

6. Read Sid Fleischman's *The Midnight Horse*, paying close attention to the author's use of figurative language, especially similes (comparisons that use the word *like* or *as*), for example, describing a face as being "as rough as moldy cheese." Select another example of figurative language and write it on the bottom of a sheet of drawing paper. Above the phrase draw a picture of what the words actually say rather than what they mean. For example, "a face as rough as moldy cheese" might be illustrated by a lumpy piece of green, moldy cheese with eyes, a nose, and a mouth. On the reverse side of the paper write what the phrase means in the book.

7. Sid Fleischman created characters that were "larger than life" in his Newbery Award-winning book *The Whipping Boy*, such as the evil men who were totally wicked, even having despicable names. After hearing the story in class, invent a character that Sid Fleischman might have included in the book. Describe the character fully, telling how he or she looks, acts, and feels. Give your character an appropriate name that is descriptive of his or her nature.

8. *Joyful Noise* and *The Whipping Boy* each won the Newbery Award. Reread either one and evaluate its contribution to children's literature. What makes it, in your opinion, an award-winning book? Document your belief with examples from the book you choose.

Closure:

Present "The Fleischman Spread," a performance in three or more acts, to other classes. Before the performance let the children make playbills similar to the one on page 55 of Sid Fleischman's *Jim Ugly* to advertise the production. Assign a student the role of stage manager to introduce each act and explain how it relates to Sid or Paul Fleischman. Acts might include costumed readings or recitations of some of Paul Fleischman's poems for two voices, a student playing Beethoven's "Rondo in C," and a presentation of the puppet play of *The Time Train*. The final act could be students performing magic tricks from Sid

Fleischman's *Mr. Mysterious's Secrets of Magic* or other magic books. Conclude the performance by having a student magician announce, "For my final act I shall now disappear." Turn off the lights or drop a curtain while the student quickly scurries offstage.

Mapping Outer Space with Seymour Simon

Objectives:

1. Define important words and create a glossary.
2. Use the strategy SQ3R (survey, question, read, review, and recite).
3. Create a diorama, clay model, or other art form.
4. Arrange events, facts, and ideas in sequence.
5. Draw inferences and make generalizations from evidence.
6. Plan and complete a group talk.
7. Apply critical thinking skills to answer questions and conduct research.
8. Demonstrate how to make an object.
9. Recognize the Dewey Decimal classification of books on space.

Recommended Readings:

Simon, Seymour. *Earth, Our Planet in Space.* Four Winds, 1984.
This slim volume introduces the earth, its cycles, and its place in space. (Objectives 1, 2, and 3)

————. *Galaxies.* William Morrow, 1988.
Colored photographs illuminate the vastness of galaxies as identified in the text. (Objectives 2, 3, 5, and 7)

————. *The Long View into Space.* Crown, 1979.
A comparative view of earth and its place in our galaxy is explained. (Objectives 1, 3, and 5)

————. *Mercury.* William Morrow, 1992.
Up-to-date facts explain Mercury's unique characteristics. (Objectives 3, 6, and 7)

————. *The Moon.* Four Winds, 1984.
Actual photographs of the moon and brief descriptions help clarify the mysteries of Earth's natural satellite. (Objectives 1, 4, and 5)

————. *The Optical Illusion Book.* Illustrated by Constance Ftera. Beech Tree, 1991.
A collection of various illusions to fool the eye is presented. (Objective 6)

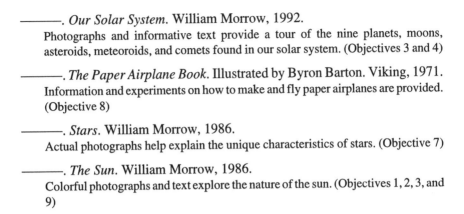

————. *Our Solar System.* William Morrow, 1992.
Photographs and informative text provide a tour of the nine planets, moons, asteroids, meteoroids, and comets found in our solar system. (Objectives 3 and 4)

————. *The Paper Airplane Book.* Illustrated by Byron Barton. Viking, 1971.
Information and experiments on how to make and fly paper airplanes are provided. (Objective 8)

————. *Stars.* William Morrow, 1986.
Actual photographs help explain the unique characteristics of stars. (Objective 7)

————. *The Sun.* William Morrow, 1986.
Colorful photographs and text explore the nature of the sun. (Objectives 1, 2, 3, and 9)

Biographical Sources:

For information on Seymour Simon see *Something about the Author*, vol. 4, pages 191–92 and *Fifth Book of Junior Authors & Illustrators*, pages 292–94.

Group Introductory Activity:

Tell the children that Seymour Simon has said many of his books are like "guidebooks to unknown territory" (*Something about the Author*, p. 192). In this unit the children will venture into and explore the new territory of space through Simon's books. Read aloud *The Long View into Space* by Seymour Simon to give an overall picture of space and distance. Simon makes several comparisons to help explain size and distance: the distance of the moon from Earth, the size of the sun compared to Earth's size, and the size of Jupiter compared to Earth. Give the students ample opportunity to recognize the vastness of space. Ask them to relate these comparisons in size or distance to objects in the room.

During this unit each student will need a notebook or folder in which to record facts and observations about space. Begin by having students define the following terms from Simon's book: *corona, solar eclipse, comet, meteoroid, binary stars, globular cluster, supernovae,* and *nebulae.* Explain to the students that they will develop a glossary of terms during the study. If desired, play background music while reading various selections in this unit; a good choice is *Also Sprach Zarathustra* by Richard Strauss (London, STS 15083, 1968), which was used as the theme for *2001: A Space Odyssey.*

Follow-Up Activities for Teacher and Students to Share:

1. To make comprehension easier for students when reading nonfiction material, introduce the "SQ3R" strategy. Model for the students how to survey, question, read, review, and recite the reading material. As Seymour Simon's

Earth, Our Planet in Space is read, have the students try out the strategy. Let the children discuss and add these words to their individual glossaries: *planet, orbit, atmosphere, magnetic field, aurora,* and *eroded.* In this book Seymour Simon explains how the earth spins like a top. Have a group of students set up a demonstration using a spinning top to show the earth's rotation. For more ideas on how to demonstrate concepts of space, refer to David A. Adler's *Hyperspace* (Viking, 1982). Follow up by having the students draw the outline of our planet on blue construction paper. They can use cotton to create a collage effect showing how the earth's surface is 70 percent water. As a further extension color salt by rubbing colored chalk into a small amount of salt. Have the children sprinkle the colored salt on black construction paper to create the effect of an aurora.

2. After reading aloud *Galaxies* by Seymour Simon and using the SQ3R strategy as explained in the above activity, gather feedback from the students on the effectiveness of the technique. Let the children discuss the quote by Alfred Lord Tennyson found on the copyright page. Ask them to speculate on why Simon chose to include the quote in his book. To help the students use their imaginations, ask them to look at the colored photographs in the book and give them titles as if each were a work of art. If possible, take a field trip to a planetarium or museum where students can view space through a telescope.

3. Seymour Simon has written a series of books on the individual planets in the solar system. *Mercury* is one of the newer books in the series. Ask teams of students to select a planet to research and report on to the class. Before beginning the research project, have each team list the facts they already know. Ask each group to place the name of the planet in the center of a large piece of paper and draw lines out to various categories such as size, location, unique characteristics, and mysteries. Have the children list facts according to the categories they decide to research. Next, ask the children to pinpoint what information they want to learn, perhaps by raising questions such as Why is Mercury dark? The final report needs to open with the stated problem (e.g., "Mercury is dark because. . . ." Each group can select an art form in which to illustrate facts about the planet. The computer-colored photographs in each book lend themselves to colorful art reproductions.

    To reach closure with all of the reports, ask open-ended questions such as: "What else did you learn?" "What was the most surprising or interesting thing you learned?" or "What have you learned that you did not know before?"

4. After sharing Seymour Simon's *The Moon* with the children, have them discuss the meaning of the following terms and add them to their notebooks: *satellite, crater, lava, Apollo, Tycho, Copernicus, Neil Armstrong,* and

Buzz Aldrin. Explain that the moon's gravity pull is one-sixth that of Earth. To help the students better understand the effect of gravity on weight, have them divide their weight by six to discover how much they would weigh on the moon.

Discuss the effects of having no air and no water. Ask the children to imagine how life would be different without air or atmosphere. Have them imagine the silence. Have the group brainstorm all the things that students now hear in their environment. Model life without sound by having a small group of students wear earplugs for a portion of the day. Ask them to share their observations at the end of that period.

5. Space often creates illusions, as do the senses. In *The Optical Illusion Book* Seymour Simon acknowledges that vision may fool the mind. Ask small groups of students to study, plan, and present a report and demonstration on selected chapters in the book.

6. After reading aloud Seymour Simon's *Stars,* have the children discuss and define the following words: *star, constellation, Alpha Centauri, Galileo, telescope, pulsar, black hole, Milky Way,* and *quasar.* Ask the students to determine what conclusions can be drawn about the vastness of stars and space. To help them imagine the number of stars in the sky, have them jab a pencil through a piece of heavy paper. Ask the children to take the paper home and, on a clear night, focus with one eye, looking through the tiny hole to count the number of stars seen in that limited space. Tell the children to record the number of stars they counted and share their findings with others in class.

7. Before reading aloud Seymour Simon's *The Sun,* share the book's dedication. Have students model the SQ3R strategy when reading this book aloud. Divide the class into teams and challenge them to list the facts they have learned about the sun. Have the students discuss and add these terms to their notebooks: *asteroid, photosphere, nuclear explosion, chromosphere, sunspot, prominences,* and *flares.* Next, have the children examine the call numbers of the books in this unit and other books on space that may be found in the library media center. Allow the children to draw a conclusion about how books are organized in the library media center. Examine the color photographs in *The Sun.* Let the students create artwork that looks like a coronagraph by using markers to draw circular designs on round coffee filters, allowing the dye to bleed through the filter. Interesting effects can be achieved by folding the filter into a wedge and dipping the pointed end briefly into a container of water. Let the filter dry thoroughly on absorbent paper towels before opening.

Follow-Up Activities for Individual Students:

1. After reading *The Long View into Space* by Seymour Simon, compose a letter to someone from the Great Galaxy in Andromeda. Think about what facts will be important for this person to know about Earth and its inhabitants. Be sure to use the return address as shown in the book:

    > Name
    > Street Address
    > Town/City   State
    > Country
    > Planet - Earth
    > System - Solar
    > Galaxy - Milky Way

2. After reading Seymour Simon's *Galaxies,* research the work of Edwin Hubble. Be as creative and imaginative as possible in presenting information on the three main types of galaxies he identified. Try to include some information on the Hubble telescope in your report.

3. After reading *The Moon* by Seymour Simon, mold a model of the moon's surface using clay or a modeling compound. Share your project and facts about the moon with the class. Or research the Apollo missions. Arrange the flights and events in sequential order.

4. Read Seymour Simon's book *Our Solar System.* Then make a table of contents for the book. Display the contents of the book on a large poster so other students may refer to it as a resource. Or use information from *Our Solar System* and art materials of your choice to create a diorama or open model of the planets in our solar system.

5. After reading Seymour Simon's *The Paper Airplane Book,* demonstrate and explain the following words: *lift, thrust, drag, gravity,* and *center of gravity.* Or choose your favorite airplane design from the book and teach other students in the class how to make it. Be sure to use the proper vocabulary, including: *aileron, lift flaps, horizontal stabilizer, elevator, vertical stabilizer,* and *rudder.*

6. Select one of the constellations named in Seymour Simon's *Stars* (e.g., Orion or Canis Major) and research it in the library media center. How and when did the star group get its name? To demonstrate the shape of the selected constellation, poke pinholes in the shape of that star group through black construction paper. Hold the paper up to a light bulb in a darkened room to show the constellation's appearance in a night sky. What conclusions can you draw about the naming of the star group, such as Orion, the Hunter?

Closure:

Collect the various terms that have been defined in the students' personal glossaries. Use these terms and other interesting facts and trivia that the students have discovered in Seymour Simon's books to form the basis for a "Space Cadet Academic Bowl Competition." If an appropriate computer program is available, input the terms in a multiple choice format. Allow 20 seconds for students to enter the correct answer. If a computer is not available, use the terms and trivia in oral questions to challenge teams of students.

Character Development with Bill Wallace

Objectives:

1. Write and perform a reader's theater script, book talk, or skit.
2. Communicate through written and oral expression.
3. Demonstrate understanding of the term *rite of passage*.
4. Make and justify evaluations of books and book characters.
5. Respond to literature through art and music.
6. Display information in graphic forms.
7. Use context clues to determine word meanings.
8. Recognize the use and meaning of contractions.

Recommended Readings:

Wallace, Bill. *Beauty*. Holiday House, 1988.
  Luke's love for Beauty, an old mare, helps him cope with his inner conflicts and offers a foundation for a relationship with his grandfather. (Objectives 1, 3, 4, and 5)

———. *The Biggest Klutz in Fifth Grade*. Holiday House, 1992.
  Pat, dubbed the Klutz, bets a rival that he can make it through the entire summer without any stitches or broken bones. (Objective 1)

———. *The Christmas Spurs*. Holiday House, 1990.
  Nick must come to terms with his feelings when his younger brother is stricken with leukemia. (Objectives 2, 3, and 6)

———. *Danger in Quicksand Swamp*. Holiday House, 1989.
  After a drought lowers the river level, Ben and Jake find a sunken boat with a treasure map that leads the boys into mystery and danger. (Objectives 3, 4, and 6)

————. *A Dog Called Kitty.* Holiday House, 1980.
An abandoned pup helps Ricky overcome the terror he has felt since he was attacked by a rabid dog. (Objectives 2, 3, and 4)

————. *Ferret in the Bedroom, Lizards in the Fridge.* Holiday House, 1986.
Liz blames her father's animals for most of her problems and feels everything would be fine if she did not "live in a zoo." (Objectives 1, 2, and 3)

————. *Red Dog.* Holiday House, 1987.
Twelve-year-old Adam must use all his wits and resourcefulness to protect his family from danger in the wilds of Wyoming in the 1860s. (Objective 7)

————. *Snot Stew.* Illustrated by Lisa McCue. Holiday House, 1989.
Two kittens quickly learn the pleasures and perils to be found when living with a human family. (Objectives 2, 4, and 8)

————. *Totally Disgusting!* Illustrated by Leslie Morrill. Holiday House, 1991.
Mewkiss and Barkus, a young cat and dog, are terrified of the rats that live in the cellar of their new family's home. (Objectives 2, 3, and 4)

————. *Trapped in Death Cave.* Holiday House, 1984.
A letter from his dead grandfather leads Gary and his friend Brian into a hunt for lost treasure, a murder mystery, and grave danger. (Objective 2)

Biographical Sources:

For information on Bill Wallace see *Something about the Author*, vol. 53, pages 178–80.

Group Introductory Activity:

Bill Wallace, a former teacher, has said, "I have found that reading aloud to students is one of the strongest motivational tools we have in creating a love of reading" (*Something about the Author*, vol. 53, p. 178). Introduce the children to Bill Wallace by sharing *A Dog Called Kitty*, the first of his novels to be published. The story was written for Wallace's fourth-grade class when he was an elementary teacher in Chickasha, Oklahoma. His students seemed to enjoy his story so he kept writing. *Kitty* was the third book-length story he had written for his class and the first to be made into a "real book." Wallace submitted the manuscript to publisher after publisher before it was finally accepted—eleven years later! Bill Wallace says, "The fourth graders whom I taught never left me. They are still with me whenever I write" (*Something about the Author*, vol. 53, p. 180).

Bill Wallace's determination and strong will are exemplified in his characters. As children read the books in this unit, they will meet many characters who must overcome difficult circumstances. The adversities the characters experience help them to mature and grow. A ceremony or event that marks the transition from childhood into maturity or adulthood is often called a "rite of passage." In literature, rite of passage refers to an event in the plot that causes the character to grow or that shows the character acting as an adult for the first time. Such events are often harsh and traumatic. Tell the children that they will find many different rites of passage in the Bill Wallace books they will read in this unit. As they read the books, they will be asked to examine the growth of each character, plot elements that contributed to that growth, and identify the rite of passage in each book.

Read *A Dog Called Kitty* aloud to the class. Stop reading after Ricky's fear of dogs has become apparent. Let the children speculate about the cause of his terror and how they think that fear will affect the story. After completing the book, let the children discuss ways the protagonist changed as the story progressed. Explain that logical change is a sign of a strong book character. These characters are called dynamic.

Introduce and explain the term *rite of passage* to the students. Ask them to recall the major events of the story in sequential order. Have the children identify the dramatic episode that served as Ricky's rite of passage. If necessary, reread chapter 12 (pp. 123–33) so the children can recognize the point at which Ricky overcame his fear. As other books in the unit are read, have the children note other climactic events that could be called rites of passage. Ask the students to write a brief description of these rites and justify their answer.

Follow-Up Activities for Teacher and Students to Share:

1. Bill Wallace's *Beauty* is appropriate as a read-aloud in small or large groups. While reading, have the children keep parallel response records in a journal. Students should mark two columns. In the left-hand column the students are to note quotes from the book. In the right-hand column the students may write reactions to the passage. Encourage the children to include passages they feel may foreshadow later events, those that show character growth, and the event that serves as Luke's rite of passage into maturity. Collect the records periodically and comment on the children's observations. After completing the book, give the children an opportunity to share their journal entries if they wish.

   As a follow-up have the children work in small groups to select a favorite scene from the story and re-create it in a three-dimensional model. The children may use purchased figures or sculpt characters from clay. While some children build the model, others may choose to prepare a book talk about this moving story. Be sure the talk includes a brief passage from the book that will make others eager to read the story. Display the model as a visual aid while groups present their book talks to the class or another group.

2. While reading Bill Wallace's *Ferret in the Bedroom, Lizards in the Fridge*, have the children record all of the animals that Liz's father keeps at their home. Divide the class into groups and ask each group to research one of these animals. Allow groups to visit the library media center to locate photographs of the animal and discover its habitat, food supply, and characteristics. Have each group present their information by drawing the animal on a 9" × 5 ½" sheet of drawing paper. Compile a Bill Wallace album by placing 9" × 11" construction paper in a binder. Cut corners from old envelopes to use as picture holders. Insert the corners of each drawing into the pockets formed by the envelope corners. Glue the backs of the corner pockets onto the album pages. Have each group label their drawing with the animal's name and its habitat. Beneath the label the group should add a brief paragraph telling the special characteristics of that animal. As a follow-up invite a naturalist or animal rehabilitation worker to visit the class, if possible, bringing a red-tailed hawk or other bird of prey to share with the students. An alternative is to have the children research and discuss how people can help protect wildlife or aid injured wildlife.

3. Read Bill Wallace's *Snot Stew* aloud to the class. Ask the students to discuss the kittens' reactions to the children's squabbles in the story. Urge the students to compare the felines' responses to their own feelings when they observe others disagreeing. Let the children evaluate Toby and Kikki's decision not to play the game "Snot Stew" anymore.

   Point out that the descriptive title of *Snot Stew* is deceiving but certainly evokes a mental image. Let the students pretend to be an advertising executive in charge of a restaurant account. Give students a list of 10 foods on the menu. Have the children write an appealing description for each food item and create a menu. Ask the students to strive to achieve a strong visual image in their menu descriptions.

4. Read Bill Wallace's *Trapped in Death Cave* aloud to the children. Then have the children each write a newspaper article about the boys' escapade. Tell the students to be sure to include the characters, what they did, when, where, why, and how. Ask the children to compose an attention-getting headline for the article.

Follow-Up Activities for Individual Students:

1. After hearing *Beauty* in class, think about the way Luke deceived himself about his father. Originally he remembered only good things about him. Write a paragraph in which you speculate about why Luke was later able to admit to himself and Beauty that their relationship was not all he had wanted it to be.

2. Bill Wallace has said he was much like Pat, the protagonist of his book *The Biggest Klutz in Fifth Grade*, when he was in fifth grade. In fact, he says on the book jacket that he still feels like a klutz at times. Perhaps because the

author bases so many of his stories on his own experiences and emotions, he frequently chooses to write in first person. After reading *The Biggest Klutz in Fifth Grade,* write a reader's theater script or play based on a passage from the early portion of the novel. The segment where Neal and his buddies tell about Pat's past accidents and make the bet (pp. 17–21) might be a good choice. Be sure to have the narrator set the scene for the action. If you need assistance, discuss reader's theater with the library media specialist. Practice with friends and perform the reading for the class to inerest others in this book.

3. After sharing *A Dog Called Kitty* or *Beauty* in class, read Bill Wallace's *The Christmas Spurs.* Prepare a story box about the book. Cover an empty fruit drink box or other six-sided box with solid color paper. Boldly write the title and author on one side of the box. On another side name and describe the main character. On a third side discuss the main problem or conflict in the story. On the fourth side record the climax or turning point of the story which acts as a rite of passage to force the character to grow. On the fifth side tell how the character resolves the conflict. Illustrate the setting on the remaining side of the story box. Tape a string onto the box and hang it from the ceiling.

4. Read Bill Wallace's *Danger in Quicksand Swamp.* Make a character development map to describe one of the characters. Start with a description of the character as he is first introduced and map important developments and events that happen to that character. Illustrate scenes and events from the story on a large sheet of paper. Draw arrows to indicate the route through the proper sequence of events. Be sure to map the turning point (climax of the story) and the rite of passage. Let X mark the spot of the conclusion. At this point describe the character as he is at the story's end. Judge how the character's experiences have changed him for the better or worse and write a justification of your answer with examples from the book.

5. After hearing *A Dog Called Kitty* in class, rewrite the opening chapters of the book in picture book form. Use simple words and illustrations to show how Ricky acquires the pet he never wanted. Ask the library media specialist to arrange for you to share your book with a group of kindergartners or first graders.

6. After hearing Bill Wallace's *Ferret in the Bedroom, Lizards in the Fridge* in class, select the scene in the story that contains Liz's rite of passage. Choose friends to help you dramatize that scene. Practice your skit and present it to the class.

7. Bill Wallace's *Red Dog* offers several opportunities to use context clues to determine the meaning of new words. Read the passages using each of the following words: *bristling* (p. 9); *pelt* (p. 35); *commenced* (p. 48); *varmint* (p. 61); *unpredictable* (p. 63); *predators* (p. 68); *pesky* (p. 82); *sneer* (p. 98); *spectacles* (p. 99); and *poised* (p. 148). The context—the way each

word is used in the sentence—should give you some clues to the meaning of the words. Write down what you think the word means based on its use. Then look the word up in a dictionary and write a shortened form of the definition in your own words. Compare the dictionary's meaning to the one you prepared from context clues.

8. In Bill Wallace's *Snot Stew*, Kikki and Toby listened to the children argue. As they spoke faster and faster, they shortened "Is not," and "Is, too" until the kittens heard "Snot" and "Stew." Words that have been intentionally shortened and combined by leaving out letters and sounds are called contractions. An apostrophe is used to indicate where letters have been omitted (e.g., "they have" becomes "they've"). Read chapter 9 again and identify 10 contractions used in the chapter. Write each contraction followed by the words it represents. Do not be confused by an "apostrophe *s*" that shows possession.

9. Read Bill Wallace's *Totally Disgusting!* What was the rite of passage and how did Mewkiss meet the challenge? On pages 108–9 Allergies tells Mewkiss, "You are special. All of us are. Our names are important, but not nearly as important as what we have inside—what we *believe* . . . if you believe in yourself, you can do most anything." Listen to a recording of "High Hopes" (*Best of Bing Crosby*, MCA, MCAC2-4045), a song about believing in yourself. How did believing in himself help Mewkiss to survive his rite of passage from kittenhood? Write your answers in a paragraph.

10. After hearing Bill Wallace's *Trapped in Death Cave*, write an advertisement for a "Death Cave" amusement park ride. Use action words and descriptors to tell about the exciting thrills riders will experience as they pass through Death Cave in their "wooden box" boats.

Closure:

Make flap books discussing the "four Ws" of Bill Wallace books. Each child should choose his or her favorite Bill Wallace book from this unit. Let children cut a 9" square of construction paper. Tell the children to fold the squares in half to make rectangles and fold the rectangles in half again to create 4 ½" squares. Have the students open the papers up and then fold each corner in so it touches the center crease. The paper should then be in the form of a square with four flaps. On the outside of one flap have children write "Who?" On the remaining flaps they should write "Where?' "What?" and "Why?" respectively. Have the children open each flap and write a description explaining the characters (who), the setting (where), the rite of passage (what), and the conflict that led to the event that was the rite of passage (why). On the back of the center square have the children write the title and Bill Wallace's name as the author of the book. If children have room, they may add simple sketches to illustrate the four elements. Let the children hang their flap books from the ceiling to create a "Who's Who in Bill Wallace's Books" display.

Word Play

Objectives:

1. Expand vocabulary through word study, literature, and class discussion.
2. Comprehend the meaning of figurative language in appropriate text.
3. Use descriptive language.
4. Communicate through a variety of written forms, such as poetry and captions.
5. Demonstrate how to use nonsense words and comparisons to create word pictures.
6. Identify parts of speech and uses of figurative language.
7. Use a dictionary definition or thesaurus to understand the meaning of a word.
8. Draw inferences from reading jokes, riddles, puns, and other forms of word play.

Recommended Readings:

Adoff, Arnold. *The Cabbages Are Chasing the Rabbits*. Illustrated by Janet Stevens. Harcourt Brace Jovanovich, 1985.
Word play is used in this poem as the vegetables reverse the cycle of nature. (Objectives 2, 3, and 8)

Carroll, Lewis. *Jabberwocky*. Illustrated by Jane Breskin Zalben. Frederick Warne, 1977.
A rhythmic poem written with inventive words tells the tale of a dreadful creature. (Objectives 2, 5, 7, and 8)

Heller, Ruth. *A Cache of Jewels: And Other Collective Nouns*. Grosset & Dunlap, 1987.
The great variety of colorful collective nouns is displayed in clear illustrations and concise rhyme. (Objectives 1 and 6)

————. *Many Luscious Lollipops: A Book about Adjectives*. Grosset & Dunlap, 1989.
Rhyming text and brilliant illustrations introduce specific terminology associated with adjectives. (Objectives 1, 2, and 6)

Merriam, Eve. *Chortles: New and Selected Word Play Poems*. Illustrated by Sheila Hamanaka. William Morrow, 1989.
Language is playfully presented in poetic settings. (Objectives 1, 4, and 7)

Most, Bernard. *Pets in Trumpets and Other Word-Play Riddles*. Harcourt Brace Jovanovich, 1991.

A collection of riddle words within other words is depicted in language and illustrations. (Objective 1)

Sarnoff, Jane, and Ruffins, Reynold. *Words: A Book about the Origins of Everyday Words and Phrases.* Charles Scribner's Sons, 1981.
Explanations of word origins are arranged by subjects. (Objectives 1 and 7)

Steig, William. *C D B!* Simon & Schuster, 1968, 1984.
Single letters of the alphabet take on new meaning in these humorous lines. (Objectives 4, 5, and 8)

Terban, Michael. *Hey, Hay! A Wagonful of Funny Homonym Riddles.* Illustrated by Kevin Hawkes. Clarion, 1991.
This collection of word play riddles is arranged by level of difficulty. (Objectives 1, 2, and 8)

————. *In a Pickle and Other Funny Idioms.* Illustrated by Giulio Maestro. Clarion, 1983.
The real and special meanings of 30 popular idioms are detailed in this humorous collection. (Objectives 1, 2, and 6)

Group Introductory Activity:

The books in this unit have been selected to show students how to enjoy having fun with words. Each poem in Eve Merriam's *Chortles: New and Selected Word Play Poems* communicates a unique play on language. Merriam says in the filmstrip *First Choice: Poems and Poets* (Pied Piper Media) that words "can chime like bells or taste as sour as pickles." Student may select favorites after these poems are read aloud. It may be fun to share potato chips after "The Ultimate Product" is read. After reading "A Token of Unspoken," have the students define the words in italics and compose sentences with the new words. Challenge the students to learn at least one new word each week. Have the children work in pairs to write their own "chortles."

To connect the word books in this unit, have each student collect words. These words can be kept on note cards or in a word notebook. Each entry should contain the new word, its pronunciation, its part of speech, its definition, and a complete sentence using the word. To encourage word collecting, celebrate a "New Word of the Day." Ask students to use a thesaurus to help them increase vocabulary and find new words. Each day one word can be selected. Place this word on a bulletin board for the students to view. If students work in groups, label a jar for each group. As students use the new word of the day add a jelly bean to the jar. Allow the children to eat the jelly beans at the end of the day.

Ask the music teacher to team teach the poem "The Egotistical Orchestra" from *Chortles.* Let the children compose an original word play musical instrument poem like Eve Merriam did. Students may use percussion or other available instruments to add appropriate musical sounds while reciting their poem.

Follow-Up Activities for Teacher and Students to Share:

1. Arnold Adoff uses the poetic devices of rhythm, sound, and figurative language to tell about a special kind of day in *The Cabbages Are Chasing the Rabbits*. Read the book aloud to the class or ask different groups to read and interpret the book. Encourage the students to listen for the word plays (puns) in the poem (e.g., "Green Onion Shoots Along"). Alliteration, the repetition of initial sounds, is easily identified as the poem is read aloud (e.g., "Warms the Wiggling Worms"). Once the groups of students have identified various devices used and the sequence of events, ask them to brainstorm other cycles in nature or life that could be reversed. As a class write a poem or story expressing this event. As a follow-up study on alliteration, play the alphabet challenge found in Cathryn Kaye's *Word Works* (Little, Brown, 1985). Refer to Rebecca Lukens's *A Critical Handbook of Children's Literature*, 4th ed. (HarperCollins, 1990) for more information on the devices of style.

2. Explain to the students that in Lewis Carroll's *Through the Looking Glass*, Alice meets Humpty Dumpty, who tells her that a name must mean something. He goes on to define an un-birthday present and tells Alice that when he makes a word do a lot of work, he always pays it extra. "When I use a word," Humpty Dumpty said, "... it means just what I choose it to mean—neither more nor less." "The question is," said Alice, "whether you can make words mean so many different things" (*Through the Looking Glass*, Random House, 1946, p. 94).

   Turn to "Annotations by Humpty Dumpty" in Lewis Carroll's *Jabberwocky* and read aloud the first four paragraphs ending with the lines, "there are plenty of hard words there." Ask the students to suggest anything they may have learned from hearing the first stanza of the poem "Jabberwocky." Allow time for the children to think of other books in which the author extended word play to its fullest by inventing new words. Children may refer to Rich Hall's *Sniglets* (Macmillan, 1984), *Daffynitions* by Charles Keller (Prentice-Hall, 1976), or Bill Peet's *The Kweeks of Kookatumdee* (Houghton Mifflin, 1985).

   After the discussion, return to *Jabberwocky* and read aloud the beginning with the dedication. Ask the students for their interpretations of the poem or of specific words. If students are not sure what words are real and what words are invented, have them look up the word or words in a dictionary. Complete the book by sharing the rest of "Annotations by Humpty Dumpty." Encourage the children to discover how many different things the invented words in the poem might mean. Linguistic children may enjoy playing "The Game of Sniglets" (Games Gang, 1990) as a follow-up activity.

3. Read aloud Ruth Heller's *Many Luscious Lollipops: A Book about Adjectives*. Reread the page that illustrates how to create an adjective. Play the "Able (Ible)" Game to help students understand this concept better. Have the children stand in a circle and let each student in turn give his or her name and an adjective beginning with the first letter or the sound of the letter of his or her first name. The result is the creation of alliterative phrases, such as Letty Likeable, Terri Teachable, Katy Capable. Urge the children to be inventive but remind them that the adjectives must end with "-able" or "-ible." As the game progresses, the next player must name all those who have come before and add his or her name. The last person will then attempt to recall all of the names and add his or her name description.

4. Have the students take turns reading aloud Bernard Most's *Pets in Trumpets and Other Word-Play Riddles,* giving their classmates an opportunity to guess each riddle's answer by finding the hidden word. Stop to let the students explain the word play when necessary. After sharing these word play riddles, list the words used in the book and on the fly pages on white poster board. Use a different color marker to outline or highlight the hidden word so the students can see and hear the riddle. Work in small groups or as a whole class to brainstorm other words that have hidden words. Color code the hidden words. These words can then be used in a spelling list or review. This activity helps children learn to spell through association.

5. Suggest that small groups of students select a topic such as "Clothes" from the book *Words: A Book about the Origins of Everyday Words and Phrases* by Jane Sarnoff and Reynold Ruffins. Each group may then decide how to present the information on word origins to the class. Students might choose to play a "Who Am I?" word game, giving origin clues to the selected word. Some of the selections lend themselves to creative dramatics. If desired, introduce the children to crossword puzzles at this time. Some of the students could use a computer crossword puzzle program, if such software is available, to generate crossword puzzles using topic words with origin clues.

6. Authors share humor in books through poetry, fine literature, jokes, riddles, and word usage. In *C D B!* by William Steig readers will laugh at the simplicity of language. Ask pairs of students to take turns reading the letter sentences aloud. When students understand the "C D" usage of letters, have them brainstorm other easy possibilities.

7. Michael Terban has written a number of books containing curious ways of playing with words. *Hey, Hay! A Wagonful of Funny Homonym Riddles* offers a useful starting point for students to develop the ability to play with words that have multiple meanings, yet only one sound. Read aloud chapter 1 and let the children write down the homonym answers. Students may continue to work with this book individually.

8. Idiomatic expressions, or "figures of speech," are groups of words that do not mean what they say. When words convey a message other than the literal meaning, they can create stumbling blocks for children. Before

sharing Michael Terban's *In a Pickle and Other Funny Idioms,* stimulate the students' curiosity by serving dill pickles. Now show a tightly packed jar of miniature sweet pickles and use the expression "in a pickle." Ask students to explain what that expression might really mean. Share aloud some favorite idioms Terban included and encourage the children to complete the suggested individual follow-up activity for the book.

Follow-Up Activities for Individual Students:

1. After hearing Lewis Carroll's *Jabberwocky,* reread the poem and list the portmanteau words (blended combinations of two other words); for example, *mimsy,* meaning "flimsy" and "miserable."
2. Depict the meaning of one of the following words from *Jabberwocky* by illustrating it: *borogove, mome raths, toves, Jabberwock, Jubjub bird, Bandersnatch, tulgey wood.*
3. After sharing Bernard Most's *Pets in Trumpets and Other Word-Play Riddles,* use the words listed in class or other words of your choice to make up original word-play riddles.
4. Jane Sarnoff and Reynold Ruffins's information book *Words: A Book about the Origins of Everyday Words and Phrases* gives the word origins for the names of the 50 states. Research in the library media center to discover the origin of the names of three to five towns or cities in your state. Be sure to add these words to your individual word book.
5. After reading *Words* by Jane Sarnoff and Reynold Ruffins, do the work of an etymologist by studying word origins. Select 10 new words to research in the library media center and share your findings with the class.
6. After reading William Steig's *C D B!* or *C D C* (Farrar, Strauss & Giroux, 1984), create a humorous license tag such as "NNNN CAR" (foreign car).
7. Examine the list of idioms from Michael Terban's *In a Pickle and Other Funny Idioms.* Use at least five of those idioms in complete sentences and illustrate either the literal or figurative meaning of each.

Closure:

Share Ruth Heller's *A Cache of Jewels: And Other Collective Nouns* with the class. Be sure to read the final page where the poet promises to write a book for each of the parts of speech. Encourage the children to see if they can locate and read Heller's other language books. Celebrate word play by asking the children to think of collective nouns for the following words: *students* (class), *musicians* (band), and *cookies* (batch). When the children correctly identify the three collective nouns, turn on a recording of a favorite musical group, give each child a homemade cookie, and "party!" Play word games as the children listen to music and munch. Children might enjoy thinking of "hinky pinkies" to rename suggested phrases; for example, a humorous rabbit (funny bunny), an obese feline (fat cat), or an angry father (mad dad).

Exploring Relationships with Alfred Slote

Objectives:

1. Recognize cause and effect.
2. Respond to literature through art, music, or creative writing.
3. Prepare and share a book talk with the class.
4. Identify foreshadowing in a story.
5. Research and present information in a variety of formats.
6. Construct math problems from life situations.
7. Predict an outcome.

Recommended Readings:

Slote, Alfred. *Finding Buck McHenry*. HarperCollins, 1991.
  Jason jumps to conclusions, deciding the African-American custodian at a local elementary school is really a former Negro-league baseball star in hiding. (Objective 1)

———. *A Friend Like That*. Lippincott, 1988.
  Robby must come to terms with more changes in his life when his housekeeper leaves to marry Beth Lowenfeld's father. (Objectives 1 and 2)

———. *Hang Tough, Paul Mather*, rev. ed. HarperCollins, 1992.
  Paul struggles with priorities in his fight to win on the baseball diamond and against leukemia. (Objectives 1 and 2)

———. *Make-Believe Ball Player*. Illustrated by Tom Newsom. HarperCollins, 1989.
  Henry is an accomplished baseball player, if only in his imagination. (Objectives 1 and 2)

———. *Moving In*. Lippincott, 1988.
  Eleven-year-old Robby Miller and his sister fear their father will marry his new business partner, and they make many efforts to prevent it. (Objectives 1, 2, and 7)

———. *My Robot Buddy*. Illustrated by Joel Schick. Lippincott, 1975.
  Jack Jameson receives a robot double, Danny One, for his birthday, and the two quickly become involved in an adventure. (Objectives 1 and 2)

————. *My Trip to Alpha I.* Illustrated by Harold Berson. Lippincott, 1978.
A computer sends Jack Jameson's consciousness into a temporary body on Alpha I, where he must save his aunt from danger. (Objectives 2 and 4)

————. *Omega Station.* Illustrated by Anthony Kramer. Lippincott, 1983.
Jack and Danny must return to C.O.L.A.R. in order to save its robot citizens from an evil mastermind. (Objectives 2 and 3)

————. *The Trading Game.* HarperCollins, 1990.
Andy Harris is willing to trade anything for the baseball card of his grandfather, worth 25 cents, even his 1952 Mickey Mantle card, valued at thousands of dollars. (Objectives 5 and 6)

————. *The Trouble on Janus.* Illustrated by James Watts. Lippincott, 1985.
Only Jack and Danny One, his robot double, can solve the mysterious trouble on the planet Janus. (Objectives 2 and 5)

Biographical Sources:

For information on Alfred Slote see *Something about the Author*, vol. 72, pages 226–30 and *Fifth Book of Junior Authors & Illustrators*, pages 298–99.

Group Introductory Activity:

Alfred Slote is a great sports enthusiast and, at his son's suggestion, often incorporates that love into his books. However, while his characters take sports seriously, "the novels are ultimately more concerned with the characters' relationships at home and at school and their growth as people" (*Something about the Author*, vol. 72, p. 228). Slote has said his books are about the things that happen to young people, not about sports specifically. He includes sports because they are an important part of many young lives.

Explain to the class that in this unit they will be sharing many of Alfred Slote's books, many of which are contemporary realistic fiction stories based on a specific sport. Others in the unit are science fiction stories, but all focus on relationships between characters and why they behave as they do.

Introduce the concept of cause and effect to the class by explaining that, when an event occurs there are usually other actions that follow because of that event. Let the children role play or discuss a cause-and-effect relationship (e.g., "A boy broke his watch while playing at the park with friends, so..." or "Coming home from the market, the shopping bag tore open, so..."). Explain that Alfred Slote's novel *Moving In* is filled with cause-and-effect situations. Tell the children to listen carefully as the story is shared to find as many such situations as possible. At the end of each oral reading session allow the children time to share cause-and-effect statements they identified. Point out to the children that cause-and-effect situations are not always spelled out with the words *because*, *then*, or *so*, and that the effect may not follow the cause immediately. Therefore, they will have to listen carefully to spot the relationships.

Read *Moving In* aloud to the group. Stop reading after chapter 3 and ask the children to predict what Robby will do to test the town. Allow the children time to share experiences or emotions they have felt when moving to a new home.

Continue reading through chapter 10. Allow the class to predict what Robby is going to do. Ask the group to explain how their speculations fit the description Robby gives at the close of chapter 10, and how it would solve the children's problem. After reading chapter 16, once again have the students predict the outcome of the situation. Have children speculate about possible effects that could come from Robby's action.

Complete the novel. Have the group discuss the way the children in the story relate to and communicate with their father. Point out that Robby was able to share feelings with Carol and Mr. Lowenfeld that he could not communicate to his dad. Urge the children to find possible explanations for the lack of communication between the father and son. As a follow-up let the students practice sharing their hopes, dreams, and fears in a "Getting to Know You" center. Stock the center with writing tools and slips of paper headed with various leading phrases such as "When I first came to this school I felt . . .," "Sometimes I worry that . . .," or "I wish that. . . ." Do not include a line for the student's name. Encourage the students to put their thoughts on paper, explaining that they need not sign their names, and post their papers in the center. At various times during the unit collect the papers from the center and share them with the group.

Follow-Up Activities for Teacher and Students to Share:

1. Read aloud the opening chapter of Alfred Slote's *Hang Tough, Paul Mather*. Students may recall that Arborville was also the setting of *Moving In*. Explain to the children that the author often uses the name "Arborville" to describe his own neighborhood in Ann Arbor, Michigan (*Something about the Author*, vol. 72, p. 227). Complete the book and then urge the children to discuss the relationships between Paul and his family and between Paul and his doctor. Ask the children who seemed to understand Paul better—his parents or his doctor. Encourage the children to speculate on why Paul's parents could not see his desperate need to play baseball. Astute children may realize that his parents were too worried about saving Paul's life to be very concerned with his baseball dreams. As a follow-up let the children write an additional sequence for the novel about what happens to Paul in the next year. Children may title their writings "Paul Mather— Still Hangin' Tough."

2. Play Peter, Paul, and Mary's recording of "Right Field" from *Peter, Paul, & Mommy, Too* (Warner Brothers, 9 45240-4, 1993) for the class. Tell the children that this song could very well be the theme song for Henry, the main

character in Alfred Slote's *Make-Believe Ball Player*. Present a book talk about the novel to the children to encourage them to read the book and complete the individual activity that accompanies it. Ask the music teacher to help the class learn to sing Peter, Paul, and Mary's song about a child who daydreams while in the outfield.

3. Read *My Robot Buddy* by Alfred Slote to the group. Have the children choose 10 words or phrases that describe the relationship that developed between Jack and his robot friend. Ask the children to write a paragraph using some of those words or phrases to describe a relationship they have with someone special. As a follow-up let the students practice walking "stiff in the knees" and try to perform some everyday tasks without bending their knees (e.g., pick up a pencil from the floor, sit down at their desks, dance, or jump up to touch the top of the door frame).

4. Share aloud Alfred Slote's *My Trip to Alpha I*. Let the children recall situations, events, or statements that gave clues to the resolution of the story. Explain that clues that hint at the coming action are examples of "foreshadowing." As a follow-up assign children to work in groups to build a model of Alpha I or another imaginary space colony. Each group should create a model of a building, vehicle, or other necessary item. Have the students prepare a diagram naming each model and describing its function in space.

5. Share *The Trading Game* by Alfred Slote with the children. Discuss the relationship between Andy and his grandfather. Let the group speculate about the relationship Andy's father had with the older man and why his father became a baseball card collector instead of a player. As a follow-up arrange with the library media specialist to set up a baseball card display in the library media center. In math class have each child use a baseball card guide to list 10 specific cards the child might have or would like to have and determine the total value of that collection. Let the children create word problems based on the collections, such as "Joe traded a rookie Ozzie Smith card for a rookie Nolan Ryan card. How much did he gain or lose on the trade?"

6. Share pages 1–30 of Alfred Slote's *The Trouble on Janus* aloud. Stop reading with the lines "Your turn now. You start a poem and we'll work on it together." Explain the ABCB rhyme scheme Slote mentions on page 30. Ask the children to predict what they think will happen to Jack and Danny on Janus and work in groups to write those predictions in poems. Write the completed poems on shapes appropriate to the story (e.g., spaceships, robots, or planets) and post them on a bulletin board labeled "Poetry That's Out of This World." Complete the book aloud, if desired, or urge the children to finish the book individually and perform the individual activity for that title.

Follow-Up Activities for Individual Students:

1. Read *Finding Buck McHenry* by Alfred Slote. The baseball card of Buck McHenry stimulated Jason's imagination. His relationship with Mr. McHenry was based on misconceptions. At the close of the novel he says, "I remembered that day. . . . The day I went looking for a legend and found a man." Write a paragraph examining the good that came from Jason and Mr. McHenry's friendship in spite of its poor foundation.

2. After reading Alfred Slote's *Finding Buck McHenry,* visit the library media center to research the Negro baseball leagues. Many of these players were among the greatest athletes to play the game but never played in the major leagues. Determine if Buck McHenry was a real or fictional character. Select the three players whose abilities impressed you the most. Share their accomplishments with the class in an oral report. Use charts or graphs to show your information. Excellent resources are Robert Gardner and Dennis Shortelle's *The Forgotten Players: The Story of Black Baseball in America* (Walker, 1993) and Michael L. Cooper's *Playing America's Game: The Story of Negro League Baseball* (E.P. Dutton, 1993).

3. After hearing Alfred Slote's *Moving In* in class, read the sequel to Robby Miller's story in *A Friend Like That.* How do Robby's relationships with his father and with Beth Lowenfeld change during the story? Prepare an illustration that shows the scene you think caused one of those relationships to change.

4. In *Make-Believe Ball Player* by Alfred Slote, Henry's imaginary games helped him become a better baseball player because of the time he spent throwing and catching in his daydreams. Think of other situations or accomplishments that require practice to do well. Write a paragraph telling which one you would choose if you were to participate in your imagination as Henry did. Note some of the actual tasks, sounds, and feelings you would experience in that fantasy.

5. C.O.L.A.R., an acronym for Colony of Lost Atkins' Robots, was introduced in Alfred Slote's book *C.O.L.A.R.* (Lippincott, 1981, o.p.). After hearing *My Robot Buddy* in class, read more about Jack and Danny One in *Omega Station* or *C.O.L.A.R.* When you have read one of these sequels, write the questions that a television news reporter might use in an interview with Jack or Danny about their adventures. Pretend to be one of the buddies and ask a friend to portray the reporter. Practice your presentation and perform it for the class, being sure to demonstrate walking "stiff in the knees." As an alternative, present a book talk to the class that will arouse curiosity and interest in the book.

6. After sharing Alfred Slote's *The Trading Game* in class, check a baseball card guide to see if the cards mentioned on pages 34–35 and pages 84–88 have changed in value since the author wrote the novel. Record your findings and report to the class.

7. After experiencing Alfred Slote's *The Trouble on Janus,* reread the description of the planets Diaperus and Canus on pages 31–32. Invent a planet of your own and decide what its inhabitants would be like. Give the planet a name that describes it or its people and illustrate a scene depicting life there.

8. On page 163 of *The Trouble on Janus,* King Paul asks Jack to name his reward, saying, "Your wish is my command." Imagine you have received four wishes that would be granted. The only limitation is that one wish must be for something to *have,* one for somewhere to *go,* one for something to *be,* and one for someone or something to *love.* Write, in poetry, about each of the four wishes, beginning each stanza with "If my wish was a command. . . ." Use any rhyme scheme you wish or write in free verse.

Closure:

Explore cause and effect in Alfred Slote's books. Begin with the following four ideas, asking the children to complete the effect portion of each sentence about Alfred Slote's characters or stories:

- Because robots were disappearing from C.O.L.A.R. . . .
- Peggy and Robby Miller thought their father would marry Mrs. Lowenfeld so. . .
- Because Andy's grandfather was overly competitive . . .
- Henry wanted to be a good baseball player but he was not, therefore . . .

Let the students think of other cause-and-effect statements about Slote's books. Divide each sentence into two portions, cause and effect. Write each part on a separate index card or sentence strip. Students may match the causes with the correct effects. Conclude by asking everyone to write an effect statement to complete "Because I've read many Alfred Slote books. . . ."

Chapter 6
Fifth Grade/Sixth Grade

Sights and Scenes with Leonard Everett Fisher

Objectives:

1. Recognize continuity between art and writing.
2. Examine the use of lines to create movement and emotion.
3. Understand the concept of the Dewey Decimal system.
4. Apply critical thinking to link historical events to the present day.
5. Locate places on a map and globe.
6. Use art as a medium of communication.
7. Research an event from history.
8. Present a report, outline, play, or demonstration to the class.

Recommended Readings:

Fisher, Leonard Everett. *The Alamo*. Holiday House, 1987.
   The historical significance of the old mission fortress is shown through photographs and original illustrations. (Objectives 1, 4, 5, and 7)

————. *Ellis Island: Gateway to the New World*. Holiday House, 1986.
   Photographs and strong text present a pictorial history of the thousands of immigrants who passed through Ellis Island into a new land. (Objectives 7 and 8)

————. *Galileo*. Macmillan, 1992.
   Paintings illustrate the life of the father of modern science. (Objectives 4 and 8)

————. *The Great Wall of China*. Macmillan, 1986.
   Black-and-white illustrations combine with brief text to recount the construction of the Great Wall. (Objectives 4, 5, and 6)

————. *Monticello*. Holiday House, 1988.
   The effort to construct Thomas Jefferson's dream home is documented in both text and illustrations. (Objectives 4, 6, 7, and 8)

————. *Pyramid of the Sun Pyramid of the Moon.* Macmillan, 1988.
The ancient Mexican pyramids are introduced through brief text and illustrations. (Objectives 6, 7, and 8)

————. *The Statue of Liberty.* Holiday House, 1985.
Full-color photographs and thorough text recount the history of America's great symbol of liberty, freedom, and opportunity. (Objectives 1, 2, 3, 6, and 7)

————. *The Tower of London.* Macmillan, 1987.
Historical events related to the symbols of royal power are depicted through emotion-laden black-and-white illustrations and text. (Objectives 1, 2, 4, 6, and 8)

————. *The Wailing Wall.* Macmillan, 1989.
A pictorial history of the Jewish people in Palestine is linked to Jerusalem's Wailing Wall. (Objectives 5 and 8)

Biographical Sources:

For information on Leonard Everett Fisher see *Something about the Author Autobiographical Series*, vol. 1, pages 89–113 and *Third Book of Junior Authors*, pages 84–85.

Group Introductory Activity:

Leonard Everett Fisher has written and illustrated more than 250 books. He says, "The creative essence that consumes me forms the pattern of my artistic learnings—expressions of form, space, form in space, space and movement, survival and continuity" (*Something about the Author Autobiographical Series*, vol. 1, p. 107). As Fisher's books are read in this unit, ask the students to look for continuity of style in writing and in his artistic expression. Through his creative expression in art and writing Fisher conveys this thought: "In a culture like ours, wherein today's material gratification seems to deny any historical link, knowledge of the past is often and mistakenly brushed aside as irrelevant to our present and future values, much less the course of our nation" (*Something about the Author Autobiographical Series*, vol. 1, p. 105). Share this quote with the students to help them judge the relevancy of historical events to today.

As *The Statue of Liberty* is read aloud, stop and have the students examine Fisher's scratchboard illustration of Alexander's Lighthouse on page 16. Let the students discuss the images, sounds, feelings, and/or sense of movement this picture evokes and how it achieves that sense. Explore the other drawings in the book to note the harmony between the photography and Fisher's original black-and-white illustrations.

Team with the library media specialist to share the books in this unit. Ask the media specialist to help the students identify the call numbers of Fisher's books and understand how they are classified as history, geography, science, or religion.

After Fisher's *The Statue of Liberty* has been read aloud, work with a small group of interested students to memorize the poem "The New Colossus," written by Emma Lazarus. Let the group present to the class the poem, which is engraved on the base of the Statue of Liberty, as a choral reading. Follow with an art activity, allowing the students to use a simulated scratchboard technique to illustrate what the poem means to them. Coat a white piece of heavy paper or mat board with a waxy substance such as crayon or melted paraffin. Paint over the white surface with black india ink or black liquid tempera to which has been added a few drops of liquid detergent (experiment with the amount of detergent needed to allow the tempera to coat the wax). When the ink or paint is thoroughly dry, let the students use various tools (e.g., pencil, scissor points, styluses, or craft sticks) to scratch lines into the black coating, revealing the white surface below. For more information on scratchboard illustration see pages 49–56 of *Literature-Based Art and Music* by Mildred Laughlin and Terri Street (Oryx Press, 1992).

Follow-Up Activities for Teacher and Students to Share:

1. After reading aloud Leonard Everett Fisher's *The Alamo,* lead a discussion on the effect the battles at the Alamo and Goliad had on American history. Study the map in the book, then have the students locate the same area on a large scale map. Several students can follow up by modeling the facade of the Alamo on cardboard. See page 48 of *Mudworks* by MaryAnn Kohl (Bright Ring, 1989) for a recipe for map modeling material.

2. Before reading Leonard Everett Fisher's *The Great Wall of China,* have each student make a "chop" indicating his or her initials. Explain that a chop on Oriental art is like the artist's signature on a painting. Let each child glue string in the reverse of his or her initials onto a wooden block. After the glue has dried thoroughly, let each child use the chop like a rubber stamp to personalize his or her papers. Just prior to sharing the book, explain that the Chinese characters on the title page translate to say "The Great Wall." As the book is read aloud, have the students speculate on the meaning of the other characters. The final page contains the English translations.

    Have the students locate the area represented on pages 4–5 on a globe. Use cardinal directions to explain where this area is located in relation to a selected town or city. Let the children discuss the Mongol threat, which motivated the building of the Great Wall. Ask the students to draw inferences based on the information in the book about the types of government in ancient China and Mongolia. Let the group speculate on the author's purpose in writing this book. Ask the children to determine what theme can be found in the story of the Great Wall's construction.

3. Note the Valley of Mexico time line on the copyright page of Leonard Everett Fisher's *Pyramid of the Sun Pyramid of the Moon.* This time line explains the decorations found on the pages of Fisher's book. Refer to this explanation

while sharing this book with the class. Lead the group to discuss the differences between the various cultures that settled in the Valley of Mexico. Have the children reproduce the decorations, moldings, or pyramids as closely as possible using clay, plaster, or other sculpting materials.

4. As *The Tower of London* by Leonard Everett Fisher is read aloud, have the children examine the illustrations for effect, continuity of story and style, emotion, movement, and information. Introduce the students to the shading possibilities in a monochromatic color scheme. Have each child use a pencil and ruler to measure and draw a 1" wide strip down one 6" side of a 6" × 9" piece of white drawing paper. Tell the children to divide the strip into six rectangles. Have the students use these rectangles to experiment with the shades of gray that can be obtained from an ordinary pencil. Ask the students to leave the top rectangle white and color the bottom rectangle as dark as possible. Starting with the second rectangle from the top, have the children fill in each square with the pencil, making each square gradually darker. The strip thus forms a value chart showing shades between white and the darkest gray obtainable with a graphite pencil. Ask the children to use their pencils to draw and shade an original picture in the remaining portion of the paper.

5. Before reading Leonard Everett Fisher's *The Wailing Wall,* have the students identify the area shown on the map in the book and locate it on a large map or globe. Allow the children to use color-topped straight pins or map tacks to mark locations described in other books by Fisher. Children may then add small tags naming each location. After reading *The Wailing Wall,* point out the chronology chart included in the volume. Ask the children to examine the chart and determine where Fisher's other books fit in the chronology of historical events.

Have the group use direct or paraphrased statements from Leonard Everett Fisher's *The Wailing Wall* to make an outline of the story and information in the book. This outlining process may be used with other books as well.

Follow-Up Activities for Individual Students:

1. After hearing Leonard Everett Fisher's *The Alamo,* research the flags that have flown over the state of Texas. Use scratchboard with color to illustrate the information you discover. Use a black crayon to color heavily on white paper. After the paper is thoroughly coated with crayon, use various tools (e.g., dull pencils, ice cream sticks) to scratch the design of the flag into the crayon. After the flag design is etched, use watercolors to lightly add the appropriate colors to the illustration.

2. After sharing in class *The Alamo* by Leonard Everett Fisher, read more about the role of Susanna Dickinson in *Susanna of the Alamo: A True Story* by John Jakes (Harcourt Brace Jovanovich, 1986). Share the information with the class in an oral presentation.

3. Read Leonard Everett Fisher's *Ellis Island: Gateway to the New World.* Pretend you were an immigrant. Write a story or produce a play depicting a first-person viewpoint of the experience.

4. After reading Leonard Everett Fisher's *Ellis Island: Gateway to the New World,* draft an outline of the book. The outline may be composed of direct statements from the book and should contain the key events in the island's history in sequential order. Conclude the outline by telling why Ellis Island holds special meaning for the author.

5. Read the biography *Galileo* by Leonard Everett Fisher. Replicate several of his discoveries such as the pendulum or principles of motion and falling objects. Demonstrate and explain these to the class. Note the historical and scientific significance of Galileo's life.

6. Leonard Everett Fisher says that American history had a strong influence in his family. "To all of us it was important to understand American institutions and their origins in order to remain free" (*Something about the Author Autobiographical,* vol. 1, p. 101). Read *Monticello.* Use the quote from Fisher to help you analyze how the life, work, and architectural interests of Thomas Jefferson may have influenced Leonard Everett Fisher.

7. In *Monticello,* Leonard Everett Fisher notes that architecture as a profession did not really exist in colonial America. Thomas Jefferson studied to become a master builder. Read and report on why the building of Monticello was a unique accomplishment in colonial America. List the stages in the construction. Speculate on how Jefferson's five-year visit to France affected Monticello's design and construction. Complete your report by making a diorama or detailed drawing of a room in Monticello. Display the diorama or illustration as you present your report to the class

8. After reading Leonard Everett Fisher's *Monticello,* further research and report on architecture or other crafts in colonial America. Refer to *The Architects* (Franklin Watts, 1970) or other books in Fisher's series, "Colonial Americans," if they are available.

9. After hearing in class *Pyramid of the Sun Pyramid of the Moon* by Leonard Everett Fisher, research the rediscovery of these pyramids. What are some of the theories about the original purpose of the pyramids? What restoration measures have been taken to preserve these ancient structures? Complete your research by building a model of one of the pyramids. Present your report to the class.

10. After reading Leonard Everett Fisher's *The Statue of Liberty,* research the seven ancient wonders of the world which so intrigued Bartholdi. Build a model of the ancient wonder of your choice.

11. After reading *The Statue of Liberty* by Leonard Everett Fisher, research one of the following men who were instrumental in establishing the Statue of Liberty: Joseph Pulitzer, Alexandre-Gustave Eiffel, Frederic-Auguste Bartholdi, or Richard Morris Hunt.

12. After hearing Leonard Everett Fisher's *The Tower of London,* replicate one of the Royal Arms shown in the book. Explain the meaning of the design and its importance to the story.

13. After hearing *The Tower of London* in class, build a model of this fortress and compare its purpose to that of other landmarks Fisher has featured in books, such as the Great Wall of China and the Alamo.

Closure:

Leonard Everett Fisher's art is very accurate and true to life. Many of his books offer maps and chronological time lines. Have students create an overall view of Fisher's extensive work by using the card or computer catalog and other resources to make a time line depicting when the books in this unit, and others written or illustrated by Fisher, were published. Note the various art techniques he used in the books. As one group of students completes the time line, have another group list all of Fisher's books by noting the Dewey Decimal number of each. Work with the library media specialist to have the students make annotated cards showing the Dewey Decimal number, title, author, illustrator, publisher, and copyright date of Leonard Everett Fisher books. Let them demonstrate their knowledge of the card catalog by showing how the cards would be filed and how to locate a book by the call number.

It's a Mystery to Me!

Objectives:

1. Recognize the elements of a mystery.
2. Demonstrate understanding of figurative language and imagery.
3. Use a thesaurus to expand vocabulary.
4. Respond to literature through the arts, math, or creative writing.
5. Research a topic.
6. Develop perceptual awareness and deductive skills.

Recommended Readings:

Bunting, Eve. *Is Anybody There?* Lippincott, 1988.
Marcus suspects Nick, a boarder, of being the culprit who has been stealing food and other small items from his home. (Objectives 2, 4, and 6)

Griffin, Pini R. *The Treasure Bird.* Macmillan, 1992.
Jessy and her stepbrother Matt hope to unravel the mystery of the lost treasure so that their family can afford to remain on Great-uncle Matthew's land. (Objectives 1 and 4)

Hahn, Mary Downing. *The Dead Man in Indian Creek.* Houghton Mifflin, 1990.
Young Matt Parker and his friend encounter danger as they try to solve a murder. (Objective 4)

Hamilton, Virginia. *The House of Dies Drear.* Illustrated by Eros Keith. Macmillan, 1968.
Thomas vows to discover the many secrets of the house of Dies Drear, a former stop on the Underground Railroad. (Objectives 4 and 5)

Howe, James. *Howliday Inn.* Illustrated by Lynn Munsinger. Atheneum, 1982.
Harold, the writing dog, shares the mystery and terror that stalked Chateau Bow-Wow while he and Chester, a cat, were boarded there. (Objectives 2 and 3)

Kehret, Peg. *Horror at the Haunted House.* E.P. Dutton, 1992.
Young Ellen encounters a ghost and a real-life mystery while working at the Historical Haunted House. (Objectives 1, 4, and 5)

Nixon, Joan Lowery. *The Other Side of Dark.* Delacorte, 1986.
Stacy awakens from a four-year coma to find her life irrevocably changed, her mother dead, and her own life in danger from the murderer. (Objectives 2, 4, 5, and 6)

Raskin, Ellen. *The Westing Game.* E.P. Dutton, 1978.
An odd assortment of heirs must solve the mystery of an eccentric millionaire's death in order to claim the bulk of the estate. (Objectives 1, 2, 4, and 6)

Roberts, Willo Davis. *Megan's Island.* Atheneum, 1988.
Megan's life is disrupted when her mother abruptly whisks her brother and her away, leaving them with their grandfather at an isolated lake cabin before vanishing. (Objective 4)

Yolen, Jane. *Piggins.* Illustrated by Jane Dyer. Harcourt Brace Jovanovich, 1987.
Piggins the butler is quick to solve the mystery of Mrs. Reynard's stolen diamond pendant. (Objectives 1 and 6)

Group Introductory Activity:

Prepare a matrix chart containing the following headings: "Setting," "Puzzle," "Clues," "Sleuth," "Suspects," "Suspenseful Events," "Figurative Language," "Speculation," and "Resolution." The chart will be used throughout the unit as a model for solving the various mysteries students will encounter in the books in this unit. Laminate the chart so that it may be used repeatedly.

Author Joan Lowery Nixon says the three most important techniques in writing are "description utilizing the five senses, use of strong action verbs which present a visual image, and opening sentences which are so interesting they reach out and firmly grasp a reader's attention" (*Something about the Author*, vol. 44, p. 136). Ask the children to listen carefully to the opening paragraphs from three mysteries to determine which of Nixon's writing techniques they demonstrate.

> "There was one week of school left on the day the peculiar things began to happen." (*Megan's Island*, p. 3)
> "The dream is too long. It slithers and slips and gurgles deeply into midnight pools in which I see my own face looking back. It pounds with a scream that crashes into earth-torn caverns and is drowned; it surges with the babble of voices that splash against my ears; it whispers over words I can't understand." (*The Other Side of Dark*, p. 1)
> "The sun sets in the west (just about everyone knows that), but Sunset Towers faced east. Strange!" (*The Westing Game*, p. 1)

Ask the children to identify the mood conveyed by each passage. Point out that the mood is established by the use of descriptive words. Explain to the class that mystery stories are characterized by several features, one of which is an eerie or suspenseful mood. Let the children brainstorm other elements of a mystery. Be sure the children include these fundamentals: suspense, the feeling that something terrible could happen at any moment; an eerie setting that helps create the atmosphere of danger and suspense; spine-tingling words and figurative language; a puzzle or crime with clues to its resolution; and mysterious or suspicious characters.

Display the mystery matrix. Explain each of the areas to the children, relating them to the elements the group brainstormed earlier. Before sharing Jane Yolen's *Piggins* with the class, point out that Jane Yolen has crafted a light-hearted mystery in this book. Ask the students to listen carefully to the story, trying to find the different mystery elements Yolen included. Stop reading after the line "Perhaps the butler did it." Explain to the children that this phrase is an old cliché about mysteries. Let the children discuss whether or not they think the butler did, indeed, "do it" in this story. Refer to the mystery elements on the matrix and have the students share the characters or events they believe should be categorized under each of the elements. Continue the reading, stopping again after the line "'None other than . . .' says Mr. Reynard." Have the children recall the clues Piggins noticed. Before finishing the reading, let the students examine the clues and suspects to see if anyone can deduce a solution to the mystery. Check the children's solutions by reading the final portion of the book.

Encourage the students to individually read several mysteries during this unit. Issue a challenge cloaked in mystery, for example, "Spine-tingling suspense, eerie atmosphere, characters who are not what they appear to be, this is the world of mystery. Come in, if you dare."

Follow-Up Activities for Teacher and Students to Share:

1.   Read Pini R. Griffin's *The Treasure Bird* aloud to the class. Throughout the book, the author foreshadows the solution to the mystery. Let the children discuss clues that they did not recognize as important until the mystery was solved. Complete the mystery matrix chart for the book. As a math follow-up, let the children determine the value of 100 pounds of gold on today's market. Children may consult *The Wall Street Journal*, the financial section of the newspaper, or a stockbroker for the price of gold per ounce. It should be pointed out that gold is measured in troy ounces, not standard ounces. (There are only 12 troy ounces in a pound rather than 16.) The children may construct and solve equations to discover how much the entire find was worth, the value of the family's share, and how much money Curtis would have received for his portion.

2.   James Howe uses effective adjectives and verbs to establish alternating moods of hilarity and terror in *Howliday Inn*. Ask the children to listen for words that evoke a mood or emotional response as the book is read aloud. Let them share examples they note during each reading session. After the book is completed, let the students speculate on how an author chooses just the right word to give the desired effect in a story. Brainstorm a list of "lazy" adjectives and verbs that are often overused in writing (e.g., *big, scary, funny, walk, went* or *said*). Let each child choose five overused words to include on a personal list. Visit the library media center, where the media specialist can introduce the children to the thesaurus. Have the children put their "lazy" words to work by using the thesaurus to find synonyms for their words that are more descriptive. Have the students write the original word in the center of a word wheel and arrange the more descriptive synonyms around the center, like spokes radiating out from a hub. Post the completed word wheels on a board labeled "Words that Go Places." This board may be used as a long-term display to aid students' creative writing.

3.   Prior to reading Peg Kehret's *Horror at the Haunted House,* have the students reexamine the mystery format on the wall chart. Ask the class to listen carefully as the book is shared, noting the various mystery elements as

they occur. After completing the book, let the children discuss the elements of the mystery, comparing their notes. Let student volunteers complete the different sections of the mystery matrix with their observations from Kehret's novel. As a follow-up, stage a Historical Haunted House, perhaps as part of a school carnival or open house. The scenes may be enacted by students if desired, but a simpler form would be to have the children construct dioramas of the various scenes. The library media specialist and social studies specialist may be of help in selecting and staging individual scenes. Children should research the historical events carefully to ensure authenticity. Invent a fictional scene as a group and see if visitors can identify the depiction that is not authentic.

4. Ellen Raskin's *The Westing Game* is a multilayered mystery that received the Newbery Award in 1979. Read this book with small groups of students in book discussion groups. This format of reading will enable the students to share their observations and speculations as the book is read. Students should keep a "detective's log" to help them track the characters and clues as events unfold. Children should record character descriptions and details about them, clues, sensory language, passages that supply comic relief, and their speculations about the resolution of the puzzle. Ask the children to note page numbers of clues that they feel are important. In each group meeting the students should discuss the entries in their logs and their reactions to the reading. After the book is completed, ask the group members to design a mystery game based on *The Westing Game*. The children may choose to create a board game similar to a classic game such as "Clue" (Parker Brothers, 1949, 1986) or invent an entirely original game based on characters and situations in Raskin's novel.

Follow-Up Activities for Individual Students:

1. Read the mystery novel *Is Anybody There?* by Eve Bunting. Consider the supplies you would need if you planned to stow away in someone's attic for an extended period of time. List the items you would collect to take with you for a two-week "hideout." Explain what purpose each object would serve.

2. As you read *Is Anybody There?* by Eve Bunting, note words and phrases that appeal to the five senses. Draw an eye, a nose, an ear, a tongue, and a finger, each about four inches high, on a sheet of drawing paper. Write at least three sensory words and the page number on which it appears on the representation of the appropriate sensory organ.

3. Read Mary Downing Hahn's *The Dead Man in Indian Creek*. Consider how the story would have changed if Tiffany had gone straight to the police with the doll instead of waiting and watching the parade. Write a new ending to the story, beginning with the words "Tiffany longed to see the

parade, but she knew the doll was important. Reluctantly she headed toward the police station, her head filled with the vision of the wonderful parade she would not see. . . ."

4. After reading Mary Downing Hahn's *The Dead Man in Indian Creek,* construct a three-dimensional scene to represent an event or episode from the story. Label the scene with the author and title of the book and display it in the classroom or library media center.

5. Read Virginia Hamilton's *The House of Dies Drear.* Hamilton has written several books, both fiction and nonfiction, addressing the issue of slavery. Research the Underground Railroad. Imagine you have been transported back in time to the era of slavery. You are a conductor on the Underground Railroad. Write a letter to a Quaker friend in Canada telling about the danger and hardships of a trip and how Dies Drear helped you on the journey. Include details about the origin and operation of the Underground Railroad.

6. After reading *The House of Dies Drear* by Virginia Hamilton, speculate on the future of Thomas and his family. Write a paragraph predicting what you believe will be done with the fortune of Dies Drear. Justify your predictions with information about Thomas, his family, and other characters and situations included in Hamilton's book. You may wish to locate and read the sequel to this story, *The Mystery of Drear House* (Greenwillow, 1987), and compare your predictions to the course Hamilton chose.

7. Read Joan Lowery Nixon's *The Other Side of Dark.* This mystery has won several awards, including the Edgar Allan Poe Mystery Writer's Award. Assume that a Hollywood producer is planning to make a film of *The Other Side of Dark* and has hired you as the casting director for the movie. You must choose an actor or actress for each role in the production. Write your list of characters and the actor or actress you'd choose for each part. Be sure to explain why you have selected each individual, in case the producer questions your judgment.

8. After reading Joan Lowery Nixon's *The Other Side of Dark,* research amnesia to discover some of the causes of the condition, methods of treatment, and the prognosis for recovery.

9. After reading Ellen Raskin's *The Westing Game,* create a mystery song game of your own. Choose a well-known song and copy the individual words onto paper squares. Make two identical sets of cards. Paper clip words in bundles of four or five, chosen at random. Divide the class into two teams and distribute the cards to each member of the team. The players in each group must examine their words and try to guess the mystery song. The first group to identify the song and arrange the words in proper order wins the game.

10. Read Willo Davis Roberts's mystery *Megan's Island.* Make character wheels describing Megan, Sandy, their grandfather, and Ben. Use a compass to draw, on construction paper, four 3" circles with 9" circles around each of them. Cut out the 9" circles and write the characters' names and the title

and author of the book inside each 3" circle. Use a protractor to divide the outer circles into eight sections of 45° each. Choose eight adjectives to describe each character. Write one adjective, going outward from the central circle, along each dividing line between sections so that the adjectives serve as "spokes" from the center hub. Draw sketches of items or scenes from the story in the areas between adjectives.

11. After reading *Megan's Island* by Willo Davis Roberts, write a diary from Megan's viewpoint. Include entries written after each of these events: Megan's mother spirits Megan and Sandy away to Grandpa's cabin; Megan and Sandy explore the island for the first time; Megan meets Ben; Megan receives the second letter from Annie; Megan finds her birth certificate; the men attack and beat Grandpa; and the villains are captured. Write a final entry that takes place after the story, telling Megan's reactions to meeting her paternal grandfather.

Closure:

Number the books in this unit that appear on the mystery matrix. Ask each child to count the number of letters in his or her first name, middle name, and last name. Have the students use the numbers to determine which setting, puzzle, and suspicious character to include in an original mystery story; for example, a student named Theodore Lee Allen would create a mystery using the setting from the eighth book, the puzzle from the third book, and a suspect similar to one in the fifth book. The other elements of mystery may be selected at random. Remind the students to use Joan Lowery Nixon's three basics for good writing: sensory descriptions, strong action verbs, and vivid opening sentences that grab the attention of the readers. Help the children to select a piece of instrumental music that sets an appropriate mood for reading the stories aloud.

Kathryn Lasky's Devices of Style

Objectives:

1. Recognize devices of style and tone in writing.
2. Focus on elements of story structure.
3. Express empathy for a book character.
4. Write a story simulating an author's style.
5. Respond to reading through art, writing, discussion, and field trips.
6. Research and communicate information in oral and written forms.

Recommended Readings:

Lasky, Kathryn. *Beyond the Divide*. Macmillan, 1983.
A young Amish girl struggles for survival of both body and spirit on the journey from Pennsylvania to California. (Objectives 3 and 5)

———. *Dinosaur Dig*. Illustrated by Christopher Knight. William Morrow, 1990.
A scientific dig is accurately depicted in a photo essay that follows a family of amateur paleontologists. (Objectives 1 and 6)

———. *Double Trouble Squared*. Harcourt Brace Jovanovich, 1991.
The telepathic abilities of twins July and Liberty lead them to an encounter with a literary ghost. (Objectives 1 and 4)

———. *I Have an Aunt on Marlborough Street*. Illustrated by Susan Guevara. Macmillan, 1992.
Young Phoebe describes her seasonal visits to her Aunt Phoebe's home in Boston. (Objectives 1 and 5)

———. *Monarchs*. Illustrated by Christopher G. Knight. Harcourt Brace Jovanovich, 1993.
The life cycle of the monarch butterfly and its mysterious migration are presented in text and photographs. (Objectives 5 and 6)

———. *Night Journey*. Illustrated by Trina Schart Hyman. Frederick Warne, 1981.
An elderly woman shares with her great-granddaughter the memory of her family's escape from Czarist Russia. (Objectives 1, 2, and 3)

———. *Sea Swan*. Illustrated by Catherine Stock. Macmillan, 1988.
An elderly woman gains a sense of independence as she discovers the joy of learning new skills. (Objectives 1, 3, and 5)

———. *Searching for Laura Ingalls: A Reader's Journey*. Illustrated by Christopher G. Knight. Macmillan, 1993.
A journey compares the land and people of Laura Ingalls's day to that of the present time. (Objectives 4 and 6)

———. *Sugaring Time*. Illustrated by Christopher G. Knight. Macmillan, 1983.
The annual process of collecting maple sap in early spring and boiling it into maple syrup is clearly defined in text and photographs. (Objective 6)

———. *Surtsey: The New Place on Earth*. Illustrated by Christopher G. Knight. Hyperion, 1992.
The birth of a new land and the emergence of life upon it are documented in a photo essay. (Objectives 5 and 6)

Biographical Sources:

For biographical information on Kathryn Lasky see *Something about the Author*, vol. 69, pages 129–32 and *Sixth Book of Junior Authors & Illustrators*, pages 160–61.

Group Introductory Activity:

Kathryn Lasky's writings include picture books, fiction, and nonfiction which is often accompanied by photographs taken by her husband, Christopher G. Knight. She has said that as a child she was always a compulsive story maker (*Something about the Author*, vol. 69, p. 131). As each of Kathryn Lasky's books is read have the children listen for and note examples of figurative language the author uses.

Rebecca Lukens defines style as "how an author says something, as opposed to what he or she says" (*A Critical Handbook of Children's Literature*, 4th ed. HarperCollins, 1990, p. 139). As Kathryn Lasky's *Night Journey* is read aloud, ask the children to focus on her style of writing. Often times the conversation between Nana Sashie and Rache shows how Sashie's line of thought is in the past while Rache's is in the present. Have the children discuss how the author handles the differing points of view between four generations of a family. As the book is read, mark passages that effectively express emotion or create a mood, such as "His body became taut . . .," (p. 30); or "Wolf looked stunned . . .," (p. 40). Reread these passages to the children and ask them to discuss the mood or emotions the words create.

The following questions can serve as guidelines to strengthen the discussion and encourage the expression of empathy for the characters in any of Kathryn Lasky's books:

- What do you think was the author's purpose for writing this story?
- Suggest the theme or underlying idea that holds the story together. Select lines that demonstrate an explicit theme.
- Who is the protagonist (main character)? What words can be used to describe the main character and his or her feelings in this story?
- Where and when does the story take place? How does the setting affect the story?
- What are the main ideas in the story?
- What problems or conflicts do the characters face? How are they resolved?
- How does the story create a mood or feeling?

Follow-Up Activities for Teacher and Students to Share:

1. Kathryn Lasky uses descriptive language and comparisons to captivate readers' imaginations in her book *Dinosaur Dig*. While reading the book aloud have the students listen to her descriptions. Stop reading periodically and ask the children to recall descriptive passages they heard (e.g., "the flat prairie has erupted," "the dun-colored landscape," and "its sculling tail tapered off..."). Ask a small group of students to write down these passages as they are reread for clarity. Follow up by having the students look at the list of passages and draw or create three-dimensional scenes to complement the language. Label the artwork with the written passage and display the scenes in the library media center.

   After reading *Dinosaur Dig* to the class, have teams of students select tasks from the following list to prepare and demonstrate for the class:

   • Draw the buttes as described in the book;
   • Use plaster of paris or clay to create an imitation fossil of a leaf or shell;
   • Draw the time line Chris Knight explained to his family;
   • Work in teams to make a very large dinosaur out of papier-mâché or corrugated cardboard and display the finished product in the media center or public library;
   • Devise a time line showing the various eras of time; or,
   • Answer the following questions: What was the most interesting or intriguing thing you learned? What have you learned that you did not know before? What questions do you still have about digging for dinosaurs?

   If possible, invite a paleontologist to show his or her equipment and talk with the class as a follow-up.

2. Kathryn Lasky heightens the reader's awareness by using language that touches the five senses. As her novel *Double Trouble Squared* is read aloud, stop after each chapter to review the descriptive passages the children notice. Let the children discuss how the language increases awareness of various senses; for example, auditory awareness is increased by "She could hear the creak of the porch swing below, pushed by a whisper of wind" (p. 1), while "she felt the crushing presence of a shape that might tumble right down on her" (p. 49) appeals to the reader's sense of touch. As the students listen, have them note at least three descriptive passages from each chapter in their writing journals. The children can then use Lasky's writing as examples or as starter sentences for their own creative writing. Students may continue this activity when reading the other books in this unit.

3. Kathryn Lasky's *Monarchs* shows the majestic beauty of the butterfly and tells of its amazing migration. After the book has been read aloud, lead a question-and-answer discussion period focusing on such questions as:

- What are the stages of metamorphosis?
- How can one tell the difference between a male and female butterfly?
- What is the difference in the life cycle between early spring and late summer monarchs?
- What is known about the monarchs' migration?
- What dangers does the monarch face on its journey?
- What is a "magic circle"?
- How do monarchs react to cold air and to carbon dioxide?
- What are some of the gifts the butterfly gives us?

As an art follow-up let the children create a scene where the monarchs look "like bunches of tissue-paper shingles" (p. 34).

4. Kathryn Lasky's *Searching for Laura Ingalls: A Reader's Journey* is a photo essay with diary entries by the author's daughter. After reading about Meribah's experience, have a group of students research the appearance of their local community 50 to 125 years ago. Ask the library media specialist to help the children take photographs of any old photographs or daguerreotypes that may be available. Let the students select the order of photographs that should be included in a photo essay of their community's history. Have one group of students write the factual entries while another group writes personal entries like those of Meribah. The completed product can be placed in the library media center.

Follow-Up Activities for Individual Students:

1. While reading Kathryn Lasky's *Beyond the Divide,* pretend to be Meribah or one of the other pioneers. Write a diary entry in first person for each of the dates and locations recorded in the book.

2. After reading Kathryn Lasky's *Beyond the Divide,* recount for the class the conflicts and hardships that Meribah faced and how she changed and grew in strength and in spirit. As you retell the accounts, use a large wall map of the United States to pinpoint the journey and the locations where each incident occurred.

3. After hearing Kathryn Lasky's *Double Trouble Squared* read aloud, pretend to have Liberty's curiosity and research the subject of twins. Demonstrate the meaning of "mirror-image twins" for the class. Share what research shows about twins separated at birth. Explain the connection between research on twins and the book characters.

4. In Kathryn Lasky's *Double Trouble Squared* the Starbuck family had a motto. Write down the motto in both Latin and English. Then explain to the class its significance. Think of your own family. Invent an appropriate motto, share it with the class, and tell why you selected it.

5. Kathryn Lasky's story *I Have an Aunt on Marlborough Street* is filled with descriptive language, the most significant being similes (comparisons using *like* or *as*). The illustrator paid special attention to the line "the chimneys have pots that look like funny hats. . . ." After reading this story select your favorite descriptive line and illustrate it in watercolors. If available, use a calligraphy pen to add the quote from the book to the finished illustration.

6. After hearing Kathryn Lasky's *Monarchs* in class, locate and read the Papago story of "How the Butterflies Came to Be" from Michael J. Caduto and Joseph Bruchac's *Keepers of the Animals* (Fulcrum, 1991). If this book is not available, ask the library media specialist to help you locate another legend on the butterfly. How does this legend compare to the nonfiction book *Monarchs*? To note your comparisons, make a three-column diagram. On the left column put the title *Monarch*. In the middle column write "How the stories are alike," and on the right column put the title "How the Butterflies Came to Be." List the information from each story in the appropriate column, being sure to indicate how they are alike. Share your findings with the class in an oral report.

7. After sharing Kathryn Lasky's *Night Journey,* create a play or a reader's theater script. The dialogue about Nana Sashie in the first 28 pages is one possible source for a script. Be sure to use a narrator to pull the story together and share enough of the story to tease listeners into reading *Night Journey* for themselves. Ask your teacher or the library media specialist to help you present your script to another class.

8. As you read *Sea Swan* by Kathryn Lasky, record examples of how the author creates sensory awareness by using language to describe what the characters see, hear, feel, taste, and smell. For example, the line "she was floating on her back and watching the sun set to the west like a huge orange pumpkin . . ." gives the reader a sense of how Elzibah enjoyed her new adventure. Share three of your favorite sensory examples with the class.

9. While reading *Sea Swan,* notice how Elzibah writes letters to Claire and Jeremy describing what she is doing and learning. Write several letters to a real or make-believe friend. In the letters first tell your friend what you do each day. Next tell something new you have learned to do and how you learned it. Then tell about an experience you had with the newly learned skill and finally tell what your future plans might be.

10. After reading Kathryn Lasky's *Searching for Laura Ingalls: A Reader's Journey,* draw a map showing the places Laura Ingalls lived in her stories. Be sure to draw the states and add the names of towns and dates when Laura lived there. In a different colored pencil show where the Knight family traveled. Point out the differences and similarities that Meribah found between her journey and Laura's.

11. *Sugaring Time* by Kathryn Lasky takes the reader chronologically through the steps in the production of maple syrup. Read the book, then develop a time line depicting the order of the steps involved. Share the information and matching photographs from the book with the class.
12. After reading Kathryn Lasky's *Surtsey: The New Place on Earth,* use the library media center to locate and read a Norse creation story and a Native American creation story. Compare the two tales for similarities, differences, and types of characters. Retell one of the stories for the class.
13. Construct a model of Surtsey after reading the book. Share the model and how the actual island came into existence with the class.

Closure:

Kathryn Lasky says that she is really not concerned with messages in her books but, rather, she hopes "that they (the readers) come away with a sense of joy—indeed celebration—about something they have sensed of the world in which they live" (*Something about the Author*, vol. 69, p. 132). Review the books that have been read in this unit with the children and have the students brainstorm what they have gained from each book. Culminate the discussion by serving foods that her characters liked, such as pancakes with maple syrup.

Thirteen Strong Women

Objectives:

1. Recognize and define types of conflict.
2. Demonstrate critical thinking skills through speaking and writing.
3. Identify and discuss ways characters from different backgrounds differ from or are similar to people today.
4. Organize thoughts and/or events sequentially.
5. Distinguish between fiction and nonfiction.
6. Recognize theme in literature.
7. Listen and read for figurative and descriptive language.
8. Write an original story, poem, or essay.

Recommended Readings:

Boyd, Candy Dawson. *Charlie Pippin*. Macmillan, 1987.
Eleven-year-old Charlie Pippin takes a stand on the issue of peace and war. (Objectives 1, 3, and 7)

Lauber, Patricia. *Lost Star: The Story of Amelia Earhart*. Scholastic, 1988.
This biography depicts Amelia Earhart's courage and commitment to her goals. (Objectives 2, 5, and 8)

Lowry, Lois. *Number the Stars*. Houghton Mifflin, 1989.
Ten-year-old Annemarie learns the meaning of bravery when she uses her wit and strength to help a Jewish family escape from the Nazis. (Objectives 2 and 8)

Lurie, Alison. *Clever Gretchen and Other Forgotten Folktales*. Illustrated by Margot Tomes. Thomas Y. Crowell, 1980.
This volume presents 15 folktales depicting women heroines. (Objectives 4, 6, and 8)

McKinley, Robin. *The Hero and the Crown*. Greenwillow, 1984.
Aerin is destined to confront the forces of evil and return the crown to her people, restoring peace to the land. (Objectives 1, 3, 6, and 7)

Myers, Anna. *Red-Dirt Jessie*. Walker, 1992.
Young Jessie displays a strong will and depth of character as she and her family cope with her sister's death and her father's withdrawal into depression. (Objectives 1 and 3)

Nixon, Joan Lowery. *A Family Apart*. Bantam, 1987.
Young Frances Mary disguises herself as a boy in order to protect her youngest brother when their family is separated. (Objectives 2, 3, and 8)

Paterson, Katherine. *The Great Gilly Hopkins*. Thomas Y. Crowell, 1978.
An 11-year-old foster child's manipulative schemes backfire when she learns to care for and respect those around her. (Objectives 1, 2, 6, and 8)

Shreve, Susan. *The Gift of the Girl Who Couldn't Hear*. Tambourine, 1991.
Two girls, each with special gifts, help each other try out for the school musical. (Objectives 1 and 6)

Stanley, Fay. *The Last Princess: The Story of Princess Ka`iulani of Hawai`i*. Illustrated by Diane Stanley. Four Winds, 1991.
This brief, illustrated biography examines the life of Hawai'i's last heir to the throne. (Objectives 2 and 4)

Zhensun, Zheng, and Low, Alice. *A Young Painter: The Life and Paintings of Wang Yani—China's Extraordinary Young Artist*. Illustrated by Zheng Zhensun. Scholastic, 1992.
Wang Yani, who began painting at the age of three, expresses her life through the arts. (Objectives 2, 3, and 8)

Group Introductory Activity:

Initiate this unit on strong women by having the class brainstorm a list of women or heroines from history to the present. After at least 10 names have been collected, let the children discuss the women and what they did. Divide the class into groups to brainstorm the qualities these women possessed. When the groups come back together, discuss the qualities the women had in common. Most of the characters in this unit are dynamic, growing and changing in the course of the story as a result of conflict and resolution. If the students have not experienced the unit on Avi or "Overcoming the Odds," explain the four types of conflict: person against nature, person against self, person against person, and person against society. Have the students define the four types of conflict in their literary notebooks. As each book in this unit is read, the students may identify which kind of conflict the protagonist faced.

Read aloud Candy Dawson Boyd's *Charlie Pippin*. As the book is read, have the group discuss the qualities the characters in the book demonstrate. Ask the students how they can relate to Charlie and her difficulties in school and at home. Have the students respond to the following questions: What difference does it make in the story that Charlie is an African-American girl? How is her background different from or similar to that of the students? Carefully examine Charlie's relationship with her sister, Sienna, described as "like a splinter, the kind that pushed in deeper and deeper" (page 5). Ask the students to write down in their literary notebooks the figurative language, descriptions, and qualities of people found in *Charlie Pippin* and other books in this unit.

While reading the book, ask the children what the phrase "responsible learners" meant to Charlie. Let the children compare her idea to their own. If the class does not share current events, determine what issues the students would choose to report on and why. On page 39 Charlie asks, "Do dreams have to die?" At this point in the reading, send a student to the library media center to locate Langston Hughes's poem "Dreams," which is included in *The Random House Book of Poetry for Children* (Random House, 1983). Share the poem with the class. Discuss the views of both the poet and Charlie's grandpa. Complete the book. Urge the children to evaluate the choices and decision Charlie and her father made in the course of the story and determine whether they were appropriate or inappropriate. Have the children examine the conflict Charlie faced to determine its source and the type of conflict.

Follow-Up Activities for Teacher and Students to Share:

1. Read aloud Patricia Lauber's *Lost Star: The Story of Amelia Earhart*. Have a group of students create a bulletin board depicting Amelia Earhart's life. Suggest a line to use as a theme, such as, "What mattered was setting herself a challenge and meeting it" (p. 3). After sharing the book, have the students

map her various flights. Let the children discuss the challenges Amelia Earhart faced in her life. Ask the group to judge how the hard years affected her determination to set and achieve goals. As she was growing up, Earhart wondered why girls in books were never allowed to have exciting adventures like boys. Ask the children to speculate on what Earhart might have thought of her biography. Urge the students to carry their speculation further by choosing contemporary books that Amelia Earhart might enjoy reading. Have the students recall the difference between fiction and nonfiction literature and then categorize this book in the proper class. Let the children discuss the symbolism in the book title, *Lost Star*. Conclude by letting the group brainstorm a list of ways in which Amelia Earhart's life demonstrated courage and commitment.

2. Folktales are known for expressing the universality of human needs and wishes. In reading groups, share the following tales from *Clever Gretchen and Other Forgotten Folktales* by Alison Lurie: "Manka and the Judge," "Mizilca," and "Molly Whuppie." Have the group members discuss the attributes of the heroine and determine the theme or comment on human nature in each tale.

    As individual students read these folktales, have them design a book jacket for each story. The book jacket should include an illustration that will entice another student to read it and a brief summary of the tale on the flap. Another source for folktales about women is Robert D. San Souci's *Cut from the Same Cloth: American Women of Myth, Legend, and Tall Tale* (Philomel, 1993).

3. To use Robin McKinley's *The Hero and the Crown* in a book discussion, read aloud to page 82 and then have the children discuss the characters, Aerin's destiny, and problems. On page 77, Aerin recognizes "the awkwardness of a father's love for a daughter he doesn't know how to talk to...." Ask the children to determine how this comment is relevant to parent/child relationships of today. Have them compare Aerin's unknown destiny to that of a child growing up in today's world. Urge the group to examine Aerin's feelings for her family members. Read to page 166, continuing to let the students discuss the heroine's destiny and the obstacles she encounters. Introduce the concept of symbolism (using an object or event to represent another thing). Encourage the children to speculate about what the dragons Aerin slays symbolize. Let them brainstorm a list of "dragons" that people face today. Have the group discuss the significance of the line "I am the shape of their fear, it (Maur) said, for you dared to slay me" (p. 137). Clarify any confusion before completing the story. In conclusion, analyze the fate of each character. Lead the children to identify the price Aerin paid in order to reach her destiny. Have the students judge the value of the rewards based

on Aerin's, Tor's, and Arlbeth's viewpoints. Let them propose and justify possible themes in McKinley's fantasy. Students need to be reminded to write in their literary notebooks their views on the conflicts faced by Aerin.

4. Before reading Anna Myers's *Red-Dirt Jessie* to the class, instruct the students to open their literary notebooks and free write what they know about the Dust Bowl or the Depression and the conflicts people faced during that period. Explain to the group that Anna Myers's book is about a family who lived in Oklahoma during the Dust Bowl days of the Depression. After the class has heard the entire book have them free write again, including how the people overcame the difficulties of that time. Have them also include how the life and times of the people in the Dust Bowl differ from today. Compare these writings with the initial papers to determine the amount of student growth and learning about this period. Encourage students to visit the library media center to find other books on the same topic.

5. Have the students describe in a book discussion or, if the book is read aloud, in their literary notebooks the major conflicts Frances Mary faces in Joan Lowery Nixon's *A Family Apart*. Ask the children to examine how she deals with those challenges. On page 152, Mr. Mueller explains to "Frankie," "The people who help slaves . . . make a sacrifice to help someone else." Urge the students to speculate on how these events affected Frances Mary's view of her own situation. Because this is the first book in a series, encourage the students to write a story based on what they predict will happen to the other members of the family. Children may then locate and read the other books in "The Orphan Train" quartet to compare the predictions to Nixon's story lines.

6. Read Katherine Paterson's *The Great Gilly Hopkins* aloud to the class or in a book discussion group. Have the children answer the following questions through discussion or writing in their literary notebooks:

   - How do Gilly's acts of defiance in the beginning of the story define her character?
   - How does Trotter's acceptance of Gilly affect her?
   - How do Gilly's problems and conflicts cause her to face reality and make decisions?
   - What type of conflict does Gilly face?
   - How do the events effect change in Gilly's view of the world?
   - What theme is implied?

7. Read aloud to the class or in a small book discussion group Susan Shreve's *The Gift of the Girl Who Couldn't Hear*. Follow the reading with a group discussion on what it means to have "limitations—real or imagined." Ask the students to think about times or situations when feelings or emotions might prevent someone from reaching a goal. As a follow-up ask the students to

compare the main character's life to that of other strong women in this unit. Have the children determine what type of conflict Gilly faced and the theme expressed in the story.

Follow-Up Activities for Individual Students:

1. After reading *Lost Star: The Story of Amelia Earhart* by Patricia Lauber, refer to newspapers and magazines to select a contemporary woman (living in the last half of this century) whose life has had a large impact on society. Report on this woman's life to the class.

2. In Lois Lowry's *Number the Stars,* 10-year-old Annemarie uses her strength and wit to help her friend Ellen's family escape from the Nazis. After reading Annemarie's story, do two of the following:

   • Write a poem or essay explaining what bravery means to Annemarie.
   • Write an essay on human decency reflecting Kim Maethe-Bruun's feelings.
   • Explain what the title *Number the Stars* and the Star of David symbolize in the book.
   • Describe through writing or art what being a strong woman means to you.

3. As you read Robin McKinley's *The Hero and the Crown,* note examples of descriptive language that refer to one or more of the five senses. Select one passage for each sense, share these five passages with the class, and explain their significance to the story.

4. *A Family Apart* and the three succeeding titles in the "Orphan Train Quartet," written by Joan Lowery Nixon, were inspired by true experiences of children on the orphan trains of the late 1800s. Use local resources to research life and living conditions of children in your locale during the nineteenth century. Compare these events to life today and/or the life of the fictitious Kelly family.

5. After reading Joan Lowery Nixon's *A Family Apart,*write a reader's theater script to share with the class or re-create and act out one of the scenes from the story, such as the train robbery incident.

6. After reading through page 60 in Katherine Paterson's *The Great Gilly Hopkins,* take time to reflect upon Gilly's temperament. Write a poem describing Gilly. When the book has been completed, write a second poem describing Gilly's characteristics toward the end of the story. Now write a third poem about Gilly from the point of view of Trotter, W.E., Mr. Randolph, or Miss Harris. Share these poems with the class.

7. The subject of a biography must have done something that makes his or her life significant. After reading the biography of Princess Ka`iulani, *The Last Princess* by Fay Stanley, write a one-page paper stating how her life was significant. The paper must contain facts to support the statement. Note the conflicts she faced and how or if she overcame them. With the help of the music teacher, locate a piece of music that is representative of Hawaii. Play this as you read your paper aloud.

8. In China it is popular to write several lines about a painting. Often these lines are very poetic. After reading Zheng Zhensun and Alice Low's *A Young Painter: The Life and Paintings of Wang Yani—China's Extraordinary Young Artist*, select several of Yani's illustrations and tell a story about them or write a poem to describe them.

9. In *A Young Painter,* the authors say that Yani feels that music, dance, and painting are related. Select or compose a piece of music and dance form that relate to one of Yani's paintings.

10. After reading about Yani's abilities and interests in *A Young Painter* summarize for the class what painting means to Yani. Explain how her skills have opened doors for her, what her personal strengths are, and how her background differs from or is similar to your own.

11. After reading at least three of the stories in this unit, go to the library media center and use the reference materials to locate information on other strong women. Write down the names of three well-known women. Read the facts on their lives and the significant contributions they have made. Write a summary statement for each of the three women. Include a bibliography of the books used in your research.

Closure:

After having read fiction and nonfiction books depicting strong women, celebrate the role of women in society by inviting women from various walks of life to speak to the class. Ask them each to relate what choices and decisions they made in order to reach their level of achievement. Be sure to include homemakers and women from rural communities, if possible.

Ask the students to each prepare a speech about a strong woman they admire. The character may be real or fictitious. Encourage the students to refer to their literary notebooks for descriptive language and personal characteristics or qualities of strong women. Use a computer software package such as *Crossword Magic* (Mindscape, available for Apple, Macintosh, and IBM), if available, to make a crossword puzzle about the strong women in this unit. Use descriptive language or events from the books as clues so students can solve the puzzle to culminate the study.

Story Time within a Rhyme: Poems that Tell Stories

Objectives:

1. Retell or examine story events from a different point of view.
2. Explore sound devices in poetry.
3. Recognize elements of story structure.
4. Research a topic.
5. Analyze and display information in a variety of forms.
6. Demonstrate understanding of various poetic forms.
7. Evaluate the effectiveness of illustrations.

Recommended Readings:

Lear, Edward. *The Owl and the Pussycat.* Illustrated by Jan Brett. G.P. Putnam's Sons, 1991.
A Caribbean setting lends vibrancy to the nonsensical narrative of an unusual courtship. (Objectives 2, 4, 6, and 7)

Lindbergh, Reeve. *Johnny Appleseed.* Illustrated by Kathy Jakobsen. Little, Brown, 1990.
Folk art paintings and quiltlike borders harmonize with the quaint charm of this biographical narrative poem. (Objectives 2, 4, 5, and 6)

Longfellow, Henry Wadsworth. *Hiawatha.* Illustrated by Susan Jeffers. Dial, 1983.
Intricate pen-and-ink drawings extend the excerpt about Hiawatha's childhood from the classic poem. (Objectives 3 and 5)

―――. *Paul Revere's Ride.* Illustrated by Ted Rand. E.P. Dutton, 1990.
Luminous watercolors breathe new life into the classic narrative poem that immortalized Paul Revere. (Objectives 2, 4, and 6)

Millay, Edna St. Vincent. *The Ballad of the Harp Weaver.* Illustrated by Beth Peck. Philomel, 1991.
The title poem from Millay's Pulitzer Prize-winning collection is extended by full-color paintings. (Objectives 1, 2, and 3)

Noyes, Alfred. *The Highwayman.* Illustrated by Charles Mikolaycak. Lothrop, Lee & Shepard, 1983.
Black-and-white illustrations with red accents add to the emotional impact of the ballad of the highwayman and his true love. (Objectives 3 and 5)

Service, Robert W. *The Cremation of Sam McGee.* Illustrated by Ted Harrison. Greenwillow, 1986.

Sam's Arctic companion is astonished when he fulfills his promise to cremate Sam's remains. (Objectives 1 and 3)

Whittier, John Greenleaf. *Barbara Frietchie.* Illustrated by Nancy Winslow Parker. Greenwillow, 1992.
The classic Civil War poem is presented with illustrations, maps, and historical notes. (Objectives 1 and 5)

Willard, Nancy. *A Visit to William Blake's Inn: Poems for Innocent and Experienced Travelers.* Illustrated by Alice and Martin Provensen. Harcourt Brace Jovanovich, 1981.
Poetry and illustrations blend flawlessly to present the guests and marvels a young boy meets during his stay at William Blake's Inn. (Objectives 3, 5, and 6)

Group Introductory Activity:

Poetry comes in many types, forms, and styles. One of the most diverse types is narrative poetry. Narrative poems may be written in any style or form, but they must tell a story. In this unit students will share several narrative poems in a variety of styles. As each poem is experienced, the children should listen or read for the elements of good story structure.

Introduce the unit by explaining five common sound devices used in poetry: alliteration, imagery, onomatopoeia, rhyme, and rhythm. Alliteration is the repetition of consonant sounds, especially in initial consonants (e.g., "Peter Piper picked a peck of pickled peppers"). Imagery is the use of descriptive words and phrases to create mental images for readers and listeners. The use of words that sound like the action they represent, for example, *crash, jingle,* or *boom,* is called onomatopoeia. The children will undoubtedly be familiar with rhyme but should be reminded that rhyme schemes are many and varied. Poets sometimes use internal rhyme, rhyming words within lines rather than only at the end of lines. Most poetry has a strong sense of rhythm, the pattern of stressed and unstressed syllables.

Write the names of the five sound devices on the chalkboard. Ask the children to listen for sound devices in the first two four-line stanzas from Nancy Willard's *The Voyage of the Ludgate Hill: Travels with Robert Louis Stevenson.* The students should recognize the rhyme and rhythm. Help the children to identify the internal rhyme in the first and third lines of each stanza. Ask the students to listen closely as the rest of the book is read aloud to find examples of each sound device. Let the children share the passages they noted and tell which device each employs. Have each student write one of the lines they chose on a 5 ½" × 9" piece of construction paper and draw an ear shape around the words. Below the line the child should write the name of the sound device it represents; for example, "monkeys with muttering maws" should be labeled "Alliteration" while "crash and tinkle and roar" should be labeled "Onomatopoeia." Have the children cut out the ear shapes and post the statements on a bulletin board labeled "We're All Ears for Poetry." The children should continue to develop the bulletin board throughout the unit, adding phrases from other books they read or hear.

Follow-Up Activities for Teacher and Students to Share:

1. *Johnny Appleseed* by Reeve Lindbergh gives readers a great deal of information about John Chapman, the man who earned the nickname "Johnny Appleseed." After reading the poem and the biographical note at the end of the book to the class, let the children research and share important facts about the pioneer by making a variation of a family tree. Outline a simple, leafless apple tree on a large sheet of brown paper. The tree should have seven large branches coming off the main trunk and a terminal branch stretching skyward. On the trunk write "John Chapman" and his date of birth. Write "Johnny Appleseed" in the root ball of the tree, perhaps even drawing the roots into the shape of the letters. Label each of the side branches with "Family Background," "General Information" (e.g., sex, race, appearance), "Personal Beliefs," "Significant Events," "Strengths and Weaknesses," "Area of Travels," and "Contribution to America." On the terminal branch write the place and date of Chapman's death. Divide the students into seven groups and have each group investigate one of the topics on the side branches. Let a representative from each group copy their findings onto the appropriate branch. Let the children arrange cut paper leaves to highlight the biographical data. Children who complete the individual activity for this book may add their concrete apple poems to the "bio-tree."

2. Read aloud Henry Wadsworth Longfellow's *Paul Revere's Ride*, asking the students to listen for and note poetic devices. Let the children discuss Paul Revere's contribution to the American Revolution. Have the students speculate on how the course of American history might have been changed if Revere and his companions had not warned the minutemen of the British advance.

   Longfellow was a poet, not a historian, and he wrote his poem almost 90 years after the Revolutionary War. Although the poem is rich in imagery and emotional impact, it is not entirely accurate. Send groups of children to the library media center to research the facts about the fateful event. Have the children investigate Revere's fellow riders and discover which man actually reached Concord. Another group might research Paul Revere's later life and his career as a silversmith. Have the groups share their information with the rest of the class in oral reports.

3. Ask the children to note any words they do not understand as they listen to Robert W. Service's *The Cremation of Sam McGee* read aloud. Let the students discuss the unfamiliar words and speculate on their meaning, based

on the context of the poem. Have different students check the group's definitions against the dictionary meaning for each word. The children should then consider the story structure within the poem. Ask the students to identify plot elements that represent the rising action, climax, falling action, and resolution of the story. As a follow-up ask the students to write a telegram that Sam's traveling companion may have sent to tell distant friends or relatives about Sam's demise. Remind the children that they should summarize the beginning, middle, and end of the story as concisely as possible because the cost of a telegram is determined by the number of words it contains.

4.   Regardless of its historical accuracy or lack thereof, John Greenleaf Whittier's *Barbara Frietchie* tells a powerful story in colorful terms. Before reading the poem to the class, share the note describing the setting. It may be advisable to also share the meanings of some of the more obscure or unfamiliar phrases as explained on the final page (e.g., "clustered spires," "dust brown ranks," and "famished rebel horde"). After reading the poem, ask the students to imagine themselves in Barbara Frietchie's place. In the era of the War Between the States, most educated people kept diaries or journals. Have the children write individual journal entries from the viewpoint of Barbara Frietchie or Stonewall Jackson.

Follow-Up Activities for Individual Students:

1. Read Jan Brett's illustrated version of Edward Lear's *The Owl and the Pussycat*. Locate and read a copy of the poem as illustrated by another artist such as Paul Galdone (Houghton Mifflin, 1987) or Janet Stevens (Holiday House, 1983). Compare the different settings and styles of the two illustrators. Which version do you believe best captures the spirit of Lear's story poem? Justify your answer.

2. After reading *The Owl and the Pussycat*, locate and read the biography *Edward Lear: King of Nonsense* by Gloria Kamen (Macmillan, 1990). Lear was a master of the limerick. As a follow-up distill the major events of Edward Lear's life into a five-line limerick. Remember, the rhyme pattern in a limerick is AABBA (i.e., lines 1, 2, and 5 rhyme with each other, as do lines 3 and 4). If the Lear biography is unavailable, rewrite *The Owl and the Pussycat* in limerick form.

3. After hearing Reeve Lindbergh's *Johnny Appleseed* in class, write a concrete poem about apples. Hold an apple and examine it carefully. Notice how it feels, looks, and smells. Bite into the fruit, noting the sound made by the bite, how it feels in your mouth, and the taste of the apple. Make a list of words that describe the apple's effect upon all five of your senses. Remember to include the sound devices found in poetry, such as alliteration and

onomatopoeia. Organize these words into a poem in the shape of an apple. Cut around the finished poem and mount it on the "bio-tree" of Johnny Appleseed.

4. The artwork on the endpapers and copyright page of Henry Wadsworth Longfellow's *Hiawatha* depicts Nokomis falling from the sky after a rival cuts her grapevine swing and weeping over her dying daughter and the infant Hiawatha. In an illustrator's note preceding the poem, Susan Jeffers points out how Wenonah's spirit watches over her son in the first few illustrations for the poem. Read the book, paying careful attention to the structure of the story within the poem. Make a pictograph showing Hiawatha's story on brown paper to simulate animal hide. Use a large, roughly rectangular piece of paper torn from a brown paper grocery bag. You may research and use Indian pictograph signs or invent your own. Draw your pictographs in pencil, then trace over them with black watercolor. When the paint is completely dry, crumple the paper and then smooth it out to give the painting an aged look. Make a key that deciphers your pictographs.

5. Many narrative poems have such a strong musical quality that they almost seem to "sing themselves" into readers' minds. These poems are called ballads. Reread Henry Wadsworth Longfellow's *Paul Revere's Ride*, noting the strong rhythm and rhyme patterns that give the poem its musical quality. Invent an original melody or musical accompaniment for this poem, turning it into a song or a rap. Practice and perform the piece for the class.

6. *The Ballad of the Harp Weaver* was the title poem in Edna St. Vincent Millay's collection that received the 1923 Pulitzer Prize when it was first published. Read the poem in the picture book version illustrated by Beth Peck. What are the main sound devices or elements of poetry exhibited in this work? Examine the story itself. Is it realistic or fantasy? Write a pyramid summary of the different story elements. Follow this form: line 1, a one-word name for a main character; line 2, two words to describe the character; line 3, three words to describe the setting; line 4, four words to tell about the climax of the story; and line 5, five words that describe a problem that still exists at the conclusion.

7. After reading Edna St. Vincent Millay's *The Ballad of the Harp Weaver*, speculate about the harp. Such instruments are very expensive. Retell the story from the mother's viewpoint. Tell how "you" came to own the "harp with a woman's head / Nobody will buy."

8. *The Highwayman* by Alfred Noyes offers a story rich in romance and adventure. Read the poem, noting the figurative language Noyes used. The night, the highwayman's clothing and weapons, Bess, and Tim are all described in vivid terms. As a follow-up construct a quadrarama depicting four scenes from the poem.

To make a quadrarama you must first make four triaramas, three-dimensional displays in the shape of a triangle. Cut four 9" squares from construction paper. Fold one corner of the square down and over to meet the opposite corner, forming a triangle. Crease the fold. Open the paper. Refold the square from an unused corner and crease. When the paper is opened there should be an "x"-shaped crease on the square. Cut in to the center along one crease line. Overlap and glue together two of the triangular sections, forming the base for the triarama. When all four triaramas have been constructed arrange and glue them back-to-back so all the top points meet at the center top. This forms a quadrarama, a four-part display. Use paper cutouts to create a scene in each section of the quadrarama. Select one scene to introduce the main characters, title, and author of the poem; one to represent the conflict; one for the climax; and a fourth scene to show the falling action or the resolution of the story. Rely on the imagery in Noyes's poem for guidance in creating the scenes.

9. The jacket flap of *A Visit to William Blake's Inn: Poems for Innocent and Experienced Travelers* states that Nancy Willard built a six-foot model of the inn while writing the poetry in the book. Create a model from boxes or draw a large cut-away view of the inn, decorating the rooms with appropriate furnishings and characters.

10. Analyze the story told in the poetry of *A Visit to William Blake's Inn*. Focus on the viewpoint of the young visitor to the inn. Fold a sheet of construction paper into thirds and use the divided sheet to make a story frame for the book. You may use pictures or words to depict the beginning, middle, and end of the story Willard tells.

Closure:

In this unit, children have experienced many poems that tell a variety of stories. Ask the students to each choose a favorite folktale or other short story and retell the story as a narrative poem. Students may use any form or style, including limericks, cinquains, and acrostics. Ask the children to use in their poems at least three of the five sound devices emphasized during this study.

Avi's Stories and Structures

Objectives:

1. Evaluate character development.
2. Identify major elements in story structure.

3. Respond to reading through art, writing, discussion, and further reading.
4. Define the type of conflict in a story.
5. Recognize the parts of a mystery.
6. Analyze style in writing.
7. Distinguish various types of genre.

Recommended Readings:

Avi. *Bright Shadow*. Bradbury, 1985.
Twelve-year-old Morwenna accidentally becomes the bearer of the last five wishes and must decide how to use them to benefit her people. (Objectives 3 and 4)

———.*Emily Upham's Revenge*. Illustrated by Paul Zelinsky. Pantheon, 1978, 1992.
A humorous melodrama unfolds as Seth Marple involves sweet Emily in a bank robbery. (Objective 3)

———. *The Fighting Ground*. J.B. Lippincott, 1984.
A young boy discovers the reality of war when he becomes embroiled in a Revolutionary War skirmish and its aftermath. (Objective 3)

———. *Man from the Sky*. Illustrated by David Wiesner. Alfred A. Knopf, 1980, 1992.
Jamie's daydreaming and cloud watching enable him to assist in capturing a thief. (Objectives 1 and 3)

———. *Nothing but the Truth*. Orchard, 1991.
A disturbance caused by a ninth-grade boy is blown out of proportion when the national news picks up the story. (Objectives 2, 4, and 6)

———. *S.O.R. Losers*. Pantheon, 1984.
A team of reluctant soccer players teaches parents and administrators a lesson about winning, losing, and having fun. (Objectives 1, 2, and 3)

———. *Something Upstairs: A Tale of Ghosts*. Orchard, 1988.
A young boy travels back in time to the days of slave trading in order to solve a murder. (Objectives 1, 2, 3, and 7)

———. *The True Confessions of Charlotte Doyle*. Illustrated by Ruth E. Murray. Orchard, 1990.
A transatlantic voyage in 1832 forever changes the life and attitude of a young passenger after she discovers the true nature of both the captain and crew. (Objectives 1, 2, 3, and 4)

———. *Who Stole the Wizard of Oz?* Illustrated by Derek James. Alfred A. Knopf, 1981.
Clever twins use clues from children's classics to solve a mystery and find a treasure. (Objectives 3, 5, and 7)

————. *Windcatcher*. Bradbury, 1991.
Young Tony finds adventure and danger as he learns to sail and spies on treasure
seekers near Connecticut's Thimble Islands. (Objectives 3 and 5)

Biographical Sources:

For information on Avi, see *Something about the Author*, vol. 14, pages
269–70; vol. 71, pages 7–15; and *Fifth Book of Junior Authors & Illustrators*,
pages 15–16.

Group Introductory Activity:

Avi, who has written books for young people in a variety of genres, believes
that the first step to writing is reading. As a child he was an avid reader, but
spelling and writing caused many difficulties for him in school (*Something about
the Author*, vol. 71, p. 9). Now as a professional writer Avi is fascinated with
technique and delights in finding new ways to structure stories (*Something about
the Author*, vol. 71, p. 12). Avi says he is more interested in finding a way to tell
a good story and to provide a means of imagining and understanding the past than
he is in teaching a specific historical fact. Like Kenny, the narrator of *Something
Upstairs: A Tale of Ghosts* Avi moved from Los Angeles to Providence, Rhode
Island, and into the historic house featured in that novel (*Something about the
Author*, vol. 71, p. 11). In *Something Upstairs* Avi states, "Writing is mostly
imagination, emotion, things you've noticed or heard about rather than things
you've done . . ." (p. 3).

Devise a chart on a bulletin board to classify and delineate the genre and
structure of Avi's books. Eight columns across the page should be headed:
"Title," "Genre," "Character," "Plot" or "Conflict," "Setting," "Theme," "Point
of View," and "Style." Under genre, students will begin to recognize these
categories: "Problem Realism and Social Issues Realism," "Historical Fiction,"
"Mystery," "Sports Story," and "Fantasy." Whenever Avi books in this unit are
read, have the students fill in the classroom chart. If reading notebooks are kept,
make a chart to be completed by individual students.

As *Something Upstairs* is read aloud, ask the children to listen for
historical facts and clues to the plot. Let the students complete the genre chart and
discuss the structure as the story is read. While reading the book in class, have
the group discuss the type of characters found in the story. Ask the students to
recall how the author revealed the characters, by their actions, speech, appearance, or comments by others? Refer to pages 39–40 of Rebecca Luken's *A
Critical Handbook of Children's Literature*, 4th ed. (HarperCollins, 1990) for
more information on character. Have the children discuss Kenny's motives,
actions, and decisions.

Follow-Up Activities for Teacher and Students to Share:

1. After reading the fantasy *Bright Shadow,* have the students define the type of conflict that exists in the story and give an example. The four types of conflict defined by Rebecca Lukens on pages 61–65 of *A Critical Handbook of Children's Literature,* 4th ed. (HarperCollins, 1990) are person against self, person against person, person against society, and person against nature. Be sure to put the children's answers on the story chart. Have the children continue the class discussion by answering Morwenna's questions from page 167: "Must the wish die with me? Or will you keep it longer?. . . Do you want the wish?" Follow the discussion by having students rewrite the ending based on one of these situations: What if the wishes had died with the wizard? What if the wizard had given the wishes to the king? A small group of students may choose to construct a castle representing the one in the story.

2. While reading aloud *Nothing but the Truth,* stop reading on page 80 to let the children write a class statement of the facts up to this point in the story. As the students recall facts or events, make sure each event is recorded from the correct point of view. Help the children recognize how different viewpoints may alter perceptions of the same event. At the end of page 129, review the class statement and let the students add or delete facts. Urge the children to discuss the climax of the story and predict the outcome. Ask the class how *Nothing but the Truth* demonstrates the wisdom of the following statement: "Act on a situation, don't react."

   When the reading is complete, have the children examine the story for conflict development, style of writing, and story structure. Ask the students to identify how this style of writing differs from other books Avi has written and discuss the meaning of "documentary novel."

3. Use Avi's *S.O.R. Losers* in a book discussion. As the book is read, children may discuss the qualities of each character and his or her believability. Ask one student from the discussion group to be responsible for filling in the genre chart. Throughout the story, the soccer team members are given pep talks. Let the group members discuss the meaning of each pep talk and compare the pep talks to experiences the students have shared. Allow the children to comment on Ed's statement, "Every one of us is good at something. . . . Why can't we just plain stink in some other places?" (p. 77). When the book is completed have each student write a page describing and giving examples of the activities at which he or she excels.

4. Read aloud Avi's Newbery Honor book *The True Confessions of Charlotte Doyle.* Examine and discuss the types of conflict found in the plot. Students need to distinguish the types of conflict by describing a passage that reflects that conflict. Have the children evaluate the character development of the protagonist, Charlotte Doyle. The students should be able to explain the

following: how she described herself in the beginning, what traits she exhibited in the beginning, and how her character changed as the events unfolded. Ask the students to describe a scene where Charlotte is affected by the events and one where the events are affected by Charlotte. Have the children speculate on what theme about human nature Avi may be suggesting in this book.

5. In mystery writing, the author often gives clues to the outcome. The presence of such clues creates foreshadowing. While reading *Who Stole the Wizard of Oz?* by Avi, have the students record in writing journals the clues they hear in the text. When the story is complete, let children discuss how the mystery genre differs from fantasy, historical fiction, and realism.

Follow-Up Activities for Individual Students:

1. Read Avi's *Bright Shadow* and Patricia MacLachlan's *Tomorrow's Wizard* (HarperCollins, 1982). Compare the role of the wizard, the value of the wishes, and the conflicts faced by the main characters in the two stories.

2. While reading *Emily Upham's Revenge* by Avi, study the drama that unfolds. Choose a scene from the story to act out or compose an acrostic poem about the book. In the acrostic poem, use the letters of the title to begin each line, for example:

   E very day she wears a different dress
   M eets a friend
   I s prissy
   L ies never
   Y ou wouldn't want to meet her.

3. Read Avi's *The Fighting Ground*. The conflict Jonathan experienced was largely caused by a failure to communicate. Jonathan's father feared for his son, but Jonathan thought his father was a coward; the corporal deliberately failed to communicate the true situation to Jonathan and the men; and the Hessians could not communicate with Jonathan and the Americans because of the language barriers. How might the situations have changed if Jonathan had been able to discern the true meaning or feelings of his father, the corporal, and the Hessians? Explain your answers in an oral report. Design a model representing a battle scene from the story to use in your report.

4. Avi says that as a child he had difficulties in writing that caused him to reverse letters or misspell words (*Something about the Author*, vol. 71, p. 9). After reading *Man from the Sky* speculate on how Avi's real-life frustrations might have helped him write about Jamie. Pretend that the story really did happen and that you are a reporter. Write an interview with Jamie based on what you know about his character.

5. After reading *S.O.R. Losers* in class, choose a partner and debate the merits of the situation created when a group of unathletic students is forced to participate in a competitive sport.

6. In *S.O.R. Losers* Avi asks the question, "What is it therefore that stands as the essential achievement in your school?" (p. 13). After you have completed the book, write an essay answering this question.

7. Avi writes in *Something Upstairs*, "Kenny now felt an urge to know about the old days . . . who were the people of this house? What did they look like? Did they wear funny suits, wigs, dresses? Were there any kids? How did they live. . . how did they die?" (p. 11). After hearing the book in class, select an historical event that has aroused your curiosity. Research in the library media center to gather facts and descriptions, then write a story about the event.

8. Miss McPherson, in Avi's *Who Stole the Wizard of Oz?,* told her students that children in upper grades should read only "useful information" books, "No mysteries, no make-believe, no romantic adventures. Children your age are beyond such nonsense" (p. 7). Read one of the classic fantasies or adventure stories mentioned in Avi's book; for example, A.A. Milne's *Winnie-the-Pooh* (E.L. Dutton, 1926), Robert Louis Stevenson's *Treasure Island* (Charles Scribner's Sons, 1945), Lewis Carroll's *Alice's Adventures in Wonderland* and *Through the Looking Glass: And What Alice Found There* (Dell, 1992), L. Frank Baum's *The Wizard of Oz* (Holt, 1982), or Kenneth Grahame's *The Wind in the Willows* (Charles Scribner's Sons, 1953), or another fantasy book. Do you agree or disagree with Miss McPherson's judgment? Write a paragraph explaining your answer. How can fantasy, science fiction, adventure, or other fiction genres be of value to readers? Do you believe the children should have turned in Mrs. Chesterton? Why or why not?

9. Read Avi's *Windcatcher*. As the mystery unfolds, keep track of the events and clues to the problem. Describe and illustrate the most suspenseful scene from the story.

10. While reading *Windcatcher,* compile a list of the main parts of a small sailboat. Prepare a captioned diagram showing those parts or construct a model of Tony's boat. Explain how Tony's new sailboat combined with his natural curiosity to create problems.

Closure:

When Avi's books have been read, the flowchart depicting the story elements will be complete. Ask the students to think about the various characters and events Avi has created. Have the children describe which character and scene they most identify with and explain why or how they feel as they do. In conclusion, have each student evaluate the variety of books and genres that Avi writes and defend the genre they like best.

Capturing Mood in the Writings of Phyllis Reynolds Naylor

Objectives:

1. Define an author's various styles of writing.
2. Develop ideas in various written or spoken formats.
3. Recognize the major elements of story structure in books.
4. Express empathy with a book character.
5. Evaluate reading materials through art, discussion, and/or drama.
6. Make inferences or draw conclusions from the stories.
7. Increase reading vocabulary.

Recommended Readings:

Naylor, Phyllis Reynolds. *The Agony of Alice*. Atheneum, 1985.
>Growing up creates many embarrassing and humiliating moments for Alice. (Objectives 4 and 5)

———. *Beetles, Lightly Toasted*. Atheneum, 1987.
>Entering and winning an essay contest takes on a new meaning for Andy after his idea stews awhile. (Objectives 2 and 3)

———. *The Bodies in the Bessledorf Hotel*. Atheneum, 1986.
>Bernie Magruder and friends search for clues and missing bodies to solve the mystery in the hotel. (Objectives 1, 5, and 7)

———. *The Grand Escape*. Illustrated by Alan Daniel. Atheneum, 1993.
>Two house cats take on the greatest adventure of their lives when they escape to the outside world. (Objective 2)

———. *How Lazy Can You Get?* Illustrated by Alan Daniel. Dell, 1992.
>Amazingly funny misadventures occur when the Megglethorp children are left in the care of Miss Brasscoat. (Objective 5)

———. *Josie's Troubles*. Illustrated by Shelley Matheis. Atheneum, 1992.
>Josie and her best friend Sarah show ingenuity and determination as they try to earn the money to repair the piano bench belonging to Sarah's mother. (Objectives 2 and 4)

————. *Night Cry*. Atheneum, 1985.
Ellen comes face to face with fear when left alone on her family's Mississippi farm. (Objectives 1, 4, and 5)

————. *Shiloh*. Atheneum, 1991.
A young boy befriends a dog that has been abused and thereby learns the value of facing problems rather than running away from them. (Objectives 1, 3, 4, 5, and 6)

————. *To Walk the Sky Path*. Dell, 1992.
Billie, a young Seminole Indian, is caught between the cultures of two worlds. (Objectives 2, 4, and 6)

————. *The Witch Returns*. Illustrated by Joe Burleson. Delacorte, 1992.
Lynn and her friend Mouse are once again involved in a spine-tingling encounter with a strange old woman. (Objectives 1, 3, and 6)

Biographical Sources:

For information on Phyllis Reynolds Naylor see *Something about the Author*, vol. 12, pages 156–57; vol. 66, pages 170–76; and *Fifth Book of Junior Authors & Illustrators*, pages 227–28.

Group Introductory Activity:

Before sharing Phyllis Reynolds Naylor's award-winning book *Shiloh*, show the filmstrip *Style* from Pied Piper Productions (*Literature for Children*, series 9, 1985). Help the students understand that a writer's style is a form of expression very much like the clothes people wear. Read the first chapter of *Shiloh* aloud. Discuss with the children the language of the characters. Lead the children to identify the author's use of an accent or dialect for the characters. Before continuing the reading, have the students gather all of the available books by Phyllis Reynolds Naylor. Read aloud the first page of each story, one by one. Have the children discuss and compare the language patterns of each to determine the style and mood the author establishes. Let the students create a mural of Phyllis Reynolds Naylor's books. The artwork should reflect the mood and style of each book it represents.

When *Shiloh* has been read aloud, have the students share their feelings and thoughts about Marty's decisions. Ask the children to compare Marty's actions with what they would have done in his position. Review the characters in the story. Have the students name the protagonist and antagonist. Analyze the attributes of each of the characters that cause them to be at odds. Tell the children to use the information they know about the characters to draw conclusions about their lives and futures.

Follow-Up Activities for Teacher and Students to Share:

1. In Phyllis Reynolds Naylor's *Beetles, Lightly Toasted,* the fifth graders at Bucksville Elementary School have the opportunity to enter an essay contest each year. The essays are judged on inventiveness and imagination. Hold an essay contest as a class project during the study of Phyllis Reynolds Naylor. Post the topics listed on pages 6–7 of the book. Read the story aloud to the class, adding the new essay topic, "conservation," to the list. Stop reading after page 43 to have the children discuss and list writing ideas using the conservation theme. Let the group brainstorm ideas for each of the other listed themes as well. Continue reading to page 113. At this point, Andy realizes what might happen if he wins the contest. Have the students predict how the book will end. When the story is completed, compare the predictions to the actual ending. Ask the students to evaluate which element was the strength of *Beetles, Lightly Toasted* (e.g., characterization, plot, style, tone, or theme). Have the children cite passages in the book to substantiate their opinions.

2. Phyllis Reynolds Naylor's *The Bodies in the Bessledorf Hotel* is a light-hearted mystery. Have a small group of children read this book or others in the Bernie Magruder mystery series. The following vocabulary words appear in *The Bodies in the Bessledorf Hotel: veterinary, citronella, wisteria, alacrity, vigilance, debarkation, hysterical, zephyrs, heliotrope,* and *laryngitis.* Have the students define these words before reading the story. As the words appear in context, students can share their meanings and explain their use within the context of the book. Children may then select five other words from the book to develop a personal spelling list. When the book is finished have the students write a script and act out a play based on the mysterious events and dialogue of the characters.

3. Phyllis Reynolds Naylor says, "All of my books begin with a mood—a feeling—which captures me and won't let go till the story is down on paper" (*Something about the Author,* vol. 12, p. 157). As *Night Cry* is read aloud or by a group of students, have the children define the mood Naylor establishes in the first chapter. Ask the children to analyze the writing to discover how the author sustains the mood. Have the group discuss the fears and feelings the main character exhibits. Ask the children to compare Ellen's fears and emotions to those they sometimes experience. Let the students discuss how the author made Ellen a credible character. Focus the discussion on the factors that motivated or influenced Ellen's actions and how those actions affected the outcome of events.

4. *To Walk the Sky Path* by Phyllis Reynolds Naylor gives readers a glimpse of two very different cultures. After reading the story aloud, ask the students to write personal accounts expressing their feelings or understanding of how

Billie and Grandfather each viewed life. Have the children write a second account explaining what they have learned about the life-style and customs of Billie's family.

Follow-Up Activities for Individual Students:

1. Phyllis Reynolds Naylor says, "Through my books I can be many different people . . . I can take a real problem I may be experiencing and work it out on paper" (*Something about the Author*, vol. 12, p. 157). *The Agony of Alice* is written in first person from Alice's point of view. Alice says, "All great writers wrote about subjects that really mattered to them and that's why she (Mrs. Plotkin) wanted us to get used to writing about feelings, not just things" (p. 97). After reading Alice's story, construct a "Me Box" depicting Alice's experiences. Paint the box. Attach things on all six sides such as pictures, photographs, drawings, or poems that represent Alice's friends, family, feelings, secrets, experiences, likes, and dislikes. Follow up by creating your own "Me Box."

   Keep a journal of your thoughts and feelings. Use art, either drawings or splashes of color, to mirror your feelings in the journal. You may wish to use clay to express yourself through sculpture.

2. After reading *The Agony of Alice*, design two posters on the theme Alice discussed, "Today is the first day of the rest of your life." One poster should represent Alice's point of view on the topic and one should reflect your own. Read other books in the "Alice" series to learn how Alice's life continues.

3. After hearing Phyllis Reynolds Naylor's *Beetles, Lightly Toasted*, reread the chapters dealing with Aunt Wanda's menu and the Soul Food Kitchen (pp. 33–52). Pretend you would like to open your own restaurant. Decide on the type of food to be served. Collect recipes and make a menu. Serve one of your favorite foods to the class. Further extend this project by calling the local Chamber of Commerce or other agency to learn what is involved in establishing a restaurant.

4. After reading Phyllis Reynolds Naylor's *Beetles, Lightly Toasted*, locate and read Thomas Rockwell's *How to Eat Fried Worms*. Compare the plot and writing style in the two books.

5. After reading *The Bodies in the Bessledorf Hotel* by Phyllis Reynolds Naylor, determine the style and mood of this mystery. Does it follow the typical format of a mystery? Explain your answer. What is it about Naylor's writing that keeps this book from being an intense murder mystery? Document your answer with passages from the book.

6. Read *The Grand Escape*, paying special attention to the antics of the cats. Speculate on whether the incidents really occurred or how the author might have come up with certain events such as the cats bobbing in the water on page 99. On the book jacket of *The Grand Escape*, Naylor says that she has two 12 pound cats at home, one of which has eaten 12 yards of ribbon while the other peers over her shoulder when she writes. Write your own cat story. First, ask people in your neighborhood or school for authentic curious or funny things that their cats have done. Begin with the factual material, then adapt it and elaborate upon it to turn it into a story like the author did. Remember to be aware of the tone and style of language you use.

7. Read Phyllis Reynolds Naylor's *How Lazy Can You Get?* As you read, write down each silly question Miss Brasscoat asked, such as "How disgusting can you get?" "How revolting can you get?" or "How annoying can you get?" Select one of the questions to answer from your point of view. The answer may be expressed in a creative story, poem, or skit.

8. After reading *Josie's Troubles* by Phyllis Reynolds Naylor, write a paragraph explaining what Josie learned about friendship. Next, write a paragraph explaining your point of view on friendship. Think about what jobs you could get at your age to earn money. Write a brief statement telling who you are, where you live, and why you are qualified for a particular job.

9. Read Phyllis Reynolds Naylor's thriller, *Night Cry*. Work with a partner to act out the book's final scene in which Maureen Sinclair interviews Ellen about the rescue. The interviewer must ask appropriate questions so that Ellen will recount the events sequentially.

10. Phyllis Reynolds Naylor's *Shiloh* won the 1992 Newbery Medal. Read and compare this book to others with similar plots, such as Bill Wallace's *A Dog Called Kitty* or Wilson Rawls's *Where the Red Fern Grows*. Compare the books based on character development, plot (conflict and resolution), setting, theme, and the author's use of style and tone.

11. After hearing *To Walk the Sky Path* by Phyllis Reynolds Naylor, write a paragraph explaining the meaning of the title and the role of the historical account of Osceola and the Seminole wars in the story. Follow up by using the library media center resources to research the account of Osceola and his men. Then write a brief account of the events. Decide whose point of view was reflected in the research and whether it fairly represented both viewpoints. If it did not, try to locate an account showing the opposing point of view. Briefly write how you believe Billie felt when his teacher confronted him about his research.

12. Phyllis Reynolds Naylor's *The Witch Returns* is the last in a series of six books involving Lynn Morley and her friend Mouse. On several occasions, the author gives the reader clues about the resolution and the theme. At one

point the theme becomes explicit; the author states exactly what the underlying message is. Quote the theme from the book and then show ways in which the theme was implied.

Closure:

Phyllis Reynolds Naylor says,

> I like to write about many different things for all ages. After writing an adventure book for younger children, I may write a poem or article for retired people. Then I might write a humorous novel for teenagers, followed by a nonfiction book for their parents. . . . There's a part of me in every book I write (*Something about the Author*, vol. 12, p. 157)

Examine the artwork on the class mural to determine how many different types of books have been read during the unit. Make a transparency of the following passage from *To Walk the Sky Path*: "And then the rains came—torrents of rain, pouring in sheets and buckets against the windows" (p. 67). Ask the students to imagine the scene depicted in the quote. Have the children practice establishing mood and style by writing three descriptions of that scene. Ask them to write one as if it were a mystery thriller, the second as a romance, and the third as a comedy. Students may take turns reading their scenes aloud, without telling the intended mood. The rest of the class may respond by identifying the mood they believe the writing expressed.

Overcoming the Odds

Objectives:

1. Classify types of conflict in literature.
2. Develop a sense of community within the classroom.
3. Summarize or compare plots and/or characters in literature.
4. Respond to literature through the arts, research, and creative writing.
5. Recognize positive traits in characters.
6. Compile a bibliography.

Recommended Readings:

Baillie, Allan. *Adrift*. Viking, 1992.
A young boy's imaginary games turn into deadly reality when he, his sister, and her cat are set adrift on the ocean in an old crate. (Objective 3)

Conrad, Pam. *Prairie Songs*. Illustrated by Darryl S. Zudeck. Harper & Row, 1985.
Louisa sees the marked contrast between her own mother and the beautiful wife of the young doctor who has come to homestead on the Nebraska plains. (Objectives 3, 5, and 6)

De Felice, Cynthia. *Weasel*. Macmillan, 1990.
Eleven-year-old Nathan struggles to overcome his thirst for revenge against the man who devastated the family homestead. (Objectives 1 and 3)

Keith, Harold. *Komantcia*. Thomas Y. Crowell, 1965; Levite of Apache, 1991.
Pedro, a sensitive young musician visiting Mexico, learns to adapt and survive after he is enslaved by a Comanche raiding party. (Objectives 1, 3, and 6)

Kudlinski, Kathleen V. *Hero Over Here*. Illustrated by Bert Dodson. Viking, 1990.
A boy discovers he is stronger than he knew when he must care for his seriously ill mother and sister during the deadly flu epidemic of 1918. (Objectives 1 and 5)

Leitner, Isabella. *The Big Lie: A True Story*. Illustrated by Judy Pedersen. Scholastic, 1992.
The horrors of the Nazi death camp are recounted by a survivor of Auschwitz. (Objectives 5 and 7)

Paulsen, Gary. *Hatchet*. Bradbury, 1987.
After the pilot has a heart attack, Brian must land the plane and survive alone in the Canadian wilderness with only a hatchet to aid him. (Objectives 5 and 6)

Radin, Ruth Yaffe. *Carver*. Illustrated by Karl Swanson. Macmillan, 1990.
Young Jon finds his own place in a new school and community while learning to be a wood-carver, even though he is blind. (Objectives 5 and 6)

Rappaport, Doreen. *Escape from Slavery: Five Journeys to Freedom*. Illustrated by Charles Lilly. HarperCollins, 1991.
Episodic chapters share the stories of five daring escapes from Southern slavery prior to the War Between the States. (Objectives 1 and 5)

Wallace, Bill. *Never Say Quit*. Holiday House, 1993.
After sixth grader Justine and her friends are excluded from the elite soccer team,

they form their own team, the Misfits, and bribe their heavy-drinking former principal to be their coach. (Objectives 1 and 2)

Group Introductory Activity:

All good stories contain conflict. Sometimes the problem is minor, sometimes it is a matter of life and death. In this unit, the children will read many stories about young people and adults facing major conflicts. The problems in books can be as many and varied as the imagination will allow, but all conflicts can be classified into one of four types: person against nature, person against self, person against person, or person against society. After reading each book in the unit, the students will be asked to identify and classify the conflict and the qualities or characteristics that enable the protagonist to overcome the odds.

Prepare a bulletin board labeled "And the Winner Is..." showing four large pairs of boxing gloves cut from paper. On one set of gloves write "Protagonist vs. Nature"; on another set write "Protagonist vs. Self"; on a third pair write "Protagonist vs. Person"; and on the fourth pair write "Protagonist vs. Society." Attach the gloves to the top of four columns on the board. Beneath the columns create 10 rows, one for each book in the unit. Carry through with the "fight" theme by labeling the rows as numbered rounds in a boxing match. As books are read, let the children write the author and title on a small pair of paper gloves and on another write the characteristics that let the protagonist triumph in the conflict. Students may attach the paired gloves to the board under the column for the type of conflict expressed in the story.

Have the children individually complete a survey of personal information. Include spaces on the data sheet for students to offer information that classmates may not know about them, for example, birthplace; parent occupation; species and names of pets; future goals; address; and favorite sports, songs, movies, television shows, and foods. Use the information on the completed data sheets to create several different "Let's Get Together" game cards. Make a grid with a number of boxes not less than the number of students. Fill each box on the grid with a bit of personal information about a class member, such as "____ lives on Washington Avenue," "____'s mother is a computer programmer," or "____'s favorite sport is racquetball." Be sure each grid contains at least one entry for each student. Duplicate enough grids so each class member will have a copy for the activity to follow later.

Over the course of several days, read Bill Wallace's *Never Say Quit* aloud to the group. At the conclusion of each reading session, give the children the opportunity to recall problems the various characters in the story have to overcome. Let the students discuss and classify the problems as to the type of conflict each represents. On the final day of reading stop after the line "If we had any sense at all, we would have quit" (p. 183). Ask the students to react to the Misfits and the way they handled their problems. Let the class judge whether the team members overcame the odds even if they did not win the final game. Have the students discuss the personal victories the children and the coach experienced, making them winners despite the outcome of the game. Conclude by telling the students that there is a bit of the book still to be read. Read the final pages in which the outcome of the game is revealed.

As a follow-up remind the students of the bonding drill the characters used to get to know each other and become a real team. Have the children get better acquainted with each other by playing "Let's Get Together." Let the students roam the room, searching for the students who are represented on their cards and completing the blanks on the grid. As a further extension, ask the music teacher to help the class learn songs about friendship or getting acquainted such as Richard and Robert Sherman's "Let's Get Together" on pages 173–74 of *The Illustrated Disney Song Book* (Random House, 1979).

Follow-Up Activities for Teacher and Students to Share:

1. Read aloud Pam Conrad's *Prairie Songs*. Prepare a Venn diagram in which the class can show the similarities and differences between Clara Downing and Emmaline Berryman. Draw two large circles on a poster board, one overlapping the other by about one-fourth of the diameter. Explain to the class that this type of diagram is used to compare two things or groups. Ask the children to think about the two characters and brainstorm a list of character traits, situations, and events that affected the women. Have the children place the words that apply to both women inside the area shared by both circles. In the outer sections the students should write words that are unique to one of the two women, placing Louisa's mother in one section and the doctor's wife in the other.

2. While reading Cynthia De Felice's *Weasel* in small book discussion groups or reading it aloud to the entire class, stop reading on page 95. Let the children discuss the conversation between Nathan and Pa about killing and revenge. Before continuing with the story, have the students predict what Nathan will do and why. When the story has been completed, have the students discuss the resolution of the story and compare it to their predictions. There may be some disagreement as the students try to classify the type of conflict in this story. Some children may see the primary conflict as Nathan's struggles against the evil Weasel, while others will identify the more prominent struggle that Nathan has with his own desire for revenge. Ask the students to justify their thoughts with information from the story. Let the children vote, if necessary, to establish the majority belief as to the conflict type before adding the entry for this "round" in the proper column.

3. After reading aloud Kathleen V. Kudlinski's *Hero Over Here*, have the students discuss the type of conflict faced by the protagonist. Send a group of students to the library media center to research the flu epidemic of 1918.

In the story, Theodore begins to dress himself in his knickers then thinks, "Never again," and chooses his brother's long pants instead. Have the students write individual paragraphs discussing the significance of his refusal. Remind the children of the term *rite of passage*, which refers to an event or ceremony that marks the transition from childhood into adulthood. Let the children discuss any formal or informal *rites of passage* with which they may be familiar (e.g., Bar Mitzvah, Bas Mitzvah, first dates).

4. Read aloud Doreen Rappaport's *Escape from Slavery: Five Journeys to Freedom*. As the book is read, have the students discuss or write out how the conflicts and resolutions in the stories are alike or different. Very few slaves escaped unaided. Virtually all successful flights to freedom were carefully planned. Have the children discuss unwanted tasks or situations from which they would sometimes like to escape. Make a group plan to avoid or escape from that situation. Remind the children to base the plan around their strengths. Have the students write individual paragraphs responding to the cliché "If you fail to plan, you are planning to fail."

Follow-Up Activities for Individual Students:

1. After reading *Adrift* by Allan Baillie, summarize and retell the story up to the climax in an accordion book. Cut a piece of butcher paper approximately 12" × 36" long. Fold the paper in half lengthwise to give your booklet added strength. Accordion-fold or fanfold the paper into equal parts. Glue a piece of manila tagboard inside both end sections to make the booklet sturdy.

   Write the title and author on the front cover with the sentence "Retold and illustrated by (your name)." Illustrate a scene of the ocean (on the left-hand side of the page) meeting the shore (on the right-hand side), as described by Baillie. On the back cover, draw the crate with the children floating on the sea. When the back page is folded out, the two covers should present a scene of the children on the crate near the shore. Extend the book fully and write your summary on each page, moving from left to right. The beginning of your text will be next to the back cover of the booklet, while the end will be next to the front cover. Stop your summary at the climax when the children are washed off the crate. Conclude with sentences urging others to read the book (e.g., "Will Flynn, Sally, and Nebu make it home? Read *Adrift* by Allen Baillie to find out"). Refold the booklet so that all the text pages are under the front cover and only the back cover is extended. Readers should pull the back page to the left as they read the book, gradually moving the children farther and farther from the shore.

2. After hearing Pam Conrad's *Prairie Songs* in class, imagine the barren plain that Conrad describes in the opening paragraph of her book. Use the medium of your choice to illustrate the scene that Louisa sees around her.

3. After hearing *Prairie Songs* and studying the Venn diagram about the two women in class, think about the contrast between the characters. Write a brief paragraph explaining why Clara survived while Emmaline could not cope with the hardships of prairie life. Copy the Venn diagram illustrating the characteristics of the two women and add any additional words you believe should be placed in the sections. Use a contrasting color to enclose or underline the terms in the diagram that describe Louisa as well.

4. Read Harold Keith's historical novel *Komantcia*. Life among the Comanche Indians of the southern Great Plains in the years following the American Civil War was not easy even for tribe members. For a prisoner and slave, it was much worse. Consider the qualities that helped Pedro to survive. What role did music play in his success? Reread chapter 6, "The Comanchero's Guitar" (pp. 83–95). Why, in your opinion, did Belt Whip react so violently? Justify your answer.

5. After reading *Komantcia*, locate and read Kenneth Thomasma's *Naya Nuki, Girl Who Ran* (Grandview, 1983). This book is based on a brief account from Lewis and Clark's journals of a reunion between Sacajawea, their Indian guide, and an unnamed friend. She and Sacajawea had been captured by an enemy war party years before, but she had managed to escape and return to her people. Compare the two stories of young slaves and their plans to escape to freedom. Fold a sheet of paper into thirds. Label the left-hand section *"Komantcia,"* the right-hand section *"Naya Nuki,"* and the center section "Similarities." Contrast the plots, the type of conflict faced, and the characters in the outer sections. List their shared features in the central area. If you prefer, you may present this information in the form of a Venn diagram.

6. Read Isabella Leitner's autobiographical account of her experiences in the German death camp at Auschwitz during World War II, *The Big Lie: A True Story*. After reading the book, develop a list of rules simulating those imposed on Jews when the Nazis first gained power. Prepare a list of rules for all students in a certain, totally arbitrary group, for example, those students born in July or those students with green eyes. Do not use ethnic or religious qualifications, however, because these factors have too often been the basis for discrimination. Refer to and adapt the list of rules for Jews on pages 21–22 of Leitner's book. Rules should revolve around what group members may or may not do while at school. Conclude your list with a disclaimer that promotes Leitner's book. You may write your own or use the following passage:

> It is hard to imagine anything like this ever really happening, but it did. European Jews under German control in the 1930s and World War II era had to follow rules that made no more sense than these. They suffered great injustice and cruelty, but some of them overcame the odds. They survived. Read Isabella Leitner's *The Big Lie: A True Story* to learn about one girl's struggle for life and freedom.

Present your list and the promotional statement to the class as a book talk.

7. After reading *The Big Lie: A True Story,* use the card or computer catalog to compile a bibliography of other books about the Holocaust available in the library media center. Before visiting the media center, brainstorm a list of possible search topics or subject headings. Ask the library media specialist to check your list and make any suggestions that might make your search more thorough or efficient. In a bibliography, books are listed in alphabetical order by the author's last name. Each book should be cited in this format:

Call number	Author's last name, first name. <u>Title</u>.
	Publishing company, copyright date.
for example:	
940.5 Lei	Leitner, Isabella. <u>The Big Lie: A True Story</u>. Scholastic, 1992.

8. Read Gary Paulsen's *Hatchet*. What skills or characteristics did Brian possess that enabled him to survive? Choose the scenes that you believe best exemplify Brian's strongest and weakest traits. Illustrate those scenes in the medium of your choice. Write a paragraph predicting how Brian's life might have changed after his harrowing experiences. You may wish to locate and read Paulsen's sequel to this book, *The River* (Delacorte, 1991).

9. After reading *Hatchet*, consider your personal strengths and weaknesses. If you were to be marooned, not in the wilderness but on a desert island, what one tool or item would you most like to have with you? Why do you think this tool would be helpful in that environment?

10. After reading *Carver* by Ruth Yaffe Radin, study the feather pattern of mallards or other waterfowl. Chart feather groups on a diagram. Carve a decoy from a bar of soap or sculpt the figure in modeling clay. Use a fine tool such as a sharp pencil point or straight pin to add small details.

11. After completing *Carver,* locate and read Jane Yolen's picture book, *The Seeing Stick* (Thomas Y. Crowell, 1977). Compare the description of "seeing" through touch in the two stories. What qualities in Jon, the princess, and the old man allow each of them to triumph over their blindness?

Closure:

Review with the group the entries for each "round" on the "And the Winner Is . . ." bulletin board. Remind the children that these characters, although faced with many difficulties, discovered a way to overcome the odds. Have the students write individual recipes or formulas for success. Ask them to include each of the ingredients required, how much of each ingredient to use, and the order and method of preparation.

Lloyd Alexander's Realms of Fantasy

Objectives:

1. Recognize components of fantasy.
2. Respond to reading through writing in various styles.
3. Empathize with a character.
4. Construct statements explaining the sequence of events, theme, or main idea of a story.
5. Evaluate the stories through art expression, drama, discussion, and further reading.
6. Understand a story with plots and subplots.

Recommended Readings:

Alexander, Lloyd. *The Beggar Queen.* E.P. Dutton, 1984.
   Mickle and Theo are thrown into conflict with an old enemy, Cabbarus. (Objective 2)

————. *The Black Cauldron.* Holt, Rinehart & Winston, 1965.
   Taran and his friends join the quest to destroy the black cauldron. (Objectives 4 and 5)

————. *The Book of Three.* Holt, Rinehart & Winston, 1964.
   Taran, the assistant pig-keeper, begins his journey to becoming a hero. (Objectives 1 and 5)

————. *The Cat Who Wished to Be a Man.* E.P. Dutton, 1973.
   Lionel the cat encounters some unexpected situations when his wizard master turns him into a man. (Objectives 1 and 2)

————. *The Foundling and Other Tales of Prydain.* Dell, 1973.
   Short stories provide information and background about the characters in the Prydain Chronicles. (Objectives 1, 2, and 5)

————. *The High King.* Henry Holt, 1968.
   Taran and his companions make one final attempt to defeat Arawn and the forces of evil. (Objectives 2 and 3)

————. *The Illyrian Adventure.* E.P. Dutton, 1986.
   Vesper Holly sets out to find a legendary treasure and an army of magical warriors. (Objectives 2 and 3)

————. *The King's Fountain.* Illustrated by Ezra Jack Keats. E.P. Dutton, 1971.
A humble man must find the strength to be himself as he faces the king. (Objective 4)

————. *Time Cat: The Remarkable Journeys of Jason and Gareth.* Illustrated by Bell Sokol. Holt, Rinehart & Winston, 1963.
Jason and his cat Gareth, who only has one life left, journey to the different times in history in which Gareth spent his first eight existences. (Objectives 4 and 5)

————. *Westmark.* E.P. Dutton, 1981.
Theo's life is intricately woven with that of many colorful characters as they serve justice and protect the kingdom from the evil Cabbarus. (Objective 6)

Biographical Sources:

For information on Lloyd Alexander see *Something about the Author*, vol. 49, pages 21–35 and *Third Book of Junior Authors*, pages 6–7.

Group Introductory Activity:

The books in Lloyd Alexander's Prydain Chronicles series were inspired by the Arthurian legends and Welsh myths and legends.

> Using the device of an imaginary world allowed me . . . to go to the central issues. . . . I used imaginary kingdoms not as a sentimentalized fairyland, but as an opening wedge to express what I hoped would be some very hard truths. . . . In the *Chronicles* there are questions about the nature and use of power, of self-aggrandizement at the expense of others, of kindness and of other humane qualities.
> (*Something about the Author*, vol. 49, p.29)

Because the Prydain Chronicles were so popular (*The High King* received the Newbery Medal in 1969), Alexander went on to write *The Foundling and Other Tales of Prydain.* He dedicated the book to "friends of Prydain who promised to read more if I promised to write more." Read aloud "The Smith, the Weaver, and the Harper" from pages 83–94 of that book. Have the children discuss the forces of good and evil at work in this story and how Alexander answered the questions the story posed about human nature.

To help the students better understand fantasy, make a master copy of the following questions:

- Describe the imaginary kingdom or setting. What new language exists, if any?
- How are the main characters, both good and evil, described?
- Show how the main character changes through the events in the book.
- Explain what the main character learns about his or her identity or strength.
- Identify the quest undertaken or problem faced by the main character(s).

- What reason did the character have for pursuing this quest? What obstacles did the characters encounter?
- What are the universal truths to be found in this fantasy?
- How has the author made the story believable?

Each time a book is read aloud, have the students discuss these questions. The children should respond in writing after individually reading other books by Lloyd Alexander.

Read aloud "The True Enchanter" from *The Foundling and Other Tales of Prydain* by Lloyd Alexander. Have the children share opinions on the discussion questions and come to a consensus on each. As a group, work together to produce a play based on the descriptions and dialogue found in the story. To set the scene for this unit, the classroom or library media center may be decorated as Prydain or another imaginary kingdom from Lloyd Alexander's works.

Follow-Up Activities for Teacher and Students to Share:

1. Before sharing Lloyd Alexander's *The Book of Three,* let the class view the sound filmstrip *Meet the Newbery Author: Lloyd Alexander* (Random House/Miller-Brody, 1974), if it is available. Read the book aloud, allowing the students to respond to the questions in the introductory activity as the book is read. Have the students listen for favorite scenes or symbols to reproduce in artwork. In the final book of the series, *The High King*, Eilonwy has attempted to embroider a cloth for Taran showing him and Hen Wen. As this book is read aloud and others in the series are read by individual students, have the children draw scenes from the books. Let a committee of children select the illustrations that best depict the Prydain Chronicles and have the students reproduce these on men's white handkerchiefs. Tape or pin the handkerchiefs to cardboard and let the children use crayon or tempera to color a chosen scene on each. The handkerchiefs have a natural border that can be decorated if desired. The finished creations can be pieced together to form a Prydain banner. If desired, 12" paper squares could be used instead of handkerchiefs.
2. As Lloyd Alexander's *The Cat Who Wished to Be a Man* is read aloud, have the students listen for the elements of fantasy. Review the questions in the introduction to help the students better understand this genre. When the story is completed, have them list at least five elements that make the story realistic and five elements that make the story a fantasy.

3. Read aloud *Westmark*, the first book in Lloyd Alexander's Westmark trilogy. Share the dedication from the book with the children. Ask the students to speculate on how it relates to the story. If *The Kestrel* and *The Beggar Queen* are available, read their dedications and let the students speculate on them as well.

    To help the students better understand plots with subplots, prepare a graph with four parallel lines and 8 to 10 columns. On the top line, chart Theo's encounters; on the second, note what Cabbarus is plotting; on the next two lines, write other simultaneous events. For example, one episode has Theo fleeing the print shop and militia in Dorning and next escaping with Las Bombas. On the next line, under the column showing Theo's escape, write down what Cabbarus was doing at that time. This will give the students a visual picture of several events happening simultaneously. The resulting graph may look like a partially completed bingo card because the author does not always reveal simultaneous events.

Follow-Up Activities for Individual Students:

1. Lloyd Alexander's *The Beggar Queen* ends the Westmark trilogy. As in the other stories, the value of personal integrity and freedom of the press are apparent. Read *The Beggar Queen*. Select one of the series of events in the book to highlight in a comic strip format. The comic strip may portray political events, opinions, or a series of episodes in the lives of the characters.
2. After reading Lloyd Alexander's *The Black Cauldron,* create a contour map of the journey Taran and his friends experienced. Explain the events that led to the climax and resolution of the quest.
3. After reading Lloyd Alexander's *The Black Cauldron,* construct a puppet to represent Gurgi. Record the sequence of events in the story from Gurgi's point of view. Be sure to include his rhyming and timing of language.
4. After hearing *The Cat Who Wished to Be a Man* by Lloyd Alexander, pretend you have the magic wishbone that Magister Stephanus gave to Lionel. Write a story about where you would wish to be and what you would wish to do if you could snap the wishbone in half.
5. In 1969 Lloyd Alexander received the Newbery Award for *The High King*. This award is presented annually to the author of the most distinguished contribution to American literature for children. Read *The High King*. On what merits do you believe it won the award? Throughout the series, Taran and his companions made tremendous sacrifices and decisions. In your opinion, what was the greatest sacrifice made by a character in *The High King* or in one of the other Prydain stories? Defend your answer.

6. In Lloyd Alexander's *The Illyrian Adventure,* Vesper Holly saved a king's life; prevented a civil war; triumphed over her father's detractors; foiled a villain; contributed to scholarly knowledge; and acquired a broken heart. After reading her story, write a series of stories, newspaper style, about Vesper's adventures. Be sure to explain who, what, when, where, why, and how in each news story.

7. The character of Vesper Holly in *The Illyrian Adventure* is quite outspoken and self-assured. Think about equal rights and freedom from Vesper's point of view. Write a story in first person (as if you were Vesper Holly) giving your opinion on the modern controversy over women's rights.

8. While reading *The King's Fountain* by Lloyd Alexander, notice the colors and sense of movement contained in the illustrations. Summarize the story in six lines. Explain to the class how the colors and placement of the characters on the pages affected the mood of the story. Use watercolors to paint a picture expressing the mood you experience when you have accomplished a difficult task.

9. While reading Lloyd Alexander's *Time Cat: The Remarkable Journeys of Jason and Gareth,* create a photograph album of the trips the characters take. Some pictures might be found in old magazines, but it may often be necessary to draw your own illustrations. Be sure to label the pictures with an explanation of the event and put them in sequential order.

10. In Lloyd Alexander's *Westmark,* Theo must teach Mickle to read and write while she, in turn, teaches him her inventive sign language. After reading the book, invent your own sign language or refer to Alvin Schwartz's *Cat's Elbow and Other Secret Languages* (Farrar, Straus & Giroux, 1982) to learn a secret code or language. Explain how the secret language was used in *Westmark* and then demonstrate how to use your secret language or code.

Closure:

Celebrate the works of Lloyd Alexander by toasting the imaginary characters in the author's stories. Have each student select a character from one of the books. (Note that in the series featuring Taran, Theo, and Vesper, the characters change and grow throughout all of the books. Therefore, more than one student could choose the same character.) Each child can then tell why that character is the funniest, friendliest, bravest, wisest, most mischievous, most stubborn, most troublesome, least likable, most cruel, most wicked, or other superlative. Share these in a "toast" format, with students in turn sharing compliments or jokes about characters.

Appendix I
Biographical Sources for
Authors and Illustrators

Fifth Book of Junior Authors & Illustrators. Edited by Sally Holmes Holtze. New York: H.W. Wilson, 1983.

Fourth Book of Junior Authors & Illustrators. Edited by Doris de Montreville and Elizabeth D. Crawford. New York: H.W. Wilson, 1978.

Sixth Book of Junior Authors & Illustrators. Edited by Sally Holmes Holtze. New York: H.W. Wilson, 1989.

Something about the Author. Detroit, MI: Gale Research. Vols. 1–71, 1978–1992.

Something about the Author Autobiographical Series. Detroit, MI: Gale Research. Vols. 1–12. 1992.

Talking with Artists: Conversations with Victoria Chess, Pat Cummings, Leo and Diane Dillon, Richard Egielski, Lois Ehlert, Lisa Campbell Ernst, Tom Feelings, Steven Kellogg, Jerry Pinkney, Amy Schwartz, Lane Smith, Chris Van Allsburg, and David Wiesner. Compiled and edited by Pat Cummings. New York: Bradbury, 1992.

Third Book of Junior Authors. Edited by Doris de Montreville and Donna Hill. New York: H.W. Wilson, 1972.

Appendix II
Directory of Publishers, Producers, and Distributors

Abingdon Press
201 Eighth Avenue South
Nashville, TN 37202

Allyn & Bacon, Inc.
7 Wells Avenue
Newton, MA 02159

Apple Island Books
Box 278
Shapleigh, ME 04076

Atheneum Publishers. *See* Macmillan
Publishing Co., Inc.

Avon Books
105 Madison Avenue
New York, NY 10016

Bantam Doubleday Dell Publishing Group, Inc.
666 Fifth Avenue
New York, NY 10103

Beech Tree. *See* Simon and Schuster, Inc.

Bradbury Press, Inc. *See* Macmillan
Publishing Co., Inc.

Bright Ring Publishing Co.
Distributed by Independent Publishers Group
814 N. Franklin Street
Chicago, IL 60610

Children's Press, Inc.
5440 North Cumberland Avenue
Chicago, IL 60656

Children's Video Library
P.O. Box 4995
Stamford, CT 06907

Child's Play
Distributed by PJC-Learning Materials
5080 Timberway Trail
Clarkston, MI 48346

Chronicle Publishing Co.
275 Fifth Street
San Francisco, CA 94103

Clarion Books
215 Park Avenue South
New York, NY 10003

Cobblehill Books. *See* Dutton Children's
Books

Columbia Records Division of Sony Music Entertainment, Inc.
550 Madison Avenue
New York, NY 10022

Coward, McCann, & Geoghegan. *See* The
Putnam & Grosset Book Group.

Thomas Y. Crowell. *See* HarperCollins
Children's Books.

Crown Publishers, Inc.
225 Park Avenue South
New York, NY 10003

Delacorte Press. *See* Bantam Doubleday
Dell Publishing Group, Inc.

Dial Books. *See* Penguin USA.

Doubleday & Co., Inc. *See* Bantam
Doubleday Dell Publishing Group, Inc.

E.P. Dutton. *See* Penguin USA.

Dutton Children's Books. *See* Penguin
USA.

Educational Activities, Inc.
1937 Grand Avenue
Baldwin, NY 11510

E.G.W. Publishing Co.
1320 Galaxy Way
Concord, CA 94520

Farrar, Straus, & Giroux, Inc.
19 Union Square West
New York, NY 10003

Four Winds Press. *See* Macmillan
Publishing Co., Inc.

Fulcrum Publishing
350 Indiana Street, Suite 350
Golden, CO 80401

Gale Research, Inc.
Book Tower
Detroit, MI 48226

Victor Gallancz
Distributed by Trafalgar Square
P.O. Box 257
North Ponfret, VT 05053

Gallaudet University Press
800 Florida Avenue, Northeast
Washington, DC 20002

The Games Gang, Ltd.
1107 Broadway, Suite 1603
New York, NY 10010

Grandview Publishing Co.
Box 2863
Jackson, WY 83001

Green Tiger Press
1061 India Street
San Diego, CA 92101

Greenwillow Books. *See* William Morrow
& Co., Inc.

Grosset & Dunlap, Inc. *See* The Putnam &
Grosset Book Group.

Harcourt Brace Jovanovich, Inc.
1250 Sixth Avenue
San Diego, CA 92101

Harper & Brothers. *See* HarperCollins
Children's Books.

Harper & Row. *See* HarperCollins
Children's Books.

HarperCollins Children's Books
10 East 53rd Street
New York, NY 10022

Heinemann Educational Books
70 Court Street
Portsmouth, NH 03801

Holiday House, Inc.
425 Madison Avenue
New York, NY 10017

Henry Holt and Company, Inc.
115 West 18th Street
New York, NY 10011

The Horn Book, Inc.
14 Beacon Street
Boston , MA 02108

Houghton Mifflin Co.
2 Park Street
Boston, MA 02108

Hyperion Books for Children
114 Fifth Avenue
New York, NY 10011

Kane/Miller Book Publishers
P.O. Box 529
Brooklyn, NY 11231

Alfred A. Knopf, Inc. *See* Random House,
Inc.

Learning Works, Inc.
P.O. Box 6187
Santa Barbara, CA 93160

J.B. Lippincott. *See* HarperCollins
Children's Books

Listening Library
One Park Avenue
Old Greenwich, CT 06870

Little, Brown & Co.
34 Beacon Street
Boston, MA 02106

Lodestar. *See* Penguin USA.

London Records
539 West 25th Street
New York, NY 10001

Lothrop, Lee & Shepard Co. *See* William
Morrow & Co., Inc.

Macmillan Publishing Co., Inc.
866 Third Avenue
New York, NY 10022

Madacy, Inc.
P.O. Box 1445
St-Laurent, Quebec, Canada H4L 4Z1

MCA Records, Inc.
70 Universal City Plaza
Universal City, CA 91608

Meadowbrook Press. *See* Simon and
Schuster, Inc.

Julian Messner
190 Sylvan Avenue
Englewood Cliffs, NJ 07632

Mindscape, Inc.
Division of Software Toolworks, Inc.
60 Leveroni Court
Novato, CA 94949

William Morrow & Co., Inc.
105 Madison Avenue
New York, NY 10016

Music for Little People
Box 1460
Redway, CA 95560

W.W. Norton & Co., Inc.
500 Fifth Avenue
New York, NY 10010

Orchard Books. *See* Franklin Watts, Inc.

The Oryx Press
4041 North Central at Indian School Road
Phoenix, AZ 85012–3397

Pantheon Books
Division of Random House, Inc.
201 East 50th Street
New York, NY 10022

Parents Magazine Press
685 Third Avenue
New York, NY 10017

Parker Brothers
50 Durham Road
Beverly, MA 01915

Penguin USA
375 Hudson Street
New York, NY 10014

S.G. Phillips, Inc.
P.O. Box 83
Chatham, NY 12037

Philomel Books. *See* The Putnam &
Grosset   Book Group.

Pieces of Learning
Distributed by Creative Learning
   Consultants
1610 Brook Lynn Drive
Beavercreek, OH 45432

Pied Piper/AIMS Media
9710 DeSoto Avenue
Chatsworth, CA 91311

Pitman Learning, Inc.
19 Davis Drive
Belmont, CA 94002

Platt & Munk, Inc.
51 Madison Avenue
New York, NY 10010

Prentice-Hall, Inc.
115 Columbus Circle
New York, NY 10023

The Putnam & Grosset Book Group
200 Madison Avenue
New York, NY 10016

G.P. Putnam's Sons. *See* The Putnam &
Grosset Book Group.

Random House, Inc.
225 Park Avenue South
New York, NY 10003

**Random House/Miller-Brody Produc-
tions**
Distributed by American School Publishers
P.O. Box 408
Hightstown, NJ 08520

Reader's Digest Association, Inc.
Pleasantville, NY 00401

Reading & O'Reilly
P.O. Box 302
Wilton, CT 06897

Reading Rainbow
Distributed by GPN
P.O. Box 80669
Lincoln, NE 68501

Nancy Renfro Studios
Box 164226
Austin, TX 78716

Scholastic, Inc.
730 Broadway
New York, NY 10003

Scholastic Software. *See* Scholastic, Inc.

Charles Scribner's Sons. *See* Macmillan
   Publishing Co.

Shorewood Fine Art Reproductions, Inc.
27 Glen Road
Sandy Hook, CT 06482

Sierra Club Books
100 Bush Street, 13th Floor
San Francisco, CA 94104

Silver Burdett Press, Inc.
190 Sylvan Avenue
Englewood Cliffs, NJ 07632

Simon and Schuster, Inc.
1230 Avenue of the Americas
New York, NY 10020

Smithsonian/Folkways
Distributed by Rounder Records
1 Camp Street
Cambridge, MA 02140

Sterling Publishing Co., Inc.
2 Park Avenue
New York, NY 10016

Tambourine Books. *See* William Morrow
& Co., Inc.

The Trumpet Book Clubs, Inc. *See*
Bantam Doubleday Dell Publishing
Group, Inc.

Viking. *See* Penguin USA.

Walker & Co.
720 Fifth Avenue
New York, NY 10019

Wallaby Records
Distributed by Seona McDowell
2971 Berkshire
Cleveland Heights, OH 44118

Frederick Warne, Inc.
374 Hudson Street
New York, NY 10014

Warner Brothers, Inc.
Division of Time Warner, Inc.
4000 Warner Boulevard
Burbank, CA 91522

Warner Brothers Records, Inc.
3300 West Warner Boulevard
Burbank, CA 91505

Weston Woods
Weston, CT 06883

Albert Whitman & Co.
5747 West Howard Street
Niles, IL 60648

H.W. Wilson Company
950 University Avenue
Bronx, NY 10452

Windham Hill Records
P.O. Box 9388
Stanford, CA 94309

Wordsong/Boyds Mills Press
Distributed by St. Martin's Press, Inc.
175 Fifth Avenue
New York, NY 10010

Workman Publishing Co.
708 Broadway
New York, NY 10003

Index

by Linda Webster